AF664464

Advanced Economics of Development

Volume–1

K.R. Gupta

Published by
ATLANTIC
PUBLISHERS & DISTRIBUTORS (P) LTD
7/22, Ansari Road, Darya Ganj,
New Delhi-110002
Phones : +91-11-40775252, 23273880, 23275880, 23280451
Fax : +91-11-23285873
Web : www.atlanticbooks.com
E-mail : orders@atlanticbooks.com

Branch Office
5, Nallathambi Street, Wallajah Road,
Chennai-600002
Phones : +91-44-64611085, 32413319
E-mail : chennai@atlanticbooks.com

Copyright © Atlantic Publishers and Distributors (P) Ltd., 2011

All rights reserved. No part of this publication may be reproduced, stored in a retrieval system, transmitted or utilized in any form or by any means, electronic, mechanical, photocopying, recording or otherwise, without the prior permission of the copyright owner. Application for such permission should be addressed to the publisher.

Printed in India at Glorious Printers, A-13, D.S.I.D.C., Jhilmil Industrial Area, Delhi-110095

Preface

Economic development is a measure of progress in an economy. It refers to the adoption of new technologies, transition from agriculture-based to industry-based economy, and general improvement in living standards of the people. Economic development entails social transformation, cultural change, establishment of a sound political system and creation of a sound work environment wherein the production of various types of goods and services is carried out and distributed among the people so that there is peace and prosperity.

Development economics is a branch of economics which deals with economic aspects of the development process in low-income countries. Its focus, according to Clive Bell, is not only on methods of promoting economic growth and structural change but also on improving the potential for the population, for example, through health and education and workplace conditions, whether through public or private channels. H.W. Arndt says that development economics involves the formulation of theories and methods that aid in the determination of policies and practices and can be implemented at either the domestic or international level. This may involve restructuring market incentives or using mathematical methods like inter-temporal optimization for project analysis, or it may involve a mixture of quantitative and qualitative methods. According to Michael Todaro and Stephen Smith, unlike in many other fields of economics, approaches in development economics may incorporate social and political factors to devise particular plans.

The last few decades have seen huge changes in the way developing countries manage their economies. Most governments have moved away from central planning toward supporting a market economy and allowing the growth of local, privately owned businesses. National economies have become more reliant on the capabilities of individual firms making their own decisions about the production of goods and services based on market signals. A wave of privatization across the globe has seen governments withdraw, in large part, from providing not only goods but also infrastructure and social services for their people.

As these in-country changes have been taking place, great changes have swept the global economy. International trade has become freer and more capital is available. Firms everywhere are encouraged to export while facing greater competition from both imports no longer subject to high tariffs and foreign firms that set up commercial operations locally. Moreover, firms based in developing countries are increasingly linked with various types of businesses abroad through franchises, subcontracts, or long-term supply relations. However, there have been many constraints to the smooth economic development. The global economic meltdown which roiled the world in 2008-09 and 2009-10 made the governments take policy decisions aiming more to put the respective economies back on track, keeping some projects of development on hold till the situation improved. The immediate concerns then were to create demand for goods and services, help businesses by reducing rates of interest, stop the rising unemployment, secure jobs, fight protectionism and develop international economic cooperation. Giving huge amounts of stimulus packages also put pressure on governments' financial sources, but it was the need of the hour. Thus, economic development is not only about pursuing the framed policies, but also about making changes as per exigencies.

The major indicators of development include equality of opportunity, rising income and living standard of people, equity in the distribution of income and wealth, an expanded role of women, minorities and other social classes in the economic, political and social life, increased opportunities for education and self-improvement, irrespective of class, race, ethnicity and religion, an efficient, competent, transparent and fairly administered public sector and a reasonable degree of competition in the private sector.

There are several factors responsible for the economic development of a country. While some of these factors are likely to be sociological and political, the major remain the economic such as the economic policies being pursued, monetary management, production of various types of goods and services, taxation, fiscal position, balance of payment position and currency reserves, among other things. There are also many pre-requisites of economic development such as the availability of natural resources in sufficient quantities as well as proper use of such resources, removal of market imperfections, an indigenous base of growth, structural changes, suitable environment, favourable social values, strong economic, social and administrative institutions, etc.

There are many theories of underdevelopment, which primarily takes place when the resources are not used to their full socio-economic potential, with the result that the development is slow. It has also been argued that under-development is caused by the complex interplay of internal and external factors that allow only lop-sided development. Similarly, the economists have propounded several theories of development. The formulation of a valid and convincing theory must give credence to the acceleration and expansion of human capabilities in all the important fields, leading to new discoveries and newer applications of established technologies, bringing improvement in the existing economic activities and capacities with better results. All these factors, aspects and theories have been discussed in the book.

The book also includes Arthur Lewis' and Gunnar Myrdal's illuminating views on economic development. They are the two most important pioneers of early economic development and were awarded with the prestigious Nobel Prize in Economics for revolutionizing the contemporary thinking on economics. Their views have been compared with those of some other major economists like J.M. Keynes.

The economic well-being of a country depends more on the quality and capability of its inhabitants than on anything else. According to Adam Smith, it is the annual labour of a nation which provides it with all the necessaries and conveniences of life. The past and present human effort and ability are the ultimate sources of all economic goods and services. The rapidly increasing population is a phenomenon common to all underdeveloped countries. It is widely believed that most of the underdeveloped countries have entered a critical phase of sharply accelerated population growth, and that the prospects for their successful economic development are crucially related to population trends. These and many other dimensions of population influencing economic development, including the famous Malthusian view, have been taken up in an exclusive chapter.

Since education is widely considered as a leading instrument for promoting economic growth, the relation between education and economic growth has been one of the central threads of economic analysis. The two leading economists—Adam Smith and Alfred Marshall—addressed the question of how individual investments in education influence the wealth of nations. Solow, Denison and Lucas considered the human capital investments similar to physical capital investments. The empirical studies since the 1980s show that education is a factor that fuels growth in national income and acts as an important engine of growth in any economy. The development aspect of education has been discussed in a separate chapter. Similarly, the role of human health in development and all its pertinent aspects like determinants of health, inequalities of health, etc. have been included.

Social capital is an empirically elusive concept, and has been subject to much debate and discussion with reference to its social regeneration, economic benefits, positive and negative aspects, indicators of measurement, gender insensitivity and its implications for a nation's development policies, etc. All these issues have been taken up.

Poverty is a major roadblock in the way of development. It is marked by deprivation of income and other sources that are needed to get the conditions of life, viz. food, material goods, amenities, standards and services. Thus, we have income poverty and consumption poverty. Nobel laureate Amartya Sen gave the concept of capability deprivation and added to the cluster of meanings of poverty. The meanings, measures and strategies of eradication of poverty have been discussed. Since the state has an important role to play in the economic development of a country, particularly an underdeveloped country, its development functions have been discussed.

The terms of trade and economic development, causes of deterioration in the terms of trade of underdeveloped countries, disequilibrium in the balance of payments of developing economies, and trade restrictions and economic development have been studied.

Economic activities are better organized in a planned economy than in an unplanned economy for a number of reasons. In unplanned economies, each individual enterprise controls a very small part of an industry, and has no knowledge of plans of other enterprises. This leads to either overproduction or underproduction. The central planning authority in a planned economy can take a wider view and form a long-term perspective of things. It can foresee the developments in advance and take remedial measures. This aspect has also been touched upon.

In the developing countries, it is public enterprise which has to lay the foundation on which the structure of a dynamic and diversified economy can be built. According to Hansen, "Whatever the ultimate perspective may be, the country anxious to develop economically has no alternative but to use public enterprise on a considerable scale, the very least in order to get things going." Thus, the rationale of public sector in economic development has been discussed.

It is believed that economic development is associated with a relative shift in the structure of the workforce away from agriculture to industry and services. Since the 1970s there has been a vast increase in the change in occupational structure as well as in the demand for skilled workers in the developed and the developing countries. These changes and their development implications have been described in a separate chapter.

Dualism can be described as a condition in which two distinct and separate economies coexist at the same time. Social, technological and regional dualism may occur together, with each type of dualism trying to reinforce the other. One of the major causes of persistence of dualism is that the more progressive sectors typically have favourable access to scarce factors of production. The urban bias also plays an important role in the process of dualism. An easy and logical way of attaining development in a dualistic economy is to transfer the resources from the low productivity rural sector to the higher productivity modern urban sector. All these aspects have been dealt with in a separate chapter.

Besides above, the other pertinent topics of economic development taken up in this book are the role of agriculture and industry in economic development; choice of techniques of development according to available resources; regional economic development; input-output analysis; linear programming, its concepts, application, problems, solving these problems, use of linear programming in development planning; and finally, project evaluation, including its techniques, applications and limitations.

Such vast coverage makes it an ideal textbook on the subject of development economics. It covers the syllabi of almost all the Indian universities on the subject and will thus prove extremely useful for the students pursuing higher level courses on development economics. The ideas have been explained in simple language and lucid manner for easy comprehension by the readers. Mathematical representations of some theories, explanations of well-labelled illustrations and diagrams, and solutions to the equations have been provided. Besides students, the book will prove beneficial for teachers of the subject as well as researchers in the field. It will immensely help policymakers, government officials, parliamentarians and all others concerned with the economic development of the country. To those who wish to know about various aspects of economic development, it will provide for a richly rewarding reading.

K.R. Gupta

Contents

Volume–2

1

Measuring Development

After going through this chapter, you will better understand:

- economic development
- difference between growth and development
- the millennium development goals
- structural changes required for development
- economic growth criterion of development
- per capita income as an index of development
- purchasing power parity (PPP) as an index of development
- the indicators criterion of development
- basic needs approach to development
- physical quality of life as an index of development
- human development as an index of development
- gender development as an index of development
- human poverty as an index of development
- capability and entitlement as an index of development

Development implies changes, and this is one sense in which the term development is used, that is, to describe the process of economic and social transformation within countries. Economic development demands and entails profound cultural change, including transformation of the political system, of individual behaviour norms, of the culture of work and production, and most fundamentally, modification in the manner in which society confronts, moulds, propels, and adapts itself to the requirements of technological progress that are the fount of economic growth and human development.

The literature indicates that there is considerable disagreement as to what constitutes economic development. However, there is little doubt that economic productivity and productivity growth are fundamental drivers of prosperity and innovation in any capitalist society. Consequently, the focus of economic development should be on supporting innovation and increasing prosperity. Thus, the economic development process is an endogenous effort designed to enhance a local community's ability to create and retain employment. It is designed to encourage business start-ups, innovation, entrepreneurship and the growth of firms already existing within a region.

Sustained increases in output and income per capita over time are of relatively recent historical origin. For much of known human history, population and total output tended to grow at about the same rate, so that per capita income remained roughly constant. Lloyd Reynolds has called this the period of extensive growth. What this meant was that for many centuries, until the early sixteenth century, the trend line of per capita production and income rose only very slowly. Most production was rurally based, there were few large urban settlements, and most people lived on and from the land, sometimes selling small surpluses in the village marketplace for other goods. Artisan and industrial-type products, such as textiles, and services, such as transportation, were also produced in the countryside, but on a very small scale. Besides agricultural production, families also produced non-agricultural goods, from clothing to cutlery to farm implements to soap and alcoholic beverages, primarily for family's own consumption. Production methods were relatively simple during this extensive period of growth, and technology was very primitive. However such technology was not static. Technological methods were constantly adapting to the growing demands of population growth, to changing land conditions, and to new crops and strains of seeds. Such technological change tended to be sufficient to keep pace with population expansion and to maintain income per person roughly constant over long periods. Annual aggregate output during the period of extensive growth was subject to periodic ups and downs, but that was primarily due to exogenous factors, such as the weather, wars, and other crises.

The transition from feudal production and social organisation to the emergence of capitalist forms of production in Europe is considered as the major "turning point" for world economic progress. Feudalism, an agricultural-based and hierarchical system of production organised around manors and based on the labour of serfs tied to the land, began to break down in the Middle Ages, especially in England, where the Industrial Revolution heralded the advent of the capitalist factory system as a new means of social and economic organisation. With incipient capitalism, the purpose of production changed from survival and stasis to the pursuit of ever-increasing profit. Capitalist production was based fundamentally on the application of new knowledge and ever-greater quantities of physical capital that could produce more, at lower cost, with the same or fewer inputs to production. Industrial capitalism established the foundation for intensive production methods, which for the first time in history created the reasonable possibility of higher levels of output and income per person without increases in population or other resources. Output and income did not depend predominantly upon the availability of resources with intensive production and industrial capitalism, as they had in pre-capitalist forms of production, including feudalism. Now, the level of output depended upon the efficiency with which available resources were used and upon the application of technology to save on the use of such resources, so that more output and income could be produced from what was available. The possibility of sustained increases in income per person, that is, in economic growth and development, is a relatively recent historical phenomenon. Further, high levels of economic sucess have been, to date at any rate, strongly associated with the spread of capitalist methods of production and the displacement of pre-capitalist methods, in both agriculture and industry.

Thus, the economic development can be explained as a complex process that is created from a successful fusion of entrepreneurship, education and skills of the community, driven largely by market forces. A favourable business environment and a supportive regulatory framework are important conditions of economic growth and development. It is generally accepted that the goal of economic development is to create new jobs, investment and improve the wealth of individuals and the community.

The concept of development, defined in the sense of an objective or a desired state of affairs, was conceived of almost exclusively in terms of growth targets, with very little regard to the beneficiaries of growth or the composition of output. Societies are not indifferent, however, to the distributional consequences of economic policy, to the type of output that is produced, or to the economic environment in which it is produced. A concept of development is required that embraces the major economic and social objectives and values that societies strive for. We can distinguish three basic components or core values of development—life-sustenance, self-esteem, and freedom.

Life-sustenance is concerned with the provision of basic needs. The basic needs approach to development was initiated by the World Bank in the 1970s. No country may be regarded as fully developed if it cannot provide all its people with such basic needs as housing, clothing, food, and minimal education. Thus, a major objective of development must be to raise people out of primary poverty and to provide basis needs simultaneously.

Self-esteem is concerned with the feeling of self-respect and independence. No country can be regarded as fully developed if it is exploited by others and does not have the power and influence to conduct relations on equal terms. Developing countries seek development for self-esteem; to eradicate the feeling of dominance and dependence that is associated with inferior economic status.

Freedom refers to freedom from the three evils of want, ignorance and squalor; so that people are more able to determine their own destiny. No person is free if they cannot choose; if they are imprisoned by living on the margin of subsistence with no education and no skills. The advantage of material development is that it expands the range of human choice open to individuals and societies at large.

All three of the above core values of development are interrelated. Lack of self-esteem and freedom result from low levels of life sustenance, and both lack of self-esteem and economic imprisonment become links in a circular, self-perpetuating chain of poverty by producing a sense of fatalism and acceptance of the established order—the accommodation to poverty.

Development has occurred when there has been an improvement in basic needs, when economic progress has contributed to a greater sense of self-esteem for the country and individuals within it, and when material advancement has expanded people's entitlements, capabilities and freedoms. The fact that many of these ingredients of development are not measurable, does not detract from their importance—the condition of being developed is as much a state of mind as a physical condition measurable by economic indices alone. The challenge of development economics lies in the formulation of economic theory, and in the application of policy, in order to understand better and to meet these core components of development. The range of issues that development economics is concerned with is quite distinctive and because of this the subject has developed its own way, although drawing liberally on economic theory, as do other branches of economics.

Economic development theory offers a new way of thinking about and seeing the everyday work. It provides an explanatory framework to describe and interpret what economic developers actually do in practice and what economic development as a professional activity is. It reinterprets the practice of economic development through a multifaceted prism of borrowed and appropriated concepts and reflect it back to the practitioners. The study of economic development helps us to understand the nature and causes of poverty in low-income countries, and the transformation of societies from primarily rural to primarily industrial, with the vast bulk of resources utilised in industrial activities and in service activities that serve the industrial sector.

The first industrial revolution gave the present developed countries an initial advantage, which they then sustained through the existence of various cumulative forces against those left behind. In the last fifty years there has been a second industrial revolution, which has propelled another bloc of countries (newly industrialised countries of South-East Asia and Latin America) into a virtually industrialised state, and many others into a semi-industrialised state. But many countries are still left behind in a semi-feudal state, including the very poorest, which have now become the prime focus of concern of the World Bank and other development agencies.

Many abstract theories about how to develop have been advanced by economists. Such theories are an integral part of development economics and provide an important historical window on how economists have thought and continue to think about development. There exists a definite moral dimension in development which is about realising very fundamental human values and finding the means to extend the fruits of these values to the greatest majority of the world's population. These human values include:

(a) the opportunity for meaningful employment and the possibility to provide for one's self and family;
(b) sufficient food, shelter, and other amenities for a decent and meaningful life above the poverty line;
(c) the opportunity to pursue education and the increased quality of life it promises;
(d) a reasonable level of health care;
(e) social security for old age;
(f) democracy and political participation in the life of the community and society;
(g) equal treatment under the law and in the economy, regardless of race, gender, class, ethnicity, religion, nationality, or other differences; and
(h) respect for individual dignity.

The above mentioned human values are some of the primary ingredients toward which development, and not just economic development, is directed.

GROWTH AND DEVELOPMENT

The term economic growth refers to either real economic growth or per capita real economic growth. Real economic growth is an increase from one period to the next in real Gross National Product (GNP). Per capita real economic growth is an increase from one period to the next in per capita real GNP, which is real GNP divided by population. In other words, economic growth is an increase in the potential output (productive capacity) of the nation. Conceptually, economic growth is represented by a rightward movement of the vertical aggregate supply curve in full employment level. If the economy operated each period at full employment as in the classical model, then economic growth could be easily measured as the annual percentage increase in real GNP.

Economic development studies the causes and cures of general poverty. Economic development refers to that process by which per capita income and economic welfare of a country increase over time. It may be noted that the terms 'economic development' and 'economic growth' are used interchangeably. But economists make a distinction between them. According to them, economic development means growth with change. Economic development refers to social and technological progress. It implies a change in the way goods and services are produced, not merely an increase in production achieved using the old methods of production on a wider scale. Economic growth implies only an increase in quantitative output; it may or may not involve development. Economic growth is often measured by rate of change of gross domestic product (e.g., percent GDP increase per year). Gross domestic product is the aggregate value-added by the economic activity within a country's borders.

The terms economic development, economic growth, and economic progress have been used as synonyms. Schumpeter, in his book *The Theory of Economic Development* (1911) clarified the distinction between economic development and economic growth. Besides, Hicks, Marshall, Kindleberger, etc. have also laid stress on the different meaning of these terms. Robert Clower, in his book *Growth without Development*, has proved that despite growth of an economy it is possible that it may not have any development.

Economic development typically involves improvements in a variety of indicators such as literacy rates, life expectancy, and poverty rates. GDP does not take into account other aspects such as leisure time, environmental quality, freedom, or social justice. A country's economic development is related to its human development, which encompasses, among other things, health and education.

Economic development is a normative concept meaning that the definition is variable however, the definition given by Michael Todaro is an increase in living standards, improvement in self-esteem needs and freedom from oppression as well as a greater choice. The most accurate method of measuring development is the Human Development Index which takes into account the literacy rates and life expectancy which affect productivity and could lead to Economic Growth.

Economic Growth is an increase in a country's real level of national output which can be caused by an increase in the quality of resources by education, etc., increase in the quantity of resources and improvements in technology. Economic Growth can be measured by an increase in a country's GDP. However this does not necessarily mean that development has occurred.

There is an issue of the distribution of income. It is thought that an increase in a country's GDP means everyone benefits however this increase might only benefit the rich. This creates alienation, encourages crime and threatens social cohesion. This can be justified on the grounds that wealth will eventually trickle down, the 'trickle down' effect. But the problem this creates is that it is far too slow compared to other development policies for example an increase in government spending on health and education.

Economic Growth does not take into account the depletion of natural resources which might lead to pollution, congestion and disease. Development however is concerned with sustainability which means meeting the needs of the present without compromising future needs. Economic Growth does not take into account the size of the informal economy. The informal economy is also known as the black economy which is unrecorded economic activity which in most cases is illegal. This stifles development because it creates urban congestion and allows disease to be spread more quickly. The informal economy also has very little regard for health and safety issues. The government cannot collect taxes from them and hence they cannot use that money to spend on health and education. Development alleviates people from low standards of living into proper employment with suitable shelter.

The main differences between economic growth and development can be summarised as:

(a) *Single dimensional and multi-dimensional*: Economic growth is single dimensional. It is concerned with increase in national and per capita income. On the other hand, economic development is multi-dimensional. It is concerned both with income and structural changes. In fact, economic development is a broad term.

In case of economic development, along with increase in national income, there is change in the economic, social, and political structure of the country. For instance, relative contribution of agricultural sector to national income declines and that of industrial and service sector increases. In other words, economic development is a multi-dimensional phenomena; it involves not only increase in money incomes, but also improvement in real habits, education, public health, greater leisure and in fact all the social and economic circumstances that make for a fuller and happier life.

On the contrary, in case of economic growth, there is increase in national income alone. There is no structural change in the economy.

(b) *Qualitative change*: The terms growth is quantitative whereas term development is qualitative. There are many important qualitative changes in development process, which take it beyond growth. These qualitative changes manifest themselves in the form of efficient functioning of the factors of production and improved technique of production. Economic development is concerned not only with increase in production but also its equitable distribution. If increased national income is not properly distributed then there will be no change in the standard of living of the people in the economy. That is why, economic development is a process that ensures growth with justice, whereas economic growth relates only to higher growth rate of national and per capita income. The latter has no concern with equitable distribution. In short, economic growth occurs when more goods can be produced, whereas economic development entails improvements in the quality of life, in the qualities of goods available or in the ways production is organised.

(c) *Spontaneous and discontinuous changes*: Development is discontinuous and spontaneous changes in the stationary state, which for ever alters and displaces the equilibrium state previously existing, while growth is a gradual and steady changes in the long run which comes about by general increase in the rate of saving and population. In short, the term development is used for spontaneous and discontinuous changes. The term growth is used for continuous and steady changes.

(d) *Economic development implies economic growth*: According to some economists, the term economic development is used to describe the determinants of economic growth, such as, changes in techniques of production, in social attitudes and in institutions. It is because of these changes that national income increases and is called economic growth. Thus, development is the determinant of growth.

(e) *Growth without development*: Main cause of rise in national income of Liberian economy is the export of primary goods. But this production is done in those gardens whose ownership is in the hands of foreign companies. Thus, in spite of rise in national income there has been no increase in production capacity of the country. On the contrary, along with the process of economic development it is essential to have economic growth to some extent.

(f) *Related to the problems of underdeveloped countries*: The term development is related to backward countries, where there is possibility of developing and using hitherto unused resources. The term growth is applicable to economically advanced countries, where most of the resources are already known and developed. Thus, the term economic development is used for the full utilisation of unutilised natural and human resources of the underdeveloped countries. The term economic growth is used for maintaining the situation of full employment in developed countries.

In short, economic growth means more output. Economic development implies not only more output but also different kinds of output than were previously produced as well as changes in the technical and institutional arrangements by which output is produced and distributed. Overall, to conclude, Growth is just one dimension of development. Economic Growth is a necessary but not a sufficient condition for development because GDP per capita might be rising but at the same time, poverty might be increasing, inequality rising and massive environmental damage might be occurring.

THE MILLENNIUM DEVELOPMENT GOALS

The latest commitment endorsed by the World Bank and the United Nations is for the percentage of the world's population living in absolute poverty to be halved by the year 2015, compared to the level in 1990. This means a reduction from 30 percent to 15 percent. To fulfill this commitment, on September 8, 2000, the United Nations General Assembly adopted the Millennium Declaration. The Millennium Development Goals (MDGs) emerged as a means to meet some of the aspirations of the Millennium Declaration.

The MDGs comprise eight broad goals and fifteen more specific 'target' policies to reach the goals. The MDGs represent concrete objectives of the entire international community for reducing the ravages of poverty by 2015. The approval of these goals by all the members of the UN demonstrates the importance the international community, including the World Bank, places upon reducing poverty, improving health care, expanding educational opportunities, and promoting sustainability for hundreds of millions of poor people around the world. This unified effort of the world community recognises that all economies are connected and that severe poverty affects us all, directly or indirectly. The Millennium Development Goals and Targets are:

Goal 1: *Eradicate extreme poverty and hunger*

Target 1: Halve, between 1990 and 2015, the proportion of people whose income is less than $ 1 a day.

Target 2: Halve, between 1990 and 2015, the proportion of people who suffer from hunger.

Goal 2: *Achieve universal primary education*

Target 3: Ensure that, by 2015, children everywhere, boys and girls alike, will be able to complete a full course of primary schooling.

Goal 3: *Promote gender equality and empower women*

Target 4: Eliminate gender disparity in primary and secondary education preferably by 2005 and in all levels of education no later than 2015.

Goal 4: *Reduce child mortality*

Target 5: Reduce by two-thirds, between 1990 and 2015, the under-five mortality rate.

Goal 5: *Improve maternal health*

Target 6: Reduce by three-quarters, between 1990 and 2015, the maternal mortality ratio.

Goal 6: *Combat HIV/AIDS, malaria, and other diseases*

Target 7: Have halted by 2015 and begun to reverse the spread of HIV/AIDS.

Target 8: Have halted by 2015 and begun to reverse the incidence of malaria and other major diseases.

Goal 7: *Ensure environmental sustainability*

Target 9: Integrate the principles of sustainable development into country policies and programs and reverse the loss of environmental resources.

Target 10: Halve, by 2015, the proportion of people without sustainable access to safe drinking water and basic sanitation.

Target 11: Have achieved, by 2020, a significant improvement in the lives of at least 100 million slum dwellers.

Goal 8: Develop a global partnership for development

Target 12: Develop further an open, rule-based, predictable, non-discriminatory trading and financial system includes a commitment to good governance, development, and poverty reduction—both nationally and internationally.

Target 13: Address the special needs of the least developed countries includes tariff and quota-free access for exports, enhanced program of debt relief for HIPCs and cancellation of official bilateral debt, and more generous official develoment assistance (ODA) for countries committed to poverty reduction.

Target 14: Address the special needs of landlocked countries and small island developing states.

Target 15: Deal comprehensively with the debt problems of developing countries through national and international measures in order to make debt sustainable in the long-term.

Target 16: In cooperation with developing countries, develop and implement strategies for decent and productive work for youth.

Target 17: In cooperation with pharmaceutical companies, provide access to affordable essential drugs in developing countries.

Target 18: In cooperation with the private sector, make available the benefits of new technologies, especially information and communications technologies.

Each of the goals addresses an aspect of poverty, and all are mutually reinforcing. For example, higher school enrolment, especially for girls, reduces poverty and mortality. Better basic health care will increase school enrolment and reduce poverty.

Many poor people earn their living from the environment, so a better environment will help poor people.

To achieve the major goal of halving the poverty rate by the year 2015 will require a sustained growth of per capita income in the countries affected, at rates much higher than experienced in the recent past, particularly in Africa. On average, the poverty rate tends to fall by about one percent for every one percent increase in per capita income, so a 50 percent increase in per capita income would be required to reduce the poverty rate from, say, 30 percent to 15 percent.

STRUCTURAL CHANGES REQUIRED FOR DEVELOPMENT

The real-world process of a country becoming more developed, of getting on the path to development, and shedding the ways of the past that resulted in low growth rates and limited progress, is not, however, simply about the efficient allocation of existing resources within a given institutional regime. It is not simply about maximising utility or profits within the constraints of what is currently available to that society and inherited from the past. Rather, development is fundamentally about regime change and about the search for an optimal growth path, or at least one that is superior to the existing allocation of resources and current efficiency levels. Further, fomenting development typically requires substantially new institutional patterns and organisational structures necessary to support such a dynamic process of change.

Marginal modifications of the economy and society simply may be insufficient to initiate the forward momentum needed to propel the system in the requisite new direction and on to a higher path of progress for the future. For less-developed nations, development compels them to undertake substantial qualitative structural change. The future cannot be just an extension of the past, of doing more of what is now being done. Change must be dramatic. The past and its weight on the present are precisely what have made these nations poor and are what need to be transcended. There are a number of major structural changes and patterns identified by development economists and economic historians that are believed to be characteristic of any successful development process. Following are some structural changes required for the development process:

(a) *Demographic characteristics*: Very poor countries are characterised by both high birth rates and high death rates. As development proceeds, death rates plummet downward. Often, birth rates remain high, before they finally follow the death rates on their downward course. In the process, a gap opens up between the birth and death rates. This leads to high population growth in developing countries.

High population growth has two effects. It means that overall income must grow faster to keep per capita growth at reasonable levels. The fact that population is growing helps income to grow, because there is a greater supply of productive labour. However, it is not clear who wins this seesaw contest—the larger amount of production or the larger population that makes it necessary to divide that production among more people. The second effect of high population growth is that the overall population is quite young. It is easy to get an intuition for this—high birth rates mean that a proportionately larger number of children are always entering the population at any given point of time. This means that the population is heavily weighted in favour of children. There are many untoward consequences of an abnormally young population, and these include poverty, child labour, and low education.

(b) *Occupational and production structure*: Agriculture accounts for a significant fraction of production in developing countries and so it forms a significant part of the lives of people living in developing countries. Economic development is strongly associated with an increasing share of a nation's output and labour force involved in industrial, especially manufacturing activities.

Parallel to the expansion of the industrial sector of the economy is a decline in the share of agricultural output in total output. This also means a reduction in the share of the total labour force employed in agriculture and a decrease in the share of the rural population within the total population.

The increase in industrialisation and the decrease in agriculture are intimately related. Surplus labour in agriculture migrates to urban areas in search of the promise of better-paid and higher productivity industrial employment. It is this shift of workers from low-productivity agricultural employment to higher-productivity industrial employment that contributes to a sharp increase in total national output when this process of internal labour migration is initiated. Technological progress and labour productivity is typically lower in the primary sector, but over time, output per person approaches the level reached in the industrial, or secondary sector as the fewer workers in agriculture produce more output per worker. In short, economic development is a process of moving from a set of assets based on primary products, exploited by unskilled labour, to a set of assets based on knowledge, exploited by skilled labour.

(c) *Changing trade patterns*: Development is marked by a maturation in the structure of trade, as a limited range of primary exports—agriculture and fishing products, unprocessed mining and other extractive minerals, and forestry products—is replaced by both a greater diversity of export products and by an evolving export mix toward manufactured goods and services.

In the process of development, country shifts from a dependence on the traditional, primary export products that marked their colonial past toward, first, simpler manufactured and non-traditional primary exports, and ultimately toward more complex commodity exports.

(d) *Increased application of human capital and knowledge to production*: Development requires increase in the productivity of labour in all sectors of the economy if incomes and the standard of living of the population are to rise. This is achieved partly through improvements in the training and education of the existing and future labour force by means of increases in what economists call human capital accumulation. This takes place not only through the formal schooling process but also via 'learning-by-doing' at the workplace.

Increased productivity of labour is also a consequence of an expansion in the use of more physical capital, that is, more machines and tools which typically embody more advanced technology and knowledge that can help to make a properly trained labour force even more efficient. Human capital accumulation, physical capital accumulation, and technology thus all contribute in a synergistic process to increase the productivity of the labour force. Greater productivity means the possibility of higher wages for labour and an easier workplace environment, both of which contribute to the potential well-being of the population.

(e) *Rapid rural-urban migration*: As development proceeds, an enormous amount of labour moves from rural to urban areas. This is an outcome of both the "push" from agriculture, because of extreme poverty and growing landlessness, and the perceived "pull" of the urban sector. The pull are reinforced by a variety of factors, ranging from the comparatively high wages and worker protections offered in the organised urban sectors to the effect of the media in promoting the urban lifestyle as a desirable end in itself.

(f) *Institutional changes*: Economic development requires fundamental institutional change. New organisations such as banks, stock and bond exchanges, and insurance companies gain added importance as an economy modernises. The role of the central government must change to facilitate and not thwart private initiatives. Physical infrastructure such as roads, ports, communications, the provision of electricity, water, and other essential services must be improved, and the state typically must play a central role in these areas, particularly during early stages of structural transformation.

The specific nature of the legal system and of property rights, the rules and regulations governing the emerging financial system of banks, stock and bond markets and other financial intermediaries, the creation and operation of a civil service system, determining what will be taught in the schools and how success will be measured and so on all must be worked out and codified by government. It is thus not only physical infrastructure that must be built, maintained, and improved, but also the soft infrastructural institutions of the state, like the law and property rights, that must be created and put into place if a more modern, productive, and equitable outcome is to be attained.

BARRIERS TO DEVELOPMENT

The level and pace of economic development are lower the greater are the barriers to economic progress and transformation in a country, and more rapid the fewer and less intractable are those obstacles. Common examples of the barriers are Poverty cycle, Institutional and Political factors, and International financial barriers. These are basically the barriers that act as a hindrance to economic growth, economic development and sometimes both. Many poor countries in Africa and Asia are known to have a poor institutional and political system and through this they are facing a variety of barriers to growth. One of the important barriers to institutional barriers is 'Lack of infrastructure'. It is known that most developing countries are lacking infrastructure even though it is important to economic growth.

Barriers to development can be classified under—(i) economic barriers, (ii) non-economic barriers, (iii) social barriers, and (iv) political and governmental barriers to economic development.

Different models of economic growth and development reveal that capital formation is an important vehicle of economic development. Capital formation essentially refers to an accumulation of capital resources that are used in the process of production (such as machines, plants, equipment, buildings, etc.). Of course, capital assets will also embody technology. Sometimes, capital formation itself can be considered to have two components—non-human and human capital. A machine or a factory shed is an example of non-human capital. Human capital formation takes the form of education and training of individuals. Both human and non-human capital formations are important as they both increase productivity and lead to economic growth. Moreover, a non-human capital asset embodying an advanced technology also requires a better-trained human operator of the machine. The view that capital formation was central to economic growth, called capital fundamentalism, was reflected in the development strategies and plans of many countries over decades. Thus, the solution to the problem of economic development was viewed primarily as securing enough investment funds to generate a certain targeted rate of economic growth.

It is now widely recognised that abundance of savings and capital formation are not adequate to guarantee an accelerated pace of economic development, in particular when capital is deployed in low-productivity projects. Moreover, investment projects financed by foreign savings, even if highly productive, may have little effect on economic growth if the recipient country's policies are not well suited to capture a fair share of returns from these projects.

While capital formation is no longer viewed as the ultimate instrument of economic development in poorer countries, it is nevertheless recognised that even a mildly robust pace of economic growth cannot be maintained over a long time until these countries invest a sizable fraction of their gross national product. At the very minimum the investment rate (the fraction of gross national product invested) should be 15 percent and in some cases it may be required to go as high as 25 percent. The 15-25 percentage interval provides a range of likely requirements—the actual investment rate would depend upon the environment in which capital formation takes place and the desired rate of economic growth.

In eyes of most economists, there is no single economic barrier to development that can explain why so few countries were able to initiate economic growth prior to the 20th century. While savings rates in many of these countries were too low to finance investments necessary to achieve economic development, the important question then remains as to why the savings rates were low. Poverty alone cannot account for low savings rates—some poor countries in the late 20th century, such as Japan, were able to generate large amounts of savings needed for growth. Japan's success in mobilising large amounts of savings was partly due to a strong governmental structure that helped extract a surplus through taxation. Thus, economic explanations alone cannot account for why particular economic barriers exist and non-economic barriers need to be considered.

Governments and political institutions play an important role in the economic development process even in capitalist countries. While early experiences with economic development, such as England's experience during the 18th century, did not involve a large role for government, the role played by the government has steadily increased in importance. At the current time, if a government is unable or unwilling to play an active role in the economic development process, then the government itself is considered an obstacle to economic development. A government can foster economic development in many ways. First and foremost, governments must create and maintain a stable political environment and a climate of peace in which modern enterprises, private or public, can flourish.

A stable government in itself, however, is not enough. In most cases, colonial governments were able to provide political stability—often for a prolonged period. This was the case for India under British rule and Korea under Japanese rule. Nevertheless, very few European or Japanese colonies experienced significant economic development. The benefits of the stable environment under colonial rule mainly accrued to a small group of traders and investors from the colonising nation. Moreover, ruling Colonial nations made no serious attempt at economic development through investment in training or through promotion of industries. Many colonial nations initiated economic development strategies after gaining independence. India provides such an example. After gaining independence from the British in 1947, the Indian government started planning to develop the country in an organised way. While India is still relatively poor, it is one of a small group of countries, seven or so, that possess space technology.

It should also be noted that political independence does not necessarily imply that a sovereign government would pursue an active policy to promote economic development. The decisions to pursue economic development involve trade-offs—some people may become better off following economic development while others may become worse off. If political power is in the hands of those who will become worse off, the country's leaders may impede efforts towards economic development. In some instances, nations have pursued social goals rather than economic development.

Economic development rides on the shoulders of entrepreneurs who venture to do things that benefit them and the society. Whether or not a society has a sufficient number of entrepreneurs to foster modern economic growth may depend on the society's values and structure. Many of the developed nations of today encouraged entrepreneurs who pursued dreams in search of reaping potential profits from innovations. What has prevented the development of entrepreneurship in under-developed economies? Some believe that certain individuals in a traditional society are blocked from becoming entrepreneurs, which normally implies more social prestige, power, and wealth. David McClelland, a Harvard University psychologist, believes that the need for achievement is a factor—certain societies produce a high number of individuals with strong desire to improve themselves financially or to be recognised by the society for their achievements. The experience of Malaya provides a historical example that illustrates McClelland's premise. Malaya was a country rich in resources, but natives of Malaya—primarily fishermen and farmers comfortable with their lives—did not become entrepreneurs until the middle of the 20th century. Meanwhile, migrant Chinese mining workers who survived diseases such as malaria became entrepreneurs in Malaya. One interpretation of this episode is that the Chinese possessed a strong desire to rise and the Malays did not.

The challenge for the development analyst is thus to attempt to identify the most significant barriers to development in each country and to formulate effective measures, including public policy, that can begin to undo, remove, or at least minimise the effects of these obstacles to progress that slow or thwart the development process. Once again barriers can be divided into two sub-heads—(i) internal barriers to development, and (ii) external barriers to development.

Some of the internal barriers to development are:

(a) the existence of substantial market failures such that market signals are not completely, or accurately transmitted to economic agents, thus distorting resource allocation, production decisions and spending patterns;

(b) the initial endowment of natural resources of a nation;

(c) geographic characteristics, for example, landlocked nations, mountainous terrain, extensive deserts, and even small country size;

(d) the level and efficiency of physical infrastructure;

(e) the role and level of development of organised banking and lending activities and of equity and other financial markets and financial intermediaries;

(f) inequalities in the existing distributions of income and wealth, including the distribution of land ownership;

(g) an ineffective or underdeveloped educational system, including low levels of general literacy and an imbalance between allocations of financing to primary, secondary, and higher education;

(h) prevailing ideological concepts and their impact on thinking and behaviour, including the influence of religious thinking, the accepted role of women and ethnic or religious minorities, the prevailing economic orthodoxy, and so on;

(i) the role of the state, that is, the power and nature of the influence of the central government, including the degree of political freedom and the strength of democratic processes;

(j) the extent and importance of political corruption and patronage and the impact of these on public policies and on economic behaviour of those governed;

(k) diseases specific to certain locations;

(l) unstability in the country due to civil war, and so on.

Some of the external barriers to development are:

(a) the economic policies of more developed nations on interest rates, for example, or on tariffs or non-tariff barriers on the global economic system;

(b) the influence of the geopolitical and strategic interests of larger economic powers *vis-a-vis* smaller and weaker economic entities;

(c) multinational corporations that control national resources;

(d) the international division of labour and the prevailing patterns of international trade;

(e) the functioning of international financial institutions, including not only the international private commercial banks but also the World Bank and the International Monetary Fund;

(f) external debt;

(g) the availability of foreign aid and investment, and so on.

For any specific nation, the list of possible internal and external obstacles can only be a guide toward the identification and detailed specification of the unique particulars of the barriers actually operating to thwart progress in that country. For every nation, the barriers to change, and then the specifics of how each obstacle acts as a restraint on progress, need to be clearly and analytically defined so that the nature of the remedy is also made more apparent. The influence of internal and external barriers can and will alter in importance over time and because of unique situations particular to specific countries. The relative influence of internal and external barriers cannot be presumed *a priori* but must be understood in each specific and changing circumstance.

INDICATORS OF DEVELOPMENT

Indicators of development are inextricably linked to definitions of development, highlighting the need for a better understanding of what development is before seeking to measure it. For most economists and policy analysts, development was seen as equivalent to economic growth, of which growth of GNP served as the main indicator. This was (and still is) usually expressed in 'per capita' terms, i.e. the gross, or total, national product was divided by a country's population to give an average figure for a country's level of economic development. However, development incorporates the diverse and broad aspirations of what might be called the 'good life' in all its economic, social, and political dimensions that each society sets for itself. Societies may have goals as diverse as:

(a) equality of opportunity;
(b) a rising income and standard of living;
(c) equity in the distribution of income and wealth;
(d) political democracy and widespread participation in society's decision-making;
(e) an expanded role for women, minorities, and all social classes in economic, political, and social life;
(f) increased opportunities for education and self-improvement irrespective of class, race, ethnicity, religion, or gender;
(g) availability of improved health care;
(h) clean and healthy environment;
(i) an efficient, competent, transparent, and fairly administered public sector;
(j) a reasonable degree of competition in the private sector;
(k) a strong law and order situation; and so on.

There are two categories of country—developed and developing. The question is how one judges the respective levels of development of different economies. It affects what factors we consider as contributing to progress, and our answer to what development is, will influence the public policies aimed at achieving a society's development goals. A variety of economic and social indicators can be used to classify countries in this way. There are two broad methodologies—economic growth criterion and the indicators criterion of development.

Economic Growth Criterion of Development

Nation's per capita income is often used as a proxy measure for evaluating the overall level of national development and welfare. The rate of growth of income per person can be used to judge the progress of economies over time. The level of economic development can be measured either by the growth of total output or of total income. Comparing GNP per capita from year to year provides a measure of economic growth relative to population size, and this therefore constitutes a measure of development progress, or the lack of it. This view of development still underlines much current official thinking.

The two most common measures used for international income and output comparisons, and hence for measuring economic growth, are gross national income (GNI) and gross domestic product (GDP). There will be no difference between GNI and GDP if an economy is completely closed to the rest of the world. Closed in this sense means that there is no migration of workers and no flows of investment between a country and the rest of the world. Exports and imports of goods, however, do not affect the measurement of GNI or GDP since trade flows do not have anything to do with differences in the values of the two income measures. It is simply that can be no labour or investment flows between economies if GNI is to equal GDP and an economy is to be considered closed. If an economy is closed in this sense, then the only income that would be received by residents of a country would be derived from new productive activity taking place within the borders of that country. There would be no income received by residents inside the country originating from sources outside the country and no flows of income created within the borders of the country going to income receipients in other nations. In this case, GDP—the income produced within the borders of the country—would equal GNI, the income received by residents of that country.

Per Capita Income as an Index of Development

Prof. Meier defines economic development as the process whereby the real per capita income of a country increases over a long period of time. According to Prof. Bran, economic development is defined as an increase over time in per capita output of material goods. To cite Buchanan and Ellis, development means developing the real income potentialities of the underdeveloped areas by using investment to effect those changes and to augment those productive resources which promise to raise real income per person.

Dividing GNI (or GDP) by the total population provides a measure of per person income, or, simply, average income. This population adjustment is essential for two reasons. First, using total GNI (or GDP) to compare different countries make little sense. To be able to compare countries in terms of their relative level of development, it is essential to use average income to account for differences in the size of economies. Otherwise, we would be trying to compare essentially non-comparable values. Total GNI or total GDP tells us nothing about the average standard of living; average GNI, or average GDP, gets us a little closer. We can thus use per capita income as a means to rank countries from richest to poorest, with difference in incomes reflecting presumed differences in the quality of life, which is the rationale behind using income per person as a proxy for overall welfare.

A second reason for using per capita income is to determine if, over time, changes in the level of aggregate income of any particular economy (a) are just sufficient to keep up with population growth, so that per capita GNI (or GDP) remains constant over time; (b) are more than sufficient to keep up with population growth, so that per capita GNI is rising over time; or (c) are insufficient to keep pace with population growth, such that per capita GNI is falling over time. Using per person income figures allows us to measure, for any particular economy, whether average income—and hence the average standard of living—is growing or not. Since, GNI per capita is simply total GNI divided by population, the percentage change in GNI per capita can be determined as

$$\begin{aligned}\text{\% change in GNI per capita} &= \%\Delta\,(\text{total GNI/total population}) \\ &= \%\Delta\ \text{total GNI} - \%\Delta\ \text{population}\end{aligned}$$

From the above relation, we find that the rate of growth of GNI per capita thus can easily be approximated as the difference between the rate of growth of total GNI and the rate of population expansion. GDP can be substituted for GNI in the above expression to determine the rate of change of GDP per capita.

Countries with high rates of population growth need to generate higher rates of growth in total income just to keep the level of per capita income constant compared to countries with lower population growth. If one country's population is growing at 2 percent per year, total GNI must increase by 2 percent per annum just to maintain a constant level of income per capita, this results in a zero percent change in per capita income. Another economy with 1 percent growth in population and the same 2 percent growth in total GNI would experience an increase in per capita GNI of 1 percent. However, it is not correct that slow population growth causes a faster rate of growth of income per person or that rapid population growth causes slower growth in income per person.

When using per capita income to measure poverty, to classify countries into rich and poor and to compare the rate of development in different countries over time, the difficulties of measuring real per capita income and real living standards between countries must be considered. There are two issues which command special attention. The first concerns the problems associated with national income accounting, particularly in developing countries. The second is the problem of converting each country's per capita income in domestic currency into a common unit of account so as to be able to make meaningful international comparisons of living standards.

Let us consider the first problem associated with the national income accounting. The first point bear in mind is that only goods that are produced and then sold in the market are included in the value of national income, measured by either the output or the expenditure method. Much output in developing countries never reaches the market, particularly in the rural sector where production is for subsistence purposes. If no allowance is made for the subsistence sector, this will bias downwards the calculation of national income, and therefore per capita income. This point also implies that any long-term growth estimates will have an upward bias as a result of the extension of the money economy and the shift of economic activities from the household and subsistence sector to the market place. If no allowance is made for the subsistence sector in some countries, it may be misleading to compare periods in these countries' history and to compare growth rates between countries. Part of the observed trend of faster GDP growth in developing countries over the last 50 years may be partly a statistical illusion arising from the changing balance between the informal subsistence sector and the modern exchange sector. Growth rates may also be biased by using prices as weights when compiling national income totals from the output statistics of different sectors of the economy, since goods with high prices, which subsequently fall, are usually the fastest growing. This is more of a danger in developing countries than in developed countries because of their less sophisticated accounting techniques, the greater difficulty in revising price weights, and the more widespread introduction of new goods with high initial prices.

Apart from the problems of bias and choice of price deflator, there is the sheer practical difficulty of measuring money national income in a rural economy where communications are bad, illiteracy rife, and many of the goods produced and consumed are not exchanged for money. Differences in the extent of the subsistence economy between developing countries, and differences in the ease and difficulty of collecting data, may markedly influence estimates of national income, and therefore of per capita income differences, between these countries and the rest of the world.

Apart from the difficulty of measuring income in many countries and the difficulty of making intercountry comparisons, using a single per capita income figure to separate developed from developing countries is inevitably somewhat arbitrary, as it ignores such factors as the distribution of income within countries, differences in development potential and other physical indicators of the quality of life. It is not so much a question of whether or not low-income countries should be labelled 'underdeveloped' or 'developing', but what income level should be used as the criterion for separating the developed from the developing countries, and whether all high-income countries should be labelled 'developed'. In many ways it should be the nature and characteristics of the countries that determine which income level should be used as the dividing line. Oil-rich countries have high per capita incomes but cannot be regarded as developed by the criteria of per capita income. Within the countries outside the industrialised bloc, the per capita income level dividing the low- and middle-income countries is arbitrary, but none is fully industrialised and all are 'developing' in this sense.

Overall per capita income is not a bad proxy for the social and economic structure of societies and perhaps it is the best single index we have. If developing countries are defined on the basis of a per capita income level so as to include most of the countries of Asia, Africa and Latin America, striking similarities are found between the characteristics and development obstacles of many of the countries in these continents. They are:

(a) a high proportion of the labour force engaged in agriculture having low productivity;
(b) a high proportion of domestic expenditure on food and necessities;
(c) an export trade dominated by primary products and an import trade dominated by manufactured goods;
(d) a low level of technology;
(e) a high birth rate coupled with a falling death rate;
(f) saving undertaken by a small percentage of the population;
(g) growing unemployment in urban areas;
(h) inegalitarian income distributions; and
(i) poor health and standards of education.

Thus, per capita income may be used as a starting point for classifying levels of development, and can certainly be used to identify the need for development. However, there is a difference between using per capita income as a guideline for classifying countries into developed or underdeveloped at a point in time and using the growth of per capita income as an index of development over time. The difficulty of using per capita income for the latter purpose is the obvious one that if, in a particular period, per capita income did not grow because population growth matched the growth of a country's total income, one would be forced into the odd position of denying that a country had developed even though its national product had increased. This leads on to the distinction between growth and development.

Development without growth is hardly conceivable, but growth is possible without development, but development is possible without a rise in per capita income. The ultimate goal of development must be to improve living standards and welfare, and while an increase in measured per capita income may not be a sufficient condition for an increase in individual welfare, it is a necessary condition in the absence of radical institutional innovations, such as an increase in public goods.

The GNI measures provides some notion of what the residents of a nation have available to them for consumption and investment, including government spending. GNI thus furnishes a measure of the sum total of new final goods and services available to the residents of a country for their final use. In economic terms, the level of output and income measured by GNI is a proximate gauge of the aggregate material welfare or well-being of the residents of a nation. If one is going to use income and the economic growth criterion as a substitute measure for the broader goals of development for a nation, it probably makes sense to use real GNI per capita as the standard, since it measures what is actually available for contributing to the standard of living of the population, both now, for current consumption, and, in the future, as investment.

The GDP on the other hand, measures all the output and income produced within the borders of a country, even though not all of that income will necessarily be received by residents of the country. It is more purely an index of the value of all new goods and services and total income produced within the frontiers of a nation rather than of the income and output available for use to the nation. Real GDP per capita is a less desirable measure to use if one is interested in a surrogate welfare measures for the broad range of development goals of nations. Real GDP per capita does give information on how output is changing in an economy, but it does so irrespective of who ultimately receives the income earned from such production. The GDP per capita measure, then, is not as closely connected to what remains in the hands of the residents of the nation for current and future consumption as the GNI per capita measure, and thus GDP per person is a more imperfect measure of a nation's overall well-being.

Which measure is employed will be determined by the use to which the income criterion is to be put. If one is solely interested in the pace of economic growth and total production for a country, then the real GDP per capita measure will serve quite nicely. If, however, one wishes to use the income proxy that best measures what is available for use by a country's residents and which can concretely contribute to their level of well-being, it makes more sense to use the real GNI per capita measures as the surrogate yardstick. However, using GDP or GNI per capita will make little substantive difference in evaluating the level of development using the income criterion.

One point should be noted that an increase in income is not a sufficient condition for an increase in welfare, because an increase in income can involve costs as well as benefits. It may have been generated at the expense of leisure or by the production of goods not immediately consumable. If development is looked upon as a means of improving the welfare of present generations, probably the best index to take would be consumption per manhour worked. This index, in contrast to an index of per capita income, focuses directly on the immediate utility derivable from consumption goods in relation to the disutility of the work effort involved in their production.

Purchasing Power Parity (PPP) as an Index of Development

According to the Law of One Price identical goods should (under certain conditions) sell for the same price in two different countries at the same time. It is the foundation for purchasing power parity (PPP) theory, which states that exchange rates between currencies are in equilibrium when their purchasing power is the same in each of the two countries. This means that the exchange rate between two countries should equal the ratio of the two countries' price level of a fixed basket of goods and services. When a country's domestic price level is increasing (i.e., a country experiences inflation), that country's exchange rate must depreciated in order to return to PPP.

In the absence of transportation and other transaction costs, competitive markets will equalise the price of an identical good in two countries when the prices are expressed in the same currency. There are three caveats with this law of one price: (i) transportation costs, barriers to trade, and other transaction costs, can be significant, (ii) there must be competitive markets for the goods and services in both countries, and (iii) the law of one price only applies to tradeable goods; immobile goods such as houses, and many services that are local, are of course not traded between countries.

The economies with lower per capita GNI will have lower prices for some items when these values are converted from the local currency to foreign currency of the country having high per capita GNI. In other words, the equivalent of ₹ 10,000 will buy different quantities of goods and services in different economies since the prices of some, *but not all*, goods and services will vary with the level of average income of an economy.

If the US dollar is used as the unit of account, the national per capita income of country X, which is a developing country, in US dollars is given by

$$\frac{\text{GNP}_X}{\text{Population}} \div \text{Exchange rate}$$

Suppose the GNP of country X is 200 billion rupees, its population is 2 million, and there are 20 rupees to the dollar, then the per capita income of country X in dollars is

$$\frac{200\,\text{billion}}{2\,\text{million}} \div 20 = \$5{,}000$$

Now, if the living standards of the two countries are to be compared by this method, it must be assumed that 20 rupees in country X buys the same living standard as $1 in the US. However, official exchange rates between two countries' currencies are not good measures of the PPP between countries, especially between countries at different levels of development. This is because exchange rates are largely determined by the supply of and demand for currencies based on goods and assets that are traded, the prices of which tend to be equalised internationally. The presumption is that the prices of traded goods will be quite similar between countries because of the forces of international competition and the potential for arbitrage[1] that large differences in prices would offer.

However, PPP depends not only on the prices of traded goods, but also on the prices of non-traded goods, which are largely determined by unit labour costs, and these tend to be lower the poorer the country. These differences will depend upon conditions internal to each country, particularly the average level of income, but also local customs, regulations, the degree of competition, and so on. For non-traded goods and services, like housing, transportation, personal services, and prepared foods that are location specific, there are no international forces of competition or the possibility of arbitrage to bring prices into line between economies. Significant price differentials for these goods and services between economies can make international GNI and GDP comparisons based on simply converting domestic currency measures to a common currency (say US dollar) measures somewhat deceiving, since a US dollar does not have the same buying power everywhere. In poor countries, a US dollar, converted into the local currency, can buy more than a dollar can in the US, since the prices of non-traded goods and services tend to be lower. As a general rule, it can be said that the lower the level of development and the poorer the country, the lower the ratio of the price of non-traded goods to traded goods and the more the use of the official exchange rate will understate the living standards of the developing country measured in US dollars.

As development proceeds the ratio of the price of non-traded goods to traded goods tends to rise as wage levels in the non-traded goods sector rise but productivity growth is slow—slower than in the traded goods sector. To make meaningful international comparisons of income and living standards, therefore, what is required is a measure of PPP, or a real exchange rate, between countries. There are several methods of constructing PPP ratios in order to make binary comparisons or multilateral comparisons in which the currency of any one of a group of countries can act as the unit of account without altering the ratios of living standards between countries.

The PPP measure make an adjustment to GNI between countries similar to the adjustment made to determine real GNI. The prices of one country, in this case the US, become the base prices for determining the purchasing power parity value of GNI per capita in other countries. Thus, purchasing power parity GNI per capita is determined as

$$PPP\ GNI\ per\ capita = \frac{\sum_{i=1}^{n} P_{i,US} \cdot Q_{i,H}}{Population}$$

where, $Q_{i,H}$ is the output vector of all newly produced final goods and services, *i*, available for use by residents of a developing country and $P_{i,US}$ is the price vector for these goods and services, *i*, in US prices. Effectively, then, what the PPP GNI measure provides is the estimated value of home country's available output valued at the prices for such goods and services prevailing in the United States. There is no need to use the exchange rate between the two countries to find the value of home country's GNI per person. Home country's output is valued directly by multiplying that production by US prices.

Another way of constructing a PPP ratio between two countries is to revalue the national incomes of the two countries by selecting a comparable basket of goods and services in each country and estimating the purchasing power equivalent of each item in country *A* relative to country *B*. Thus, if P_{ia} is the price of item *i* in country *A* and P_{ib} is the price of item *i* in country *B*, the purchasing-power equivalent of item *i* in country *A* relative to country *B* is P_{ia}/P_{ib}. By extending this calculation to all goods and applying the price ratios to the average quantities consumed of each item in the two countries, we obtain a formula for the overall purchasing power equivalent in country *A* relative to country *B* as

$$\frac{\sum_{i}^{n} Q_i P_{ia}}{\sum_{i}^{n} Q_i P_{ib}}$$

where, Q_i is the geometric mean of the quantities of each good consumed in the two countries. The purchasing-power-equivalent ratio can then be used to convert one country's national income measured in local currency into another country's currency as the unit of account. For example, suppose that the official exchange rate between the Indian rupee and the US dollar is 10:1, while the purchasing-power-equivalent ratio is 2.5:1. This means that converting the Indian national income into US dollars at the PPP rate will quadruple the amount received at the official exchange rate.

Large differences not only in the prices of non-traded goods and services between the two countries but of the mix of traded to non-traded goods in total national output will affect the PPP measure of GNI per capita compared to the value obtained from the official exchange rate conversion. The PPP per capita income is more meaningful when comparing incomes among economies at any point in time. For the less developed countries, PPP GNI per capita > the exchange rate determined value of GNI per capita.

The PPP measure of income gets us a little closer to understanding the levels of income among diverse economies. The actual purchasing power of income in lower-income countries tends to be understated by simply converting local GDP or GNI per capita to US dollars using the official exchange rates as a result of the lower prices of non-traded goods and services, such as housing, retail services, local food products, and local transportation in poorer nations. These prices are lower because the lower income of these countries keeps the prices of these non-traded goods below what they are in more developed nations. The more developed economies tend to have PPP GNI per capita values closer to that calculated at the official exchange rate because of the greater openness to world trade, a mix of production with more traded goods relative to non-traded goods, and because of their more modern structures of production, which result in greater efficiency in production in both traded and non-traded goods and service sectors.

The Indicators Criterion of Development

The poverty can be defined as the inability of people to attain a minimum standard of living.[2] This definition gives rise to three questions: (i) How do we measure the standard of living? (ii) What is meant by a minimum standard of living? (iii) How can we express the overall extent of poverty in a single measure?

An individual's real income or expenditure can be considered one of the most obvious measure of living standards. However, the same level of real income and expenditure in different countries may be associated with different levels of nutrition, life expectancy, infant mortality, schooling and so on, which must be considered as an integral part of 'the standard of living'. Therefore, measures of living standards based on per capita income may need to be supplemented by further measures that include these other variables.

The International Labour Organisation, the World Bank, and independent researchers, all were against the use of per capita income and the rate of economic growth criterion as the exclusive measures of development. They proposed several measures alternative to GNI, GDP, per capita income, or PPP GNI per capita such as basic needs approach, physical quality of life index (PQLI), and some other composite measure.

Basic Needs Approach to Development

On becoming independent, developing countries adopted a planned interventionist approach aimed at the promotion of growth and industrialisation. In some respects this was successful, as growth and industrialisation did accelerate, and social indicators, such as infant mortality and literacy rates, also improved. However, a dualistic pattern of development resulted, with a small relatively privileged modern sector leaving the rest of the economy with low incomes and investment. Growth in employment, especially in the industrial sector, lagged behind population growth and unemployment and underemployment emerged as serious problems. The incidence of poverty remained very high as a proportion of the population in most developing countries, and the absolute numbers of people falling below a given poverty line increased. Problems of employment and poverty led to new approaches to development. Initially, the ILO suggested that employment expansion should be the overriding goal. But, it was soon accepted that employment is not wanted for itself, but for the recognition, production, and above all incomes that it brings. Consequently, the focus moved to the incomes of the poor, formalised in the publication, *Redistribution with Growth*[3], which advocated giving much higher weight to the incomes of the poor in the development objective. The associated development strategy was to continue to promote growth, but to redistribute the fruits of growth to the poor in the form of productive assets.

It was argued that what the poor need is not money income alone, but essential goods and services to give everyone the opportunity to lead full lives, that is, basic goods and services. Money incomes might not be sufficient to secure adequate supplies of basic needs goods and services because important core elements, such as education, health services and drinking water supplies, depend on public production and distribution, not private incomes.

Thus, the provision of health services, education, housing, sanitation, water supply and adequate nutrition came to be known in development economics as the basic needs approach to economic development. Since the early 1970s the focus of thought about economic development in less developed countries has shifted from a purely growth-oriented approach to approaches that put as much emphasis upon equity as upon growth. One such approach is the basic needs approach that shifts attention from the goal of output maximisation to poverty minimisation. Basic needs is both an analytical concept and a strategy of aid and development. It calls for the elimination of urban bias in both product and technology, and for the reorientation of development efforts in at least two ways—(i) more emphasis on producing those goods and services consumed by the poor, and (ii) creation of employment for the target groups by using appropriate technology and providing public services, especially in the areas of education, health, and housing, until the poor can pay for these basic needs. The rationale of the approach was that the direct provision of such goods and services was likely to relieve absolute poverty more immediately than alternative strategies that would simply attempt to accelerate growth or would rely on raising the incomes and productivity of the poor.

The basic needs approach can be supported by following arguments:

(a) the poor tend not to spend their income wisely, and certain facilities such as water supply and sanitation can be provided only publicly,
(b) the productivity and incomes of the poor depend in the first place on the direct provision of health and education facilities,
(c) growth strategies usually fail to benefit those intended,
(d) it may take a long time to increase the incomes of the poor so that they can afford basic needs,
(e) it is difficult to help all the poor in a uniform way in the absence of the provision of basic needs.

The provision of basic needs could be regarded as a form of consumption transfer (away from investment) so that growth will be retarded and the basic needs strategy will then not be sustainable in the long run. On the other hand, the provision of basic needs could be regarded as a form of investment in human capital, which might be as productive as investment in industry.

The basic needs approach is often identified with a list of particular goods and services that must be made available to all. It has thus been accused of being materialistic[4] and paternalistic by dictating the consumption patterns of the poor. The ILO defines basic needs as 'the minimum standard of living which a society should set for the poorest groups of its people', which they state includes meeting the minimum requirements for personal consumption of food, shelter and clothing; and access to essential services such as safe drinking water, sanitation, health, education and transport; and 'the satisfaction of needs of a more qualitative nature—a healthy, humane and satisfying environment, and popular participation in the making of decisions that affect the lives and livelihood of the people and individual freedoms'. By making participation part of the approach, the ILO indicates that what is to be provided is not intended to be determined paternalistically, but people themselves should contribute to defining their needs. The ILO has emphasised in its various publications that the satisfaction of basic needs depends crucially on the establishment of a new international economic order, the aim of which, according to the Lima Declaration of 1975, was to increase the developing countries' share of world manufacturing output to 25 percent by the year 2000.

The major architects and proponents of the basic needs approach agree that the list of basic needs should not be determined arbitrarily and from outside. Several approaches were proposed for identifying basic needs. One is participatory—getting people themselves to determine their own basic needs; another is consultative—requesting governments to identify the core needs. A third approach is to start by defining the quality of life that should be aimed for—both with respect to its main characteristics, for example, being healthy, nourished, educated, and also the minimum acceptable levels of these characteristics—and then derive the goods and services needed empirically as those that would be necessary to produce the opportunity for a such a 'full' life. This relationship has been described as the meta-production function by Fei, Ranis and Stewart[5] as $FL = f(a, b, c, d, \ldots)$ where, *FL* is a vector of full-life characteristics that might include health, nutrition, educational achievements, participation, employment, political rights and so on; and *a, b, c*,...are the goods and services needed to achieve the minimum acceptable *FL* characteristics.

Thus, potentially the basic needs approach is quite complex, encompassing non-material as well as material needs, and allowing for participation and observation of the meta-production function in order to determine what the actual basic needs requirements are in terms of goods and services. But in practice, the basic needs approach is typically interpreted as involving a quite specific list of requirements—normally including education, health services, food requirements, and sometimes shelter and clothing. The minimum levels are generally defined roughly—for example, enough food to avoid malnutrition, universal access to primary education, universal functional literacy, clean water for all, universal access to primary healthcare, and reasonable quality of shelter for all. Fulfilling these needs would mean huge progress towards eliminating poverty.

The basic needs strategy and structural transformation in the direction of industry lead to the same conclusion as far as industrial growth is concerned. Whether both objectives are achieved largely depends on the overall economic strategy pursued. The basic needs approach suggests a threefold approach to macro planning—supply, demand and organisational. For success, it is necessary to ensure that supplies of the basic needs goods and services are adequate. This is a sharp departure from the income-orientated approach of *Redistribution with Growth*, or many other poverty-reduction strategies, because they focus only on demand (that is, incomes) of the poor, and just assume sufficient supplies would be forthcoming. But since many of the basic needs goods and services are public goods, like health and education services, sanitation and water supplies, this cannot be assumed, but must be planned; moreover, food is a key element and supply rigidities in food production could lead to inflation and failure, unless adequate supplies are ensured. However, it is also essential to focus on the demand side, and see that the poor have sufficient incomes, through employment and self-employment or income transfers to be able to buy adequate food, and to make full use of schools, health clinics and so on. There is also the important issue of ensuring adequate allocation of resources within the household towards basic needs goods. Finally, there is an organisational aspect of planning for basic needs. Because so many basic needs goods and services are produced in the public sector, public sector efficiency needs to be secured in each of the basic needs sector. It is apparent that basic needs approach does not substitute for economic growth, but requires it since economic growth is essential to generate the incomes the poor need and the public revenue to ensure that the sector supplies are adequate. Relatively equal distribution of income is needed, as well as appropriate allocation of public revenue to the basic needs sectors.

The basic needs approach lost support largely because other concerns came to dominate the donor community—namely stabilisation and adjustment—while it was never taken up with enthusiasm by developing countries partly because it tended to be understood, wrongly, as meaning an end to industrialisation and growth. One set of problems with the approach, for which there are a variety of answers but no single solution, is the apparent arbitrariness in choice of the core basic needs goods and services and in the determination of the levels to be aimed at. More fundamentally, the basic needs approach lacked theoretical elegance, and seemed to be an approach that developed countries advocated for developing countries but did not apply to themselves. Countries with a poor performance in the provision of basic needs illustrate that a basic needs strategy must be comprehensive, otherwise failure in one respect will nullify progress in others.[6]

Physical Quality of Life as an Index of Development

Per capita income and structural factors are useful measures for assessing levels of economic development. However, many economists believe they are insufficient or perhaps even misleading, as they ignore other kinds of social well-being. Indeed, many analysts believe that focusing on income levels tends to obscure the real purpose of poverty-alleviation programs. They argue that raising income levels is merely an instrumental goal. The real objective is improving the physical quality of life and the basic standard of living for people in developing countries. To assess a country's progress towards development, they say, one needs to measure improvements towards those goals.

Rapid economic growth raised average living standards in many countries around the globe in the 1960s and the early 1970s, but inequality also emerged as an issue. Prosperity bypassed large segments of the population, especially in developing countries, which stimulated a search for meaningful measures of poverty that were readily calculable. Some people saw progress in the segments of the population that lacked essential human needs, such as clean water, basic medical care, suitable housing, and adequate calories. An early effort to rank countries solely on the basis of the physical and social well-being of their population was the Physical Quality of Life Index (PQLI). It was developed for the UK Overseas Development

Council in the mid-1970s by Morris David Morris, as one of a number of measures created due to dissatisfaction with the use of GNP as an indicator of development.

PQLI is a measure of performance in meeting the basic needs of poor populations that lends itself well to international comparisons. This ranked three factors—life expectancy at age 1, infant mortality and literacy—on a single index, without any direct reference to income levels. Life expectancy at age one and infant mortality were selected because they sum up the combined effects of social relations, nutritional status, public health, and family environment. During infancy, patterns that affect feeding and rearing, specifically those reflected in maternal and family practices are extremely important. This suggests that infant mortality is a reflection of specific environmental influences and family characteristics, a great part of which are affected by the role and position of women. Beyond infancy, life expectancy at age one is an indicator of the much broader and all embracing environmental impact on life and death chances. The third indicator, literacy provides information about the potential for development and the extent to which poor groups can share the possibilities and advantages of development activity. A simple average of these three indicators is taken, after transforming the demographic variables to scales of 0–100 representing the feasible ranges for their values.

For each indicator, the performance of individual countries is rated on a scale of 1 to 100, where 1 represents the worst performance by any country and 100 the best performance. For life expectancy, the upper limit of 100 was assigned to 77 years (achieved by Sweden in 1973) and the lower limit of 1 was assigned to 28 years (the life expectancy of Guinea-Bissau in 1950). Within these limits, each country's life expectancy figure is ranked from 1 to 100. For example, a life expectancy of 52, midway between the upper and lower limits of 77 and 28, would be assigned a rating of 50. Similarly, for infant mortality, the upper limit was set at 9 per 1,000 (achieved by Sweden in 1973) and the lower limit at 229 per 1,000 (Gabon, 1950). Literacy rates, measured as percentages from 1 to 100, provide their own direct scale. Once a country's performance in life expectancy, infant mortality, and literacy has been rated on the scale of 1 to 100, the composite index for the country is calculated by averaging the three ratings, giving equal weight to each.

It is found that significant improvements in the basic quality of life can be achieved before there is any great rise in per capita GNP or, conversely, that a higher level of per capita GNP is not a guarantee of a better quality of life. There was a loose correlation between income levels and PQLI performance, but the disparities in some instances were striking. Some countries with high-income levels had PQLI rankings at levels below the average for the poorest countries, while some very low-income countries had PQLI levels comparable to those for many upper middle-income states. Particularly noteworthy were the contrasts between Saudi Arabia and Sri Lanka; health and education rankings were much higher at the time in the latter country despite its lower average income.

If we want to measure the changing condition of the world's poor, we need a better measure of what is happening to them. The measure must tell us not how much has been spent, but how effectively lives have improved. The Physical Quality of Life Index (PQLI) is one way of measuring development. Although far from the threshold of paradise, human well-being and development as measured by infant mortality, life expectancy, and literacy rate has been improving in some countries better than others. Viewing the map of South America and Africa, it is obvious that South America exhibits a higher PQLI than Africa. From this one can assume that South America have better living standards in which their infant mortality, life expectancy, and literacy rate should be greater than Africa's. Compared to Africa, South America must contain better living condition, which means that the people living there should have enough money to buy food. Rising PQLI numbers show that there is vitality, and organisational potential that can be mobilised to directly improve the conditions of poor countries. The gains have come from the mobilisation of indigenous people.

PQLI might be regarded as an improvement but shares the general problems of measuring quality of life in a quantitative way. It has also been criticized because there is considerable overlap between infant mortality and life expectancy. In principle one could use the PQLI in much the same way as any measure of human welfare, including policy design and assessment, or as a phenomenon to be explained by economic or social models. Econometric work, however, has been limited, in part because imitators and successors have crowded the field. Although the PQLI was designed as a minimal measure of social performance and partly as an antidote to undue emphasis on gross national product (GNP) per capita, its critics have noted that health is counted twice (infant mortality and life expectancy at age one are highly correlated) and that the index omits the material side of the quality of life. Soon other indexes appeared, some with more than 40 components or indicators, including crime, pollution, and suicide rates. Among these, the Human Development Index (HDI) of the United Nations has been the most widely discussed and applied.

Human Development as an Index of Development

Development means the material advancement of people, especially the world's poor. But material advancement, especially if understood as simple economic growth, is not enough by itself, and, indeed may not even be realised without other components of development which includes the capacity to ensure adequate distribution of the benefits of such growth, ecological sustainability in the way growth is achieved, and the governance to ensure that the processes to achieve such growth are agreed in a politically inclusive manner and operate under the rule of law. If we accept that development in its fullest form represents more than material advances and economic growth, then the measurement of development needs to reflect this broader definition. To overcome the limitation of taking a single measure of per capita income as an index of development and the problem of using per capita income as a measure of living standards, the United Nations Development Program (UNDP) has developed two alternative indices by which to compare the level of development and the progress of countries—Human Development Index (HDI) and Human Poverty Index (HPI). These indices give alternative measures of the economic well-being of nations that do not necessarily accord with the usual measure—the level of per capita income. As the UNDP says in its *Human Development Report* (2004) 'although GNP growth is absolutely necessary to meet all essential human objectives, countries differ in the way that they translate growth into human development'. This depends not only on income but also on other social indicators such as life expectancy, education, literacy and health provision.

As a method of measuring development the best known alternative to the economic indices is the Human Development Index, which relies upon multiple criteria and which is partly based on the work of the Indian economist Amartya Sen. The HDI is calculated on the basis of 'three dimensions' to human development—first, a *long and healthy life*, measured by life expectancy at birth; second, *knowledge*, measured on the basis of adult literacy rates and the combined gross enrolment ratio for primary, secondary and tertiary schools; third, a *decent standard of living*, measured by GDP per capita. The actual index uses estimates of life expectancy at birth, the adult literacy rate, school enrolment ratios, and PPP GDP per capita to calculate an HDI value for each economy. The HDI encapsulates a concept of development as a process of enlarging people's choices, allowing them the opportunity to live longer, to acquire knowledge, etc. Thus, the narrow focus on economic growth and transformation is widened to embrace a variety of other (economic but also non-economic) factors. The 1980s saw a further crucial variable thrown into this definitional pot, that of environmental sustainability. In its most famous articulation, from the Brundtland Commission, 'Sustainable development is development that meets the needs of the present without compromising the ability of future generations to meet their own needs.'[7]

The HDI measure of development is thus broader than the simple income per person yardstick, though income does enter into the calculation of the HDI. At the same time, the HDI gives direct value to those factors, particularly education, which help create opportunities for individuals to reach a higher and more fulfilling standard of living that may not be captured by the income measure alone. The actual calculation of the HDI value for any country is based on that country's deviation from the maximum values for each component of the index—a maximum life expectancy of eighty-five years at birth; 100 percent literacy and 100 percent combined (primary and secondary) school enrollment; and a maximum PPP GDP per capita income of $40,000. Thus, HDI measures the relative position of an economy compared to the maximum (and minimum) levels of achievement. In other words, the HDI is a measure of how far away a country is from the current maximum achievable values on the selected variables that enter the HDI.

With the 1995 issue of the *Human Development Report*, the HDI is calculated as a weighted average of educational attainment, life expectancy at birth, and income. All components of the index measure the relative distance between a country's achievement and what is possible. Thus, for any component of the HDI, the individual indices can be computed according to the general formula:

$$\text{Index value} = \frac{\text{actual value} - \text{minimum value}}{\text{maximum value} - \text{minimum value}}$$

Educational attainment (E) is measured as a combination of two indices, one for adult literacy (minimum value = 0 percent; maximum value = 100 percent) and of the combined primary, secondary, and tertiary enrolment ratio (minimum = 0 percent; maximum = 100 percent) with the following weights:

$$E = 2/3 \text{ adult literacy rate} + 1/3 \text{ combined enrollment ratio}$$

Life expectancy (L), for purposes of calculating the HDI index, has a minimum value of 25 years and a maximum value of 85 years.

Income (Y) enters the HDI as a log value of the purchasing power parity (PPP) measure of GDP per capita. As the UN Development Program puts it, "income serves as a surrogate for all the dimensions of human development not reflected in a long and healthy life and in knowledge".[8] PPP GDP per capita income beyond $40,000 adds nothing further to the Y index.

Let us calculate the HDI of India for year 2007. The basic data needed to calculate L, E, and Y are: Life expectancy at birth

= 63.4 years; Literacy rate = 66 percent; combined enrollment rate = 61 percent; and PPP GDP per capita = $2,753.

The life expectancy index, L is determined as

$$L = \frac{63.4 - 25}{85 - 25} = 0.64$$

To determine the education index, E, a two-step procedure is necessary. First, the adult literacy index, A, component of educational attainment is calculated as

$$A = \frac{66 - 0}{100 - 0} = 0.66$$

Second, the combined enrollment index, C, the other component of education attainment, is determined as

$$C = \frac{61 - 0}{100 - 0} = 0.61$$

The educational attainment index, E, is calculated as

$$E = \frac{2}{3}A + \frac{1}{3}C = \frac{2}{3}(0.66) + \frac{1}{3}(0.61) = 0.6433$$

The income index, Y, using PPP GDP per capita income is

$$Y = \frac{\log(2,753) - \log(100)}{\log(40,000) - \log(100)} = \frac{3.4398 - 2}{4.6020 - 2} = \frac{1.4398}{2.6020} = 0.553344$$

The value of the HDI is then calculated as a weighted average of L, E, and Y, with each components having a value of 1/3. Since each of these is a "deprivation" measure, what is being calculated is the gap between a particular country's achievement level and what might be attained. Thus, the HDI for India in 2007 is a simple weighted average of L, E, and Y, given by

$$\begin{aligned} \text{HDI} &= \frac{1}{3}L + \frac{1}{3}E + \frac{1}{3}Y \\ &= \frac{1}{3}(0.64) + \frac{1}{3}(0.6433) + \frac{1}{3}(0.553344) \\ &= 0.612215 \end{aligned}$$

The HDI simplifies the comparison among countries by combining the achievement on a number of different variables into a single number. The value of the HDI index can vary between 0 and 1, with an HDI score closer to 0 indicating greater distance from the maximum to be achieved on the aggregate of the factors entering the HDI. An HDI value closer to 1 indicates greater achievement relative to the maximum attainable on the variables that comprise the index and thus a higher level of human development.

Although such comparisons of ratios simply do not make sense, the ranking generated by the HDI are of some interest because they illustrate how it is possible for a relatively high-income country to face so badly in meeting basic socio-economic goals that its HDI index falls behind that of a relatively poor country. One way to show how this happens is to present the HDI ranking for different countries as well as the ranking induced by per capita GDP. It is then possible to study the difference in the two rankings induced by these two measures. A positive difference means that the country has done better in "human development" relative to its position in the GDP rankings; a negative ranking means the opposite.

The HDI measure was created with the purpose of attempting to take into account the fact that countries, meaning both governments and individuals, make choices on their spending and use of resources among alternative uses. The use of these resources affects the range of choices open to people and their level of well-being, with effects that may not always be captured in the income per person ranking of nations. For instance, among the less-developed nations, it is found that though one-quarter of national income is spent via government, less than 10 percent of this share, on average, is dedicated to identifiable human development expenditures, such as education, health care, and social security. The largest area of government spending is on the military, the contribution of which to human development is, at best, controversial. Of course, different nations will allocate their public expenditures in different ways, both to achieve particular development goals, as well as to accomplish other priorities, such as defence, that are deemed significant.

The impact of these choices, at least partly, will be captured by the variables included in the HDI, and thus, it is argued, provide a more robust view of the average level of development of an economy than is possible by simply looking at per capita income.

Just as it is useful to adjust the GDP or GNI income figures so that they provide a more reliable standard for evaluating the level of development if one is to use that measure, so too are there some modifications that can be made to the HDI that refine the information it provides. Gender development index (GDI) and human poverty index (HPI) are the modified version of the HDI.

Gender Development as an Index of Development

The Human Development Index (HDI), the single composite measure of education, health and living standards, was the first serious attempt to assess development that goes beyond the income dimension. However, HDI does not take into account the disparity between males and females. Hence, subsequently need for comprehensive investigation of gender inequality in economic and social arrangements was felt and a program to develop a framework for gender-equity-sensitive indicators was launched under HDR in 1995. The status of women is central to the economy because if one half of the society suffers so does the rest. Hence, it was imperative to have an index, which incorporates the extent of inequality between males and females in achievements.

Gender and development are complementary to each other having both-way causality. Gender disparities lead to weaker economic growth and that stronger economic growth leads to reduced gender disparities. It is found that reducing gender inequality and improving the status of women may contribute to higher economic growth and bring about greater macroeconomic stability, whereas women's relative lack of opportunities in developing and least developed countries inhibits economic growth. Economic growth leads to an improvement in the condition of the disadvantaged groups, including gender. Gender inequality is not only the most marked form of inequality in a society, but also the most pervasive within all socio-economic groups. In most developing countries, gender inequality is a major obstacle to meeting the Millennium Development Goal (MDG) targets. In fact, achieving the goals will be impossible without closing the gaps between women and men in terms of capacities, access to resources and opportunities, and vulnerability to violence and conflict. Also literature shows that women in control of their household's resources spend more on basic necessities and on the development of their children's potential than men do in similar circumstances.[9] Thus, equality of gender at both micro and macro level is bound to lead to more of human well-being.

Both qualitative and quantitative presence of women in the workforce is important not only for lowering the disproportionate levels of poverty among women, but also for taking a step towards raising household income and encouraging economic development in countries as a whole.[10] As women tend to be less corrupt than men, societies where women enjoy greater participation in public life have 'cleaner' businesses and governments.[11] Corruption is attributed to lack of women voice in policy-making, which in turn produces poorer quality of institutions, lower quality investment, and weaker growth. Sen (1999) has also advocated the notion where the societies need to see women less as passive recipients of help, and more as dynamic promoters of social transformation, evidence suggesting that the education, employment and ownership rights of women have a powerful influence on their ability to control their environment and contribute to economic development. Gender inequalities in human capital and other productive inputs lead to slower growth and because growth can reduce the disadvantaged condition of women, there is merit to the idea of a virtuous circle of growth and reduction in gender inequalities. Being sensitive to gender concerns has intrinsic as well as instrumental advantages. In the measurement of Human Development this is echoed through the Gender Development Index (GDI).

GDI is one of the two gender sensitive measures by UNDP to assess overall development with a note on inequality.[12] GDI is a gender-adjusted HDI measured in the equally weighted components, same as the HDI, but formulated in a way to take note of the gaps between men and women on each of these components. The three components are income at purchasing power parity; education, measured in terms of weighted average of adult literacy rate and enrollment ratio;[13] and health in terms of life expectancy at birth.

Calculation of the GDI involves three steps:

Step 1: Unit-free indices between 0 and 1 are calculated for both females and males for life expectancy, education (the adult literacy rate and the combined primary to tertiary gross enrollment ratio), and estimated earned income at purchasing power parity.

$$\text{Female Life Expectancy Index} = \frac{\text{female life expectancy} - 27.5}{87.5 - 27.5}$$

$$\text{Male Life Expectancy Index} = \frac{\text{male life expectancy} - 22.5}{82.5 - 22.5}$$

Female and Male Education Indices

$$= \frac{2}{3} \cdot \frac{\text{adult literacy rate of gender}}{100} + \frac{1}{3} \cdot \frac{\text{gross enrollment rate of gender}}{100}$$

Female and Male Income Indices

$$= \frac{\log(\text{earned income of gender}) - \log(100)}{\log(40{,}000) - \log(100)}$$

Step 2: For each area, the pair of gender indices are combined into an equally distributed index that rewards gender equality and penalises inequality. It is calculated as the harmonic mean of the two indices as

Equally Distributed Index

$$= \left(\frac{\text{female share of population}}{\text{female index}} + \frac{\text{male share of population}}{\text{male index}} \right)^{-1}$$

Step 3: The GDI is the unweighted average of the three equally distributed indices—equally distributed life expectancy index, equally distributed education index, and equally distributed income index.

Let us calculate the GDI of India for the year 2007 considering following data:

Female life expectancy at birth = 64.9 years
Male life expectancy at birth = 62.0 years
Adult literacy rate for female = 54.5%
Adult literacy rate for male = 76.9%
Gross enrollment rate for female = 57.4%
Gross enrollment rate for male = 64.3%
Earned income for female = 1304 (PPP US$)
Earned income for male = 4102 (PPP US$)
Share of female in total population = 48.26%
Share of male in total population = 51.74%

$$\text{Female Life Expectancy Index} = \frac{64.9 - 27.5}{87.5 - 27.5} = 0.6233$$

$$\text{Male Life Expectancy Index} = \frac{62 - 22.5}{82.5 - 22.5} = 0.6583$$

$$\text{Female Education Index} = \frac{2}{3}\cdot\frac{54.5}{100} + \frac{1}{3}\cdot\frac{57.4}{100} = 0.55466$$

$$\text{Male Education Index} = \frac{2}{3}\cdot\frac{76.9}{100} + \frac{1}{3}\cdot\frac{64.3}{100} = 0.727$$

$$\text{Female Income Index} = \frac{\log(1304) - \log(100)}{\log(40,000) - \log(100)}$$

$$= \frac{3.11527 - 2}{4.6020 - 2} = 0.42862$$

$$\text{Male Income Index} = \frac{\log(4102) - \log(100)}{\log(40,000) - \log(100)}$$

$$= \frac{3.61299 - 2}{4.6020 - 2} = 0.61990$$

Equally Distributed Life Expectancy Index

$$= \left(\frac{48.26}{0.6233} + \frac{51.74}{0.6583}\right)^{-1} = 0.006409$$

Equally Distributed Education Index

$$= \left(\frac{48.26}{0.55466} + \frac{51.74}{0.727} \right)^{-1} = 0.006322$$

Equally Distributed Income Index

$$= \left(\frac{48.26}{0.42862} + \frac{51.74}{0.6199} \right)^{-1} = 0.005101$$

Thus,

Gender Development Index (GDI)

$$= \frac{100\,(0.006409 + 0.006322 + 0.005101)}{3} = 0.5944$$

The value of GDI lies between 0 and 1. If the GDI, which is simply a gender-adjusted HDI value, is less than the average HDI, reflects the lower average level of attainment of women compared to men on the variables entering the HDI. Some countries do better than others on gender equality, however, so that the GDI ranking of all countries is different from the HDI ranking, rising for those nations for which the average achievement of women is closer to that of men and falling for those nations where the achievement of women is more distant from that of men as a group. If we consider Saudi Arabia and China, the former is ranked seventy-sixth and the latter eighty-first on the HDI. However, looking at the GDI values of each country, we see that China scores higher than Saudi Arabia and thus China ranks higher on the GDI, sixty-fourth versus seventy-second for Saudi Arabia. Still, no country had a GDI equal to or greater than its HDI. Closing the gaps in education, health, income, and political participation between men and women is essential for full development of a nation, and the GDI gives us some indication of the success of countries in achieving gender equity.

The GDI measure is criticised because of its failure to make a cross-country comparison as the absolute level of human development is conflated with gender equality. Income component of measurement is also criticised because of its urban bias and non-consideration of control over family income. There is problem associated with earned income component of the GDI and how it dominates over the health and education dimensions. The rationale of uniform weight schemes to all dimensions and non-consideration of age specific mortality in health dimension are also questioned. It has further been suggested that the scope of GDI by expanded to include subtle gender inequalities like bias in educational choices, access to employment and consumption of goods. Morrisson and Jutting (2005) have identified GDI's failure to account the institutional framework which encompasses the influence of traditions, customs, and explicit and implicit laws regarding the role and positions of women.

Human Poverty as an Index of Development

HDI does not indicate what is happening to the poorest members of society, except to the extent that this is reflected in the overall HDI value via, say, the impact of poverty on average life expectancy. To attempt to capture the conditions of living of the poor more directly, the UNDP introduced Human Poverty Index (HPI) that utilises slightly different variables from either the HDI or the GDI and hence is not directly comparable.

If human development is about enlarging choices, poverty means that opportunities and choices most basic to human development are denied. Thus, a person is not free to lead a long, healthy, and creative life and is denied access to a decent standard of living, freedom, dignity, self-respect and the respect of others. From a human development perspective, poverty means more than the lack of what is necessary for material well-being. For policy-makers, the poverty of choices and opportunities is often more relevant than the poverty of income. The poverty of choices focuses on the causes of poverty and leads directly to strategies of empowerment and other actions to enhance opportunities for everyone. Recognising the poverty of choices and opportunities implies that poverty must be addressed in all its dimensions, not income alone.

The Human Poverty Index (HPI) is an attempt to bring together in a composite index the different features of deprivation in the quality of life to arrive at an aggregate judgment on the extent of poverty in a community. It is a composite measure set in the capability and human development space, drawing on the several important perspectives that have enriched our understanding of poverty. In this framework, poverty is the deprivation side of human development—the denial of basic choices and opportunities to lead a long, healthy, creative and free life; to enjoy a decent standard of living; and to participate in the life of the community including political freedom and cultural choices. HPI is a measure of capability deprivation; it aims to capture 'human poverty' as distinct from 'income poverty', i.e. failures to achieve the basic capabilities needed for human functioning rather than any given level of consumption or income. But like the HDI, the HPI is a highly incomplete measure and does not capture many of the dimensions of a full life, nor the social conditions that are necessary. Sen refers to five 'instrumental freedoms' as essential to a life of dignity, namely economic facilities, social opportunities, political freedom, security and transparency guarantees. Neither the HPI nor HDI include indicators of political freedom, security and transparency.

Important aspects of human poverty, notably those relating to participation such as political freedom and cultural choices, are simply not quantifiable or lack data and thus not included. Still, HPI is a more adequate measure of deprivations in human lives than the income poverty measure. HPI focuses on three of the four key dimensions of HDI: the capability to:

(i) survive, measured by vulnerability to early death defined as before 40 years;

(ii) be knowledgeable, measured by the adult illiteracy rate; and

(iii) have access to private income as well as public provisioning, measured by the percentage of malnourished children under five and by the percentage of people without access to safe water.

These particular measures are not so relevant in the richer industrial societies. Therefore an adjusted HPI was developed with indicators more suited to high income Organisation for Economic Co-operation and Development (OECD) countries. Thus, we have two measures for the human poverty index—one for developing countries and other for developed OECD countries.

The human poverty index for developing countries (HPI-1): The HPI-1 measures deprivation in the three basic dimensions of human development in the developing countries.

(a) A long and healthy life—vulnerability to death at a relatively early age, as measured by the probability at birth of not surviving to age 40.

(b) Knowledge—exclusion from the world of reading and communications, as measured by the adult illiteracy rate.

(c) A decent standard of living—lack of access to overall economic provisioning, as measured by the unweighted average of two indicators, the percentage of the population not using an improved water source and the percentage of children under weight-for-age.

Calculating the HPI-1 is straightforward since the indicators used to measure the deprivations are normalised between 0 and 100 and so there is no need to create dimension indices as for the HDI. Calculation of HPI-1 involves two steps:

Step 1: Measuring deprivation in a decent standard of living—an unweighted average of two indicators is used to measure deprivation in a decent standard of living.

Unweighted average

$$= \frac{1}{2}(\text{population not using an improved water source}) + \frac{1}{2}(\text{children under weight-for-age})$$

Step 2: Calculating the HPI-1—the formula used to calculate the HPI-1 is

$$HPI\text{-}1 = \left[\frac{1}{3}\left(P_1^{\alpha} + P_2^{\alpha} + P_3^{\alpha}\right)\right]^{\frac{1}{\alpha}}$$

where,

P_1 = probability at birth of not surviving to age 40,

P_2 = adult literacy rate,

P_3 = unweighted average of population not using an improved water source and children under weight-for-age, and

α = 3.

Let us calculate the human poverty index for India using the data of 2007.

Probability of not surviving to age 40 = 15.5%

Adult illiteracy rate (15 and above) = 34%

People not using an improved water source = 11%

Children underweight-for-age (aged under 5) = 46%

Thus, we have

$P_1 = 15.5,$

$P_2 = 34,$

$P_3 = \frac{1}{2}(11) + \frac{1}{2}(46) = 28.5$

$\alpha = 3$

$$\text{HPI - 1} = \left[\frac{1}{3}\left\{(15.5)^3 + (34)^3 + (28.5)^3\right\}\right]^{\frac{1}{3}}$$

$$= \left[\frac{1}{3}(3723.875 + 39304 + 23149.125)\right]^{\frac{1}{3}}$$

$$= \left(\frac{66177}{3}\right)^{\frac{1}{3}} = (22059)^{\frac{1}{3}} = 28.045$$

The human poverty index for OECD countries (HPI-2): The HPI-2 measure deprivations in the same dimensions as the HPI-1 and also captures social exclusion. Thus, it reflects deprivations in four dimensions:

(a) A long and healthy life—vulnerability to death at a relatively early age, as measured by the probability at birth of not surviving to age 60.

(b) Knowledge—exclusion from the world of reading and communications, as measured by the percentage of adults (ages 16-65) lacking functional literacy skills.

(c) A decent standard of living—as measured by the percentage of people living below the income poverty line (50 percent of the median adjusted household disposable income).

(d) Social exclusion—as measured by the rate of long-term unemployment (12 months or more).

HPI-2 can be calculated using the formula,

$$\text{HPI - 2} = \left[\frac{1}{4}\left(P_1^{\alpha} + P_2^{\alpha} + P_3^{\alpha} + P_4^{\alpha}\right)\right]^{\frac{1}{\alpha}}$$

where,

P_1 = probability at birth of not surviving to age 60,

P_2 = percentage of adults lacking functional literacy skills,

P_3 = percentage of population below income poverty line,

P_4 = rate of long-term unemployment (lasting 12 months or more), and

α = 3.

Let us calculate the human poverty index for Norway using the data of 2007.

Probability of not surviving to age 60 = 6.6%

People lacking functional literacy skills = 7.9%

Population living below 50% of median income = 7.1%

Long-term unemployment = 0.2%

Thus, we have

$P_1 = 6.6$

$P_2 = 7.9$

$P_3 = 7.1$

$P_4 = 0.2$

$\alpha = 3$

$$\text{HPI - 2} = \left[\frac{1}{4}\left\{(6.6)^3 + (7.9)^3 + (7.1)^3 + (0.2)^3\right\}\right]^{\frac{1}{3}}$$

$$= \left[\frac{1}{4}(287.496 + 493.039 + 357.911 + 0.008)\right]^{\frac{1}{3}}$$

$$= \left(\frac{1138.454}{4}\right)^{\frac{1}{3}} = (284.6135)^{\frac{1}{3}} = 6.577868$$

In calculating HPI-1 and HPI-2, the value of α has an important impact. If α = 1, the HPI is the average of its dimensions. As α rises, greater weight is given to the dimension in which there is the most deprivation. Thus, as α increases towards infinity, the HPI will tend towards the value of the dimension in which deprivation is greater. The value 3 is used to give additional but not overwhelming weight to areas of more acute deprivation.[14]

The correlation between income poverty and human poverty is weak, and there is a large spread in levels of human poverty among countries with similar levels of income poverty. Some countries with high levels of human poverty around 40 percent such as Pakistan and Yemen have relatively low levels of income poverty around 15-17 percent like Ecuador and China, which have reduced human poverty to around 10 ercent. These data highlight both achievements and challenges for governments. Some countries with very low GDP per capita have achieved significantly more reduction in human poverty than countries with higher levels of income. Tanzania for example reduced human poverty to 36 percent, which is still high, though not when compared to their income poverty of 58 percent and per capita GDP of only PPP $ 674. This level of human poverty is similar to or lower than countries with much higher incomes, such as Pakistan (36%) and Bangladesh (44%), where per capita GDP is respectively PPP $ 2225 and PPP$ 1870.

Following are some of the characteristics of the HPI estimates.

(a) *Policy priorities:* Countries that show higher levels of human poverty in relation to income poverty or per capita income point to a need for greater policy attention on low social achievements, especially public provisioning related to health and education. Although HPI does not capture the full extent of deprivations in human lives, it covers the essential aspects of life that relate to social and economic policies, and that go beyond income alone.

(b) *Feasibility:* The HPI demonstrates the relevance and the feasibility of a multi-dimensional aggregate measure to monitor human as opposed to income poverty.

(c) *Data availability*: HPI uses internationally comparable data. While there are many gaps, the gaps in these data are fewer than the gaps in the PPP $1 a day estimates. HPI is estimated for 102 developing countries while the PPP $1 a day estimate is available for 94 countries.

(d) *Coverage*: HPI covers 95 countries as compared with 174 countries for HDI.

(e) *Global and regional estimates*: HPI is of particular interest for monitoring global trends in the way that the $1/day income poverty estimates do. Global and regional estimates of HPI should be attempted.

HPI estimates show the relevance of aggregate, internationally comparable measures of multidimensional poverty. Intercountry comparisons of HPI sharpen the focus on human poverty that requires policy attention, and should be further developed to provide a global monitoring tool. According to UNDP, the cost of eradicating poverty across the globe is relatively small compared with global income, and that 'political commitment, not financial resources, is the real obstacle to poverty eradication'. Basic social services could be made available to all people in developing countries at the cost much lower than the defence expenditure of the country. Less than one percent of the world income is required to eradicate income poverty across the world.

Capability and Entitlement as an Index of Development

Amartya Sen's vision of development is defined in terms of the expansion of entitlements and capabilities, the former gives life sustenance and self-esteem; and the latter gives freedom. Life-sustenance is concerned with the provision of basic needs and self-esteem is concerned with the feeling of self-respect and independence. No country can be regarded as fully developed if it is exploited by others and does not have the power and influence to conduct relations on equal terms. Developing countries seek development for self-esteem; to eradicate the feeling of dominance and dependence that is associated with inferior economic status. And freedom refers to freedom from the three evils of 'want, ignorance and squalor' so that people are more able to determine their own destiny.

Entitlement is defined as 'the set of alternative commodity bundles that a person can command in a society using the totality of rights and obligations that he or she faces', and entitlements generate the capability to do certain things. Economic development should be thought of in terms of the expansion of entitlements and capabilities, which are not well captured by aggregate measures of output growth.

Sen views freedom as the primary objective of development, as well as the principal means of achieving development. Development consists of the removal of various types of 'unfreedoms' that leave people with little choice and opportunity. Major categories of 'unfreedom' include famine and undernourishment, poor health and lack of basic needs; lack of political liberty and basic civil rights, and economic insecurity. Development should be regarded as a process of expanding the real freedoms that people enjoy.

Capability

The capability approach has been pioneered and developed by the economist and philosopher Amartya Sen and the philosopher Martha Nussbaum.[15] According to this approach, the proper evaluative space in questions of justice, equality, and development is not income, not resources, not primary goods, not utility (i.e., happiness or the sum of pains and pleasures) or preference satisfaction. Its proponents argue that the focus should be on human capabilities. Capabilities have been described as "what people are effectively able to do and be",[16] or the (positive) freedom that people have "to enjoy 'valuable beings and doings'".[17] These beings and doings are called "functionings" by Sen.

The capability approach advocates a focus on people's capabilities when making normative evaluations, such as those involved in poverty measurement, cost-benefit analysis, efficiency evaluations, social justice issues, development ethics, and inequality analysis. It contains three central concepts—functioning, capability, and agency. A functioning is a valuable activity or state that makes up people's well-being. A capability is a person's ability to do valuable acts or reach valuable states of being. Agency is a person's ability to pursue and realise goals he has reason to value. The human development and capability approach is multi-dimensional. It contains four key principles—equity, efficiency, participation/empowerment and sustainability.

Functionings "together constitute what makes a life valuable"[18] and are "constitutive of a person's being".[19] Examples of functionings are such diverse things as working, resting, being literate, being healthy, being part of a community, being able to travel, and being confident. "The distinction between achieved functionings and capabilities", as Robeyns explains, "is between the realized and the effectively possible; in other words, between achievements on the one hand, and freedoms or valuable options from which one can choose on the other".[20] According to Alkire, one reason to focus on capabilities instead of functionings is that we value free choice. A person who is fasting is in a state of undernutrition, which may seem very similar to a person who is starving. But in the one case, the fasting person could eat and chooses not to; whereas the starving person would eat if he could. Moreover, the capability approach recognises the importance of both "well-being freedom" and "agency freedom". The latter acknowledges that people pursue not only their own well-being, but may also choose to pursue other ends; for example, the well-being of others, living up to religious ideals, or following moral norms.

The difference between a functioning and a capability is like the one between an achievement and the freedom to achieve something, or between an outcome and an opportunity. All capabilities together correspond to the overall freedom to lead the life that a person has reason to value. Sen stresses the importance of 'reason to value', because he argues that we need to scrutinise motivations to value specific lifestyles, and not simply value a certain life without reflecting upon it.

By advocating that normative evaluations should look at people's capabilities, Sen criticises evaluations that focus exclusively on utilities or income. He argues against a utility-based evaluation of individual well-being because such an evaluation might not reveal important dimensions and lead to misleading interpersonal or intertemporal comparisons. A person may be in a desperate situation with little food and poor shelter, and still be contented with life if he has never known it differently. A utilitarian evaluation will only assess her satisfaction, and will not differentiate between a happy healthy and well-sheltered person, versus an equally happy, but unhealthy and badly sheltered person who has mentally adapted to his situation.

The capability approach also rejects normative evaluations based on commodities, income, or material resources. Resources are only the means to people's well-being and advantage, whereas the concern should be with what matters intrinsically, namely people's functionings and capabilities. Resources-based theories do not acknowledge that people differ in their abilities to convert these resources into capabilities, due to personal, social or environmental conversion factors, such as physical and mental handicaps, talents, traditions, social norms, social customs, legal rules, a society's public infrastructure, public goods, and climate.

One of the crucial insights of the capability approach is that the conversion of goods and services into functionings is influenced by personal, social, and environmental conversion factors; and that it should not be taken for granted that resource provision leads to increased capabilities or functionings. The reason why capability theorists prefer these capabilities over utility or preference satisfaction is the phenomenon which Sen has called "adaptive preferences".

The capability approach is increasingly being applied in different areas. In 2006, Robeyns identified nine different types of applications of the capability approach:[21]

(a) general assessments of human development of countries,
(b) assessing small-scale development projects,
(c) identifying the poor in developing countries,
(d) poverty and well-being assessment in advanced economies,
(e) deprivation of disabled people,
(f) assessing gender inequalities,
(g) debating policies,

(h) critiquing and assessing social norms, practices, and discourses, and

(i) functionings and capabilities as concepts in non-normative research.

One very important debate is about which capabilities matter and who (how, when) is to decide this. Different visions exist on this issue. One of several differences that Robeyns mentions between the contributions of Nussbaum and Sen is that, "whereas in Sen's work the notion of capabilities is primarily that of a real or effective opportunity (as in social choice theory); Nussbaum's notion of capability pays more attention to people's skills and personality traits as aspects of capabilities". And while Nussbaum comes up with a concrete and—so he believes—universally applicable list of important capabilities, "Sen has always refused to endorse one specific well-defined list of capabilities", or to set priorities among different capabilities. His reasons are that the proper list of capabilities may depend on purpose and context, and should be a result of public reasoning and democracy; not something a theorist should come up with.

Nussbaum and Sen's versions of the capability approach have different theoretical assertions, and their approaches entail different conceptions of what the list should be doing. Nussbaum's list is a list of normative things-to-do. Her list has a highly prescriptive character and she makes strong universalistic claims regarding the scope of her theory. Nussbaum has used the capability approach to develop a universal theory of the good—it applies to all social justice issues, and to the global world. This does not imply, she argues, that her list is not sensitive to culture and context. Her list is formulated at a highly abstract level, and for each country or community, it can then be made more specific depending on the local context. Hence, in Nussbaum's theory, there is one universal general list, which can be translated in more detailed and specific lists so as to suit the context.

Sen's capability approach, in contrast, has broader and less specified theoretical pretensions—Sen's capability approach is only a *framework*, not a *theory*. Given the intrinsic under-specification of Sen's capability approach, there cannot be one catch-all definite list. Instead, each application of the capability approach will require its own list. For Sen, a list of capabilities must be context dependent, where the context is both the geographical area to which it applies, as well as the sort of evaluation that is done. Applications of Sen's capability approach can be very diverse. They can be academic, activist, or policy-oriented. They can be abstract and philosophical, or applied and very down to earth. They can be theoretical or empirical. These applications can concern social, political, economic, legal, psychological or other dimensions of advantage, either all taken together, or considering only a few. The capability approach can be specified for a global or a local context.

The fact that the capability approach is not a fully fleshed-out theory means that its further specifications can be very diverse. For each of these further specifications, we will need a relevant list of capabilities. How should this selection be done, and what type of list of capabilities is appropriate? When drawing up a list of functionings, the following criteria should be met.

(a) *The criterion of explicit formulation*: The most basic criterion is that the list should be made explicit, discusses, and defended. To political and moral philosophers this might seem an obvious requirement. But the current practice in welfare economics does not reflect this principle. The existing applications in welfare economics operate virtually exclusively at the level of quantitative empirical analysis, and use whatever functionings can be found in the available datasets, without defending *a priori* list of functionings.

(b) *The criterion of methodological justification*: This criterion states that when drawing up a list, we should explain how we have reached that list. In other words, we have to clarify and scrutinise the method that has generated the list, and justify that this is the appropriate method for the issue at hand.

(c) *The criterion of sensitivity to context*: The list should be pitched at the level of abstraction and within the theoretical framework that is most appropriate for the aim for which we use the capability approach. This criterion therefore proposes a pragmatic attitude towards drawing up a list. It acknowledges that it is important to speak the language of the debate in which we want to get involved. For example, in philosophical discussions the list will be specified at a highly abstract level, whereas for political, social, or economic discussions the list will be less abstract. And even within the latter discussions the level of abstraction can vary—using the capability approach in the context of legal rights will require a list at a higher level of abstraction than when the capability approach is applied to socio-economic inequality measurement.

(d) *The criterion of different levels of generality*: It states if the specification aims at an empirical application, or wants to lead to implementable policy proposals, then the list should be drawn up in at least two stages. Each stage will generate a list at a different level, ranging from the level of ideal theory to more pragmatic lists. This means that only from the second stage onwards will constraints and limitations related to the measurement design and data collection, or to political or socio-economic feasibility in the case of policy-oriented applications, be taken into account. Distinguishing between the ideal and the second-best level is important, because these second best constraints might change over time, for example as knowledge expands, empirical research methods become more refined, or the reality of political or economic feasibility changes. The multiple-stage procedure is one possible tool to correct for biases stemming from the social situations of researchers and policy-makers.

(e) *The criterion of exhaustion and non-reduction*: This criterion states that the capabilities on the list should include all elements that are important—no dimensions that are relevant should be left out. Moreover, the elements of the list should not be largely reducible to other elements. There may be some overlap, as long as the overlap is not substantial. This does not exclude the possibility that a subset might have such an important status that it is important to consider it on its own, independent from the larger set.

The selection of the capabilities requires careful attention as it is a potential source of androcentric and other biases. For example, following is the list of capabilities at the ideal level for the conceptualisation of gender inequality.

(a) *Life and physical health*: being able to be physically healthy and enjoying a life of normal length;
(b) *Mental well-being*: being able to be mentally healthy;
(c) *Bodily integrity and safety*: having the freedom not to be exposed to violence of any sort;
(d) *Social relations*: being able to be part of social networks; and giving and receiving social support;
(e) *Political empowerment*: being able to participate in and having some influence on political decision-making;
(f) *Education and knowledge*: having the freedom to be educated, and to use and produce knowledge;
(g) *Social reproduction and nonmarket care*: being able to raise children and take care of other people;
(h) *Paid work and other projects*: being able to work in the labour market or to do projects such as arts;
(i) *Shelter and environment*: being able to be sheltered and to live in a safe and pleasant environment;
(j) *Mobility*: having the freedom to be mobile;
(k) *Leisure activities*: being able to engage in leisure activities;
(l) *Time-autonomy*: having autonomy in allocating one's time;
(m) *Respect*: enjoying the freedom to be respected and treated with dignity;
(n) *Religion and spirituality*: having the freedom to practice a religion or live one's life according to spiritual principles.

The above mentioned list is only indicative. A widely published list of capabilities has been proposed by Nussbaum. Her list has ten dimensions—life; bodily health; bodily integrity; sense, imagination and thought; emotions; practical reason; affiliation; other species; play and control over one's environment. Nussbaum's interpretation of functionings and capabilities is different from Sen's. While for Sen capabilities are opportunities, for Nussbaum they also include talents, internal powers, and abilities. This implies that in Nussbaum's theory, Sen's three conversion factors are integrated in the concept of capability itself.

For policy-related issues and debates in the social sciences, especially the measurement of individual advantage and the design of socio-economic policy proposals, the criterion of context would lead to a recommendation to use Sen's conceptualisations. Nussbaum's list will be more appropriate in other discussions, mainly those about moral philosophical principles that might result in legal rights and political declarations. Nussbaum's list differs in character from other lists. She takes it for granted that the government will have to deliver minimum levels of the capabilities on her list. This belief in the government stands in sharp contrast to much critical theory, which sees the government as part of the problem of injustices. Sen's capability approach allows for an analytical distinction between the distribution of well-being on the one hand, and policies of redistribution and rectification on the other. Thus, even if the same capabilities would figure in Nussbaum's list and the list proposed by Sen, their character and normative assertions are distinct.

Another important list has been generated by the Swedish approach to welfare, which has been developed since 1965. This approach stipulates that a person's standard of living is his "command over resources in the form of money, possessions, knowledge, mental and physical energy, social relations, security, and so on". The Swedish approach differs from the capability approach because it focuses on resources. The components of Swedish list are health and access to health care; employment and working conditions; economic resources; education and skills; family and social integration; housing; security of life and property; recreation and leisure; and political resources. The Swedish list includes economic resources, which Sen has excluded from his list, as it is not a capability. Further, the Swedish list is narrower, and somewhat more direct towards the material dimensions of life. It is also gender-biased, as it does not include care and household work, or time-autonomy.

Strengths and weaknesses of the capability approach: The first advantage is that functionings and capabilities are properties of individuals, hence the capability approach is an ethically individualistic theory. This means that each person will be taken into account in our normative judgments. Ethical individualism implies that the units of normative judgment are individuals, and not households or communities. At the same time, the capability approach is not ontologically individualistic. It does not assume atomistic individuals, nor does it assume that our functionings and capabilities are independent of our concern for others or of others' actions. The social and environmental conversion factors also allow to take into account a number of societal features, such as social norms and discrimination. In sum, the ethically individualistic and ontologically non-individualistic nature of the capability approach is a desirable characteristic for well-being and inequality analysis. This is also attractive for feminist research, because ethical individualism rejects the idea that women's well-being can be subsumed under wider entities such as the household or the community, while not denying the impact of care, social relations, and interdependence.

The capability approach is therefore a major improvement over standard well-being approaches in welfare economics or political philosophy. Accounts of inequality and well-being in political philosophy often use implicit assumptions about gender relations and the family, which are unrealistic and deny or ignore intra-household inequalities. In welfare economics, inequality theories are generally ethically individualistic, but this principle gets lost in applied work. Individuals and families are often sloppily equated as when it is assumed that partners pool their income, so that both partners receive an equal share. There is by now a substantial literature on intra-household allocations, but this literature had no significant impact on the inequality measurement in welfare economics. Frances Woolley and Judith Marshall have argued that "standard approaches to inequality measurement presume that there is no inequality within the household". However, this turns out to be an unrealistic assumption, as not all partners share the total household income equally. Even if household income were shared completely, it is problematic to assume that it is irrelevant for a person's well-being whether he earned this money himself, or whether it was earned by his partner. Conceptualising and measuring gender inequality in functionings and capabilities will avoid these problems, as it looks at the lives that individuals can and do choose to live.

The second advantage of the capability approach is that it is not limited to the market, but looks at people's beings and doings in nonmarket as well as market settings. This is an important characteristic of the capability approach, as many aspects of well-being are not visible in the market. Including nonmarket dimensions of well-being in our normative analysis will reveal complexities and ambiguities in the distribution of well-being that an analysis of income or wealth alone cannot capture. This is especially important for gender inequality research. Feminist economists have been arguing for some time that economics needs to pay attention to processes and outcomes both in the market and nonmarket economy. Inequality comparisons based only on the market economy, for example by comparing income, earnings, and job-holding, exclude some important aspects of well-being such as care labour, household work, domestic violence or how much one can rely on social networks. This also applies in particular to gender inequality analysis—we need to take into account aspects of people's well-being and advantage related to both the market and nonmarket aspects of life, as women are spending much more time outside the market than men.

The third strength of the capability approach is that it explicitly acknowledges human diversity, such as race, age, ethnicity, gender, sexuality, geographical location, whether people are handicapped or pregnant, or have caring responsibilities. Sen has criticised inequality approaches that assume that all people have the same utility-functions, or are influenced in the same way and to the same extent by the same personal, social, and environmental characteristics. Investigations of equality—theoretical as well as practical—that proceed with the assumption of antecedent uniformity, thus miss out on a major aspect of the problem. Human diversity is not a secondary complication; it is a fundamental aspect of our interest in equality. Again, this characteristic of the capability approach is important for gender inequality analysis. Sen's concern with human diversity contrasts strikingly with the tendency in standard welfare economics to take men's lives as the implicit norms, for example by assuming equal sharing within the household and by neglecting nonmarket labour. Women are thus excluded from the inequality analysis for those aspects of their lives which clash with the masculine norm. Equality is ultimately measured in male terms. Feminist scholars have argued that many theories of justice pretend that they address the lives of men and women, but by closer scrutiny men's lives are taken as the standard or gender inequalities and gender injustices are assumed away, and thereby often indirectly justified. By conceptualising gender inequality in the space of functionings and capabilities, there is more scope to account for human diversity, including the diversity stemming from people's gender.

The capability approach also has one major drawback, which results from its underspecified nature. Capability egalitarianism strictly speaking only advocates that when making inequality assessments, we should focus on capabilities. However, every evaluative assessment implicitly or explicitly endorses additional social theories, including accounts of the individual, social and environmental conversion factors, and a normative theory of choice. Depending on the social theories that we add to the capability framework, we can come to quite divergent normative conclusions. If these social theories are racist, homophobic, sexist, ageist, Eurocentric or biased in any other way, this will be reflected in the capability evaluation. For example, gender discrimination in the market can reduce one's capability set; or gendered preference formation mechanisms, such as gender socialisation, can have an impact on the different choices that women and men make from their capability sets. The main concern for feminists is that the capability approach is vulnerable to androcentric interpretations and applications.

Sen's ideas have invited certain critiques—some are general skepticism and some on specific aspects of his work. For example, the capability approach, while highly regarded, has been called "an unworkable idea" by some, and accused for being insufficiently specified by others (Robeyns, 2000). In fact, Sen has intended it to be used for a wide range of purposes; therefore, the capability approach has been deliberately left "incomplete", rather than precise and prescriptive, as most other development theories are (Robeyns, 2005). Sen has been reluctant, despite criticisms, to prescribe a list of functionings to be taken into account, or an aggregative principle, and for good reason. Such a formularised prescription, and the process of coming up with it, will be questionable given the vastly discrepant circumstances, conventions, and social pressures that people face. Therefore, the application of the capability approach, such as an evaluative, should be carried out on under specific circumstances.

Entitlements

Entitlements have been defined by Sen as "the set of alternative commodity bundles that a person can command in a society using the totality of rights and opportunities that he or she faces". It should be noted that this is a descriptive rather than a normative concept; entitlements derive from legal rights rather than morality or human rights. It provides a particular focus for the analysis of famines. It does not specify one particular causation of famine—only the general one that a famine reflects widespread failure of entitlements on the part of substantial sections of the population.

The entitlement approach to starvation and famine concentrates on the ability of people to command food through the legal means available in the society, including the use of production possibilities, trade opportunities, entitlements *vis-à-vis* the state, and other methods of acquiring food. A person starves either because he does not have the ability to command enough food, or because he does not use this ability to avoid starvation. The entitlement approach concentrates on the former, ignoring the latter possibility. Furthermore, it concentrates on those means of commanding food that are legitimised by the legal system in operation in the society. While it is an approach of some generality, it makes no attempt to include all possible influences that can in principle cause starvation, for example illegal transfers, and choice failures.

A person's "entitlement set" is the full range of goods and services that he or she can acquire by converting his or her "endowments" (assets and resources, including labour power) through "exchange entitlement mappings". In the context of poverty and famine, the entitlement approach aims comprehensively to describe all legal sources of food, which Sen reduces to four categories:

(a) production-based entitlement—growing food,

(b) trade-based entitlement—buying food,

(c) own-labour entitlement—working for food, and

(d) inheritance and transfer entitlement—being given food by others.

The exchange entitlement mapping depends on the legal, political, economic, and social characteristics of the society in question and the person's position in it. Individuals face starvation if their full entitlement set does not provide them with adequate food for subsistence. Famine scales this up—occupationally or geographically related groups of people face famine if they simultaneously experience catastrophic declines in their entitlements.

Ownership of food is one of the most primitive rights, and in each society, there are rule governing this right. The entitlement approach concentrates on each person's entitlements to commodity bundles including food, and views starvation as resulting from a failure to be entitled to a bundle with enough food. In a fully directed economy, each person *i* may simply get a particular commodity bundle, which is assigned to him. To a limited extent this happens in most economies, e.g. to residents of old people's homes or of mental hospitals. Typically, however, there is a menu, possibly wide, to choose from. E_i is the entitlement set of person *i* in a given society, in a given situation, and it consists of a set of alternative commodity bundles, any one of which the person can decide to have. In an economy with private ownership and exchange in the form of trade (exchange with others) and production (exchange with nature), E_i can be characterised as depending on two parameters—the endowment of the person (the ownership bundle) and the exchange entitlement mapping (the function that specifies the set of alternative commodity bundles that the person can command respectively for each endowment bundle).

Perhaps the most valuable contribution of the entitlement approach to famine theorising is that it shifts the analytical focus away from a fixation on food supplies—the Malthusian logic of "too many people, too little food"—and on to the inability of groups of people to acquire food. Food insecurity affects people who cannot access adequate food (e.g. because of poverty) irrespective of food availability—a famine can occur even if food supplies are adequate and markets are functioning well. This is a crucial insight. As Sen emphasized, there is no technical reason for markets to meet subsistence needs—and no moral or legal reason why they should. An equally important insight—and one that has generated much confusion and controversy in the literature—is that famine can be caused by "exchange entitlement decline" (adverse shifts in the exchange value of endowments for food, e.g. falling wages or livestock prices, rising food prices) as well as by "direct entitlement decline" (loss of food crops to drought, for instance). The entitlement approach does not exclude the latter possibility.

Bringing in production will make entitlement mapping depend on production opportunities as well as trade possibilities of resources and products. It will also involve legal rights to apportioning the product, e.g. the capitalist rule of the 'entrepreneur' owning the produce. Sometimes the social conventions governing these rights can be very complex indeed, for example those governing the rights of migrant members of peasant families to a share of the peasant output. Social security provisions are also reflected in the entitlement mapping, such as the right to unemployment benefit if one fails to find a job, or the right to income supplementation if one's income would fall otherwise below a certain specified level. And so are employment guarantees when they exist—as they do in some socialist economies—giving one the option to sell one's labour power to the government at a minimum price. Entitlement mappings will depend also on provisions of taxation.

Let the set of commodity bundles, each of which satisfies person *i's* minimum food requirement, be F_i. Person i will be forced to starve because of unfavourable entitlement relation if and only if he is not entitled to any member of F_i given his endowment and his exchange entitlement mapping. The 'starvation set' S_i of endowments consists of those endowment bundles such that the exchange entitlement sets corresponding to them contain no bundles satisfying his minimum food requirements.

Person i can be plunged into starvation if his endowment collapses into the starvation set S_i either through a fall in the endowment bundle, or through an unfavourable shift in the exchange entitlement mapping. Following figure illustrates the distinction in terms of the simple case of pure trade involving only two commodities, food and non-food.

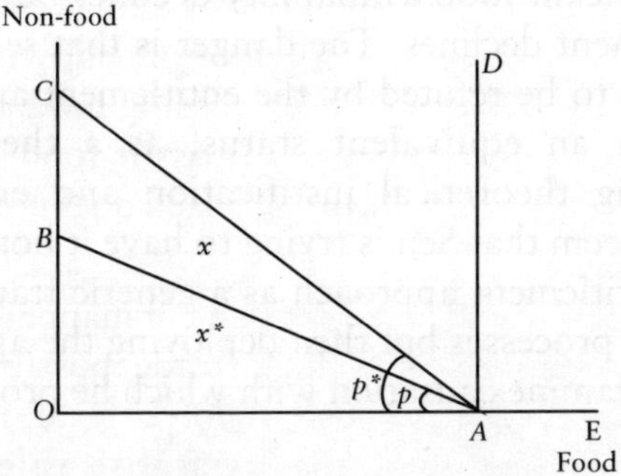

The exchange entitlement mapping is taken to assume the simple form of constant price exchange. With a price ratio p and a minimum food requirement OA, the starvation set S_i is given by the region OAB. If the endowment vector is x, the person is in a position to avoid starvation. This ability can fail either (i) through a lower endowment vector, e.g. x^*, or (ii) through a less favourable exchange entitlement mapping, e.g. that given by p^*, which would make the starvation set OAC. Starvation can develop for a certain group of people as its endowment vector collapses, and there are indeed many accounts of such endowment declines on the part of sections of the poor rural population in developing countries through alienation of land, sale of livestock, etc. Shifts in exchange entitlement mapping are rather less palpable, and more difficult to trace, but starvation can also develop with unchanged asset ownership through movements of exchange entitlement mapping. This would be impossible only if the endowment vector itself contained enough food, for example, in the above figure if it belonged to the region *DAE*.

Although Sen is careful to emphasise that the entitlement approach is descriptive rather than theoretical, and empiricist rather than normative—"a general framework for analysing famines rather than one particular hypothesis about their causation"—he chooses to set up the entitlement approach in theoretical opposition to something he labels 'FAD', for *food availability decline*, and he invests much intellectual energy in *Poverty and Famines* in attempting to demonstrate that the four 20th-century famines he chooses as case studies were not precipitated by significant food availability declines but instead by exchange entitlement declines. The danger is that setting up FAD as a hypothesis to be refuted by the entitlement approach places the latter in an equivalent status, as a theoretical proposition requiring theoretical justification and empirical verification. It does seem that Sen is trying to have it both ways, by presenting the entitlement approach as a generic framework for analysing famine processes but then deploying the approach to refute a theory of famine causation with which he profoundly disagrees.

Early critiques of entitlement theory concentrated on the complex relationship between "food availability decline" and "exchange entitlement decline" in famine events, and specifically on Sen's assertion that several 20th-century famines were not triggered by catastrophic declines in food production or food availability. A vigorous empirical debate followed around the analysis or interpretation of food production and availability data for specific famines. This literature has two strands:

(a) *Refutation of entitlement theory by reinterpretation of data*: In *Poverty and Famines*, Sen recalculated data from four famines to demonstrate—(a) adequate food availability and/or negligible decline from pre-famine food availability; (b) exchange entitlement collapse for specific population groups as a proximate cause of famine. Some critics have challenged Sen's use of food production, trade and price statistics, to claim that Sen underestimated the extent to which food availability decline was in fact an important element in these famines.

(b) *Refutation of entitlement theory by counter-example:* A related strand of the critical literature attempts to demonstrate that the entitlement approach does not adequately explain some famines that were not examined by Sen in *Poverty and Famines*. The argument is that Sen's preoccupation with exchange entitlement collapse (adverse shifts in food price/wage or food price/livestock price ratios) understates the significance of FAD—specifically food production failure—as a causal trigger of many famines, especially in Africa, and that if famines can be found that were not triggered by catastrophic "exchange entitlement failures", this somehow refutes entitlements' claims as a general theory in opposition to FAD.

Whatever the merits of the competing analyses of various famines, this strand of the debate is fatally flawed. It is predicated on the false premise that food availability decline is a "non-nested alternative" to entitlement decline, whereas in fact FAD is incorporated within the entitlement framework as "direct entitlement decline" or failure of "production-based entitlement". A more significant challenge is provided by cases of famine that are characterised by radical violations of legally defined entitlement relations—such as recent famines in the Horn of Africa, where assets are transferred or destroyed not by voluntaristic exchange in markets or by natural disaster such as drought but by political conflict and war. Entitlement collapse offers a fresh perspective on the famine process, but its critics are correct to complain that entitlements is too apolitical and ahistorical to tell us much about the structural causes of famines. However, the point remains that the entitlement approach is not a theory of famine causation in competition with other theories such as FAD or Malthusianism. It is a framework for the analysis of famine processes at the micro-level.

In *Poverty and Famines*, Sen recognised four limitations of the entitlement approach, which are:

(a) *There can be ambiguities in the specification of entitlements*: Entitlement analysis is predicated on the implicit assumption that a food shortage triggers an automatic behavioural response, namely the conversion of endowments into food for survival. Thus, a person's "starvation set" is defined as "those endowment bundles such that the exchange entitlement sets corresponding to them contain no bundles satisfying his minimum food requirements". Sen's concession that people "sometimes *choose* to starve" in the short-term to enhance their future entitlements drew on findings from Indian droughts and anticipated research into "coping strategies" during African famines of the 1980s that would highlight consumption rationing as a strategic response to livelihood shocks. However, Sen later stressed that he regards such choice behaviour as applying to "persistent hunger" rather than to "famine".

While the early literature on "coping strategies" reflected an assumption that strategic behaviour is dominated by the search for food, later research found that consumption rationing is an austerity measure that is adopted almost routinely. Evidence from many famines confirms that "coping strategies" during food crises are preoccupied with avoiding asset depletion rather than with maintaining consumption levels. People facing food shortage make strategic decisions not only about how to bridge their consumption deficit, but also about how to balance this priority against its longer term economic and social costs. The sequence of coping strategy adoption is determined not only by each strategy's effectiveness in terms of bridging a food gap, but also by the cost and reversibility of each action. Strategies that incur little long-run cost are adopted first (including rationing food consumption), while those that incur higher costs and are difficult to reverse are adopted later (e.g. selling the household plough to buy food). Seen in this light, decisions to ration food consumption, even severely, can be understood as attempts to manage the current endowment set, including food, to maximise the individual's or household's long-term entitlements. Endowments are not always exchanged for food because consuming productive assets undermines future viability.

Sen's focus on the household as the principal unit of analysis confounds the entitlement approach, as does its failure to engage with social relations and power inequalities, in this case at the intrahousehold level. Curiously, Sen has never drawn on his related work [e.g. on "co-operative conflict" (Sen, 1990), his seminal contribution to the intrahousehold bargaining models literature, or on female mortality risk in South Asia] to examine how differential power within the household translates into differential mortality risk during famines.

(b) *The entitlement approach focuses on starvation, which has to be distinguished from famine mortality, since many of the famine deaths—in some case most of them—are caused by epidemics*: In *Poverty and Famines*, Sen writes about people being "plunged into starvation" when their entitlement to food collapses. In fact, frank starvation is rarely recorded as the cause of death in famines. More often, death is attributed to hunger-related diseases such as diarrhoea or gastro-enteritis, and is explained by heightened susceptibility as lack of food undermines biological resistance to these illnesses. This is not of course incompatible with a "food entitlement decline" theory of famine. For entitlement failure to retain explanatory power, however, requires demonstrating an association between, mortality during famines (due to whatever proximate cause) and entitlement collapse, as proxied, say, by destitution. Sen finds an association between occupation status and mortality risk during the Bengal famine of 1943 and the Bangladesh famine of 1974, with low-paid occupations such as landless labourers suffering the highest rates of destitution and death. But the evidence is less clear for African famines, and sometimes appears to contradict Sen. In famines where mortality is triggered by epidemics, it is not the undernutrition caused by the famine but the social disruption caused by it that is critical in causing excess deaths. Therefore, famine mortality is a consequence of the social process of famine, rather than the economic process (entitlement collapse)—lack of food or poverty at the individual level.

The relationship between food shortage and morbidity or mortality outcomes reflects "behavioural synergies" (which might include increased exposure due to famine-induced distress migration) as well as "biological synergies" (increased susceptibility to infection). In terms of both explanations, exposure to disease is accepted as the proximate cause of death, but the underlying cause of death remains as "entitlement failure". Famine mortality reflects both increased susceptibility and increased exposure to diseases, some of which are hunger-related while others are not—but both reflect a common origin in disrupted access to food (epidemics that are not triggered by food scarcity are not, definitionally speaking, famines). The relative contribution to mortality of starvation, hunger-related morbidity and epidemic diseases will vary from one famine to another, but all three contributory factors are intrinsic to the famine process, and all three can arguably be accommodated within a broadly framed entitlement analysis. One feature that the "health crisis" model does highlight, though, is the recognition of famine as a social crisis rather than an economic crisis scaled up from the household to the group level. Once again, the entitlement approach proves to be unable to explain collective outcomes (in this case, disease epidemics) because of its analytical focus on the individual or household unit.

(c) *While entitlement relations concentrate on rights within the given legal structure in that society, some transfers involve violations of these rights, such as looting or brigandage*: In his original formulation of the entitlement approach, Sen was concerned only with legal ownership by individuals of alienable commodities. He ignored possibilities for weaker claims over resources, such as access and usufruct rights, as well as contexts where property rights are exercised institutionally, such as common property regimes, rather than individually. These two sources of "fuzziness" confound the central tool of entitlement analysis—namely the mapping between an individual's endowments and their entitlements.

(i) *Fuzziness with respect to units of analysis*—In his elaboration of the entitlement approach, Sen chooses the individual, the household, or an "economic class" of people (sharecroppers, pastoralists) as his unit of analysis, and he shifts seamlessly between these levels of aggregation, as if they are interchangeable. Osmani justifies this blurring of individuals and groups as follows: "The basic unit of analysis is an individual person. For practical purposes, however, the analysis can also be conducted at collective levels such as household, group, or class by using the standard device of assuming a 'representative individual'."

In any context where ownership relations between individuals or institutions and resources or commodities are multi-layered, complex and even contested by different individuals or groups of people, the "standard device" that Osmani endorses becomes difficult to justify. This is particularly the case when "fuzziness" in terms of units of analysis arises because different individuals and institutions exercise distinct claims over the same resource. In such cases, agreed rules must be established for allocating rights over the resource to the various claimants. When several groups of people each hold socially legitimated rights over the same resource endowment, entitlements flowing from that resource cannot be modelled as if they accrue to a single person, and the notion of a "representative individual" simply cannot be applied.

Access to natural resources (or to entitlements derived from these resources) is strictly governed by rules and norms that are established on the basis of "belonging" (citizenship, ethnicity), "seniority" (age, gender) and other axes of inclusion or exclusion. These filters act as rationing mechanisms, selectively allocating resources to individuals who display the preferred characteristics and marginalising the claims of others who do not share these characteristics—which are often inherited (ascribed) attributes such as ethnicity or age that cannot be changed (or acquired). To the extent that a community or society is structured along rules or norms of inclusion and exclusion an individual's personal characteristics become a major determinant of his or her ability to access resources (i.e. to accumulate endowments and to realise entitlements). As Gasper points out, "Beyond legal rights, effective access within institutions typically depends not only on formal rules but on particular relationships of authority and influence."

Leach *et al.* (1997) agree that Sen's definition of entitlements as legal rights only is too restrictive, and they develop the concept of "environmental entitlements", which attempts to "extend the entitlements framework to the whole range of socially sanctioned as well as formal-legal institutional mechanisms for gaining resource access and control". This formulation recognises that certain entitlements—for example usufruct rights to land or trees in communal tenure regimes—are neither conferred nor enforceable by formal legal systems, but instead are validated by community-level institutions on the basis of social membership rather than private ownership.

(ii) *Fuzziness with respect to property rights*—The notion of entitlements is conceptually and empirically inseparable from an economic system founded on private property and the legal rights associated with exclusive ownership by individuals of assets as commodities. "Exchange entitlements" are defined by the conventions of commodity exchange in capitalist regimes, being subject to the laws of contract and occurring as an impersonal "'exchange of alienable things between transactors who are in a state of reciprocal independence'. By contrast, traditional precapitalist societies are the domain of non-commodity (gift) exchange defined as 'an exchange of inalienable things between transactors who are in a state of reciprocal dependence'." This implies that the entitlement approach is analytically weakest in precisely those socio-economic contexts for which it was designed, namely, famine-prone communities whose vulnerability is partly defined by their weak or unfavourable incorporation into markets, where common property and open access regimes for resources dominate private property and market-based exchange. To the extent that commodity exchanges in precapitalist communities (or poor communities that retain significant precapitalist features) occur outside the contractual rules of the market-place, the entitlement approach is effectively inapplicable.

Of the four main resource regimes—private property, state property, common property and open access—entitlements are "fuzziest" with respect to common property regimes. Under private and state property regimes, entitlements are clearly defined and ownership is vested in individuals or state institutions. In open access regimes, entitlements are freely available to whoever chooses to take advantage of the resource. Under common property regimes, however, it is necessary to separate out ownership, control and access to a resource (endowment) from ownership, control and access to the utilities derived from that resource (entitlement). This introduces a critical "ambiguity" (though not necessarily, as Sen puts it, "vagueness") around the specification of ownership relations. Take the case of "communal land" which is owned by the state, controlled by community leaders (village headmen) and accessed or utilised by individual farmers. In return for allocating usufruct rights over land to local farmers, village headmen might extract rent for its use in the form of tribute or "gifts". The state might also extract rent, in the form of a head tax on livestock or grazing fees. There is, in this example, a structural separation between the resource endowment and entitlement to utilities derived from that resource.

(d) *People's actual food consumption may fall below their entitlements for a variety of other reasons, such as ignorance, fixed food habits, or apathy*: Edkins, following a deconstructivist approach, has argued persuasively that what Sen chooses to marginalize or exclude from the entitlement approach is more significant than Sen acknowledges. Two crucial exclusions are "extra-entitlement transfers" and deliberate starvation. By confining his analysis to legally enforceable property rights, Sen explicitly favours a restrictive view of famine as an "economic disaster" and he privileges "poverty and market forces as the root of famine". This characterisation had earlier been criticized for neglecting the determination of entitlements. It also avoids engaging with the highly politicised context within which famines invariably occur.

The entitlement approach overlooks the centrality of political processes, many of which involve gross violations of human rights, including the right to food, in precipitating or exacerbating famines. Sen's characterisation of famine as "entitlement failure" excludes intentionality as a possible causal trigger, and ignores the reality that famine produces beneficiaries as well as victims, who may play an active role in perpetuating or prolonging famine conditions. It is often asserted that the entitlement approach by definition cannot address "war famines", since "entitlement theory has no place for violence". In a very general sense this is true, but the impact of war and violence needs to be unpacked before any analytical role for the entitlement approach is rejected, since one of its most powerful contributions is in examining the distributional impact of a livelihood shock, whatever its source. Conflict impinges on all sources of entitlement to food, but not all of these involve "extra-entitlement transfers".

(a) *Production-based entitlements*: During a war, the ratio of food producers to food consumers falls; farmers are conscripted, displaced, disabled or killed; soldiers requisition food and livestock. "Scorched earth" tactics include destruction of granaries, burning of fields of standing crops and poisoning of wells.

(b) *Employment-based entitlements*: During a war cash crop production and marketing networks collapse, employment opportunities (demand for agricultural labour, petty trading activities) contract and farmers and pastoralists are attacked for food and livestock. Internally displaced persons and refugees lose their normal livelihoods. Lacking assets, incomes and access to food, they become dependent on external assistance.

(c) *Trade-based entitlements*: Conflict disrupts normal trading activities in various ways, including: (i) by disrupting trade routes—roads are mined and bridges are destroyed, trucks and fuel are diverted to military uses; (ii) by direct attacks on markets, e.g. the Ethiopian government bombed village markets in Tigray and Eritrea during the 1980s until markets had to be held at night; (iii) by appropriating food from traders or looting food stores; and (iv) by laying siege to towns or districts, thereby blockading movements of people and food. All these disruptions reduce food supplies and raise food prices in conflict zones, thus creating famine conditions.

(d) *Transfer entitlements*: War disrupts both "private" and "public" transfers. Conflict shatters social support networks. The 1998 famine in southern Sudan was named the "famine of breaking relationships" by local people. Transport problems and roadblocks might make it impossible for relatives to send remittances. Food aid is frequently prevented from entering conflict zones, either by government decree or because of security risks. Relief convoys and planes are attacked and food aid is seized.

These effects of war can be disaggregated into three distinct clusters. The first cluster covers the disruptive effects of conflict on local economies and livelihoods. In theory, these disruptions—such as farmers volunteering for military service, or the contraction of local markets—could be incorporated within the entitlement approach, much as the effects of drought can be modelled in so far as they affect endowments and entitlement mappings. The second cluster is Sen's illegal "extra-entitlement transfers" such as the requisitioning of grain from farmers, raiding of livestock from pastoralists, or seizing of food aid from relief convoys. There is no escaping from Sen's own judgment that these typical features of "war famines" render the entitlement approach "defective". The third cluster of effects is equally problematic for the entitlement approach, and refers to various "unruly practices" associated with war that do not directly transfer entitlements but create "conditions which are deliberately and socially engineered to undermine entitlement". Perhaps the paradigmatic case is a siege that denies access to food, in order deliberately to bring about starvation of the besieged community.

Thus from the above analysis, we can say that development has occurred when there has been an improvement in basic needs, when economic progress has contributed to a greater sense of self-esteem for the country and individuals within it, and when material advancement has expanded people's entitlements, capabilities and freedoms. The fact that many of these ingredients of development are not measurable does not detract from their importance—the condition of being developed is as much as a state of mind as a physical condition measurable by economic indices alone.

NOTES

1. Arbitrage is the process in which goods are purchased in one market to be resold in another at a higher price and with a known and certain profit.
2. The 1990 and 2000/2001 World Development Report, published by the World Bank, were devoted to a consideration of the measurement,

magnitude and nature of poverty in the Third World, and how to tackle it.

3. Chenery et al., 1979.
4. Subject to commodity fetishism, according to Sen, 1993.
5. Stewart, 1985, ch. 2.
6. For an evaluation of country experience and of the complementarities and trade-offs in the provision of basic needs, see Streeten et al. (1981) and Stewart (1985).
7. Martinussen 1997, p. 150.
8. UNDP Human Development Report 2003, p. 341.
9. Stotsky, 2006a.
10. World Economic Forum (WEF), 2005.
11. Dollar et al., 2001, World Bank, 2001.
12. The other measure is Gender Empowerment Measure (GEM). Likewise GDI, GEM is measured in the three components; political participation —measured by women's and men's percentage of shares of parliamentary seats, economic participation—measured by share of jobs classified as professional or technical, and administrative or managerial going to women and men and power over economic resources—measured by women's and men's estimated earned income (UNDP, 2007).
13. Adult literacy rate is given 2/3rd weight and enrollment ratio is given 1/3rd weight.
14. For a detailed analysis of the HPI's mathematical formulation, see Sudhir Anand and Amartya Sen's "Concepts of Human Development and Poverty: A Multidimensional Perspective" and the technical note in *Human Development Report 1997.*
15. See Martha C. Nussbaum, *Women and Human Development: The Capability Approach* (New York, Cambridge University Press, 2000).
16. Ingrid Robeyns, "The Capability Approach—A Theoretical Survey", *Journal of Human Development* (2005).
17. Sabine Alkire, "Why the Capability Approach?", *Journal of Human Development* (2005).
18. Ingrid Robeyns, "The Capability Approach—A Theoretical Survey."
19. Sabine Alkire, "Why the Capability Approach?"
20. Ingrid Robeyns, "The Capability Approach—A Theoretical Survey."
21. Ingrid Robeyns, "The Capability Approach in Practice," *Journal of Political Philosophy* (2006), 351-76.

2

Factors in Economic Development

After going through this chapter, you will better understand:

- pre-requisites for economic development
- economic factors affecting development
- capital-output ratio and economic development
- technology and development
- entrepreneurship and development
- non-economic factors affecting development
- economic obstacles to development
- government obstacles to development
- social values as obstacles to economic development
- international obstacles to development
- dualism
- cumulative causation

Why did some societies develope sooner than others? Why have some societies experienced such rapid increases in living standards while others have lagged behind? Why has development not spread equally in all societies?

The answer to all the above questions is that at different stages of development, different constraints on progress operate. While some of these factors are likely to be sociological and political, the major constraints are likely to be economic. An underdeveloped country aspiring to make its way up the economic ladder should necessarily possess some pre-requisites for economic development. But, in order to attain economic development it is not enough to remove the obstacles to development. According to Prof. W.A. Lewis, the proximate causes of economic growth are—the effort to economise, the increase of knowledge and its application in production, and increasing the amount of capital or other resources per head. These three causes, though clearly distinguishable, conceptually are normally found together. According to Lewis, an underdeveloped country should do something to acquire these three pre-requisites for economic development. But, since economic growth is closely tied with human endowments, political conditions and social attitudes and historical accidents, only economic pre-requisites for growth are not enough. Social, political, cultural and psychological requirements are as important as economic requirements. As Professor Cairncross rightly remarks, "Development is not just a matter of having plenty of money nor is it purely an economic phenomenon. It embraces all aspects of social behaviour, the establishment of law and order, scrupulousness in business dealings, including dealings with the revenue authorities, relationships between the family, literacy, familiarity with mechanical gadgets and so on."

Followings are the pre-requisites for economic development:

(a) *Availability of abundant and rich natural resources*: A country which possesses rich natural resources, will have better scope for development than country which lacks them. But, this does not mean that a country with poor endowment of natural resources cannot attain a high level of development. Japan and Switzerland provide examples of countries which have attained a high level of development inspite of their poor natural resources. We simply want to point out the decisive advantage which a country enjoys if it possesses good and abundant natural resources. The domestic availability of natural resources reduces its dependence on other countries and this imparts certainty to schemes of economic development.

(b) *Removal of market imperfections*: Market imperfections restrict transfer of factors from less productive to more productive forms of employment, handicap the expansion and development of markets and restrict the impact of expansion in one sector on another sector. They must, therefore, be removed. Alternative forms of social and economic organisations are needed to remove the market imperfections. The opportunities for greater productivity within the existing state of knowledge and with the existing resources should be more widely exploited. The knowledge of market opportunities and new techniques of production should also be increased. Monopolistic practices through the domestic production and marketing sectors should be curbed. The capital market should be widened; better credit facilities should be made available to peasants, small traders and small businessmen. The entrepreneurial horizons of the small traders and manufacturers should be widened by spreading new knowledge, workers should be made aware of better employment opportunities elsewhere and producers should be made aware of existing domestic and international market opportunities. The removal of market imperfections is particularly necessary if development in one sector is to spill over to other sectors. If rigidities and inflexibilities are reduced foreign trade would have much greater impact throughout the economy.

(c) *An indigenous base*: The process of development should have an indigenous base within the underdeveloped economy. If the forces of growth are implanted from outside, the stimulating effect will not be lasting. "The implanted forces can, at the most, ginger up the growth process for a short time but they can hardly initiate the process of feed-back within the economy."[1] Meier and Baldwin also observe, "If the process is to become cumulative and long-lasting, the development forces must be fundamentally based within the developing country."[2] All parts of the economy should grow in proportion to their importance in the functioning of the economy. An excessive growth of any part would ultimately inhibit the smooth growth of economy.

(d) *Structural changes*: The process of development has not only to make a fuller use of existing resources but also to expand resources. The problem has to be attacked at two fronts. In the first place, the productive opportunities within the existing resources and know-how have to be exploited to the maximum possible extent through our optimum allocation of resources.

Secondly, the 'production frontier' has to be widened through sizable structural changes.

The amount of development that can be achieved by a mere better allocation of the existing resources, however, is very much limited. Schultz has aptly remarked, "in most poor countries there is not much economic growth to be had by merely taking up whatever slack may exist in the way of the available resources being utilised".[3] In fact, the supply of the productive factors has to be expanded to give an outward push to the production frontier. For this a number of structural changes have to be brought about.

The structural change in the underdeveloped agricultural countries may begin with a reduction in the proportion of population engaged in agriculture and an increase in that employed in non-agricultural activities. "The speed or rate of economic development may then be described by the rate at which the 70:30 ratio in economic structure is approximated to the 20:80 ratio which represents ultimate equilibrium at a high level of development."[4] The transfer of agricultural population to the non-agricultural sector has to be accompanied by an increase in agricultural production to provide food and raw materials for the latter sector and for the mutual increase of population in both the sectors. This requires sizable changes in the agricultural set-up, *viz.,* land reforms, new credit institutions, increase in the supply of productive factors in agriculture, dynamic market mechanism, new incentives, changed socio-economic relationship, etc.

Economic phenomena are interwoven in the social system. This is particularly true of underdeveloped countries where productive activities and expenditure patterns are substantially influenced by social institutions, habits and attitudes. The pattern of savings and investment, for instance, is considerably shaped by cultural and social considerations. Any structural change in the economy of the country will, therefore, necessarily require a change in the social structure of the society. A dynamic economy and a static social set-up cannot pull together. Meier and Baldwin aptly remark, "New wants, new motivations, new ways of production, new institutions need be created if national income is to rise more rapidly. Where there are religious obstacles to modern economic progress, the religion may have to be taken less seriously or its character altered."[5] Professor Gadgil states that all attitudes, habits of mind, patterns of behaviour, etc. are born out of chiefly historical institutional modes of living. These modes of living in most underdeveloped countries have had in the past little direct connection with economic development. If now rapid economic development is to become the main objective of these societies, their attitudes and habits of mind must change correspondingly.[6]

(e) *Favourable environments*: Economic development cannot be achieved unless the prevailing atmosphere is conducive to it. There must exist among the people a desire for economic progress and the political, legal and religious institutions should be conducive to it. Development is not a function simply of capital and technology. If the atmosphere in a country is not very conducive to development, mere investment cannot lead to economic development. Investment in such an economy can at the best give it a kick and it will return to its original position after some time. Investment can lead to self-sustained development only if the general atmosphere is favourable to development. When atmosphere is favourable, initial investment leads to automatic cumulative growth.

(f) *Belief in possibility of development*: People must be convinced that development is possible. Development will not be desired in a country where people are doubtful about the feasibility of achieving it. Belief in the possibility of development leads to a scientific and experimental outlook. Human beings experiment with different techniques of production, different techniques of organisation, different social institutions and so on. Experimental attitude is very essential for economic development. Modern methods of production, methods of organisation and social institutions existing in advanced countries are the result of experiments carried over centuries.

(g) *Desire for development*: Even when it is widely believed that development is possible, it won't be realised if there does not exist a strong desire among the people for material advancement. The religious philosophy in several backward countries teaches people to be less materialistic and to care more for the other world than for the world in which they are living. Meditation and worship of God is considered to be a more fruitful use of life than the production of goods and services. People are taught to strictly limit their wants and to lead a simple life. Such philosophy is not very conducive to economic development and its eradication is very essential for rapid economic development.

After elementary needs have been met, the marginal leisure-preference becomes very high. This kind of attitude is not very favourable to economic development. Such behaviour prevails, primarily, because of lack of education, social mores and prejudices. It is rigid but not unalterable.

(h) *Absence of taboos and prohibitions*: Economic development may be inhibited by a series of taboos and prohibitions. Use of certain products and the adoption of certain processes may be made difficult by these. Progress in certain occupations, very essential for economic development, may be inhibited because these are ranked low. Even where there exist no social or religious prohibitions, economic development may be inhibited by traditions and habits built through practices continuing since generations. Self-employed workers on farms and in cottage industries, for instance, are not accustomed to punctuality in hours of work and regular attendance which are very essential for factory life. Unless these traditions, attitudes and habits are shed off, people won't be very responsive to economic development.

(i) *Favourable social values*: Urge to work for producing wealth will be lacking if the social prestige which people desire can be acquired more easily in other ways. In a feudal or aristocratic society where inherited wealth is far more important than the earned wealth, the urge to produce wealth will be lacking. People born outside feudal and aristocratic families cannot acquire their status and prestige however hard they may work for producing wealth. On the contrary, work for producing wealth is often considered to be contemptuous and below the prestige of well-bred people. In such societies, people ambitious of social prestige, therefore, turn to professions other than producing wealth, which command high social esteem and give them power, *viz.*, military, law, literature, theology, journalism, music, etc. For economic development, it is essential that those people should be held in the highest esteem who are actively engaged in the production of wealth. Social status of a person should depend upon the wealth produced by him and not upon that inherited by him.

(j) *Law and order*: Strict maintenance of law and order is very essential for economic development. Incentive to produce wealth will be lacking if the people are not sure to enjoy the fruit of their labour. In several underdeveloped countries governments are weak and internal disorders frequent.

(k) *Economic, social and legal institutions*: Prevalence of joint family system acts as a disincentive to enterprise. A person won't have the incentive to work hard if he knows that he has to share the fruit of his hard labour with a number of other persons. Individualistic system of society is more conducive to economic development. The institution of veil deprives the economy of a considerable portion of the working population.

Incentive for enterprise will be lacking if the legal system of the country is defective and fails to secure a person the fruit of his efforts. A tenant, for instance, will have no incentive to make investment in land if the law does not provide for compensation for the unexhausted investments at the time he vacates the land.

Under private enterprise system, communal ownership of property is not very conducive to enterprise. An enterprising cultivator, for instance, cannot effect improvements on land if it is held jointly by the whole community. Institution of the individual ownership of property is very essential for economic development.

Innovation should not be hindered by law or by custom. In certain societies, techniques and rituals in agriculture are prescribed by priests and any person introducing innovations is considered to be committing sacrilege. Even in advanced countries, there exists considerable opposition to the introduction of improved technology.

Every person in society should be provided full scope for economic advancement so that talent potentialities do not go unutilised in persons who are denied opportunity to show their worth. In many backward countries, persons born in poor families do not get an opportunity to demonstrate their abilities. If provided with an adequate opportunity, some of them may contribute to the national product far more than that contributed by most of those who get opportunity simply because they are born in rich families. Opportunity for economic advancement is denied to a large section of society not only by inequalities in the distribution of wealth but also by caste, colour and creed bars. Rapid economic development is not possible if vertical mobility is hindered either by law or by custom.

Potential enterprisers should not be denied opportunity to organise new units of production. Opportunity to potential enterprisers may be denied in a number of ways. Enterprisers coming from certain classes may not be permitted to buy land. Banking concerns may discriminate against certain classes of enterprisers. Horizontal mobility of resources is no less important than the vertical social mobility. In certain industries, entry of new enterprisers may be excluded by the existing monopolistic organisations.

Above all, leaders of the country at all levels—politicians, teachers, engineers, doctors, business leaders, trade unionists, priests, journalists—should desire advancement of the country and work for it honestly and sincerely. No progress can occur if the leaders who are to guide and inspire the masses are corrupt and selfish.

The economic, social, political and institutional obstacles to rapid economic development mentioned above should not discourage us in launching a development programme in underdeveloped countries. In their earlier stages of development, Western countries were not free from such obstacles. Experience shows that once the development process starts, these obstacles start disappearing gradually. Calculation replaces traditions and deep-rooted habits. The force of social and religious prohibitions weakens. People develop a strong desire for material advancement. New techniques and products become more acceptable. Economic and materialistic values get higher place in life. Vertical mobility increases. Nuclear families replace joint families. Rural workers get accustomed to factory discipline. Appropriately designed education and publicity can considerably help in rapidly removing social and institutional obstacles.

Besides the above mentioned pre-requisites which are essential for development, there are some economic and non-economic factors without which development cannot be possible.

ECONOMIC FACTORS

One of the most critical factors in the early stages of development is the health of the agricultural sector, because without a surplus of food production over subsistence needs, little else can be done. There would be no surplus labour, no saving and no food to feed labour working in alternative activities. Unless agriculture is settled, there is no prospect of agricultural productivity increasing to provide the basis for the development of non-agricultural activities, the building of cities and so on. In many developing countries today, agriculture is still extremely backward. Low productivity is a major cause of poverty and retards development of the whole economy.

The important economic factors which affect economic development are—(i) land, (ii) labour, (iii) capital, (iv) technology, and (v) entrepreneurship.

Land

The term 'land' is used here in a wider sense including not only soil but everything bestowed by nature. The quantity and quality of the available natural resources is an important factor determining the rate of economic development. Natural resources include character of the soil, the forest resources, topography as favouring or hindering cheap transportation, mineral resources, availability of water, rainfall, and temperature. The geographical situation of the country considerably influences the opportunities for profitable trade.

The quality of land can markedly affect the level of agricultural productivity in the early stages of economic development, and in turn the importance of agricultural development can be clearly seen within the production-function framework. Rising agricultural productivity permits the release of labour from agriculture to industry, which in turn leads to increasing returns, rising income per head and greater capital accumulation. Given the dominance of the agricultural sector in the economic structure of developing countries, such factors as the physical attributes of land (topography, fertility, and so on), the land-tenure system, the ratio of labour to land and the extent of natural resource endowments are likely to exert a major influence on the speed of development, as determinants of the pace of agricultural advance and the pace of industrialisation based on a healthy agricultural sector or the exploitation of indigenous resources. Geographical factors such as the nature of the land, and God-given factors such as the weather, must be included in any list drawn up to answer such questions as: why have some countries developed earlier than others, and why have some countries remained in a traditional or transitional state longer than others? This is the concept of geographic determinism, which can be advanced as a hypothesis of underdevelopment in its own right.

An economy can react to an unequal distribution of land in a variety of ways. A proper functioning of land market is very important for the overall development of the economy. If land is held unequally and many individuals fail to obtain access to it, they are likely to leave agriculture in search of a less precarious source of living. This can lead to a situation in which large numbers of migrants crowd the cities, a situation that can be politically, environmentally, and economically unpalatable.

The importance of land has a tendency to decrease with the advancement of an economy. As the economy advances, capital accumulates and technology improves. Improvements in technology reduce the input of land per unit of output. These make possible substitution of other factors of production, particularly capital, for land. With the advancement of an economy, services requiring little land from a larger and larger portion of the total product. But land is fixed in quantity while the supply of other factors of production can be increased. Consequently, other things remaining the same, growth of an economy will have a tendency to increase the relative scarcity of land. If the rate of discovery of unknown land and/or the rate of improvement in technology economising lands and substituting other factors of production for land is greater than that of the growth of other factors of production, the relative scarcity of land may not increase. "...despite the increasing importance of 'services' in the total product of economically advanced countries, a fairly large amount of 'goods' appears to be a necessary prior condition."[7]

Labour

The basic presumption of economic development is an efficient use of basic production factors, i.e. labour, land, and capital. As a decisive production factor, we can mark labour. Labour as a purposeful activity, the bearer of which is man, actives other production factors and transforms natural objects into such shape which serves people to meet their needs and is a presumption of their existence. In this way, it creates conditions for its own reproduction as a factor at a still higher level and at the same time it creates sources for reproduction and improvement of other production factors. Efficiency of labour use as a production factor is generally expressed by the level of labour productivity. Labour productivity is defined as the efficiency of human work utilised in creation of useful goods. It is expressed by the amount of these goods per unit of the labour input.

The higher the marginal product of labour in agriculture, the greater the force of the neoclassical argument that it is the growth of the agricultural surplus that determines the growth of non-farm employment. If the marginal product of labour in the rural sector is positive, the withdrawal of labour from the subsistence sector will reduce total output. What if labour in agricultural sector was being utilised in an extremely inefficient manner, to the degree that, by taking agricultural workers out of this sector and employing them in industry, agricultural production would not decline at all, while industrial output was increased with the influx of greater employment? What if there were actually a surplus of agricultural workers, such that by transferring some labour from agriculture to industry the remaining workers could work longer hours, or more efficiently, and total agricultural production could remain constant or even rise? Or, alternatively, agricultural producers who had been selling to the export market could replant their fields with an eye to the potential profits created by the growing domestic market resulting from the process of industrialisation. In any event, if there was surplus labour in agriculture, then that "hidden reserve" could be tapped for industrialisation, and development perhaps would not prove to be so difficult to attain after all.

The development via unlimited supplies of labour is feasible and relatively painless, if we assume zero marginal product of labour. But the question arises of how workers can survive on the land if their marginal product is zero, or even positive but below subsistence. We will discuss this in later chapters.

Capital

Capital is a factor of production that is not wanted for itself but for its ability to help in producing other goods. Classical economics regards capital as a factor of production, distinguishing between financial capital and physical capital. Financial capital is accumulated or inherited wealth held in the form of assets, such as stocks and shares, property, and bank deposits, while physical capital is wealth in the form of physical assets such as machinery and plant. The capital accumulation enhances a country's capacity to produce goods in the future and enables it to grow faster. There are many types of capital goods such as:

(a) Plant and machinery—used in factories and offices, which yield no utility directly but produce consumption goods and services that do.
(b) Infrastructure investment—partly provides goods and services directly, and at the same time makes other forms of investment more productive.
(c) Research and development investment—improve the productivity of labour or capital or both; and lead to new inventions and then to innovation.
(d) Social expenditure—such as investment in health and education, which provides some utility directly but at

the same time makes individuals and society more productive.

If capital is defined as any asset that generates an additional future stream of measurable income to society, many goods and services that might be thought of as primarily consumption goods ought strictly to be included as part of a country's capital stock. Developing economies lay great emphasis on the importance of capital accumulation, and stress the need to raise the level of investment in relation to output. Thus, the only way to build up a country's productive potential and raise per capita income is to expand the capacity for producing goods, this need not refer simply to the provision of physical capital such as plant and machinery, but also to roads, railways, power lines, water supply, schools, hospitals, houses and even incentive consumer goods such as consumer durables—all of which can contribute to increased productivity and higher living standards.

Development is associated with industrialisation and industrialisation with capital accumulation. Many development economists also see investment as the most important single factor in the growth process. W.W. Rostow defines the process of 'take-off' into sustained growth in terms of a critical ratio of investment to national product, and Arthur Lewis has described the process of development as one of transforming a country from being a 5 percent saver and investor to a 12 percent saver and investor. To achieve a particular rate of growth or to prevent per capita income from falling, each country has to calculate a precise ratios of investment to national income, which requires assumptions about the normal relation between capital and output. H.G. Johnson singles out capital accumulation in its widest sense as the distinguishing characteristic of development, and has described the structural transformation of economies as a generalised process of capital accumulation. In his words, "The condition of being developed consists of having accumulated, and having established efficient social and economic mechanisms for maintaining and increasing large stocks of capital per head in the various forms. Similarly, the condition of being underdeveloped is characterised by the possession of relatively small stocks of the various kinds of capital."

The scope for capital to permit more roundabout methods of production and increase productivity will be greater in developing countries where specialisation is minimal than the countries where specialisation has already reached a high level of sophistication. In a labour-abundant economy with a low capital-labour ratio, the very act of capital deepening make a substantial difference to total product, much more so than in countries where the process of capital deepening has been a continuing process for some length of time. All these factors represent important contributions that capital can make to economic progress, which may be relatively more important the smaller is the initial capital stock of a country relative to its population.

Capital-Output Ratio

The concept of capital-output ratio has been employed in the well-known models of Harrod, Hicks, Domar and others. The link between capital and output is embodied in the concept of the capital-output ratio, which can measure in physical units, or in value terms, either the average or the marginal relation between capital and output. The average capital-output ratio of an economy is the stock of capital divided by the annual flow of output *(K/Y)*, while the marginal or incremental capital-output ratio (ICOR) measures the relation between increments to the capital stock and increases in output ($\Delta K/\Delta Y$ or $I/\Delta Y$). If the economy is at full capacity, the incremental capital-output ratio will approximate to the average.

The concept is, often, used to determine the current rate of national income growth. Current rate of national income growth can be obtained by multiplying the current investment rate by the reciprocal of the marginal capital-output ratio. To express it algebraically let Y be the net national income, ΔY the absolute increase in the national income, I the investment, $\frac{I}{Y}$ the investment rate and $\frac{I}{\Delta Y}$ the marginal capital-output ratio. The rate of net national income is $\frac{I}{Y} \cdot \frac{\Delta Y}{I} = \frac{\Delta Y}{Y}$. To take a numerical example, if the rate of net investment is 12 percent and the marginal capital-output ratio 4, the rate of national income growth will be 12/4 = 3 percent. Taking both time-series and cross-section data, there is substantial empirical evidence of a strong inverse relation between growth and the value of the ICOR and good theoretical reasons for believing that the ICOR is the dependent variable in the relation. There are two main reasons for this. First, the investment rate tends to be more stable than other factors, so that growth may increase or decrease while the rate of capital accumulation remains virtually unchanged. The inverse relation would be less marked if capital-output ratios were computed by taking a measure of capital services, rather than the stock of capital, but this is not normally done. Second, if the significance of non-capital inputs in the growth process is greater than that of capital, there will be an inverse relation between the investment rate and the capital-output ratio. This means that if the relation between growth and the investment rate is positive, the relation between growth and the capital-output ratio will be negative.

In the short run, a low measured ICOR more probably implies that growth has been rapid, and not that relatively rapid growth will be associated with a low ratio of investment to output because the ICOR is low. The use of the incremental capital-output ratio for estimating the amount of investment required to increase output by a given amount was inspired by the work of Harrod and Domar. Although their work was originally designed to establish the conditions for equilibrium growth, their fundamental equations have been put to various alternative uses. Harrod's basic growth equation is $gc = s$, where g is the rate of growth ($\Delta Y/Y$), c is the ICOR ($I/\Delta Y$), and s is the saving ratio (S/Y). By substituting terms it can be seen that the equation merely expresses the *ex post* identity that saving equals investment, which follows from the accounting identities that income equals consumption plus investment, and income equals consumption plus saving. Nonetheless, it is this equation that has been endlessly manipulated to give the savings (or investment) ratio (s) necessary to achieve a particular target rate of growth (g), given the value of c, and to calculate the value of c, given g and s. The Harrod equation predicts an inverse relation between growth and the ICOR, but since *c* is assumed constant in Harrod's original model, it is the ICOR that determines growth and not the other way round.

The adjusted ICOR is sometimes referred to as the net incremental capital-output ratio; that is, the ICOR on the assumption that other factors do not change. Net or adjusted ICORs are difficult to estimate, but the variability of the factors that cooperate with capital in the productive system can play havoc with calculations of the actual ICOR from data on past growth and the investment ratio alone. When calculations are made of saving and investment requirements to achieve target rates of growth for, say, a 5-year to 10-year planning period, the normal assumption is that the incremental capital-output ratio will approximate to the average and that over the long-term the factors that cooperate with capital will be forthcoming, as in the past. For a planning period in excess of 5 years this assumption may not be unreasonable. Criticisms of the use of the incremental capital-output ratio in investment planning relate more to its use in the short run because of its cyclical variability. If the ratio does stay fairly constant over long periods, capital requirements for growth may be estimated with some accuracy over a long enough time horizon. Planning investment requirements for anything less than a 5-year period on the assumption of a stable capital-output ratio, may not be suitable.

The usefulness of the concept of capital-output ratio as a tool of economic analysis is very much limited because of its dependence on the behaviour of a number of other variables. The rate of growth of national income depends, in addition to rate of investment, upon a number of other factors. Capital is normally used in combination with other agents of production. An important factor determining the capital-output ratio is the amount of other agents combined with a certain amount of capital. The same rate of investment will lead to different rates of growth of national income according to the different amounts of other factors combined with a certain amount of capital. Capital-output ratio may be changed by changes in the nature of availability of 'free factors', *viz.*, rainfall, climate, etc., which play an important role in the production process. A favourable change in natural factors will lower the capital-output ratio and an unfavourable one will raise it. Capital-output ratio may be changed by changes in the extent of the utilisation of installed capacity. To separate out the effect of changes in capital on the changes in the rate of growth of income, we may use the concept of net capital-output ratio which means capital-output ratio on the assumption that all factors other than capital remain constant. Because normally changes in capital are associated with a change in other agents of production, to be nearer to reality, we may use the concept of adjusted capital-output ratio which means capital-output ratio when a change in capital is combined with a specified change in other factors of production. In what follows, we won't use the modified concept mentioned above and use the concept of gross capital-output ratio, i.e., ratio between the change in the rate of investment and the rate of growth of income irrespective of changes in other variables.

Capital-output ratio in economic planning: Given different values of s and c, different rates of growth of income can be obtained. For obtaining the maximum rate of growth, what a country has to do is to manipulate the economic forces in such a manner that the value of s is raised to the highest possible level and that of c lowered to the lowest possible level.

Capital-output ratio is not an infallible measure of capital productivity. It may not always be in the interest of a country to make investment in fields in which capital-output ratio is the lowest one. Capital-output ratio may be very high in the case of public utilities like roads, railways, irrigation, electricity, yet the importance of these cannot be overemphasized for accelerating economic development. The concept of capital-output ratio does not take into acccount the indirect contribution of capital to output. Public utilities facilitate production and thus contribute to production mostly indirectly. The concept of capital-output ratio does not take into account the contribution to production of an equipment over its whole period of life. In the long run, durable machinery which gives service for a long period may turn out to be more productive and cheaper than the non-durable one which is cheaper but gives service only for a short period.

The danger of using the capital-output ratio as a basis for investment planning may be—(i) Exclusive attention to the capital-output ratio may exaggerate the need for investment when output may be increased by other simpler means. For example, before calculating the additional capital required to produce a target output, it would be wiser for a developing economy to think first of the output that might reasonably be expected from increased utilisation of existing factors and better methods applied to old capital. (ii) The accuracy of any calculations of the capital-output ratio may be called into question in backward economies that lacks comprehensive and reliable statistics. (iii) The aggregate ICOR is bound to disguise sectoral differences, and when calculating overall investment requirements some allowance should be made for the changing sectoral distribution of resources.

Capital-output ratios calculated from past data can be used for forward planning only if they remain constant over a long period. They, however, remain changing along with changes in other variables, *viz.,* level of utilisation of capacity, interest rates, prices of factors of production, technological developments, type of economic organisation, etc. They differ not only in a country over time but also from country to country. The usefulness of the concept of capital-output ratio as a tool of economic planning, therefore, is very much limited.

Relation between capital-output ratio and economic development: What is the relation between the capital-output ratio and the economic development? Does capital-output ratio increase, decrease or remain constant with the increase in per capita income? Very little statistical information is available on the subject. Analytically speaking, some factors suggest that capital-output ratio is likely to decline with economic development while other factors suggest quite the reverse. On the whole, the former kind of factors seem to be more forceful than those of the latter kind and, therefore, there is the likelihood that the capital-output ratio will decline with economic development. Let us consider the important arguments on both sides. First we start with the considerations which suggest a rise in the capital-output ratio.

Economic development generally leads to an increase in the demand for labour and thereby to a rise in wage rates. Productivity of labour rises with economic development. This supports the demand of labour for an increase in wages. Rise in wage rates encourages substitution of capital for labour. Substitution of capital for labour will raise capital-output ratio. Wage rates may not rise if the increase in incomes is followed by a considerable increase in the rate of growth of population which generally happens in the initial stages of economic development. Ultimately, however, economic development is followed by a decrease in the rate of growth of population and, therefore, wage rates are likely to rise.

Economic development consists of a utilisation of known potentialities. Gradual utilisation of exhaustible and non-replaceable natural resources raises their price. Capital-output ratio will rise to the extent such resources enter into the production of capital goods. The argument is based on the assumption that known natural resources are fixed in volume or that the rate of utilisation of resources is higher than that of the discovery of new resources. The natural resources of underdeveloped countries, however, have not been properly surveyed and investigated. If sufficient outlay is made in discovering new natural resources, the rate of the discovery of natural resources may be higher than the rate of utilisation of these. In case it is so, economic development will be associated with a fall in the price of natural resources. In fact, it is very difficult to say anything definite about the rate of discovery of new natural resources.

Because of the existence of abundant unexploited opportunities in the field of technology capital will be highly productive in the early stages of economic development. Modern techniques developed in advanced countries cannot be used in underdeveloped countries because of lack of capital. If capital is available, production can be spectacularly increased by the introduction of modern techniques. Once the latest known techniques have been used, additional capital will not lead to so rapid advances in production.

Let us now examine the arguments which suggest that the economic development is likely to lead to decline in the capital-output ratio.

Colin Clark held that the capital-output ratio should decline because economic development consists in a shift of production from primary to tertiary industries which use comparatively lesser capital.[8] But economic development also consists in a shift of production from primary to secondary industry which are comparatively more capital intensive. This kind of shift will tend to raise capital-output ratio.

A rise in incomes increases efficiency of labour in a number of ways. It enables labour to acquire more knowledge and skills, to consume better food, to avail of greater medical facilities, to live in better housing, all of which add to efficiency. Expenditure on the improvement of human beings is generally classified as consumption and not as investment. Availability of larger capital increases the scope for division of labour which increases its productivity. Increase in the productivity of labour decreases the capital-output ratio.

An increase in production, generally, leads to a number of internal and external economies of production which tend to lower capital-output radio.

Generally, the more durable the capital, the higher will be the capital-output ratio. In the initial stages of development, a large part of the capital is invested in the construction of economic and social overheads which are more durable than the industrial machinery which accounts for considerable expenditure in the latter stages.

As development proceeds, the demand for fixed factors increases. An increase in the demand for fixed factors leads to rise in their rent. Rent component in the total cost (and total volume of output), therefore, will be smaller in the early stages of development than in the later stages.

In the initial stages of development, countries are more efficient in the production of consumption goods than in that of capital goods; this raises the cost of capital in relation to income.

In the early stages of economic development, the countries do not know the proper use of capital and this leads to a considerable wastage of it. Workers are not properly trained and they handle the equipment less carefully. Depreciation rates are very high because the roads, buildings and machines are not properly maintained. Capital is not properly allocated between different sectors and between different industries in each sector. This is partly because of lack of knowledge about the profitability of different investment opportunities. Capital tends to stick to beaten tracks even if there exist more profitable opportunities in other lines.

Standardisation and capital-output ratio: Standardisation of products and processes is an important method of economising capital, and thus of lowering the capital-output ratio. This is particularly so in the manufacture of industrial intermediates, spareparts, necessaries, and certain common tools, equipment and machinery used in industries. A fuller use can be made of fixed capital in many interlinking units by standardising their output.

Technology

The significance of technological change to economic growth and development has been verified again and again in empirical studies. The research based on neoclassical growth models has found that the basic factors of production, capital and labour, cannot explain all, or even much, of economic growth. It is often the "residual", that is, the unidentified variables, which contribute the most to increased productivity. The non-included variables, which can encompass such diverse items as technology, business and governmental organisation, institutional structures, the legal system, property rights, and so on, carry the weight of explaining economic growth over time and the differences in growth rates amongst countries.

Improvements in the art of production, which is the most literal interpretation of technical progress, result from a combination of research, invention, development and innovation. Research and invention are the activities that create knowledge, and development and innovation are the activities that apply new knowledge to the task of production. These are all basically economic activities.

Technology, one of the most important contributors to economic progress, is knowledge applied to the production process. It permits an outward shift of a nation's production possibilities frontier and creates the potential for greater output and income from the same resources. Technological progress reduces costs, increases productive efficiency, conserves society's resources, and establishes the capacity for a higher standard of living for greater numbers of persons. However, technology is often a difficult concept to understand. This is because it is not any particular object, but rather is a way of doing things and a way of thinking. Technology involves not only the entire accumulated complex of scientific and machine-tool knowledge and the tools and machines which encapsulate this knowledge. It also encompasses the country-specific human understanding, skills, education, and training essential for making use of this knowledge, the machines, and the tools.

One major source of improvement in technology and progress is the inventive and innovative activity of the native population. All societies are endowed to some degree with a potential supply of inventors, innovators and risk-takers, and in the absence of imported technology and personnel, it is on the emergence of this class of person that technological progress will primarily depend during the early stages of development. Economic backwardness in many countries may quite legitimately be traced back to a relative shortage of inventors, innovators and risk-takers. It is fairly well established that some cultures and some environments are more amenable to change than others, and in the past have produced a greater supply of entrepreneurs. The view is frequently expressed that the major source of growth during Britain's industrial revolution was primarily technological progress fostered by an abundant supply of inventors, innovators, entrepreneurs and risk-takers, with the accumulation of capital playing an essentially secondary role.

Technology is thus specific to each economy. The same physical manifestations of technology, such as a computer or a lathe, can have quite different effects on productivity since these tools are combined with labour forces in each economy, even each firm, with specific accumulated skills operating within a larger institutional and organisational framework. Technological knowledge is thus economy-specific, depending not just on the tools, machines, and other manifestations of technology in place, but also dependent on the skills and effectiveness of the operators and users of those tools and that knowledge.

The more rapidly technological knowledge is able to be adapted and put to work in an economy, the more rapid will be the pace of economic growth. This requires that workers and entrepreneurs have hands-on experience using such ideas in the act of producing. Slower technological progress means, *ceteris paribus*, slower economic growth and reduced possibilities for augmenting or creating the social mechanisms that promote greater equity and the higher level of human development that technological progress make feasible.

In economies where social and economic institutions are relatively weak, facilitating, and complementary to change, or can be made so by appropriate state policies, technological knowledge has a better chance of being combined in the production process to contribute to greater productivity and to higher levels of output. On the other hand, in societies where the social and economic institutional structure is retrograde, especially powerful, and non-facilitating of change, and where the state does not act to debilitate these adverse structures and ways of thinking, new knowledge is less apt to be applied to production.

The importance of technology has been widely identified as a major contributor to economic growth beginning with the empirical work of Edward Denison (1967). His research found technology to be responsible for over 40 percent of growth in the US and the UK over the period studied. Simon Kuznets's work also identified the significance of technological change, broadly interpreted, to productivity and economic growth. Solow (1988) noted that perhaps over 90 percent of the increases in output can be accounted for by the combined forces of technology and education.

Endogenous growth models have identified the importance of both technology and of human capital as fundamental complementary inputs affecting the rate of economic growth and the level of per capita income. To appreciate endogenous growth theory, it is useful to briefly review neoclassical growth theory, its forerunner, developed principally by Solow. The neoclassical growth model posited that a region's rate of economic growth is a function of the stock of capital and its stock of labour. There is assumed to be some rate of technological progress, but this is exogenous, i.e., it cannot be affected by any actions or policies within a region. In the short-term a region can grow because of an increase in either its supply of capital or an increase in its labour supply. But a region's supply of capital and labour are determined solely by differences in wage rates and rates of return to capital among regions. The model predicts that there is a steady-state growth path applicable to all regions. This is due to the equilibrating tendencies for labour to migrate to higher wage regions, increasing wage rates in the lower wage region and decreasing the wage rates in the higher wage region, and for capital to flow to regions where there is higher expected rates of return, with the effect of decreasing the returns to capital in the region with the initial higher rates of return. A key determinant of the equilibrium behaviour of this model is that both labour and capital are subject to decreasing returns.

With endogenous growth theory, this assumption of a "given" and spatially constant rate of technological progress is withdrawn. Specifically, endogenous growth theory is built upon the notion that a region's rate of technological progress is at least partially determined within the model, and specifically by the production of knowledge and by investment in human capital. Indeed, knowledge and technology play the key role in stimulating and sustaining a region's economic growth because these particular inputs display, unlike physical capital and labour, increasing returns to scale. The reason for this is that at least some component of knowledge has the attributes of being non-rival and at least partially non-excludable. Non-rival means that individual firm A's ability to make use of an input, say a new idea, is not diminished by firm B's use of that same idea. This attribute leads to the production of positive externalities from the point of view of the individual firm, each firm able to utilise the knowledge input receives a pecuniary benefit it otherwise would not have. In turn, this takes the form of a knowledge spillover effect, since there tends to be a strong negative spatial gradient to knowledge flows, especially of tacit forms of knowledge.

It is precisely because of the existence of these positive externalities and spillovers available within a spatially defined area that lead to unequal rates of technological progress among regions. It is by this factor that endogenous growth theory provides an explanation for why any cumulated advantages a particular region might have do not dissolve as a result of the equilibrating tendencies for capital to flow across regions in search of the highest expected return, and labour to migrate to regions with the highest wage rates.

The endogenous growth theories also show how the ability to apply technological knowledge varies dramatically amongst economies, so that a convergence of income has not taken place in the simple fashion suggested by the neoclassical growth model. This is because technological knowledge in use is economy-specific as a result of differences in the capacity of end-users to apply knowledge in the production process. This way of looking at technology focuses attention on the need for social investment in specific human capital and organisational inputs if such knowledge is to be utilised to its full effect. This way of understanding technology also recognises that there can be technology gaps among economies and that each economy must develop its own relatively unique technological base. Technology is specific knowledge, not general knowledge. It cannot be applied everywhere in the same way. Each country must make a substantial investment in its social and human resource capital base if it is to gain the capacity "to do" technology in a way that maximises the gains that are implicit in any particular component of knowledge applied to production.

A technological strategy of development: Economic development is indistinguishable from the ongoing application of technological knowledge to production. Without continuing technological change, economic growth slows and eventually development falters. Technological change is the result of scientific discovery, experiment, and innovation which must be financed either by the private sector or the state. The successful introduction of technology into the domestic production process in any country, what can be called domestic innovation, requires a domestic scientific establishment capable of understanding, adopting, and adapting new, often foreign-created, technological knowledge to the specific needs of the domestic economy. Machines and tools often have to be customised to fit local conditions. This is the adaptation stage of technological progress where existing knowledge is borrowed from the world supply and made to fit the local economy. Later, some countries might move into the creation state of technological progress, which involves the conducting of new research, the designing of experiments, and the dissemination of new knowledge that adds to the world supply of technological competency and to the possibility of ever higher standards of living. These two distinct stages are referred by Ronald Doreas, respectively, independent technology learning capacity (ITLC) and independent technology creating capacity (ITCC). An ITLC might also be called, interchangeably, technological autonomy. Creating an ITLC and achieving technological autonomy is the first step toward greater self-sufficiency, a higher level of domestic efficiency and the creation of an internal dynamic for any economy. It is an ITLC that undergirded the Japanese, Korean, and Taiwanese development successes. The easy import substitution and easy export substitution phase of industrialisation in those countries provided the creative space for domestic entrepreneurs and workers to be able to attain higher levels of skill that permitted them to become increasingly technologically competent. It is this learning capacity which permitted the East Asian economies to grow faster, on average, than other less-developed countries which apparently shared roughly the same initial endowments, such as the level of investment.

Recent empirical studies have found that a nation's research and development expenditures are significant in explaining sustained growth rates over time. Other research has suggested that within the overall goal of increasing the stock of human capital, scientists and technicians involved in R&D are an important sub-category of human capital which should be emphasised to better appropriate the benefits of technology. Both R&D and the training of R&D researchers contribute to the creation of specific national technologies and to the learning required to be able to utilise technological knowledge effectively.

While the rate of economic growth and technological change are path dependent in the sense of being the consequence of past decisions on the economic strategy, on expenditures for human capital purposes, on the exchange rate and inflation rate, and so on, modification of the path are always possible when a country decides to make a change. Though the current rate of economic and human development may be path dependent, the future path has multiple branches at any moment in time. The decisions the state sector makes on expenditures for education, health, the military, on tariffs, on tax laws, on patents and other intellectual property rights, on the treatment of multinational corporations, and on a whole range of other factors today will determine along which path the economy and society will traverse in future. Private firms, individuals, and the state make decisions within the confines of the parameters for economic decision-making determined by the state and within the cultural and historical confines of each specific society. They choose the path now via spending and other decisions which affect future growth and development prospects and determine the future path dependency of the economy.

Technology and total factor productivity: The impact of various inputs to production on economic development can be assessed using a growth accounting methodology. Basically, this is an attempt to measure how much of any increase in an economy's output can be accounted for by additional units of the inputs added to production, for example physical capital (K) and additional labour (L). Any economic development left unaccounted for by increases in the quantity of physical inputs is called total factor productivity (TFP). And the countries able to combine both new capital, which typically embodies new technological knowledge and a growing and improving human capital stock which is better able to make use of and unlock the technological knowledge incorporated in new capital, will be better equipped to move toward and keep pace with the world production possibilities "best practice" frontier and will tend to have the highest rates of TFP. World Bank opined that in explaining the growth of TFP, the main additional element is the quality of labour, that is, human capital accumulation.

Through total factor productivity, we can get an idea about how efficient a country is as it progresses along its path of economic development. Let us consider an example. Suppose the GDP per person of some country is growing at an average rate of 7.5 percent per year, but its TFP is zero. What a TFP = 0 means is that there has been a zero increase in efficiency, implying no increase in the productivity of inputs involved in achieving the increased GDP. Here the question arises, how is it possible to have a growth in the economy without any growth in the efficiency of inputs?

The only way an economy's total output can increase if there is zero increase in productivity is if more inputs are added to production, inputs that are of the same quality as in the past. Typically those inputs are physical capital and labour, but there could be other inputs as well such as different types of workers, R&D, or any other input that might be identified. Whenever GDP increases because there has been an increase in the inputs added to production, we call this extensive economic growth, i.e., economic growth resulting from adding more inputs to production. If TFP = 0, and a country has nonetheless experienced growing GDP, then all the increase in GDP has been due to the use of more labour and capital in production, and all economic growth is extensive.

On the other hand, if a country has TFP > 0, then that means that some part of the country's economic growth is due to greater efficiency. When TFP > 0 that amount of growth is called intensive economic growth implying that with the same quantity of inputs a country can produce more GDP than it could otherwise and at a faster rate than can be achieved by just adding new inputs to production. Having TFP > 0 is how countries can achieve even faster economic progress over the long-term than would be possible otherwise.

Total factor productivity can be estimated by subtracting from the growth rate of total output the share of that total growth attributable to increase in the quantity of physical capital and increases in the labour force, each weighted by their contribution to total production. In other words, TFP measures the synergistic effect of combining an economy's physical capital and its human capital, which can result in productivity increases beyond the contribution of more physical quantities of the individual inputs. Consider the following example.

Let us assume an economy with two inputs to production, labour (*L*) and physical capital (*K*). If annual output growth was 7.5 percent; physical capital, *K*, grew by 3 percent per year and *K's* contribution to production was 30 percent; and the labour force, *L*, which contributed 70 percent to aggregate production, grew by 2 percent per year; then,

TFP = total percentage change in output
– (percentage change of K × contribution of K to production, as a decimal) – (percentage change of L × contribution of L to production, as a decimal)
= 7.5 percent – (3 percent × 0.3) – (2 percent × 0.7)
= (7.5 – 0.9 – 1.4) percent = 5.2 percent

The 5.2 percent is the annual rate of TFP, that is, it is that part of total economic growth that cannot be explained by having added more inputs to the production process. It is the amount of intensive economic growth.

TFP is an attempt to capture the impact of all the factors that contribute to the greater productivity of the inputs, *K* and *L* (or any broader definition of inputs used). Included in the TFP measure are:

(a) technological change and technological catch-up;

(b) improvement in the efficiency and learning capacity of the labour force due to human capital accumulation;

(c) the positive productivity effects of the structural transformation from agriculture to industry and other strategy switches;

(d) changes in state policy that contribute to greater efficiency, such as lower inflation rates or an improved tax structure;

(e) organisational and institutional alterations, such as better management practices and improved financial control mechanisms in the banking system, and so on.

In a general sense, all of the variables which might affect an economy's total factor productivity are related to an economy's acquisition of an independent technology learning capacity and a national technological capacity to do technology and to be more effective users of resources.

Technology-centred development: When technology is viewed not as an exogenous given or as a public good freely available to all but as an endogenous process to some extent dependent on indigenous factors specific to each economy, then education and the improvement of human skills in general and the creation of a core R&D cadre must become essential components of any development strategy aimed at real structural transformation. In the words of Simon Kuznets, "Far more important [than physical capital to economic growth]...are the economic and social characteristics that reside in the capacities and skills of an economy's population, determine the efficiency of the institutions that direct the use of accumulated physical capital, and guide the current production into proper channels of consumption and capital investment."

Technology exists as an intangible and accumulating body of knowledge at the world level capable of being utilised by any given country only to the degree it has developed a technologically sophisticated community, which can use and adapt the existing supply of knowledge to employ the implements of production to advance economic progress. It is thus not possible for countries to effectively borrow the manifestations of technology, such as physical capital, tools, and machines which are so often the focus of the technology transfer literature, and expect to become developed if the human skills, culture, and institutions required to make effective use of this technological knowledge are absent or poorly formed within the borrowing economy. Thus, people, not tools, are the real agents of technology transfer and diffusion.

A technologically sophisticated country is composed not only of knowledge workers, like scientists, engineers, and researchers, but also of skilled workers on the shop floor who can utilise new ideas in the ways they are meant to be utilised, perhaps even improving upon them in their specific, local application. There must exist or be created an indigenous entrepreneurial nucleus of determined agents capable of appreciating the potential of new ways of producing and who are able and willing to make use of new technology through constant innovation in the domestic production process. Rather than serving as a complement to local technological development and as a boost to locally controlled and locally directed production and to the establishment of a dynamic national technology, foreign inputs can become substitutes for the local factors of production and for the building of a domestic technological capacity. This is especially likely to occur in those countries where the necessary components of a technological autonomy strategy have not been implemented, and particularly where general education levels and technical education levels are low.

Macropolicies and technological change: Policies of the state as they affect the economy have an important impact on the level of total factor productivity. Policies which create an environment in which private firms are enabled and encouraged to produce and invest in technological acquisition and to be efficient are likely to have a greater positive impact on output growth than policies that are less facilitating. In particular, macro-economic policies can either encourage or discourage private entrepreneurs to innovate and change. Also, policies that help to keep inflation rates and the balance of payments in check also would be expected to contribute to growth, national technological change, and development. To acquire technology, countries can import it embodied in capital and consumer goods; they can obtain it on licence from patent holders, or they can attract foreign direct investment which brings technology with it. The spread of technology and ideas may also be expected to come about naturally in the general process of commercial intercourse and the exchange of information through trade. This is one of the dynamic gains from trade. But not all countries have equal access to technology. Geography, culture, and the quality of human capital matters. The speed with which modern technology is absorbed by economically backward countries will depend on the same class of factors as the diffusion of knowledge within countries.

Despite the dimensions of inappropriateness, technology developed in rich countries is often transferred intact for use in poor countries. Because well over 90 percent of the world's expenditure on technology research and development is made in rich countries. Third world countries invite multinational corporations to invest in their leading sectors. They obtain equipment through official aid programs. The investors and aid givers can only provide what they know and are available. When technology available from the developed countries is inappropriate, where is more appropriate technology to be obtained? Four possible sources can be distinguished:

(a) LDCs can use developed-country technologies but make peripheral modifications, for example, in materials handling.

(b) They can borrow old technologies from the industrial countries.

(c) A possible source of appropriate technology is selective borrowing from the industrial countries.

(d) Developing countries can do their own research and development work to evolve technologies specifically designed to fit local conditions.

It is sometimes said that traditional indigenous technologies which have been developed over the years by locals provide a promising basis for development. But if these alternative channels of technological development are really open, why does much of the technology used in the third world remain so obviously inappropriate? One important reason is when competitive pressures are absent, incentives to adapt to local conditions are weak. Another barrier is communication difficulties. Communication barriers have been an especially serious impediment to the adoption of older technologies from the industrial countries.

Frances Stewart has distinguished three schools of thought on technology policies for third world countries. The first group, which she calls "the price incentive school", stresses "getting the prices right", in the belief that factor prices which reflect social costs will not only lead to the selection of the most efficient techniques out of the currently available range, but will also create incentives for more appropriate technologies to be developed. The opposing "technologist school" believes that this mechanism of induced innovation cannot be relied on to do the job, that a conscious decision to invest more in technological development is needed. Finally, there is "the radical reform school", which takes a broader view of the matter. This school argues that both the array of goods produced and the methods used to produce them are inherent features of social systems. One cannot expect anything but capital-intensive methods and products targeted for middle-class consumption from the multinational corporations. Creation of appropriate technologies and use of appropriate factor proportions, this last group argues, requires that production be reoriented toward a multitude of cheap items for mass consumption. This in turn requires a massive redistribution of income, which cannot be achieved without a social revolution. Hence the problem of inappropriate technology and inadequate job creation can only be solved in the context of a radical reform of society.

While the contributions of endogenous growth theory for helping to fashion more effective technology-based economic development strategies are evident, Malecki and others have criticised the theory for paying insufficient attention to the institutional context and institutional adaptivity as prerequisites for successful knowledge-based regional economic development. With the focus on increasing firm productivity—consistent with endogenous growth theory—Porter's diamond model has highlighted a number of institutional conditions that allow firms within certain sectors to be able to gain national (or regional) competitiveness. The diamond—the four sets of interacting determinants of national (or regional) competitiveness—consists of (i) firm strategy, structure, and rivalry; (ii) demand conditions; (iii) factor (input) conditions; and (iv) related and supporting industries. Porter argues that economic development policy and government more generally have important roles to play in each of these four determinants of competitiveness. These roles may be direct, such as timely and responsive investments in physical infrastructure, information technology, K-12 education, and instruction and R&D at public universities.

Entrepreneurship

The concept of the entrepreneur or entrepreneurship was developed by Joseph Schumpeter, who put the entrepreneur at the centre of his *Theory of Economic Development* originally published (in German) in 1911. The entrepreneur is the man who sees the opportunity for introducing a new technique or a new commodity, an improved organisation, or for the development of newly discovered resources. He raises the money to launch a new enterprise, assembles the factors of production, chooses top managers, and sets the organisation going. He need not be a capitalist—he may not provide any funds of his own. He may not be a day-to-day manager. Nor is he usually an inventor or explorer. Inventions or discoveries by themselves have little economic effect, Schumpeter argues.

It is one thing to develop a new technique or invention, but unless someone actually put that technique to practical use, to turn it into an innovation, it will have little or no impact on economic development. The entrepreneur who plays this crucial role is someone who has the imagination to see the potential for profit from the innovation, the initiative actually to carry out the task of introducing the innovation, and a willingness to take a calculated risk that the effort might fail and lead to a loss rather than a profit.

Schumpeter himself raised basic questions about whether entrepreneurship was really necessary once industrial development had reached an advanced level. In advanced industrial economies innovation tends to become routinised. Corporations have their own large research laboratories and managers more or less automatically turn the results of that research into new products or new methods of producing old products. Innovations no longer require the bold imagination of a few unique entrepreneurs. Schumpeter's insight concerning advanced industrial economies is directly relevant to developing countries. If innovation can be routinised in advanced economies, why not in developing economies as well? After all it does not take much imagination or daring to see that a railroad or a chemical fertiliser plant may make a major contribution to a developing country's economy. The value of such innovations is clear to all, and the task for the developing nation is to find the capital and managerial talent to pay for and run the new enterprise.

Like Marx, Schumpeter lay considerable stress on sociological factors, and some of these are not easily reduced to simple mathematical expressions. This stricture applies to Schumpeter's concept of the "social climate", a complex phenomenon reflecting the whole social, political, and socio-psychological atmosphere within which entrepreneurs must operate. It would include the social values of a particular country at a particular time, the class structure, the educational system, and the like. It would certainly include the attitude of society toward business success, and the nature and extent of the prestige and other social rewards, apart from profits, which accompany business success in the society. A particularly important factor in "climate" is the entrepreneur's understanding of the "rules of the game", the conditions under which he must operate. Sudden changes in the rules of the game are particularly deleterious to an increasing flow of enterprise.

In underdeveloped countries, the central role is played not by the entrepreneur but by the government acting in social and national interests. Welfare of the masses rather than the maximisation of profits of the entrepreneur is the main guiding force. In underdeveloped countries, the divergence between social and private returns is so wide that the entrepreneur interested only in maximising his private profits cannot be assigned a central role. Initiation of the development process requires considerable investment in social and economic overheads, the return from which is mostly indirect and not taken into account by the entrepreneur. In underdeveloped countries, the innovating class of entrepreneurs is not very important because innovations do not play an important role and the process of development primarily involves the application of known technology existing in advanced countries. The emergence of planning has thrown the entrepreneur in the background.

In the words of Henry C. Wallich, "No longer is he the hero of the piece, admired by economists, and, more important, by his compatriots. The law does no aid and abet him and his property interests on all sides, as it did during the heyday of capitalism. He seems to be regarded as a byproduct of economic development, to be tolerated because of his usefulness but to be watched and curbed because of his selfish propensities. If in most of the less-developed countries his wealth escapes heavy taxation, it is mainly due to administrative inadequacies."[9]

Loss of faith in *laissez faire* policy and the emergence of socialistic ideology has considerably decreased the importance of entrepreneur even in developed countries. Schumpeter himself predicted the ultimate fall of the entrepreneur as, "A more or less stationary state would ensue.... There would be nothing left for entrepreneurs to do. They would find themselves in much the same situation as generals would in a society perfectly sure of permanent peace. The social function (of an entrepreneur) is already losing importance and is bound to lose it at an accelerating rate in the future even if the economic process itself of which the entrepreneur was the prime mover went on unabated. For, on the one hand, it is much easier now than it has been in the past to do things that lie outside familiar routine—innovation itself is being reduced to routine. Technological progress is increasingly becoming the business of teams of trained specialists who turn out what is required and make it work in predictable ways. The romance of earlier commercial adventure is rapidly wearing away because so many more things can be strictly calculated that had of old to be visualized in a flash of genius.... Thus, economic progress tends to become depersonalized and automatized. Bureau and committee work tends to replace individual action."[10]

Even if it is difficult, if not impossible, to establish a clear casual connection between certain types of minority-group status and entrepreneurship, there remains the question of whether one can say anything about what causes people to become entrepreneurs whether or not they are members of minorities. One idea first put forward by the Harvard psychologist, David McClelland, is that of *need for achievement*, or *n-achievement* for short. The principal idea behind this term is that certain societies produce a large number of people who have a high level of desire to improve themselves in order to get ahead financially or be recognised as the best at some form of endeavour. Societies where people possessing this kind of motivation are plentiful will produce large numbers of entrepreneurs and hence will experience economic development.

There seems to be little reasons to dispute the notion that success in business as in many other activities is somehow connected with a need to achieve. The controversy surrounding the term instead centres around two other issues. There is first of all the question of whether one can come up with plausible and independent methods of measuring n-achievement levels that can then be compared with economic performance to see if there is a relationship. Proponents of the concept argue that they have developed such measurable concepts and that the correlation clearly exists, whereas the considerable body of skeptics remains to be convinced. A second question is whether n-achievement is something that must exist in adequate amounts before development can occur or whether appropriate motivation is something that arises more or less automatically as economic development creates opportunities for people to exploit.

The problem of appropriate motivation for economic development exists in some developing societies and for a variety of reasons certain cultures seem more resistant to change than others. It is also clear that the problem of motivation is not confined to the issue of what creates entrepreneurs. Development requires effective managers and a hardworking and disciplined labour force, and motivation presumably has something to do with these people as well. But once one has made these obvious points it is difficult to say much more with any conviction. We have only a general idea of what the appropriate kinds of motivation are for economic development to be successful, and an even hazier notion of how that motivation is created.

NON-ECONOMIC FACTORS

Development, a leading sector in national transformation, is rooted in nonmaterial factors and requires a positive feedback between culture, economy, and polity. The need for economic growth in a developing country has few if any economic springs. It arises from a desire to assume full status by taking part in an industrial civilisation, participation in which alone enables a nation or individual to compel others to treat it as an equal. Inability to take part in it makes a nation militarily powerless against neighbours, administratively unable to control its own citizens, and culturally incapable of speaking the international language.

In addition to economic factors, non-economic factors play an important role in economic development. Economic and non-economic factors act and react on each other. Economic changes have far-reaching political and social consequences. Similarly, political and social changes have important economic consequences. Ignoring or assuming away non-economic factors leaves the economic theory extremely sterile. The motivation for economic development is provided as much by non-economic forces as by economic forces. The non-economic factors are crucial to the theoretical explanation of differences in growth rates in the advanced and poor countries. The distinction between economic and non-economic factors has aroused sharp criticism from several economists.

In words of Jacob Viner, "It is incumbent on the economist to recognise and proclaim that economic improvement is not merely a matter of more capital, or more coal in the ground, but also of a growth of effectiveness of management and of manual effort through better education, better health, better motivation, and better political and social organisation. If he fails to do so, he is liable to himself throwing the blame for national poverty wholly on physical circumstances beyond human remedy, or on factors external to that economy, to the neglect of internal human, social, political and moral factors which may carry a large part of the true responsibility."[11]

In words of Gunnar Myrdal, "In reality there is no distinction between facts corresponding to our traditional scholastic division of social science into separate divisions. A realistic analysis of problems can never stop at such lines of division. The distinction between factors that are 'economic' and those that are 'non-economic', is, indeed, a useless and non-sensical device from the point of view of logic.... It will have to be discarded as illogical and, consequently, misleading. Economic analysis will have to deal with all the relevant factors if it wants to be realistic; general economic theory will have to become social theory...concrete problems are never simply economical, sociological, psychological and political. A theory of underdevelopment and development which works only with 'economic variables' is for logical reasons doomed to be unrealistic and thus irrelevant."[12]

There is, however, the problem that if all factors—economic, political, social, cultural, religious and psychological—are considered together, the phenomenon becomes so complex as to make any generalisations almost impossible. Because social, political, cultural, psychological and several economic elements are not amenable to rigorous treatment, there is a tendency on the part of the economists to concentrate only on a few variables, assuming away all other variables. Recently, it has become a fashion to build elegant models taking into consideration only a few variables and assuming away all realities. If the assumptions behind these models are not fully kept in view, use of these may lead to wholly unrealistic and grossly mistaken conclusions and policy recommendations. As the economy advances, however, the influence of non-economic factors diminishes.

In backward countries, exogenous or non-economic factors exercise relatively most influence; the autonomy of an economic system as such increases as the society including it progresses, and therewith the applicability of economic theory.[13]

OBSTACLES TO DEVELOPMENT

It is easily said that poverty and backwardness are due to a general shortage and inefficient use of the key factors of production. But, it is very hard to determine precisely why there should be a dearth of some factors and an abundance of others, and why development may be a slow and lengthy process. The present development gap has arisen largely through industrial development in certain selected areas of the world, which in turn has generated its own factor endowments. In this section we shall consider some of the potential obstacles to development in the present developing countries, and the mechanisms through which unequal advantage between developed and developing countries is perpetuated.

Economic Obstacles to Development

Poverty is mainly the result of economic forces within the developing nation. The two most commonly cited economic barriers to development are the vicious circle of poverty and the limited extent of the market in developing nations.

The vicious circle of poverty: The vicious circle of poverty is only one of many 'vicious circles' that exist in the less-developed world. The idea behind it is that it is easier for rich people to save and invest than it is for poor people. By analogy, therefore, it is more difficult for poor nations to save and invest enough to raise themselves out of poverty. Given that investment is crucial for development, poor nations thus stay poor. To break this vicious circle either one must discover a way of extracting more savings out of very poor people, or one must find funds for investment from outside the poor country. The 'vicious circle of poverty' argument, not surprisingly, is a frequently heard justification for why foreign aid from advanced nations is essential if the poor nations of the world are ever to achieve substantial progress. In effect if developing nations are too poor to save for themselves, richer countries must do part of the job for them.

The limited extent of the market: The relationship between the limited extent of the market and economic underdevelopment is based on the idea that economies of scale in industry are a key feature of economic development. If industrial enterprises must be large in order to make most efficient use of modern technology, then the size of the markets on which the goods of those enterprises are to be sold must also be large. But, it is argued, the size of markets in developing countries is small precisely because incomes and hence demand in such countries are low.

There are several drawbacks in this argument. First, economies of scale exist in some industrial sectors such as steel and chemical fertilisers, but it is often possible to produce quite efficiently in comparatively small enterprises in sectors such as machinery or textiles. Second, while per capita incomes in developing countries are low, there are often large numbers of people in these countries so that total income and hence demand can be quite large. If most of the people in the developing world live in comparatively large nations, there is still an important sense in which the domestic markets of these nations are not large. Because of the poor transport and commercial systems that are characteristic of most developing nations, these nations are not one integrated market but a collection of many smaller fragmented markets. Thus, the scale of cement plants in less-developed country may be small because it costs too much to ship cement long distances over poor or nonexistent roads. But, even the existence of fragmented markets does not succeed in completely rehabilitating the notion that the limited size of markets is a major cause (and effect) of underdevelopment. It is possible to argue that the limited size of the market is a problem for some industries in some countries, but only in rare instances it is a major cause of lack of development in a nation as a whole.

The existence of foreign trade also undermines the popularly held belief that a nation must be rich in natural resources in order to be successful in achieving development. As long as a nation can sell what it does produce abroad, it can use the foreign exchange earned to purchase the natural resources it needs. For example, Japan, one of the most natural-resource-poor nations in the world, has done precisely that for nearly a century.[14]

While there are economic causes for the prevalence of poverty in large parts of the world, it is apparent that economic explanations alone cannot account for why so many nations are poor. Economists are uncomfortable when they leave the realm of economic explanations in part because the tools of economic analysis are of only limited help outside the sphere for which they were designed. But if one is seriously interested in understanding poverty in nations there is little choice but to explore the relationship between economic development on the one hand and political systems and social values on the other.

Government Obstacles to Development

There is a great deal of evidence to suggest that disparities in the level of development between countries are related to governance and that poor governance is an obstacle to development. Economic development in England in the eighteenth century began with little direct assistance from the government, but since that time the role of government in development has risen steadily to a point where successful growth is not really possible without the active support of a government. An active positive role for government is essential. It follows that if a government is unwilling or unable to play such a role, then the government itself can be considered a barrier to development or a fundamental cause of poverty.

Political stability: Governments must be able to create and maintain a stable environment for modern enterprises, whether public or private. At a minimum, civil war, sustained insurrection, or invasion by hostile forces must be avoided. Investors will not put their money into projects that pay off only over the long run if in the short run a change of government could lead to the project's being confiscated or rendered unprofitable by new laws and other restrictions. Where instability is particularly rife, a common solution has been to not invest in the local economy at all.

Political independence: A stable environment alone is not enough for the development. For example, colonial governments were usually quite stable, often for very long periods of time. Most colonial governments had a very specific interest in creating a stable environment for private business and yet few if any European or Japanese colonies experienced anything that could be described as sustained economic development. Part of the explanation is that the stable environment created was often only for the benefit of a small number of traders and investors from the colonising nation whereas the citizens of the colonies themselves received little such support. Probably a more important part of the explanation, however, is that most colonial governments made only limited investments in training local people, in developing electric power resources, or in promotion of industry. It follows, if not quite automatically, that political independence was in most cases necessary before modern economic growth was possible.

Government support for development: There are many governments of developing countries today that for domestic reasons of their own are not willing to do what is necessary to achieve growth. Since virtually all leaders of developing nations regularly make speeches about the need to grow and appoint commissions to draw up development plans, there would seem to be little point in discussing governments unwilling to do what is necessary to achieve growth. The decision to pursue economic development like most other economic decisions involves hard choices or trade-offs. While there are many people whose position is improved by economic development, in the early stages at least there are usually people whose position becomes worse off. If those who become worse off in the short run are in a position to topple the government, that government will be unwilling or unable to take the steps necessary to promote growth. The nature of the problem is best illustrated by the experience of a number of developing nations that have attempted either to devalue their currencies, to eliminate excessive staffing of public enterprises, or to remove subsidies on basic consumer goods.

Some nations feel that certain international goals should take precedence over domestic development goals. For example, President Sukarno in Indonesia, during the period he held real power (1948-1965), was more interested in international affairs such as leadership of the third world or military confrontation with Singapore and Malaysia than in economic development. A number of Arab states have devoted a sizable share of their surplus resources to three decades of confrontation and war with Israel. No doubt both President Sukarno and the leaders of these Arab states would have preferred to have economic development as well as confrontation, but their resources were limited and they had to choose between goals. In choosing they did not opt for economic development.

Some nations have concentrated their energies on achieving what could be termed social goals rather than economic development. Economic development includes both growth and wide distribution of the benefits of growth. While some nations have pursued growth but not development, there are several nations that have sacrificed growth at least for a time in order to achieve wider distribution and other social goals. For example, Cuba in the 1960s experienced little economic growth in large part because energies were concentrated on achieving a major redistribution of income, education, and other benefits in favour of the poorest elements of the society. China's Cultural Revolution (1966-1970) was even more ambitious. There the ultimate goal of at least some of the nation's leaders was to eliminate all class distinctions and to greatly reduce the role of material incentives, and the leaders were willing to sacrifies growth at least temporarily to achieve those objectives.

Thus, one of the reasons many nations are still underdeveloped is that the governments of those nations have been unable or unwilling to pursue policies that would achieve development. Governments after all represent various interests in the society and in some cases it has proved impossible to pursue developmental goals and maintain sufficient support from those interests to stay in office, while in other cases government leaders themselves have preferred to pursue objectives that were in conflict with development.

Social Values as Obstacles to Economic Development

Certain individuals in a traditional society are prevented from rising to the more conventional sources of prestige, power, and wealth, such as high government office. The reason they are prevented from rising up through the conventional hierarchy may be that they are members of a religious minority subjected to discrimination or because they are immigrants from abroad and not natives of the country. If these blocked minorities had previously enjoyed a high status, they have a particularly keen desire to restore themselves to a position of wealth and prestige. Since they cannot join the army or the civil service, the one route open to them is to become wealthy through entrepreneurship. The examples of blocked minorities that supplied large numbers of entrepreneurs is a long one. The list includes Parsees in India, Jews in Europe, Chinese in Southeast Asia, Indians and Lebanese in Africa, and so on. In looking at the early developing nations of England, northern Europe, and North America, the connection between minority status and entrepreneurs becomes more remote except in a fairly trivial sense. Everyone in the United States is a member of a minority group of some kind, for example, but only a few of those minorities have been blocked from rising up any of the ladders of power and prestige, and those blocked minorities have not yet been the major suppliers of entrepreneurship.

Development is a comprehensive economic, social, cultural and political process that aims at constantly improving the well-being of the entire population on the basis of everyone's active, free and meaningful participation and the fair distribution of the available resources. Racism and other forms of discrimination are not only human rights violations but also major obstacles to achieving development. Such obstacles can be conflicts that stem from racial tensions and disrupt local, national and regional development, or the marginalization of vulnerable groups resulting in missed development opportunities. Racial discrimination and poverty often form a vicious cycle. Experience reveals that in many cases victims of racism, racial discrimination, xenophobia and related intolerance are among the poorest. Eliminating racial discrimination promotes social cohesion and development. Indeed, combating discrimination helps prevent conflicts and social unrest, and contributes to economic growth. Equality is fundamental to social harmony; it is essential for the promotion of good governance, sustainable development and the fair allocation of available resources. Equality and development reinforce each other.

International Obstacles to Development

If we consider that the obstacles to development are concentrated on economic conditions, political systems, and social values that are internal to the less-developed world, to the extent that these internal conditions are the main causes of poverty, successful development will depend on internal solutions. But, many economists and others argue that the main barriers to development today lie not with these internal elements but with conditions external to the developing world. Specifically, the existence of already rich and industrialised nations, it is argued, creates international pressures that hamper the growth efforts of today's poor nations.

The theory of comparative advantage states that nations with different endowments of capital, labour, and natural resources will gain by specialising in those areas where their relative costs are low and importing where their relative costs of production are high. Further, the greater the difference in endowments between countries—and the differences between rich and poor countries are great indeed—the greater are these gains from trade likely to be. In certain extreme cases, but ones that occur in the real world, a nation possesses one resource or factor such as land or oil in such abundance that it is impossible to make effective use of all of that resource internally. Trade makes it possible to use this surplus resource because one can export what is not needed at home for things that are needed. Saudi Arabia could not possibly use all the petroleum it is capable of producing, or Canada all of the wheat from its great plains. Trade thus becomes what is sometimes referred to as a *vent for surplus*. Other gains from trade include the fact that real capital goods can only be transferred from rich to poor nations (and *vice versa*) through trade. In addition there is the fact that some countries' enterprises producing for export are among the most progressive in the nation because they have to be to survive international competition. And the example of these progressive firms influences domestic enterprises as well to follow the progressive example set.

While almost everyone acknowledges the potential advantages of being able to learn from the experience of others, many have argued that this potential is seldom realised in practice because the advanced nations create barriers to the progress of poor nations. Many economists have attempted to explain the nature and sources of these barriers imposed on the less-developed world. Development is severely inhibited by the fact that its surplus is being drained off abroad by multinational companies leaving little money of its own to invest and at the same time the nation is receiving only small amounts of investment from abroad.

Some scholars argue that what was lost was a potential rather than an actual surplus. The drain of profits from the developing countries might not be large, but measures taken by the capitalist nations prevented the developing nations from producing the surplus that would have existed in the absence of capitalist pressures from abroad. Some argued, for example, that free-trade policies imposed on the developing world made it impossible to protect infant industries and hence those industries did not develop. The resources that would have gone to produce industrial output and funds for further investment instead lay idle. Free trade, leading to imports of manufactured cloth and the like, also destroyed local handicrafts, it is argued, thereby further contributing to the unemployment of domestic resources. Still other scholars have argued that the drain of profits was real enough but hidden by the way prices are set for goods transferred from the industrial to the developing nation. Multinationals charge much higher prices when they sell to developing countries than when they sell the same product at home.

As for what happens to the poor nation attempting to develop, emphasis has shifted away from the role of a direct drain of surplus to collusion between advanced-nation capitalists and antigrowth forces within the developing nation. The issue is not as much the drain of surplus abroad as it is the misuse of that surplus at home. Some scholars argue that it is in the interest of advanced-nation capitalists to keep developing-nation markets open to their products and to keep cheap supplies of developing nation raw materials flowing. Industrial growth within the developing nation would be harmful to both goals since local industrial products would compete with imports and would also bid for local raw materials. Domestic companies tend to side with foreign investors because they do not want competition from multinationals. The end result is an alliance of foreign investors backed by their governments and merchant capitalists who together keep a government in power that does little to promote development.

The poor nations in the early stages of development tend to have a very unequal distribution of income. As a result demand for industrial products in these societies tends to be concentrated on luxury products such as automobiles since the poor have little money left over after purchasing food and housing. It is precisely luxury goods that are usually either imported from abroad or produced domestically by foreign firms. Local enterprises and investors lack the capital or know-how to produce such sophisticated products in the early stages of development. Foreign investors have an interest in keeping the distribution of income unequal because that is what keeps up demand for products only they can produce. The local ruling class has the same interest because they are the beneficiaries of this unequal distribution. Growth is slow because foreign investors only invest the minimum necessary to keep control of the local market.

Dualism

Dualism describes a condition in which developing countries may find themselves in the early stages of development, referring to economic and social divisions in an economy, such as differences in the level of technology between sectors or regions, differences in the degree of geographic development and differences in social customs and attitudes between an indigenous and an imported social system. In all its aspects, it is a concomitant of the growth of a money economy, which may either arise naturally as a result of specialisation or be imposed from outside by the importation of an alien economic system. Therefore, a dual economy is characterised by a difference in social customs between the subsistence and exchange sectors of the economy, by a gap between the levels of technology in the rural subsistence sector and the industrial monetised sector, and possibly by a gap in the level of per capita income between regions of a country if the money economy and industrial development are geographically concentrated. In fact it is not unusual for geographic, social and technological dualism to occur together, with each type of dualism tending to reinforce the other. Also, the more 'progressive' sectors typically have favourable access to scarce factors of production, which is a major cause of the persistence of dualism.

If the basic origin of dualism is the introduction of money into a subsistence barter economy, and development depends on the extension of the money economy, development must contend with the existence of dualism in all its aspects.

Now the question is, what development problems does the existence of dualism pose for an economy, and how can dualism impede and retard development? As far as social dualism is concerned, the obstacles appear to be similar to those presented by a traditional society with no modern exchange sector at all. The task is one of providing incentives in the subsistence sector and drawing the subsistence sector into the money economy. The fact that the indigenous subsistence sector may be reluctant to alter its traditional way of life and respond to incentives is not peculiar to a dual economy. It is, therefore, true that underdevelopment tends to be associated with social dualism, but it is perhaps misleading to regard social dualism as an underlying cause of backwardness and poverty. It would be difficult to argue that development would be more rapid in the absence of a monetary sector, from which the existence of dualism stems. Even if the growth of the exchange sector makes little impact on attitudes in the indigenous sector, it is bound to make some contribution to development by employing labour from the subsistence sector and disseminating knowledge. Without the growth of the money economy it is difficult to envisage any progress at all. In short, it seems more realistic to regard social dualism as an inevitable consequence of development rather than as a basic cause of underdevelopment. Different development strategies will be required to cope with dissimilar conditions in the two sectors, and this may involve real resource costs that are not encountered by the developed economy. It is in this sense that the dual economy is at a comparative disadvantage.

Technological dualism is the result of a foreign enclave, a proportion of the profits generated in the industrial sector will be remitted to the home country, reducing the level of saving and investment below what it might have been. If in the rural, or non-monetised, sector of the economy production processes are characterised by labour-intensive techniques and variable technical coefficients of production, while production processes in the industrial, technologically advanced sector are capital-intensive and possess relatively fixed technical coefficients, it is possible that the technology of the industrial sector may impede progress in the agricultural sector, upon which the development of the total economy in part depends. First, relatively fixed technical coefficients (that is, a low elasticity of substitution between factors) means that labour can be absorbed from agriculture into industry only as fast as the growth of capital, and second, capital intensity itself will restrict employment opportunities in the industrial sector, contributing to urban unemployment and perpetuating underdevelopment in the rural sector. Hence productivity growth in the agricultural sector, which is recognised as being necessary to establish a secure basis for take-off into sustained growth, may be slowed down.

Cumulative Causation

Cumulative causation, associated with Gunnar Myrdal, is being used as an explanation of the backwardness of developing nations. This hypothesis is applicable to nations and regions within nations, which can be advanced to account for the persistence of spatial differences in a wide variety of development indices, including per capita income, rates of growth of industrialisation and trade, employment growth rates and levels of unemployment.

In the context of development both economic and social forces produce tendencies towards disequilibrium, and that the assumption in economic theory that disequilibrium situations tend towards equilibrium is false. Myrdal replaces the assumption of stable equilibrium with what he calls the hypothesis of circular and cumulative causation, arguing that the use of this hypothesis can go a long way towards explaining why international differences in levels of development, and interregional differences in development within nations, may persist and even widen over time.

To describe the process of circular and cumulative causation, let us consider a country in which all regions have attained the same stage of development, as measured by the same level of per capita income, or by similar levels of productivity and wages in the same occupations. Then assume that an exogenous shock produces a disequilibrium situation with development proceeding more rapidly in one region than another. The proposition is that economic and social forces will tend to strengthen the disequilibrium situation by leading to cumulative expansion in the favoured region at the expense of other regions, which then become comparatively worse off, retarding their future development.

In explaining cumulative causation, Myrdal has considered a type of multiplier-accelerator mechanism producing increasing returns in the favoured region. Instead of leading to equality, the forces of supply and demand interact with each other to produce cumulative movements away from spatial equilibrium. Since the wage level is the basic determinant of per capita income, we shall consider wages and wage differences to illustrate the process of cumulative causation.

Let us consider two regions of India, Kolkata and Delhi, and assume that wages are determined by supply and demand as shown in Fig. 2.1.

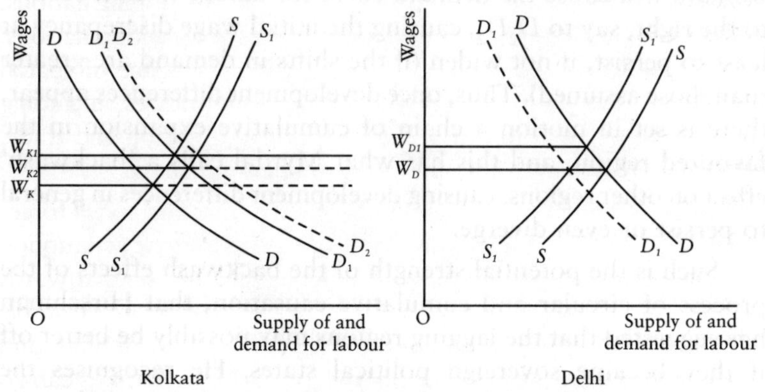

Fig. 2.1

Suppose that wage levels are identical in the two regions, that is, $W_K = W_D$. Then assume that a stimulus of some sort causes the demand for labour, and therefore wages, to rise in Kolkata relative to Delhi; that is, the demand curve for labour in Kolkata shifts to D_1D_1, causing wages to rise to W_{K1}. Since labour tends to respond to differences in economic opportunities of this sort, the wage discrepancy may be assumed to induce labour migration from Delhi to Kolkata. Equilibrium theory then predicts that there will be a tendency for wage levels to be equalised once more through a reduction in labour supply in Delhi from *SS* to S_1S_1 and an increase in labour supply in Kolkata from SS to S_1S_1, giving a wage in Kolkata of W_{K2}, equal to a wage in Delhi of W_{D1}.

However, according to the hypothesis of cumulative causation, changes in supply may be expected to react on demand in such a way as to counteract the tendency towards equilibrium. Migration from Delhi denudes the area of human capital and entrepreneurs, and depresses the demand for goods and services and factors of production, while movements into Kolkata, on the other hand, will tend to stimulate enterprise and the demand for products, adding to the demand for factors of production. In short, migration from Delhi will cause the demand curve for labour to shift to the left, say to D_1D_1, and migration into Kolkata will cause the demand curve for labour to shift further to the right, say to D_2D_2, causing the initial wage discrepancy at least to persist, if not widen (if the shifts in demand are greater than those assumed). Thus, once development differences appear, there is set in motion a chain of cumulative expansion in the favoured region, and this has what Myrdal calls a 'backwash' effect on other regions, causing development differences in general to persist or even diverge.

Such is the potential strength of the backwash effects of the process of circular and cumulative causation, that Hirschman has suggested that the lagging regions may possibly be better off if they became sovereign political states. He recognises the continued existence of backwash effects and argues that, to offset them, a nation that is concerned with developing its backward regions should provide certain equivalents of sovereignty, such as a separate tax system and the right to protect certain activities. Policies must be designed to reduce what he calls the 'polarisation' effects of interregional differences in development and to strengthen the 'trickle down' effects. The 'trickle down' effects are the favourable repercussions on backward regions emanating from expanding regions, which Myrdal calls 'spread' effects. These trickle-down or spread effects consist mainly of an increased demand for the backward areas' products and the diffusion of technology and knowledge. In Myrdal's view, the spread effects are weaker than the backwash effects, and if interregional differences are to be narrowed, nations must rely on state intervention through regional policies.

NOTES

1. D.S. Nag, *Problems of Underdeveloped Economy* (Agra, 1962), p. 111.
2. Gerald M. Meier and Robert E. Baldwin, *Economic Development, Theory, History and Policy* (New York, 1957), p. 112.
3. T.W. Schultz, *The State of the Social Sciences* (1956), p. 372.
4. H.W. Singer, "The Mechanics of Economic Development", *Indian Economic Review* (August, 1952).
5. Meier and Baldwin, n. 2, p. 112.
6. D.R. Gadgil, "Pre-Conditions of Economic Development", *Indian Economic Review* (February, 1952), p. 19.
7. Joseph L. Fisher, "The Role of Natural Resources" in H.F. Williamson and J.L. Buttrick (ed.), *Economic Development* (New York, 1954), p. 22.
8. Colin Clark, *Conditions of Economic Progress* (London, 1951), pp. 500-04.
9. Henry C. Wallich, "Some Notes Towards a Theory of Derived Development" A.N. Agarwala and S.P. Singh (eds.), *The Economics of Underdevelopment* (Bombay, 1958), p. 191.
10. Schumpeter, n. 2, pp. 131-33.
11. Jacob Viner cited in J.W. Williams, *Economic Stability in a Changing World*, p. 16.
12. Gunnar Myrdal, *Economic Theory and Underdeveloped Regions*, pp. 22, 112, 175.
13. Joseph J. Spengler, "Economic Factors in Economic Development", *American Economic Review, Papers and Proceedings*, 47 (May, 1957), p. 42.
14. Japan today imports 99 percent of its crude oil requirements, 100 percent of its tin, nickel, and aluminium, and over 80 percent of its timber requirements.

3

Theories of Underdevelopment

After going through this chapter, you will better understand:

- an underdeveloped economy
- characteristics of underdeveloped countries
- Hagen's theory of the transition to economic growth
- low-level equilibrium trap model
- dependency models—Frank Kay, Furtado, Samir Amin
- different versions of exploitation models—direct and indirect exploitation

Underdevelopment takes place when resources are not used to their full socio-economic potential, with the result that local or regional development is slower in most cases than it should be. Furthermore, it results from the complex interplay of internal and external factors that allow less developed countries only a lop-sided development progression. Underdeveloped nations are characterized by a wide disparity between their rich and poor populations, and an unhealthy balance of trade.

According to United Nations definition, underdeveloped countries are those with per capita incomes less than one-quarter those of the United States. There is a difference between underdeveloped countries and underdeveloped areas. In some countries with quite high average incomes large regions have very low per capita income. Striking examples of this are Italy, with its "developed" north and its "underdeveloped" south; Venezuela and Iran, with a rich petroleum industry superimposed on an otherwise little developed economy; Malaya, with its trade-rich Singapore and its relatively poor Malayan peasants. Even in such countries as Canada and the United States, one can find regions in which per capita income is low enough to warrant the use of the term "underdeveloped".

Paul Rosenstein-Rodan (1943) famously argued that at an early stage of development, the investments of industrializing firms in one sector may increase the profitability of other sectors throughout the economy. Simultaneous industrialization of many sectors of the economy could be profitable for them all, even though no sector would be profitable industrializing alone. As a result, an underdevelopment trap was possible. Even the market mechanism need not succeed in coordinating the activities needed to ensure development.

In modern terms, there could be a coordination failure, where individuals' inability to coordinate their choices leads to a state of affairs that is worse for everyone than some alternative state of affairs that is also an equilibrium. The obstacle to achieving the better state of affairs is not a matter of technological opportunities (or even knowledge of those opportunities), nor resources or preferences, but only of coordination. In the 1950s, the possibility of underdevelopment traps or "vicious circles of poverty" was elaborated on by many others (including Nurkse 1953 and Leibenstein 1957). But individuals are rarely convinced by those who do not address their concerns. Without a well-developed theory of the sources of externalities (spillover effects), the idea of an equilibrium trap had little influence on neoclassical economists of that period. They continued to use their models to argue that the market mechanism could coordinate the changes needed for development (Krugman 1992, 1995, and the comment by Stiglitz 1992).

The term 'underdeveloped' has come into wide usage with the organisation of programs for technical and capital assistance since World War II. A country is added to the active list of countries under consideration for aid by the agencies administering these programs when its government becomes sufficiently interested in development to apply for assistance, and if it is regarded as a potential candidate for such aid by the agency. For policy purposes, we might even define an "underdeveloped country" as one with announced goals and policies for economic development which is regarded as a candidate for assistance through the foreign aid programs of the United States and other Western nations.

CHARACTERISTICS OF UNDERDEVELOPED COUNTRIES

If poverty were always accompanied by other characteristics, we might hope to find in these characteristics a clue to the causes of poverty. There cannot be an increase in living standards and the eradication of poverty without an increase in output per head of the working population, or an increase in labour productivity. Rich developed countries have high levels of labour productivity; poor developing countries have low levels of labour productivity. The questions that naturally arise are: what are the major causes of low productivity, and what are the primary sources of productivity growth?

Examination of statistics and descriptive information pertaining to underdeveloped countries reveals that there is indeed a correlation between national poverty and other features of the country's economic and social organisation.

Economic Characteristics

General

(a) A very high proportion of the population in agriculture, usually some 70 to 90 percent.

(b) "Absolute overpopulation" in agriculture; that is, it would be possible to reduce the number of workers in agriculture and still obtain the same total output.

(c) Evidence of considerable "disguised unemployment" and a lack of employment opportunities outside agriculture.

(d) Very little capital per head.

(e) Low income per head and, as a consequence, existence near the "subsistence" level.

(f) Practically zero savings for the large mass of the people.

(g) Whatever savings do exist are usually achieved by a landholding class whose values are not conducive to investment in industry or commerce.

(h) The primary industries, that is, agriculture, forestry, and mining, are usually the residual employment categories.

(i) The output in agriculture is made up mostly of cereals and primary raw materials, with relatively low output of protein foods.

(j) Major proportion of expenditures on food and necessities.

(k) Export of foodstuffs and raw materials.

(l) Low volume of trade per capita.

(m) Poor credit facilities and poor marketing facilities.

(n) Poor housing.

Basic Characteristics in Agriculture

(a) Although there is low capitalisation on the land, there is simultaneously an uneconomic use of whatever capital exists due to the small size of holdings and the existence of exceedingly small plots.

(b) The level of agrarian techniques is exceedingly low, and tools and equipment are limited and primitive in nature.

(c) Even where there are big landowners as, for instance, in certain parts of India, the openings for modernised agriculture production for sale are limited by difficulties of transport and the absence of an efficient demand in the local market. It is significant that in many backward countries a modernised type of agriculture is confined to production for sale in foreign markets.

(d) There is an inability of the small landholders and peasants to weather even a short-term crisis, and as a consequence, attempts are made to get the highest possible yields from the soil, which leads to soil depletion.

(e) There is a widespread prevalence of high indebtedness relative to assets and income.

(f) The methods of production for the domestic market are generally old-fashioned and inefficient, leaving little surplus for marketing.

(g) A most pervasive aspect is a feeling of land hunger due to the exceedingly small size of holdings and small diversified plots. The reason for this is that holdings are continually subdivided as the population on the land increases.

Demographic Characteristics

(a) High fertility rates.

(b) High mortality rates and low expectation of life at birth.

(c) Inadequate nutrition and dietary deficiencies.

(d) Rudimentary hygiene, public health, and sanitation.

(e) Rural overcrowding.

Cultural and Political Characteristics

(a) Rudimentary education and usually a high degree of illiteracy among most of the people.

(b) Extensive prevalence of child labour.

(c) General weakness or absence of the middle class.

(d) Inferiority of women's status and position.

(e) Traditionally determined behaviour for the bulk of the population.

Technological and Miscellaneous Characteristics

(a) Low yields per acre.

(b) No training facilities or inadequate facilities for the training of technicians, engineers, etc.

(c) Inadequate and crude communication and transportation facilities, especially in the rural areas.

(d) Primitive technology.

Underdeveloped countries have a high proportion of their gainfully occupied population in agriculture and also they produce relatively large proportions of their national income in the agricultural sector. The share of income in agriculture is less than the share of employment in agriculture, reflecting the relatively low productivity per man-year in the agricultural sector. According to J.K. Galbraith a purely agricultural country is likely to be unprogressive even in its agriculture. And Gunnar Myrdal adds, "Industrialisation creates technology which can then be applied to agriculture but not *vice versa*."[1]

Even in the production of major staples underdeveloped countries are frequently less efficient than advanced countries for which the same commodity is a minor export. In underdeveloped country the most important local agricultural product is produced at very high cost and cannot compete in the free market with imports from advanced countries.

Thus, whereas all the countries with income below one quarter per year of the United States income might be considered underdeveloped, in the sense that their future development is a matter on which policy decisions are being made both in those countries and in the advanced countries with aid programs, and although all such countries exhibit common characteristics, we see that there are important subdivisions to be made among them. In the first place, there is a marked difference between a country with a per capita income of $300 to $500 per year and one with $50 to $100 per year. The former might be considered to have future development within its own grasp, even if it is not currently growing. It is the latter group of countries that present the most appalling problems, particularly if they are stagnant as well as poverty-stricken.

CATEGORIES OF UNDERDEVELOPED COUNTRIES

At least four categories of underdeveloped countries can be distinguished. First, there are countries which have per capita incomes low enough to put them into the underdeveloped category, but which have unutilised known resources, and which are currently undertaking enough industrialisation and agricultural improvement to bring substantial increases in per capita income. In these countries, growth is very unevenly distributed among social groups and among regions. The problem in these countries is one of sustaining growth, reducing open and disguised unemployment, and spreading the benefits of growth more widely.

Second, there are countries whose per capita incomes are currently very low, which do not appear to have abundant resources relative to the size of their populations, but where per capita income is currently rising. In these countries the rise in income must be accelerated, not just sustained.

Third, there are countries which are poor and stagnant, in the sense that per capita incomes show no rising trend, but which are relatively rich in resources. In such countries, especially if the rate of population growth can be held within bounds, the hope for raising per capita income significantly would appear to be much better than in resource-poor countries. But where per capita income is stationary, or falling, or rising very slowly from a very low level, there is little hope that growth will become cumulative without a transformation of the economy. Here the task is not merely to sustain or direct growth already under way, but to launch a process of growth that can become cumulative at some level of per capita income.

Finally, there are countries which are very poor, which are stagnant, and which are also poor in resources. Such countries need a special kind of plan, emphasising improvement of existing economic undertakings more than structural change.

Such differences in basic economic situation obviously bring with them differences in the nature of the policies to be prescribed. A list of common characteristics is instructive and helps us to understand the nature and magnitude of the problem, but it does not spare us the need to analyse carefully the causes of underdevelopment. Still less does it indicate policies to overcome it.

HAGEN'S THEORY OF THE TRANSITION TO ECONOMIC GROWTH

On the assumption that there is a (i) need for system analysis; (ii) need for integration of social science theory; and (iii) need to relate childhood to history, Prof. Everett Hagen's devotes his efforts to building a general system model from interdisciplinary views of human behaviour. He also assumed that (i) traditional societies possess the technological creativity to begin the process of economic growth, but that (ii) they lack the requisite capital to do so. For Hagen, the contrary assumptions are closer to the truth—peasant societies have the economic capacity to finance the investment which is necessary for a rising per capita income, but they do not have, for a variety of historical reasons, the requisite technological creativity.

Hagen put his theory in the form of a model. He considers following variables:

(a) The structure of production:
  (i) techniques,
  (ii) rate of technical progress,
  (iii) composition of output,
  (iv) rate of saving and investment, and
  (v) composition of investment.

(b) The social structure:
  (i) geographic scope of—economic community and political community,
  (ii) structure of class relations—concentration-diffusion of control of production, social distance between classes, and concentration-diffusion of political power, and
  (iii) pattern of interpersonal relations—basis for selection of associates: quality-performance, diffuseness-specificity of rights and obligations.

(c) The structure of personality:
  (i) scope of knowledge—knowledge of science and techniques, knowledge based on external experience,
  (ii) world-view—physical, social,
  (iii) needs—dependency-need achievement, affiliation-need autonomy, dominance, and
  (iv) values concerning occupations.

These variables are essentially quantitative in nature, and could be set forth in the form of a set of simultaneous equations with appropriate leads and lags. Because of the difficulties of measurement, Hagen did not consider it worthwhile translating his model into a set of formal equations.

Capital formation is frequently regarded as the process immediately responsible for continuing economic growth—growth in per capita output and income in a society. But it is clear that capital formation is important only as it is the carrier or agent of technological progress.[2] The essential task is to isolate the forces which bring about the transition from virtually stationary technology to continuing progress. By continuing technological progress Hagen means technological advances sufficiently frequent and of sufficient effect on production so that output per worker in a society as a whole increases considerably each decade for as many as three successive decades. He believes that the various social sciences have now progressed to a point at which a first halting general statement of a theory of a transition of a society from virtually stationary technology to continuing technological progress is possible.

Hagen begins his analysis by setting up an idealised form of a peasant society, which he then contrasts with an industrialised society in order to isolate the distinguishing characteristics. A peasant society, he says, is first of all a dual society. It consists of a number of agricultural villages with one or more centres, which are trading cities or the king's courts. There is little migration into or out of each village. The occupation of the majority of the people is small-scale agriculture, although there are a few craftsmen and traders. The family form is usually the extended family. Relationships among villages may be limited to a trickle of trade. The elite live in the centre, except for a few officials, teachers, and rent collectors who represent the central government in the villages. The society has little contact with foreign countries, though a small trickle of trade, and with it a small trickle of ideas across national borders, occurs. When one considers the vigorous international trade in Asia in the sixteenth century and earlier, it is clear that Hagen's peasant society is a deliberate abstraction rather than a precise description of underdeveloped countries at any particular phase in their history. All these characteristics, in Hagen's view, are the exact opposites of the technologically progressive society.

To isolate the differences more systematically, Hagen groups the major variables which determine the nature of a society under five headings, conforming more or less to the variables set forth above. He begins with the structure of production, and the structure of class relationships. In a psychological sense he states, the elite and the villagers of the peasant society live literally in different worlds and have extremely few interests in common. In a technologically progressive society, on the other hand, there is a more rapid circulation of the elite, more social mobility through economic success, and a substantial middle class. Again, the peasant society is characterised by crude concepts of the physical world, a rudimentary state of the physical sciences, primitive methods of production, and low literacy. In a technologically progressive society, the physical sciences are well developed and the concepts of the nature and operation of the physical world are refined.

In contrast to the technologically advanced society with its high n-achievement, high need-autonomy (need to be independent of others), and high need-dominance (need to be a leader) the peasant society is characterised by a high need-affiliation (need to please friends and to have their affection, to cooperate with them) and high need-dependency (need to feel inferior to someone; to have ideas and attitudes approved by persons regarded as superiors). With this motivational pattern, the rate of technological progress is likely to be slow. For the essence of innovation is the solution of problems involving unknown or unique elements and no one could consistently and effectively apply his energies to the attacking of problems unless he possessed a high need achievement.[3]

Hagen discusses the contrast between peasant and technologically progressive societies in terms of interpersonal relationships, using the Talcott Parsons concept of pattern variables. In the village, he says, one's attitudes toward other people does not depend on their capability or needs, but upon their status. The peasant does not seek the most efficient worker to help him in his field, he employs members of his family without question. In technologically advanced societies, by contrast, the tendency is to seek the best man for the job. He concludes that all these characteristics of peasant society are inimical to rapid technological change.

Five possible forces tending to cause changes in the structure and functioning of peasant society have been suggested by Hagen. They are:

(a) creeping progress of understanding of the physical world and of technology;

(b) social tensions among the elite; it is possible that high need achievement, aggression and dominance may exist among the elite of a peasant society and the effects of possible tensions among the elite groups merit exploration;

(c) pressure which may threaten the structure of social relationships within the society;

(d) altered economic opportunities;

(e) imposition of change through physical force, such as colonial rule.

The last three causes of change are forces outside the society. This analysis leads Hagen to somewhat gloomy prognosis for underdeveloped countries. Whatever the initiating force may be, it will not bring about change from creeping technological progress to continued technological progress without an intervening process of gradual change in the values of all the variables of the model presented above. The individual's view of his relationship with the world must change radically, scientific knowledge and the scope of experience must widen, occupational values must undergo basic alteration, class relationship must alter in their social, economic, and political aspects, and the values of pattern variables must change considerably. Moreover, drastic change in the value of any one variable in the peasant society while the others remain at their peasant society level seems unlikely. The entire set of values must probably shift to considerable degree, though of course not equally, before any of them can shift drastically. Hagen considers it extremely difficult, though not impossible, for the entire set of changes to take place within one generation. Historical development does not suggest gradually accelerating technological progress, he says, but "a surge of change". This line of thought leads Hagen to his theory of entrepreneurship. He agrees with most analysts of economic development that the entrepreneurial function is fundamental in the process of economic change.

The principle that "only a group driven by an urge to regain or maintain a rightful social status will carry out the revolutionary actions which complete the transition to continuing technological advance", Hagen calls "the law of the subordinated group". The members of the innovating group must have the combination of world-view and motivational structure which results in a vigorous attack on their problem rather than resignation to their fate. Hagen seems to be saying that if people are to have economic growth they must "want it"—in the sense that a sufficient number of the subdominant elite are motivated toward economic activity of a sort bringing technological progress and economic growth, while the motivation of the rest of the society is such as to permit technological progress to spread throughout the society. If this reaction is to occur, the society as a whole must have common cultural bonds to be innovated. They must not be so alien, so different from other groups that their activity creates emotional antipathy rather than desire to achieve equal success by doing likewise.

Hagen's theory might be restated as another kind of psycho-sociological dualism—a dualistic society, with technological progress confined to a small sector of the economy influencing only a small proportion of the population, is unlikely to develop. The conditions suggested above should not be regarded as prerequisites for economic development, but as forces tending to cause or to prevent change, whose interplay determines the path and speed of movement of the society. External forces may help to break the vicious circle. For example, expansion of the market provides favourable economic opportunities, and increases the intensity of incentives to channel energies into technological progress. However, Hagen maintains that expansion of the export market did not play an important role in the later stages of transition for the developed or developing countries. Technical knowledge imported from abroad may help, but not much. The mere availability of the technical knowledge of other countries does not permit a society to by-pass that long cumulative growth of scientific and technical knowledge sketched above. While the time period involved can be telescoped considerably, a process of essentially the same nature must be gone through whether the society is developing its own science and the technology or has the knowledge from abroad available.

The people of underdeveloped countries cannot learn science and advanced technology as they might learn a foreign language. They cannot apply science in their thinking until basic change has occurred in their world-view, motivations, and values. In any case, a complex of production techniques in one society cannot simply be copied in another, as one man might wear another man's clothes. Relationship within a factory or other production organisation also depend on the culture of the society. The production process may have to be altered if it is to function efficiently in a society with different patterns of behaviour.

An external threat to a nation as a whole may be a powerful force toward development, especially if combined with internal factors in planning the country toward technological change. This kind of combination of internal and external pressures, in Hagen's view, explains the relatively rapid transformation of the Japanese society from a stagnant one into one with sustained technological progress.

LOW-LEVEL EQUILIBRIUM TRAP MODEL

The model of low-level equilibrium trap attempts to integrate population and development theory by recognising the interdependence between population growth, per capita income and national income growth. This type of model, which originated in the 1950s, is designed first to demonstrate the difficulties that developing countries may face in achieving a self-sustaining rise in living standards, and secondly to provide pointers to policy action.

This model provides a tool for analysis of the effects of various policies; and certain pitfalls that are not intuitively obvious are brought to light. The model shows that, even if production techniques are not improved and even in the absence of a crash investment program, the trap may still be escaped if the socio-political environment is favourable. Richard Nelson (1956) uses an essentially simple model with three equations. First, there is an income determination equation. This is fundamentally the same as the production function—income depends on the stock of capital, the size of the population, and the level of technique. The labour force is assumed to bear a constant relationship to the size of the population. Second, net investment consists of savings-created capital plus additions to the amount of land under cultivation. The savings-created portion is roughly the same as investment in the industrial sector; it represents additions to stock of tools and equipment. No such investment will take place until income rises above the subsistence level, after which it rises with per capita income. The amount of new land brought under cultivation tends to increase with the population, but cultivating fresh areas becomes more difficult as good land becomes scarce. There is a "floor" to disinvestment; "one cannot eat torn-up rail-road track no matter how hungry one gets". Finally, there is a population growth equation. These three equations imply assumptions about technology and human behaviour.

Capital Formation

Net capital formation is an increase in the quantity of the capital input of the production function. In this model there are two sources of capital formation—capital may be created out of current income at the alternative cost of consumption, and, if there is unused arable land, capital may be increased by bringing this land under cultivation. Land and savings are valued in deflated money units. Capital formation takes place through saving and new land brought into cultivation, that is,

$$dK = dK' + dL \qquad \text{... (3.1)}$$

where,

K = capital,

K' = savings-created capital, and

L = land under cultivation.

The rate at which additional deflated money units of land are brought under cultivation is positively related to the increase in population, negatively related to the proportion of total arable land already under cultivation, represented as

$$dL = g\left[\frac{L^* - L}{L^*}\right] dP \qquad \text{... (3.2)}$$

where,

L = land under cultivation,

L^* = total arable land, and

P = population.

As land area under cultivation increases, the difficulty of bringing into cultivation additional land units of equal productivity increases.

Reproducible capital: Per capita savings are determined by per capita income, and all savings flow into investment. Keynesian unemployment of labour and capital is a phenomenon of a money-market economy of specialised producers. The theory is not appropriate to an economy based on self-sufficient units, with money market playing a minor role. Foreign investment is autonomous. The per capita rate of investment from savings, then, is determined as

$$\frac{dK'}{P} = b\left(\frac{Y}{P} - X\right); \quad \left(\frac{Y}{P}\right) > \left(\frac{Y}{P}\right)'$$

$$= -C \quad ; \quad \left(\frac{Y}{P}\right) \leq \left(\frac{Y}{P}\right)' \qquad \text{... [3.3(a)]}$$

or,

$$\frac{dK'}{Y} = b - bX \cdot \left(\frac{P}{Y}\right); \quad \left(\frac{Y}{P}\right) > \left(\frac{Y}{P}\right)'$$

$$= -C \cdot \left(\frac{P}{Y}\right) \quad ; \quad \left(\frac{Y}{P}\right) \leq \left(\frac{Y}{P}\right)' \qquad \text{... [3.3(b)]}$$

where,

K' = investment from savings,

X = the zero savings level of Y/P,

$(Y/P)'$ = the level of per capita income below which the rate of net disinvestment is the maximum technically possible.

Until a certain level of per capita income is reached, all income will be spent on the necessities of life; hence the positive X-intercept. This can be shown by Fig. 3.1.

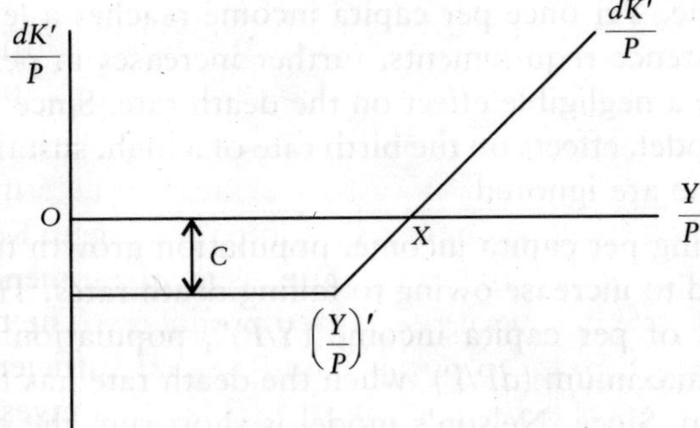

Fig. 3.1: Rate of savings and per capita income.

Negative investment is limited by the rate of depreciation of the capital stock and the incentive to tear down existing equipment; hence the break in function at $(Y/P)'$. There is a maximum rate of capital depletion. Soil depletion through failure to apply fertiliser is a principle source of capital depletion in poor agricultural economies. Changes in the distribution of income shift the $\frac{dK'}{P}$ function to the right along the Y/P axis if the change is toward greater equality. The more unequal the income distribution, the lower the level of per capita income that is sufficient to support a given level of positive savings. Government policy may force capital formation from an economy with a per capita income so low that no investment would be forthcoming in the absence of government policy. Changes in government policy, distribution of income, and the social incentive system shift the $\frac{dK'}{P}$ curve along the *Y/P* axis.

Population Growth

The rate of population growth is simply the birth rate minus the death rate plus the rate of net immigration. For the purpose of the present model immigration is autonomous. The neo-Malthusian assumptions about population growth are made. In areas with low per capita incomes short-run changes in the rate of population growth are caused by changes in the level of per capita income. Yet once per capita income reaches a level well above subsistence requirements, further increases in per capita income have a negligible effect on the death rate. Since this is a short-run model, effects on the birth rate of a high, sustained per capita income are ignored.

With rising per capita income, population growth (*dP/P*) is first assumed to increase owing to falling death rates. Then at a critical level of per capita income $(Y/P)''$, population growth reaches the maximum $(dP/P)^*$ when the death rate has fallen to the minimum. Since, Nelson's model is short-run, the effect of per capita income on the birth rate is ignored but the relation can easily be accommodated if desired. Hence,

$$\frac{dP}{P} = p\left(\frac{Y}{P} - S\right); \quad \left(\frac{Y}{P}\right) < \left(\frac{Y}{P}\right)''$$

$$= \left(\frac{dP}{P}\right)^* \quad ; \quad \left(\frac{Y}{P}\right) \geq \left(\frac{Y}{P}\right)'' \qquad \text{... (3.4)}$$

where,

S = subsistence level of per capita income,

$(dP/P)^*$ = maximum rate of population growth,

$(Y/P)^2$ = level of per capita income above which increases in per capita income have negligible effect on the death rate.

The relation between population growth and per capita income can be represented as in Fig. 3.2.

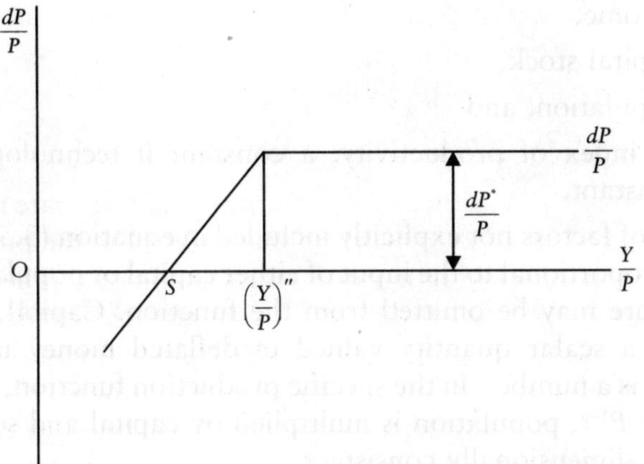

Fig. 3.2: Population growth and per capita income.

The function assumes a given income distribution, a given social structure, and given medical techniques. A shift in income distribution toward greater equality shifts the *dP/P* function to the left along the *Y/P* axis. The more unequal the income distribution, the smaller the population a given aggregate income can support. The introduction of modern medical practices in certain areas since the second world war has enabled a sharp cut in the death rate; yet nutrition and housing standards have fallen sharply in some of these areas. If the death rate is viewed as a function of per capita income, then improved medical technique should be viewed as shifting the function to the left.

Growth of National Income

Income is the net aggregate supply of want-satisfying goods distributed in a period of time and is a scalar quantity measured in deflated money units. Given the social-political environment and existing technology, income is assumed to be a linear homogeneous function of two variables, capital and labour. If both capital and labour are increased n-fold, and if there is no change in techniques, income produced increases n-fold.

$$Y = Af(K, P);$$

$$nY = Af(nK, nP) \quad \text{... (3.5)}$$

where,

Y = income,

K = capital stock,

P = population, and

A = an index of productivity, a constant if technology is constant.

Inputs of factors not explicitly included in equation (3.5) are assumed proportional to the input of either capital or population and therefore may be omitted from the function. Capital, like income, is a scalar quantity valued in deflated money units. Population is a number. In the specific production function, such as $Y = AK^{\alpha} P^{1-\alpha}$, population is multiplied by capital and so the equation is dimensionally consistent.

The population input: The labour input is assumed to be a constant percentage of the population, given the social-political environment. The omission of the constant multiplier in equation (3.5) does not affect the analysis, and permits simpler notation.

The capital input: Capital consists of produced goods and arable land used in the production process. Land and produced capital are perfectly substitutable in the production of aggregate income. In other words, n money units of land, and n money units of produced capital can produce either the same product, or different products valued equally.

The social and technological environment: The assumption of linear homogeneity is reasonable only if the social structure and the technology used are constant. Cultural inertia is conducive to economic inertia. But the reverse is also true. Where economies are stagnant, where capital is not accumulating, cultural rigidity is encouraged by a rigid economic circular flow.

Improved use of existing resources, either by fuller utilisation of available inputs or by use of better alternative techniques, enables greater income from given inputs. Economies caught in the low-level equilibrium trap are often marked by considerable slacks; that is, existing inputs are not producing the maximum amount of output that man's knowledge will allow. If these economies are properly stimulated, income may be increased with no increase in factor supplies. Increase in the productivity of existing factor supplies may be defined as innovation and is represented in the model by an increase in *A* in equation (3.5).

From the assumptions of the model, the income growth curve can be drawn as in Fig. 3.3, considering *S* = *X*, population is stationary, the rate of savings-created capital per head is zero, and therefore income will be stationary (*dY*/*Y* = *0*).

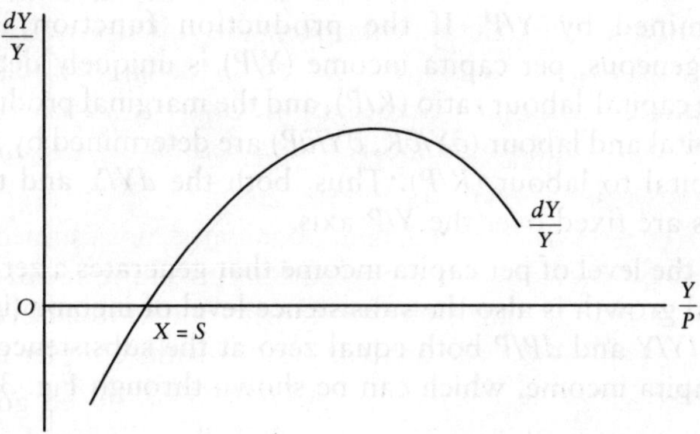

Fig. 3.3: Income growth curve.

With rising per capita income beyond this stationary equilibrium, growth increases because of increases in the labour force and capital per head. As population growth reaches a maximum, however, and savings as a percentage of national income approach a constant, income growth will level off. In the absence of technical progress, growth will ultimately decrease owing to the law of variable proportions, in this case due to a fall in the capital-labour ratio.

The assumption imply certain shapes of the *dY*/*Y* and *dP*/*P* curves plotted against the *Y*/*P* axis. Given the state of technology, the quantity of unused land, and the social-political environment, *dY*/*Y* and *dP*/*P* are uniquely determined by the level of per capita income. The rate of growth of income, *dY*/*Y*, is explained by the equation:

$$\frac{dY}{Y} = \frac{\partial Y}{\partial K} \cdot \frac{dK}{Y} + \frac{\partial Y}{\partial P} \cdot \frac{dP}{Y}$$
$$= \frac{\partial Y}{\partial K}\left(\frac{dK'}{Y} + \frac{dL}{P} \cdot \frac{P}{Y}\right) + \frac{\partial Y}{\partial P} \cdot \frac{dP}{P} \cdot \frac{P}{Y} \qquad \text{... (3.6)}$$

Since dK'/Y, dL/P and dP/P are determined by the level of per capita income through equations (3.2), (3.3) and (3.4), if $\partial Y/\partial K$ and $\partial Y/\partial P$ are determined by Y/P, then dY/Y is certainly determined by Y/P. If the production function is linear homogeneous, per capita income (Y/P) is uniquely determined by the capital-labour ratio (K/P), and the marginal productivities of capital and labour ($\partial Y/\partial K$, $\partial Y/\partial P$) are determined by the ratio of capital to labour (K/P). Thus, both the dY/Y and the dP/P curves are fixed over the Y/P axis.

If the level of per capita income that generates a zero rate of capital growth is also the subsistence level of income (if S = X), then dY/Y and dP/P both equal zero at the subsistence level of per capita income, which can be shown through Fig. 3.4.

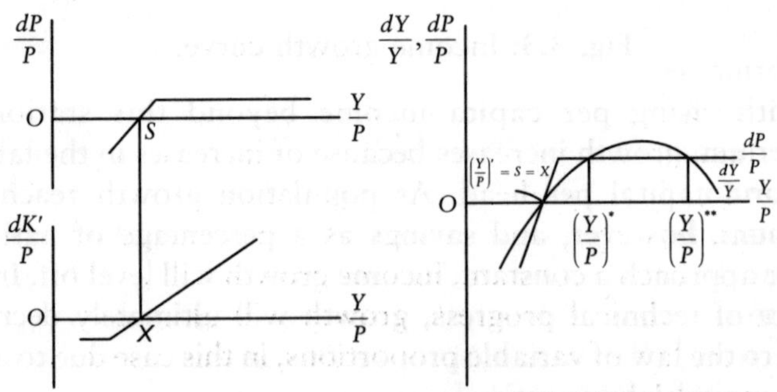

Fig. 3.4: Low-level equilibrium trap.

If the zero-investment level of per capita income exceeds the subsistence level of per capita income (if X exceeds S), then dY/Y is negative at S, and equals zero some point to the right of S and to the left of X. At this point the increase in income caused by a rising labour force is just offset by the decrease in income caused by a declining capital stock. If X is less than S, then the zero dY/Y level of per capita income is to the left of S and to the right of X.

To the right of its zero value the dY/Y curve rises with increasing per capita income as dP/P, the rate of population growth, and dK'/Y, savings as a fraction of income, increase. As per capita income further increases, dP/P becomes a constant, and savings as a percentage of income approaches a constant; hence the dY/Y curve flattens out. As per capita income rises still higher, the dY/Y curve may turn down. If the production function is linear homogeneous, the greater per capita income, Y/P, the smaller must be the output-capital ratio, Y/K, and since dK/Y approaches a constant, the proportional rate of growth of capital, $dK/K = (Y/K)\cdot(dK/Y)$, will tend to fall as per capita income increases. Since dP/P is a constant, dY/Y will tend to fall.[4]

If the rate of growth of income exceeds the rate of growth of population (if the dY/Y curve lies above the dP/P curve at a given level of Y/P) then per capita income will increase from that level. Conversely, if the dP/P curve lies above the dY/Y curve at a given level of Y/P, then per capita income will fall from that level. Levels of per capita income at which dY/Y equals dP/P are equilibrium levels of per capita income. Population and income grow at an equal rate at that level of per capita income. However, an intersection of the dY/Y and dP/P curves will only be a stable equilibrium level of per capita income if the slope of the population growth curve exceeds the slope of the income growth curve at the intersection. If the dP/P curve lies above the dY/Y curve to the right of the intersection, below it to the left of the intersection [$Y/P = S$ and $Y/P = (Y/P)^{**}$ in Fig. 3.4] then if per capita income increases above the equilibrium level the increase in population will exceed that of income and per capita income will fall back toward the equilibrium. If per capita income falls below the equilibrium value, the rate of population growth will drop below the rate of income growth and per capita income will climb back toward the equilibrium. Conversely, if the slope of the dY/Y curve exceeds the slope of the dP/P curve at an equilibrium level of Y/P, the equilibrium is unstable [$Y/P = (Y/P)^{*}$ in Fig. 3.4], and deviations from that level will tend to grow.

The low-level equilibrium trap is a phenomenon caused by the shape of the dY/Y and dP/P curves at their point of intersection at or in the neighbourhood of S, the subsistence level of per capita income. This low-level equilibrium will henceforth be symbolised as $(Y/P)^t$ (where t means trap). Economies whose social, political and economic organisation generate a dP/P curve that exceeds in slope, the dY/Y curve at $(Y/P)^t$ are caught in a low-level equilibrium trap—the equilibrium is stable. But there is no reason why the intersection $(Y/P)^t$ need be or remain a stable equilibrium. If the social, political and economic conditions generate a dY/Y curve of greater slope than the dP/P curve at $(Y/P)^t$, then there is no tendency for an economy to stagnate at the low-level equilibrium. If the production function is linear homogeneous, then output per capita can only be increased if the amount of capital per worker is increased. In other words, the dY/Y curve lies above the dP/P curve at a given level of per capita income if and only if the rate of capital increase exceeds the rate of population increase at that level of per capita income.

At an equilibrium level of per capita income both capital and population are constant, or are changing at an equal rate so that their ratio is constant. If the ratio $\dfrac{d(dP/P)}{d(dK/K)}$ at the equilibrium $(Y/P)^t$ is less than one, the equilibrium is unstable and there is no trap. If the ratio is greater than one, the economy is trapped at $(Y/P)^t$. If $S = X$ and $dK/K = dP/P = 0$ at $(Y/P)^t$, then the ratio can be written as:

$$\frac{K}{P}\cdot\frac{d^2P}{d^2K}=\frac{K}{P}\cdot\frac{p}{b+g\left[\left(L^*-L\right)/L^*\right]p} \quad \text{... (3.7)}$$

where, p [from equation (3.4)] shows how responsive the rate of population growth is to changes in per capita income; b, from equation (3.3), is the marginal propensity to invest in per capita terms; $(L^* - L)/L^*$, from equation (3.2), is the percentage of total arable land that is still free and available for increased agriculture production, and g, from equation (3.2), is a measure of the propensity of new population to clear new arable land. The first fraction (*K/P*) summarises the technological efficiency of the economy. The lower the ratio, the smaller the quantity of capital per labourer needed to support a given level of labour productivity. The second fraction:

$$\frac{p}{b+g\left[(L^{*}-L)/L^{*}\right]p}$$

summarises an economy's response to increases in per capita income from $(Y/P)^t$. The lower the ratio, the greater the induced increase in capital relative to the induced increase in population. The greater the marginal propensity to invest, and the easier it is to bring new land into cultivation, the lower will be the ratio.

Thus, the social and technological conditions conducive to trapping an economy are:

(a) a high correlation between the level of per capita income and the rate of population growth,

(b) a low propensity to direct additional per capita income to increasing per capita investment,

(c) scarcity of uncultivated arable land, and

(d) inefficient production methods.

Opposite conditions are conducive to an unstable equilibrium at $(Y/P)^t$. If the population maintains control over its rate of growth, if the propensity to invest is high and free land plentiful, and if production methods are efficient, then the economy will not be caught in the low-level equilibrium trap.

The strength of the trap: Assuming for the moment that the *dY/Y* and *dP/P* curves are shaped so as to trap the economy at $(Y/P)^t$, the trap may be tight or loose. The strength of the trap is defined as the gap between $(Y/P)^t$ and $(Y/P)^*$, the value of per capita income that must be achieved before the pull of the trap is escaped (Fig. 3.4). The relative values of *S*, the subsistence level of income, and *X*, the zero investment level of income, are important factors in determining the strength of the trap. If *S* is less than *X*, then the *dP/P* curve cuts the *Y/P* axis to the left of the point where the *dY/Y* curve cuts the axis. In this case the gap between $(Y/P)^t$ and $(Y/P)^*$ is increased, which has been shown in Fig. 3.5.

If X moves to the left, S to the right as income inequality increases, then, *ceteris paribus*, the more unequal the distribution of income, the weaker the hold of the trap.

Improvement in medical technique and knowledge reduces the level of per capita income that is consistent with a stable population, and, according to the model, would seem to make escape from the trap more difficult. However, this effect may well be compensated for by the increase in labour productivity (shifting and lifting the dY/Y function) that better health may permit. This example points out an important implicit assumption of the model that parameter values are assumed independent of each other. *Ceteris paribus*, the smaller the difference between the slopes of the dP/P and dY/Y functions at $(Y/P)^t$, the weaker the hold of the trap. The factors that act to trap an economy determine, in their degree, the tightness of the trap and the difficulty of escape.

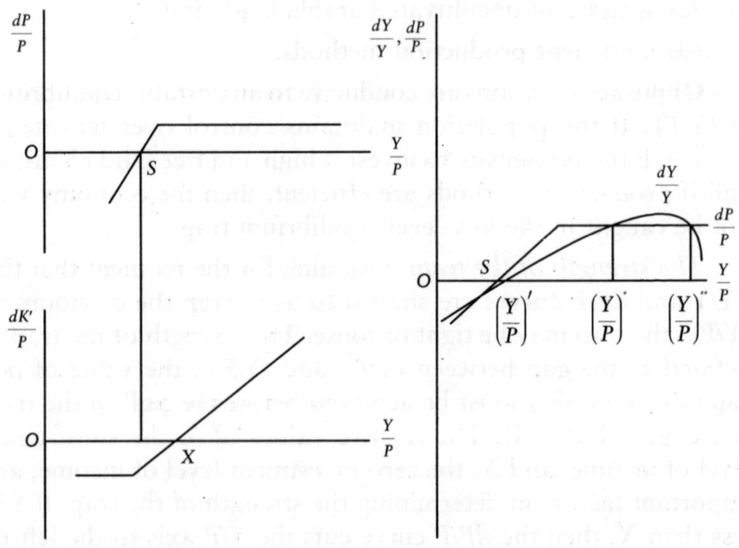

Fig. 3.5: Low-level equilibrium trap.

The model suggests the tentative hypothesis that until the technology advances of the eighteenth and nineteenth centuries, rapid continuous growth, such as that of the United States, Western Europe and Japan, could never have taken place, and only economies with ample free land (or that were exploiting colonies or subject states) could for long support a level of per capita income greater than $(Y/P)^t$. Only economies with free land faced a dY/Y curve of greater slope than the dP/P curve at $(Y/P)^t$. The state of technological knowledge necessitated a far large amount of capital per labour to support a given level of labour productivity than is needed with modern knowledge. The ratio $\frac{K}{P}\cdot\frac{d^2P}{d^2K}$ was large because K/P at $(Y/P)^t$ was large. If free land [a large $(L^*-L)/L^*$] permitted easy capital accumulation, a level of per capita income in excess of subsistence needs could be supported by productive agriculture, but as population increased and crowded the land, $(L^*-L)/L^*$ would decrease and the dY/Y function would pivot clockwise about S and $(Y/P)^t$ would become a stable equilibrium, which has been shown in Fig. 3.6. Once the land became crowded all economies were trapped. It has only been since the industrial revolution that man's knowledge has permitted densely populated economies to remain prosperous.

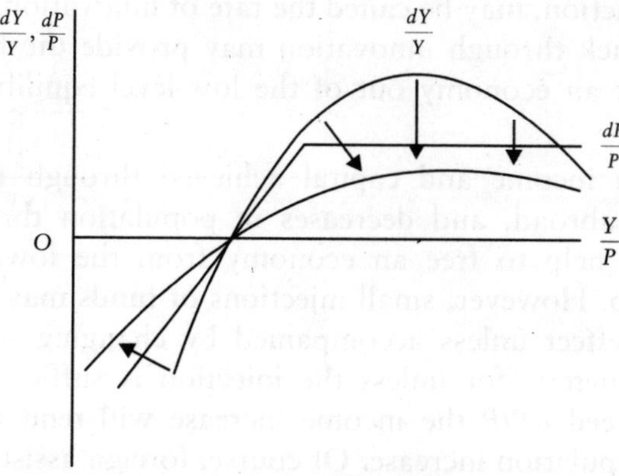

Fig. 3.6

The escape from the trap: The low-level equilibrium may be escaped in several different ways. Historically, escape has been achieved through the simultaneous use of several means. Changing social structure (a greater emphasis upon thrift and entrepreneurship, greater incentives to produce in quantity, increased incentive to limit family size), increased percentage of the population in the labour force, changing distribution of income enabling accumulation of wealth by investors, a government investment program, all act to shift and pivot the income growth and population growth functions and thereby weaken the strength of the trap; perhaps eliminate the trap by pivoting the dY/Y curve to a greater slope than the dP/P curve at $(Y/P)^t$. If this model summarises the maladies of stagnant economies, then it is clear that policies directed toward eliminating social inertia may play an important role in loosening the trap.

Social and political change has usually been accompanied by application of improved production techniques. The raising of the marginal productivity of capital and labour pivots the dY/Y function counter-clockwise. If the improvement in techniques is applied to all production, as well as to new production, then the taking up of slack lifts the dY/Y function over its entire range and enables an income increase that is achieved without increasing factor supplies. If the production function is written $Y = Af(K, P)$, then dA/A, the proportional increase in productivity of existing factors of production, may be called the rate of innovation. The taking up of slack through innovation may provide the boost necessary to lift an economy out of the low-level equilibrium trap.

Increases in income and capital achieved through funds obtained from abroad, and decreases in population through emigration can help to free an economy from the low-level equilibrium trap. However, small injections of funds may have no permanent effect unless accompanied by changing social-economic parameters, for unless the injection is sufficient to make dY/Y exceed dP/P the income increase will tend to be swamped by population increase. Of course, foreign assistance, together with internal change, can play an important role in boosting an economy from the hold of the trap. Once per capita income has increased beyond $(Y/P)^*$ growth will be self-generative, since $(Y/P)^*$ is an unstable equilibrium. Per capita income will either rise to a stable equilibrium value $(Y/P)^{**}$ if the *dY/Y* curve turns down to cut the *dP/P* curve from above; or, if the *dY/Y* curve stays above the *dP/P* curve, per capita income will continuously increase. The gap between the *dY/Y* and *dP/P* curves determines the rate of growth of per capita income.

Thus, growth can be rapid and explosive if the *dY/Y* curve stays above the *dP/P* curve, or growth may be of the slow, shifting-equilibrium type. Through time, technological innovation may shift the *dY/Y* function, and a decline in the birth rate may drop the *dP/P* function, thus shifting $(Y/P)^{**}$ to the right and accelerating growth. However, the model can only be, at best, suggestive of the determinants of the rate of growth of economies with a high per capita income.

The model is based on the assumption of a rapid response of population and net capital formation to changes in the level of per capita income. Differential rates of response can affect the nature of the low-level equilibrium trap. If, after an increase in per capita income, savings out of increased incomes are quickly directed toward capital creation which quickly starts new production, while population growth occurs only after a substantial time-lag, then the trap model is meaningless as a description of the world, and the model clearly does not explain stagnation. However, if the *dP/P* response occurs at the same speed, or with greater speed than the *dY/Y* response, then the different rates of response do not weaken the trap. The response of the death rate to increases in per capita income is probably rapid in areas where the level of per capita income is very low, and where death rates are high because of the low per capita income. On the other hand, income not consumed becomes productive only with a time-lag. Investment projects must be completed before income is created out of past increases in income. Differential rates of response are probably not of the sort that eliminate the low-level equilibrium trap.

To take account of factors other than population growth that may depress per capita income, and factors other than increases in capital per head that may raise per capita income, the low-level equilibrium trap model can be extended and generalised by adopting Leibenstein's terminology of income-depressing forces and income-raising forces. Leibenstein's approach is illustrated in Fig. 3.7.

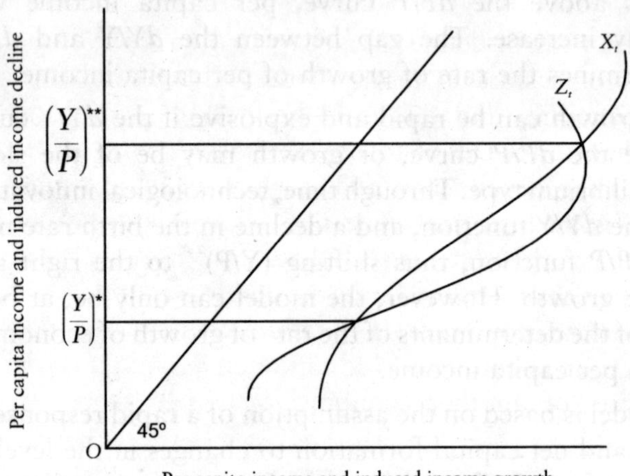

Fig. 3.7: Leibenstein's approach.

The curve representing income-depressing forces, Z_t, is measured horizontally from the 45° line, and the curve representing income-raising forces, X_t, is measured vertically from the 45° line. Per capita income level $(Y/P)^*$ is the only point of stable equilibrium. Between $(Y/P)^*$ and $(Y/P)^{**}$ income-depressing forces are greater than income-raising forces and per capita income will slip back to $(Y/P)^*$. Only beyond $(Y/P)^{**}$ are income-raising forces greater than income-depressing forces such that a sustained increase in per capita income becomes possible. $(Y/P)^{**}$ is the critical per capita income level necessary to escape the low-level equilibrium trap.

DEPENDENCY THEORY

Dependency Theory developed in the late 1950s under the guidance of the Director of the United Nations Economic Commission for Latin America, Raul Prebisch. Prebisch and his colleagues were troubled by the fact that economic growth in the advanced industrialized countries did not necessarily lead to growth in the poorer countries. Indeed, their studies suggested that economic activity in the richer countries often led to serious economic problems in the poorer countries. Such a possibility was not predicted by neoclassical theory, which had assumed that economic growth was beneficial to all (Pareto optimal) even if the benefits were not always equally shared.

Dependency can be defined as an explanation of the economic development of a state in terms of the external influences—political, economic, and cultural—on national development policies.[5] Theotonio Dos Santos emphasizes the historical dimension of the dependency relationships in his definition—Dependency is an historical condition which shapes a certain structure of the world economy such that it favours some countries to the detriment of others and limits the development possibilities of the subordinate economics...a situation in which the economy of a certain group of countries is conditioned by the development and expansion of another economy, to which their own is subjected.[6]

Dependency analysis built on the ideas of the structuralists, specifically Prebisch's distinction between the centre and the periphery. The centre was viewed as *cause* and the periphery as *effect*. According to dependency writers, the less-developed nations had to be understood as part of a global process. Their fate was merely to provide the inputs to the advanced nations or to receive their cast-off, low-wage manufacturing processes under trading conditions which were likely to worsen. Dependency theory found the causes for the lack of development to be external to the socio-economic formations of the less-developed nations. Characteristics of economic dependency can be outlined as follows:

Underlying conditions

(a) The export sector dominates the economy, imports are large in relation to the GDP.

(b) Exports are dominated by one, or a few commodities.

(c) Export firms are primarily foreign-owned.

(d) Mineral/petroleum commodities are produced under conditions of vertical integration.

(e) Foreign ownership dominates the financial sector and the industrial sector.

Structural results

(a) Income, employment, and growth are determined by:
   (i) prices and demand conditions in international markets, and
   (ii) the willingness of transnational corporations to invest.
(b) Income, employment, and growth are conditioned by:
   (i) economic fluctuations abroad,
   (ii) changes in taste and fashion or technologically created substitutes, and
   (iii) changes in the price and type of imports.
(c) Foreign capital, foreign technology, and management are dominant economic actors.
(d) Profits are normally repatriated, not re-invested.
(e) Production for the export industries is dependent on imported inputs.
(f) Backward and forward linkages in export activities are rare.
(g) Economic growth is not self-activating.

Internal backward or dysfunctional institutions of the less-developed nations were not treated seriously by dependency writers as a subject of analysis, or were seen as extensions of external domination. Internal institutional structures, such as the role of state corruption, large and unproductive landholdings, the extreme concentration of wealth, unresponsive political institutions, and so on, were played down. Instead, the negative influence of transnational corporations, multilateral institutions like the World Bank and the International Monetary Fund, and the extensive influence of foreign governments in the internal affairs of less-developed nations were highlighted.

Prebisch's initial explanation for the phenomenon was very straightforward—poor countries exported primary commodities to the rich countries who then manufactured products out of those commodities and sold them back to the poorer countries. The "Value Added" by manufacturing a usable product always cost more than the primary products used to create those products.

Therefore, poorer countries would never be earning enough from their export earnings to pay for their imports.

Prebisch's solution was similarly straightforward—poorer countries should embark on programs of import substitution so that they need not purchase the manufactured products from the richer countries. The poorer countries would still sell their primary products on the world market, but their foreign exchange reserves would not be used to purchase their manufactures from abroad.

Three issues made this policy difficult to follow. The first is that the internal markets of the poorer countries were not large enough to support the economies of scale used by the richer countries to keep their prices low. The second issue concerned the political will of the poorer countries as to whether a transformation from being primary products producers was possible or desirable. The final issue revolved around the extent to which the poorer countries actually had control of their primary products, particularly in the area of selling those products abroad. These obstacles to the import substitution policy led others to think a little more creatively and historically at the relationship between rich and poor countries.

At this point dependency theory was viewed as a possible way of explaining the persistent poverty of the poorer countries. The traditional neoclassical approach said virtually nothing on this question except to assert that the poorer countries were late in coming to solid economic practices and that as soon as they learned the techniques of modern economics, the poverty would begin to subside. However, Marxists theorists viewed the persistent poverty as a consequence of capitalist exploitation. And a new body of thought, called the *world systems approach*, argued that the poverty was a direct consequence of the evolution of the international political economy into a fairly rigid division of labour which favoured the rich and penalised the poor.

Several factors contributed to the rise of dependency analysis. Of utmost importance was the influence of "modernisation" theory on social science analysis and policy, which promised quick and sweeping development. Rosenstein-Rodan, Nurkse, Hirschman, Rostow, and others had maintained that the attainment of development for the less-developed countries was only a matter of time. Since most nations had already reached the "pre-take-off" stage, using Rostow's stage categorisation, spectacular results were to be anticipated in little more than a decade. Yet in the 1950s and 1960s in most of the less-developed nations, growth was only modest. Population growth had slowed gains in per capita income. Furthermore, confirming Myrdal's work, a process of cumulative causation leading to greater dualism could be observed. Economic growth had created poles of prosperity in a sea of despair.

The debates among the liberal reformers (Prebisch), the Marxists (Andre Gunder Frank), and the world systems theorists (Wallerstein) was vigorous and intellectually quite challenging. There are still points of serious disagreements among the various strains of dependency theorists and it is a mistake to think that there is only one unified theory of dependency. Nonetheless, there are some core propositions which seem to underlie the analyses of most dependency theorists.

There are three common features to the definitions which most dependency theorists share. First, dependency characterises the international system as comprised of two sets of states, variously described as dominant/dependent, center/periphery or metropolitan/satellite. The dominant states are the advanced industrial nations in the Organisation of Economic Cooperation and Development (OECD). The dependent states are those states of Latin America, Asia, and Africa which have low per capita GNPs and which rely heavily on the export of a single commodity for foreign exchange earnings.

Second, most definitions have in common the assumption that external forces are of singular importance to the economic activities within the dependent states. These external forces include multinational corporations, international commodity markets, foreign assistance, communications, and any other means by which the advanced industrialized countries can represent their economic interests abroad.

Third, the definitions of dependency all indicate that the relations between dominant and dependent states are dynamic because the interactions between the two sets of states tend to not only reinforce but also intensify the unequal patterns. Moreover, dependency is a very deep-seated historical process, rooted in the internationalisation of capitalism. Dependency is an ongoing process.

In short, dependency theory attempts to explain the present underdeveloped state of many nations in the world by examining the patterns of interactions among nations and by arguing that inequality among nations is an intrinsic part of those interactions.

Different forms of dependence can be distinguished, as they have evolved historically. First, there is colonial dependence, based on trade and the exploitation of natural resources. Second, there is financial-industrial dependence, which consolidated itself at the end of the nineteenth century and has geared the economic structure of dependent nations to the needs of the centre. Third, a new type of dependence has emerged from 1945 based on multinational corporations, which began to invest in industries geared to the internal market of developing countries. This is technological-industrial dependence. Dos Santos argues that each of these forms of dependence has so conditioned the internal structure of peripheral countries, that this itself has become part of the dependency relation; for example the highly dualistic structure, the income inequality and conspicuous consumption of the wealthy classes, a dependency mentality and the ingrained habit of seeking outside help, and the unholy alliance between the domestic ruling elite and foreign interests all conspire to impede internal development. Thus, Don Santos maintains that dependency is not simply an external phenomenon; it also has to do with the supportive power groups within the poor countries themselves who find the status quo profitable.

Baran, Frank, and Amin focus their attention more squarely on the traditional Marxist mechanisms by which capitalism in general, and international capitalism in particular, aid the rich in exploiting the poor. Emphasis is placed on the expropriation and transfer of the surplus produced by labour to the owners of capital, which operates at different levels. The multinational corporations are seen as the modern instrument for the expropriation of surplus value. Neo-Marxists allow for a residue of surplus, but argue that if it is reinvested in the periphery or left in the hands of local elites, it will not be used appropriately for development purposes. As in Don Santos' model, the system hinges on the collaboration of the governing elite who live in the capital city, who think like, and identify with, their ex-colonial masters. So poor countries, despite formal political independence, remain locked into an old system of economic dependence that perpetuates underdevelopment.

Like Dos Santos, for Frank underdevelopment is a natural outcome of the world capitalist system since the development of some countries inevitably means the distorted development or underdevelopment of others. Development itself perpetuates underdevelopment, a process that Frank has called 'the development of underdevelopment'. Frank sees the origins of the process in colonisation, which started as a form of economic exploitation and has distorted the economic structure of Third World countries ever since. The developing countries were forced into the position of being suppliers of raw materials to industrial countries, thus effectively blocking industrial development in the primary producing countries themselves. In the words of Frank, "...historical research demonstrates that contemporary underdevelopment is in large part the historical product of past and continuing economic and other relations between the satellite underdeveloped and the now developed metropolitan countries. Furthermore, these relations are an essential part of the capitalist system on a world scale as a whole."[7]

According to this view, the capitalist system has enforced a rigid international division of labour which is responsible for the underdevelopment of many areas of the world. The dependent states supply cheap minerals, agricultural commodities, and cheap labour, and also serve as the repositories of surplus capital, obsolescent technologies, and manufactured goods. These functions orient the economies of the dependent states toward the outside: money, goods, and services do flow into dependent states, but the allocation of these resources are determined by the economic interests of the dominant states, and not by the economic interests of the dependent state. This division of labour is ultimately the explanation for poverty and there is little question but that capitalism regards the division of labour as a necessary condition for the efficient allocation of resources. The most explicit manifestation of this characteristic is in the doctrine of comparative advantage.

Moreover, to a large extent the dependency models rest upon the assumption that economic and political power are heavily concentrated and centralized in the industrialized countries, an assumption shared with Marxist theories of imperialism. If this assumption is valid, then any distinction between economic and political power is spurious: governments will take whatever steps are necessary to protect private economic interests, such as those held by multinational corporations.

Not all dependency theorists, however, are Marxist and one should clearly distinguish between dependency and a theory of imperialism. The Marxist theory of imperialism explains dominant state *expansion* while the dependency theory explains *underdevelopment.* Stated another way, Marxist theories explain the reasons why imperialism occurs, while dependency theories explain the consequences of imperialism. The difference is significant. In many respects, imperialism is, for a Marxist, part of the process by which the world is transformed and is therefore a process which accelerates the communist revolution. Marx spoke approvingly of British colonialism in India, "England has to fulfil a double mission in India: one destructive, the other regenerating—the annihilation of old Asiatic society, and the laying of the material foundations of Western society in Asia."[8]

For the dependency theorists, underdevelopment is a wholly negative condition which offers no possibility of sustained and autonomous economic activity in a dependent state. Additionally, the Marxist theory of imperialism is self-liquidating, while the dependent relationship is self-perpetuating. The end of imperialism in the Leninist framework comes about as the dominant powers go to war over a rapidly shrinking number of exploitable opportunities. World War I was, for Lenin, the classic proof of this proposition. After the war was over, Britain and France took over the former German colonies. A dependency theorist rejects this proposition. A dependent relationship exists irrespective of the specific identity of the dominant state. That the dominant states may fight over the disposition of dependent territories is not in and of itself a pertinent bit of information (except that periods of fighting among dominant states affords opportunities for the dependent states to break their dependent relationships). To a dependency theorist, the central characteristic of the global economy is the persistence of poverty throughout the entire modern period in virtually the same areas of the world, regardless of what state was in control.

Finally, there are some dependency theorists who do not identify capitalism as the motor force behind a dependent relationship. The relationship is maintained by a system of power first and it does not seem as if power is only supported by capitalism. For example, the relationship between the former dependent states in the socialist bloc (the Eastern European states and Cuba, for example) closely paralleled the relationships between poor states and the advanced capitalist states. The possibility that dependency is more closely linked to disparities of power rather than to the particular characteristics of a given economic system is intriguing and consistent with the more traditional analyses of international relations, such as realism.

The Central Propositions of Dependency Theory

There are a number of propositions, all of which are contestable, which form the core of dependency theory. These propositions include:

(a) Underdevelopment is a condition fundamentally different from *undevelopment*. The latter term simply refers to a condition in which resources are not being used. For example, the European colonists viewed the North American continent as an undeveloped area: the land was not actively cultivated on a scale consistent with its potential. Underdevelopment refers to a situation in which resources are being actively used, but used in a way which benefits dominant states and not the poorer states in which the resources are found.

(b) The distinction between underdevelopment and undevelopment places the poorer countries of the world is a profoundly different historical context. These countries are not "behind" or "catching up" to the richer countries of the world. They are not poor because they lagged behind the scientific transformations or the Enlightenment values of the European states. They are poor because they were coercively integrated into the European economic system only as producers of raw materials or to serve as repositories of cheap labour, and were denied the opportunity to market their resources in any way that competed with dominant states.

(c) Dependency theory suggests that alternative uses of resources are preferable to the resource usage patterns imposed by dominant states. There is no clear definition of what these preferred patterns might be, but some criteria are invoked. For example, one of the dominant state practices most often criticized by dependency theorists is export agriculture. The criticism is that many poor economies experience rather high rates of malnutrition even though they produce great amounts of food for export. Many dependency theorists would argue that those agricultural lands should be used for domestic food production in order to reduce the rates of malnutrition.

(d) The preceding proposition can be amplified: dependency theorists rely upon a belief that there exists a clear "national" economic interest which can and should be articulated for each country. In this respect, dependency theory actually shares a similar theoretical concern with realism. What distinguishes the dependency perspective is that its proponents believe that this national interest can only be satisfied by addressing the needs of the poor within a society, rather than through the satisfaction of corporate or governmental needs. Trying to determine what is "best" for the poor is a difficult analytical problem over the long run. Dependency theorists have not yet articulated an operational definition of the national economic interest.

(e) The diversion of resources over time (and one must remember that dependent relationships have persisted since the European expansion beginning in the fifteenth century) is maintained not only by the power of dominant states, but also through the power of elites in the dependent states. Dependency theorists argue that these elites maintain a dependent relationship because their own private interests coincide with the interests of the dominant states. These elites are typically trained in the dominant states and share similar values and culture with the elites in dominant states. Thus, in a very real sense, a dependency relationship is a "voluntary" relationship. One need not argue that the elites in a dependent state are consciously betraying the interests of their poor; the elites sincerely believe that the key to economic development lies in following the prescriptions of liberal economic doctrine.

The Policy Implications of Dependency Analysis

If one accepts the analysis of dependency theory, then the questions of how poor economies develop become quite different from the traditional questions concerning comparative advantage, capital accumulation, and import/export strategies. Some of the most important new issues include:

(a) The success of the advanced industrial economies does not serve as a model for the currently developing economies. When economic development became a focused area of study, the analytical strategy (and ideological preference) was quite clear: all nations need to emulate the patterns used by the rich countries. Indeed, in the 1950s and 1960s there was a paradigmatic consensus that growth strategies were universally applicable, a consensus best articulated by Walt Rostow in his book, *The Stages of Economic Growth*. Dependency theory suggests that the success of the richer countries was a highly contingent and specific episode in global economic history, one dominated by the highly exploitative colonial relationships of the European powers. A repeat of those relationships is not now highly likely for the poor countries of the world.

(b) Dependency theory repudiates the central distributive mechanism of the neoclassical model, what is usually called "trickle-down" economics. The neoclassical model of economic growth pays relatively little attention to the question of distribution of wealth. Its primary concern is on efficient production and assumes that the market will allocate the rewards of efficient production in a rational and unbiased manner. This assumption may be valid for a well-integrated, economically fluid economy where people can quickly adjust to economic changes and where consumption patterns are not distorted by non-economic forces such as racial, ethnic, or gender bias. These conditions are not pervasive in the developing economies, and dependency theorists argue that economic activity is not easily disseminated in poor economies. For these structural reasons, dependency theorists argue that the market alone is not a sufficient distributive mechanism.

(c) Since the market only rewards productivity, dependency theorists discount aggregate measures of economic growth such as the GDP or trade indices. Dependency theorists do not deny that economic activity occurs within a dependent state. They do make a very important distinction, however, between economic growth and economic development. For example, there is a greater concern within the dependency framework for whether the economic activity is actually benefiting the nation as a whole. Therefore, far greater attention is paid to indices such as life expectancy, literacy, infant mortality, education, and the like. Dependency theorists clearly emphasize social indicators far more than economic indicators.

(d) Dependent states, therefore, should attempt to pursue policies of self-reliance. Contrary to the neo-classical models endorsed by the International Monetary Fund and the World Bank, greater integration into the global economy is not necessarily a good choice for poor countries. Often this policy perspective is viewed as an endorsement of a policy of autarky, and there have been some experiments with such a policy such as China's Great Leap Forward or Tanzania's policy of *Ujamaa*. The failures of these policies are clear, and the failures suggest that autarky is not a good choice. Rather a policy of self-reliance should be interpreted as endorsing a policy of controlled interactions with the world economy: poor countries should only endorse interactions on terms that promise to improve the social and economic welfare of the larger citizenry.

Dependency Models

Andre Gunder Frank

The theory of dependency that formed in the 1960s played a more crucial role than any other conceptual framework in developing a critique of the world market supportive of liberation and anti-capitalist movements in Africa and Latin America. The general theme of dependency theory can be captured by the idea that the economic surplus generated in post-colonial societies is appropriated by foreign interests and domestic elites in a way that reinforces a pattern of economic backwardness. In its starkest formulation, development in the North and underdevelopment of the South are not opposites, but a common process.

Andre Gunder Frank, who was born in 1929 in Germany, was one of the foremost proponents of dependency theory. Frank did much to develop and translate the radical dependency analysis being developed in Latin America through the 1960s to a wider audience, particularly in the English-speaking world. The argument of dependency theory was that capitalist markets produce inherent structural inequalities. In Gunder Frank's view, the underdevelopment of the periphery was an inevitable reflection of the development of the core. He argued that the industrial 'metropolis' extracts a surplus from its 'satellites' in order to sustain its own dynamic growth. Exploitative metropole-satellite relationships are reproduced between countries in the periphery, and even within countries. While internal political and social structures contribute to the process of underdevelopment, they can only be understood as a function of this external dominance. Given the ongoing extraction of locally-generated capital, Frank doubted whether development was possible in dependent countries.

The important characteristics of the Frank's model are:

(a) Close economic, political, social and cultural ties between each metropolis and its staellites, which result in the total integration of the farthest outpost and peasant into the system as a whole. This contrasts with the supposed isolation and non-incorporation of large parts of society according to the dualist model.

(b) Monopolistic structure of the whole system, in which each metropolis holds monopoly power over its satellites; the source of form of this monopoly varies from one case to another, but the existence of this monopoly is universal throughout the system.

(c) As occurs in any monopolistic system, misuse and misdirection of available resources throughout the whole system and metropolis-satellite chain.

(d) As part of this misuse, the expropriation and appropriation of a large part or even all of and more than the economic surplus or surplus value of the satellite by its local, regional, national or international metropolis.

Instead of a photograph at a point in time, the model may be viewed as a moving picture of the course of history. It then shows the following characteristics:

(a) Expansion of the system from Europe until it incorporates the entire planet in one world system and structure. (If the socialist countries have managed to escape from this system, then there are now two worlds—but in no case are there three.)

(b) Development of capitalism, at first commercial and later also industrial, on a world scale as a single system.

(c) Polarising tendencies to important historical changes in the source mechanism of monopoly which the capitalist world metropolis exercises over its satellites.

Baran and Frank emphasize, in their dependency (spatial) components, as opposed to their neo-Marxist (class) components, that surplus extraction was the cause of the initial division of the world into rich and poor areas, and that the extraction is essentially an aspect of the relationship among countries, not strata. The tools of the extraction/appropriation process, in the colonial period, took the form of direct, overt appropriation of products (looting and plundering), while in the modern period it takes the form of indirect, covert repatriation of profits. What in essence is suggested is that capitalism does not develop primarily on the basis of the exploitation of the proletariat, but upon the basis of the exploitation of countries.

Hence external delinking, internal participation, socio-political mobilisation, and socialist restructuring are the solution's components of Frank. Short of that, the alleviation of underdevelopment can only occur during periods of retreat or withdrawal by the industrial capitalist economies (an ineluctable form of delinking). Contrary to the Reaganite-Thatcherite argument that less social development is necessary for more economic development, therefore, Frank stipulates that the prior development of human capital through education, health and improved social relations would lead to social and economic development.

Frank's dependency perspective also counters the thesis, advocated, e.g., by W. Arthur Lewis, according to which the underdeveloped world's first priority need is foreign investment and capital aid on the premise that the principle obstacle to its development is its shortage of capital. He counters this supply side theory with the essentially Keynesian demand side concept that the real economic obstacle is insufficient market demand for productive national investment. Frank, thus, argues that policies of "structural adjustment" are insufficient to expand the internal market and generate development. Hence, development would not result from minor changes in dual economies/societies, hoping that the modern sector would expand and eliminate the traditional one.

Frank, thus, eventually concludes that escape from underdevelopment, and subsequent development, are no longer possible for the UDCs as part of the capitalist system, and only liberation from that system offers that possibility; that continued participation in the same world capitalist system could only mean continued development of underdevelopment, that is, there would be neither equity, efficiency nor economic development. The course of action he recommends therefore is to deliberately and revolutionarily delink from the system externally, and to transit to self-reliance internally in order to make independent or nondependent economic development possible.

Frank's difficulty in his dependency circle stems, however, from his theories of underdevelopment and dependency, which are meant to conflate the transfer of value through spatial relations with the Marxist emphasis on the appropriation of surplus value through the class relationship. The exploitative relationship between the capitalists of the core and the peasants of the satellites is seen to exist through a network of spatial relations. This exploitation brand has therefore never satisfied orthodox Marxists, and Frank's work has thus been considered neo-Marxist due to its emphasis on the metropolis-satellite relationship at the expense of the quintessential class relationship of Marxist theory. Neo-Marxist analysis of capitalist exploitation emphasizes the core-periphery division on an equal basis to the quintessential class division.

Frank (1978) subsequently espoused Arghiri Emmanuel's thesis of unequal exchange (1972), which provides a different account of surplus extraction through trade. An important element of Frank's rendition is his emphasis upon surplus appropriation through trade, implicitly equating capitalism with relations of exchange rather than a system of production. He argued that monopolistic merchant capitalism had penetrated the remotest reaches of all underdeveloped economies via a series of trading networks in which small scale merchants in rural areas were linked to larger monopolistic suppliers, and monopsonic buyers, and so on up the chain to large scale import-export activities dominated by foreign interests.

Frank used this thesis as the basis of his affirmation that all branches of underdeveloped economies have been incorporated into the world capitalist system. Underdeveloped economies have bypassed the phase of competitive capitalism due to the mode of their incorporation into the international economy. Their monopoly capitalists are content to appropriate existing rigging profits and have no interest in promoting a competitive, dynamic capitalist sector. Meanwhile the strata that control the use of the surplus also hold political power, and they use this power to maintain the status quo. In these circumstances, the only possible way forward is delinking through a social and political revolution that will replace the existing alliance of the domestic dominant bourgeoisie and foreign capitalists with a socialist regime committed to social and economic development.

In the early 1970s the critique concentrated on Andre Gunder Frank (1967, 1969), not necessarily because he was the most typical of the dependency school, but for a number of other reasons. First, Frank wrote in English—the Spanish of the other dependentists seems to have been too inaccessible to the critics. Second, Frank was both polemical and outspoken in his arguments. He was also sometimes placed with the world systems theorists because he not only wrote about Latin America but also about the historical development of the capitalist world system, and the 'true' world system writers based themselves on his work.

We will now look at one element of this criticism, as it led to the formation of the modes of production theories and emphasised the contrast between Marxists and neo-Marxists. Frank asserted that Latin America could be characterised as capitalist practically from the start of the colonial period. There was no question of the dual society proposed by modernisation theorists. There was something approximating production for the world market and there was a system for appropriation of the economic surplus. The way in which the surplus was appropriated varied over time (from plunder to unequal trade), but the surplus was always usurped in oneway or another.

Frank's assertion that Latin America was capitalist from the beginning of the colonial period brought him under heavy fire, particularly from the Argentinean economist Ernesto Laclau (1971). Laclau argued that Frank had used a mistaken definition of capitalism, that capitalism was a mode of production, rather than a mode of exchange. He concentrated on the sort of labour relations, which created a product in the first place, rather than on what happened to the surplus. If, rather than the manner of production, matters such as production for a market and appropriation of the surplus were of prime importance in defining capitalism, reasoned Laclau, then capitalism should be defined as having existed since the Ancient Greeks. According to Laclau, such a definition turns capitalism into a meaningless concept. In the meantime, the modernisation theorists had recovered from their shock, and began to direct their criticism at the inadequate empirical evidence supporting the dependency thesis that differences in degree of dependency were causally related to differences in economic development. In general this criticism followed the tactic of erecting a straw man (of dependency theories) which was then knocked down. Soon, however, modernisation theorists became more interested in computerised global growth models (Kahn and Wiener 1967, Rostow 1978, Kahn et al. 1979).

Cristobal Kay

Since the debt crisis of the early 1980s, there has been a radical series of transformations in the economic, political, social and cultural spheres of Latin America. This can be termed a paradigmatic shift, such has been the scale of the ideological transformation, particularly of governments and their advisers. The previous paradigm can be said to have lasted from the early 1930s to the mid 1980s and developed in a similar way as a response to an economic crisis. It was characterised by greater involvement in the management of the economy, an attempt to reduce the linkages with the wider world economy and promote industrialisation. This paradigm spawned structuralist and dependency theories, which tried to interpret events that had already occurred.

Latin American school of development and underdevelopment which emerged in the postwar period, has two major strands—the structuralist reformist and the marxist revolutionary. What unites these two strands is that they both argue against neoclassical and modernization theory and that they define underdevelopment as being the outcome of a process of world capitalist accumulation which continually reproduces both poles of the world system. They argue that underdeveloped countries have peculiarities of their own and for this reason neoclassical and modernization theory have little relevance for understanding this reality, and worse, the policies which are derived from these theories do not address the fundamental problem of underdevelopment and can even aggravate it. The major difference between these two paradigms is that the structuralists think that by reforming the international and national capitalist systems it is possible to overcome underdevelopment. Meanwhile for the Marxist only world socialism can ultimately overcome underdevelopment and the inequalities of the contemporary world capitalist system.

Both Haya and Mariategui characterised the mode of production in the countryside as feudal or semi-feudal, condemned the landlord class and imperialism for Latin America's underdevelopment, and advocated industrialization. Finally, both agreed that the development process in Latin America differed from the classical European model and that the bourgeoisie in Latin America was unable to perform the progressive role it did in Europe. In Haya's view the revolution had to be anti-feudal and anti-imperialist. It could not be a socialist revolution as, in his view, it was not possible to skip the historical stages of development, and thus it was necessary first to develop capitalism fully. This revolution was to be led by the middle class, the proletariat being too small and the peasantry too backward. Haya called for the establishment of an anti-imperialist state which, owing to the weakness of the national bourgeoisie and the strength of the feudal class and imperialism, had to be state-capitalist. However, he recognised some progressive aspects of imperialism (modern technology and industrial capital) and thus the struggle was only against the negative aspects of imperialism. The objective of the revolution was to achieve Latin America's economic independence and development within capitalism.

Mariategui can be considered as the first Latin American neo-Marxist who anticipates many of the dependency arguments. He attacked Haya's dualist position by arguing that feudal and capitalist relations are part of one single economic system. Furthermore, imperialist capital is seen as linked to, and profiting from, pre-capitalist relations. Contrary to Haya, Mariategui saw no scope for the development of an autochthonous or independent national capitalism. In his view the development of capitalism would not eliminate pre-capitalist relations and would only intensify the domination of imperialist monopoly capital. While Haya considered that the national bourgeoisie was oppressed externally by imperialism and internally by feudalism and that the struggle for national liberation should therefore take precedence over the class struggle, Mariategui held the opposite view. Mariategui argued that the local bourgeoisie was organically linked to imperialism and feudalism and that they jointly oppressed and exploited the urban and rural workers. Thus, the fight for national liberation did not neutralise the class struggle and, on the contrary, was subordinated to it.

Furthermore, the local bourgeoisie was unable to fulfil this task and only the working class could accomplish it.

The centre-periphery paradigm: While various writers developed the structuralist paradigm, Raul Prebisch's original ideas were pivotal in launching this perspective, whose influence has extended beyond Latin America. The structuralists' perspective is both holistic and historical. The originality of the structuralist paradigm lies in the proposition that the process of development and underdevelopment is a single process, and that the disparities between the centre and periphery are reproduced through international trade. Thus, the periphery's development problems are located within the context of the world economy. It is an historical perspective as structuralists probe into the origins of the integration of Latin American economies into the dominant capitalist system as producers of primary products. This pattern of development in the periphery is called the 'primary-export model' or 'outward-oriented development model'. In such case, an import-substituting industrialisation policy is advocated which would help peripheral countries to switch to what they termed an 'inward-directed' development process.

The cornerstone of structuralism is the centre-periphery paradigm. This paradigm attempts to explain the unequal nature of the world economic system. It also suggests a series of policies to narrow the gap between countries of the centre and those of the periphery. According to this paradigm the duality in the world economy originated with the industrial revolution in the centre when the possibilities for increasing the productivity of the factors of production rose dramatically. The diffusion of this technical progress was, however, very large uneven throughout the world. The centre countries internalised the new technology by developing an industrial capital-goods sector and by spreading the improved technology to all economic sectors. This resulted in the development of an homogeneous and integrated economy. In the periphery, by contrast, new technologies were largely imported and mainly confined to the primary-commodity-producing export sector. As a consequence, the peripheral economy became both disarticulated and dualist—disarticulated because it had to import the advanced technology from the centre; and dualist because a large gulf in productivity developed between the export and subsistence sectors. A sizable low-productivity pre-capitalist sector survives in the periphery producing a continuous surplus of labour. This large surplus of labour keeps wages low and prevents the periphery from retaining the fruits of its own technological progress as productivity increases in the export sector are largely transferred to the centre owing to the deterioration of the terms of trade.

Other aspects of the structuralist school are:

(a) *The deterioration of the terms of trade*: The assertion that the central and peripheral countries are linked by a series of asymmetric relationships which reproduce the system represented a key departure from the evolutionist and mechanical stage theories of development. Furthermore, CEPAL's[9] thesis on the deterioration of the periphery's terms of trade sought to challenge conventional economic theories of international trade and to question the international division of labour by proposing an import-substituting industrialisation strategy for the periphery.

An increase in productivity can result in either a fall in the price of a commodity where this technical progress has occurred, thereby benefiting the consumers; or in a rise in the payment to factors of production (i.e. wages and profits), thereby benefiting the producers; or in a combination of both. According to Prebisch the existence of trade union power and oligopolies in the centre means that prices have not fallen, or have fallen to a leaser extent than the increase in productivity. Thus, workers and capitalists in the centre are able to gain the fruits of their technical progress via rises in wages and profits. Meanwhile the opposite has happened in the periphery due to the weakness or non-existence of trade unions and the greater competition facing export-producers. However, the main argument put forward by Prebisch to explain the inability of workers to capture a significant part of the increase in productivity is the existence of a large surplus labour force. An additional factor is the low productivity of the pre- and semi-capitalist sectors with their low subsistence incomes and wages which act as a restraint on wage increases in the export sector where most of the productivity increases in the periphery occur.

(b) *Import-substituting industrialisation*: Prebisch favoured the periphery's industrialisation because he believed that this would reduce its vulnerability to international economic crises, lead to greater increases in productivity and incomes, and reduce unemployment, thereby removing one of the causes of low wages in the periphery, and avoid further deterioration in its commodity terms of trade. CEPAL was initially optimistic about the benefits industrialisation would bring to the periphery. It was regarded as the panacea which would not only overcome the limitations of the outward-directed development process but would also provide social and political benefits such as enhancing the middle and working classes and democracy.

One of the first criticisms to emerge of import-substituting-industrialisation policy came from within the CEPAL fold itself. CEPAL's Manifesto had already voiced misgivings about Latin Amercian industrialisation, and by the early 1960s CEPAL published a series of critiques of the import-substituting industrialisation process. These have often been overlooked by both neoclassical and dependency critiques undertaken in the late 1960s and early 1970s. Structuralists criticised the 'actually existing' import-substitution process as both concentrating and exclusive in that the fruits of technological progress brought about by industrialisation were concentrated in the hands of the owners of capital, excluding the majority and exacerbating inequalities in the distribution of income. At the same time this development process failed to absorb the surplus labour. Also this model resulted in 'structural heterogeneity' as difference between economic sectors (such as those between a backward agriculture and a modern capital-intensive industry) and those within economic sectors (such as those between the informal and formal parts of any one economic sector) were exacerbated. Furthermore, it had aggravated the economy's external vulnerability and led to an increasing foreign control of the industrial sector.

(c) *The structuralist-monetarist controversy on inflation*: During the mid-1950s a group of Latin American economists, largely associated with CEPAL, started to challenge the conventional wisdom on the nature and cures of inflation. This gave rise to a long debate between 'monetarists' and 'structuralists' which has sporadically resurfaced since. The fundamental disagreement between monetarists and structuralists is over the cause of inflation. Monetarists regard inflation as a monetary phenomenon arising from excessive demand while for structuralists inflation arises from structural maladjustments and rigidities in the economic system.

Structuralists situate the problem of inflation within the context of the problem of development of the Third World while monetarists are less prone to do so. Thus, structuralists would forego price stability for development while the monetarists' attitude is the opposite. This difference arises because for the structuralists, inflation in Latin America arises from the socio-political tensions, sectoral imbalances and expectations generated by the process of development itself. Meanwhile, for the monetarists it is the inflationary process which is the major obstacle to growth.

Dependency analysis: The dependency literature has stimulated many debates and provoked a bewildering array of critiques. While some critics of dependency theory have made a positive contribution many other critics have revealed an ignorance of key dependency writings and spread many distortions thereby creating much confusion. In particular, there exists an imbalance (especially common in the English-speaking world) regarding the diffusion of dependency theory. Although some propositions are shared, many important differences remain between dependency writers. Two key positions can be differentiated—reformist and Marxist. The ideas of the reformist dependency writers are best seen as a further development of the structuralist school as they attempt to reformulate CEPAL's developmentalist position in the light of the crisis of import-substituting industrialisation. Marxist dependency camp, best considered as neo-Marxists as they query the progressive role of capitalism in dependent countries.

Dependence is not regarded simply as an external variable as reformist do not derive the internal national socio-political situation mechanically from external domination. Although the limits for manoeuvre are largely set by the world system, the particular internal configuration of a country determines the specific response to the same external events. Thus, they do not see dependency and imperialism as external and internal sides of a single coin, with the internal reduced to a reflection of the external. They conceive the relationship between internal and external forces as forming a complex whole by exploring the interconnections between these two levels and the ways in which they are interwoven.

Recent studies have confirmed the continuing deterioration of the periphery's terms of trade in relation to that of the centre countries, a fact first highlighted by structuralism and incorporated into dependency's unequal exchange theory. This means that LDCs have to export an increasing amount of commodities to the developed countries so as to able to import the same amount of commodities from the developed countries. However, this does not necessarily mean that foreign exchange earnings have declined—often the case has been the contrary due to the continued rise in the volume of commodity exports from the periphery. But, this unequal exchange does mean that part of the periphery's economic surplus is transferred to the centre countries. LDCs should shift their export structure to higher value added commodities and services rather than continuing to export basic primary commodities which can lead to resource depletion and negative environmental consequences.

Looking back at history, Kay sees the rise of the neoliberal approach as a result of both internal and external dynamics. Highlighting the internal, he pointed to the failure of ISI (Import Substitution and Industrialization) as a development model, resulting in the debt crisis of the 1980s and the "lost decade of Latin America", where massive unemployment, high inflation, and rampant poverty and inequality were widespread. With the failure of ISI, Latin American countries found themselves cash strapped to pay back their debts, opening up the way for the World Bank, the IMF and their package of structural adjustment policies (SAPs).

In analysing the impact of external factors, Kay pointed to other countries that had experimented with the model. International financial institutions such as the World Bank and

IMF were quick to point to the rapid economic success of the Asian Tigers as evidence that the neoliberal model was the only way to take Latin American countries out of the current economic crisis, bring about sustainable economic development and breathe life into their stagnant economies. Strict policy prescriptions accompanied this shift in paradigm, with an emphasis on privatization, promotion of exports, deregulation, foreign investment, paying back the debt and a shrinking back of the state.

With the implementation of the neoliberal model, countries like Argentina began to experience a drop in inflation, initially giving the model much needed legitimacy. Exports became the most dynamic sector in the economy with the highest rate of growth. However, after the initial phase, the export boom, controlled mostly by a few multinationals, had not created much employment and had benefited only a small group of elites. Some of the negative impacts that accompanied the implementation of the model included the weakening of labour unions, increasingly precarious working conditions, instability of Latin American financial markets, a significant drop in wages, and greater inequality in income distribution. For all the expectations that neoliberal restructuring would bring about unprecedented growth rates, the actual figures since the 1980s show a growth rate less than half of what it had been from the 1950s to the 1980s under ISI.

After highlighting some of the failures of the neoliberal project in Latin America, Kay went on to discuss the relevance of past development theories to today's context, specifically addressing the relevance of dependency theory. He pointed out that now more than ever there is a case to be made for a centre-periphery view of the world, where the income gap between rich countries in the North and developing countries in the South continues to grow. The mechanical transfer of wealth from the North to the South continues and increasingly evident is the asymmetry within the region of Latin America, as evidenced in the income gap between poorer countries like Bolivia and Guatemala, and more economically advanced countries such as Chile and Mexico. There has also been a tremendous growth in the informal sector where low wages and precarious employment are the norm. Financial dependence on international financial institutions has increased immensely, resulting in greater vulnerability and decreased state control over policy and governing of their own countries. As Kay pointed out however, an inherent problem with the dependency model is that it fails to prescribe an alternative set of policies that governments can implement.

With the failure of neoliberalism and the lack of an alternative offered by dependency theorists, Kay proposed that we pay closer attention to neo-structuralism and what it can offer as an alternative development model. This approach emerged as an alternative during the 1990s as a structuralist strand of dependency theory. It was touted as development from within—a new structuralist approach to Latin America—after the failure of dependency theory to offer any concrete alternatives. ECLAC (Economic Commission for Latin America and the Caribbean) has been one of the main proponents of this alternative approach. The goal of the model is to promote growth with equity. It prescribes the introduction of new technology and an increase in productivity with a more aggressive move into export markets. A highly skilled labour force is thus an imperative, requiring a substantial investment in the education of its population. A sustainable increase in productivity also means a reliance on competitive advantage and not comparative advantage, created through industrial, education and development policy. As Kay emphasised in his discussion, the point is to increase the productive capacity of labour, to have a skilled intensive population, and thus a higher demand for labour. As for integration into the world market, it is left up to the country to choose how they want to integrate themselves globally. It is not a decision for the IMF or the World Bank to make.

Celso Furtado

Celso Furtado, born on July 26, 1920 in Pombal, Brazil and died on November 20, 2004 in Rio de Janeiro, was one of the most influential Latin American economists of the 20th century. His eventful life includes a wartime experience in the Italian front and a partnership with the famous Argentinean economist Raul Prebisch in the initial stages of the United Nations *Economic Commission for Latin America* (ECLA), where he was head of the development division and helped to formulate the structuralist approach to economics. He also assumed an important role as a policy-maker in Brazilian pre-military governments and, after the political banishment (1964), achieved a wide academic experience in American and European universities. His 1959 *Formação Economica do Brasil* is the classic interpretation of the economic history of Brazil. In 1961 he published a collection of essays about the notion of underdevelopment and development as interdependent phenomena. Furtado's last contribution was his careful discussion in the 1970s of the concept of cultural and economic dependence in underdeveloped countries.

Although in Europe and in the United States his name is mainly associated with the early versions of the 'dependence theory', or with the establishment of a 'theory of underdevelopment',[10] in Brazil Furtado's memories include his moral stature, his prolific activity as a writer and polemicist and, among economists, his decisive contribution to the diffusion of economic thinking.

Furtado's approach to economic theory: Furtado's assessment of economic theory was entirely guided by his lifelong involvement with economic development. Having the economic development as a point of reference, he praised the classical economists' and Marx's focus on the economic surplus and deplored, on the other hand, the neoclassical theory of prices and distribution for having extinguished the surplus approach. He objected to the classical fixation on the stationary state as well as Marx's difficulties in admitting the increase of the wage rates, a confirmed historical trend. Among the neoclassical, Furtado recognized Schumpeter's efforts to reconcile innovation with economic theory, although he thought any general equilibrium framework incompatible with the economic development approach.

In his overall evaluation of economic theory, all the great theoretical systems—the classical, the neoclassical and the Marxist—failed in providing a decisive contribution to the comprehension of the phenomenon of economic development, as they lacked the due combination of abstract reasoning and embedment in historical reality. According to Furtado, the main methodological issue in economic studies is "...the definition of the level of generality—or of concretion—in which any relation with explaining value applies."[11] In what concerns the development theory, the abstract models were seen as especially defective, as they missed two points—the irreversibility of the historical processes and the structural differences between economies according to their distinct stages of development. In other words, Furtado's view the of economic science takes on account its dual character, i.e., its abstract and historical character. The economic analysis is bound to deal with such dual character and analysts must draw the boundaries limiting the validity of the abstract models. Effectively, this was Furtado's lifelong commitment—the application of general principles to (historical) economic realities.

The dynamism of the export-driven economy depends on the external demand, while the dynamism of the industrialization process depends on internal demand and on the economy's capacity to adapt its supply structure and overcome some bottlenecks. The most important bottlenecks are the discontinuities in the internal industrial structure, the infrastructure deficiencies and the small size of the market (given the existence of economies of scale in the industrial sector). Anyhow, the growth of the internal industrial production can be seen as a response to the changes in the relative prices, which are byproducts of the exchange rate moves following the collapse of the country exports. Tariffs and other administrative controls impel further changes in the relative prices and stimulate the production of local products. The continuous expansion of the internal market and the industrial production keeps the import capacity under a permanent squeeze, thus the import substitution proceeds.

Features of Furtado's economic analysis: Furtado's economic analysis has four nuclear elements—absorption and release of resources and productivity; in kind versus monetary transactions; surplus versus subsistence economy; and relative prices. Furtado's uses of economic concepts are not always straightforward, consistent or compatible with the general understanding of the economists. An attempt to clarify the meanings Furtado attributes to some of the concepts will contribute to establish the range, and also the limits, of his analysis.

In Furtado's view, the colonial economies are stores of idle or under-used factors of production: land, natural resources and labour (when the population is dispersed in the subsistence sector). The discovery of gold and silver mines or the cultivation of highly appreciated products—sugar, coffee, cocoa and rubber—connects these resources to the world economy. In other words, the international trade awakes idle resources and shakes a dormant economy enhancing its productivity. When these export-driven pushes collapse before the adoption of an alternative substitute or prior to the achievement of economic diversification and the development of an internal market, the economy retrogresses and the resources disperse into idleness. As already noted, the new retrograde state is not identical to the pre-expansion state; nevertheless, the resources go back to an under-using condition.

The above description brings to surface two important elements of Furtado's system—the role of the external trade and the mechanisms that determine a rise/fall in productivity. The external trade plays the virtuous role of awakening internal factors, otherwise dormant. Due to historical reasons, some countries (USA, Australia) succeeded in making the transition from this first stage—export-led growth—to the second—development of an internal market. Other countries, as Brazil, underwent a late transition and, most importantly, under different conditions and with different consequences. Another significant element of Furtado's system is the specific conceptions of productivity he adheres to in different parts of his work. There are three relevant conditions to an increase in productivity—(a) the absorption of under-used resources; (b) a rise in prices, typical of primary exports; and (c) a 'Smithean' rise in productivity, typical of manufacture and industry.

The first and the second situations are the most relevant, as they underline Furtado's understanding of the process of economic development. The simple establishment of a successful export front, the expansion of an already established export business or a rise in the export prices, can be taken as events that increase the overall productivity of the system. There are two reasons for this increase—(a) the resources are being transferred from less to more productive uses; and (b) in the case of a rise in prices, the same amount of resources gives access to more commodities abroad. In other words, a positive change in the terms of trade and the simple transfer of resources into more productive uses—in the sense of connected to high demand and high prices—increase the overall productivity of the economy.

On the other hand, there are increases in productivity related to the organisational process, or to technical progress. This increase in productivity is physical—a greater output per unit of resources. According to Furtado, the technical progress scarcely applies to agriculture, at least in Latin America. The productivity is higher in the sugarcane plantation than in the 'subsistence sector', basically due to the sugar price. And, since labour and land are abundant, there is no competition among the producers, thus no induction to technical progress in the sugarcane business.

In the analysis of the import substitution process, the relative prices do play a role. Furtado's scheme incorporates the terms of trade and the impacts of the exchange rate moves on the internal prices. The domestic industry becomes viable exactly because the exchange rate and the occasional additional protection place it in a competitive condition *vis-à-vis* the international suppliers. In other words, the import substitution process entails an adjustment between the supply and the demand structures commanded by changes in the relative prices. However, the price relations of the internally produced commodities do not appear in Furtado's scheme.

Furtado's contributions to structuralism: Furtado made three major contributions to the structuralist framework. First of all, Furtado endowed structuralism with a long-term historical perspective (1959 to 1970) and showed that, throughout centuries of alternating cycles of growth and contraction each period has generated social and economic dualities (or heterogeneities), as well as a low level of diversification of production.

Secondly, Furtado launched the debate on the difficulty of modern urban sectors to absorb the massive workforce streaming from countryside to city. He may have been the first to suggest that underemployment might become a long-term problem in Latin America and that the duality analysed by Lewis (1954) might persist. He was also one of the first to contend that the increase in productivity in modern sectors can coexist over a long period with low wages, thereby maintaining the poor secular distribution of income in Latin America. Furtado warned that, even if growth were sustained, it would be difficult to absorb the huge workforce available in Latin American societies; indeed, even if growth is sustained over a long period, the problems of unemployment and underemployment, technological heterogeneity, income concentration and social injustice can persist.

Furtado's third major contribution to structuralism appeared some years later, when he deepened his analysis of the relationship between growth and income distribution. He argued that the sectoral composition of investment and technological options were predetermined by income and wealth concentration, giving the modern fraction of the Latin American production structure a capital density similar to that of the developed countries. The technology used can help to maintain full employment and high wages in the latter, but is insufficient in Latin America to absorb the abundant labour supply and raise wages systematically. This model of investment implies maintaining unemployment, low wage levels and income concentration, which in a vicious circle, reinforces an inappropriate investment mix. Here again, he contrasted the periphery to the centre as a way of showing that, unlike what occurs in the countries of the centre, growth patterns in those of the periphery tend to preserve the abundance of labour and prevent improvements in productivity from being reflected in workers' income.

From a historical and structuralist perspective, a pattern of growth is a historically-determined, countryspecific combination of a number of structural elements which are responsible for the dynamic of growth, investment, productivity, employment and wages. The most important of these elements are: (a) the principal investment agents (the State, local and foreign capital); (b) the financial equation for investment (retained profits versus domestic and foreign finance); (c) the composition of production and of foreign trade, together with the associated technological choices; (d) the direction of growth—inward, outward, or both; (e) trends in employment and underemployment; and (f) trends in income and wealth distribution.

These factors, taken in conjunction with the macroeconomic regime and financial relationships with the rest of the world and institutions existing in each country, provide a good road map for an investigation into what is going on today in each Latin American country. On this basis, it may be possible to come up with a map of similarities and differences in the behaviour of individual countries that may help to design development projects for each nation and construct a broad and diversified strategic agenda for the region as a whole.

Concept of economic underdevelopment: It was in attempting to explain the backwardness of Brazil that Furtado hit upon the idea that underdevelopment and development are two interdependent phenomena which appear simultaneously as part of the evolution of industrial capitalism. The theme was elaborated in his 1961 book, where Furtado put forward concepts of economic underdevelopment and development that have been largely accepted in the literature. An underdeveloped structure is one in which full utilization of available capital is not a sufficient condition to complete absorption of the working force at a level of productivity corresponding to the technology prevailing in the dynamic sector of the economy. Underdeveloped economies (as distinct from simply backward ones) are hybrid structures characterized by technological heterogeneity of the various sectors. This comes from the historical fact that the import-substituting industrialisation process in those economies led entrepreneurs to adopt a technology compatible with a cost and price structure similar to that prevailing abroad. Technology becomes, therefore, an independent variable in economies where industrialisation is induced from outside. Whereas industrialisation in underdeveloped economies was determined by demand, the formation process of capitalist European economies in the 18th and 19th centuries was dominated by supply factors, which led Furtado to define economic development as the introduction of new combinations of production factors which increase labour productivity. Underdevelopment is regarded as a permanent feature of the centre periphery system, not as a stage on the road to development. Those ideas originally appeared in an essay written as the first critical comment on Ragnar Nurkse's notion of balanced growth, where Furtado pointed out that the dynamics of demand (internal and external) in underdeveloped economies should be studied in tandem with the process of accumulation. According to Furtado, underdeveloped countries lack incentives to save (because of the consumer habits of higher income groups), not to invest. The accumulation process should be examined from the point of view of changes in the process of generation, utilization and appropriation of the economic surplus, especially as affected by foreign trade. Furtado first developed these ideas in an essay originally written in Portuguese in 1955 (two years before Paul Baran made the concept of surplus a central notion of his own approach to development) and further elaborated it as part of a comment on Paul Rosenstein-Rodan's theory of "big push", made at the International Economic Association conference on economic development held in Rio in 1957, and in his 1967 and 1980 textbooks.

Foreign trade and dependency: One of the main aspects of the industrialisation process of Latin American countries is the persistent tendency towards balance of payment crises and inflationary pressures. Anticipating some elements of the two-gap model later developed by Chenery and Bruno (1962), Furtado showed in a two sector model featuring a modern and a backward sector how balance of payment disequilibrium could constraint the economic growth process under the assumption that the coefficient of imports in the investment sector is larger than in the consumption sector, as is typically the case in underdeveloped countries. Such chronic disequilibrium has structural (not monetary) causes and may lead to the strangulation of economic growth. Another obstacle to growth is that, after the end of the easy phase of the substitution of imported consumer goods, as industrialisation advances to the production of intermediate and capital goods, the rate of profit falls because of the higher capital output ratio accompanied by increasing income concentration and lower aggregate demand. This was an essential element of Furtado's interpretation of the slowdown of economic growth in Latin America in the early 1960s, but, as the Brazilian economy recovered in the late 1960s and early 1970s, Furtado's stagnationist argument was criticised by economists in Brazil.[12] Furtado eventually concluded that, after the two earlier periods of economic growth—determined respectively by comparative advantages and import-substitution—the Latin American economy had entered a new dynamic path in which consumption demand by high income groups could under certain conditions become the leading factor of the system. This led him to explore in detail a theme that had often come up in his writings in the 1950s: *dependency theory*.

Furtado argued that underdeveloped economies feature cultural dependence, that is, consumption patterns are historically transplanted from developed countries by the upper strata of the underdeveloped areas as a result of their appropriation of the economic surplus generated through comparative advantages in foreign trade. Such modernised component of consumption brings dependence into the technological sphere by making it part of the production structure. Dependent structures are also dualistic systems with unlimited supply of labour at a subsistence wage, as first described by Furtado (1950) in his investigation of the dynamics of the labour market in Brazilian economic history. This is close to Arthur Lewis's (1954) classic model, but, in contrast with Lewis, Furtado's conclusion is that industrialisation within a dualist dependent structure reproduces this dualism and does not bring about a homogeneous system with real wages increasing in tandem with the average productivity of the economy. The relationship between the centre and the periphery in the world economy is defined not just by the unequal sharing of the benefits of development and technical progress (as in Prebisch's terms-of-trade argument), but by dependence involving domination and control of access to modern technology by transnational corporations. In Furtado's view, economic growth does not entail economic development in dependent and reflex economies, since it implies an aggravation of both external and internal exploitation, and thereby tends to make underdevelopment even more acute.

Samir Amin

Samir Amin, born in 1931 in Egypt, is a well-known neo-Marxist and one of the most publicly acclaimed African economists. He is a revolutionary economist because he was taught that "surrender to an unjust order is not acceptable." He supports socialism for a reason of "a revulsion against the wretchedness to which local children were condemned". He believes in a world society that must "ensure genuine equality for all human beings in all countries of the world". He is anti-imperialist because he saw "the connection between the wretched social institutions of the Egyptian people and the country's submission to imperialist domination". He has written many books and articles over the last forty years, analyzing capitalism, globalization, and imperialism as well as their institutions. He has concluded that these forms do exploit the majority of people over the globe and create chaos. Accordingly, he rejects the bourgeois economics because of its tendency to legitimize capitalism by formulating models devoid of power and social conflict. Consequently, economic policy based on this science is the "art of managing capitalist expansion".

Dependency and neo-Marxist theories have exerted a substantial impact upon development economics. Western development analysts are becoming more aware of the important role that social groups and their political struggles play in the development process. However, controversy over some key issues of world development rages between the neo-Marxist and dependency theorists and neoclassical economists. A chief element in this controversy is a conviction among dependency theorists that development in backward areas is related through the international market to the developed countries and is blocked because of its integration into the world capitalist system. Moreover, this integration is hypothesized to lead to the underdevelopment of Third world societies. Dependency theorists contend that because of the introduction of capitalism from outside, Third World economies are weak and national business groups in these countries are unable to launch and sustain industrialisation. Furthermore, they argue that relations between developed countries and underdeveloped nations are relations of dependence. Dependence is defined as "a situation in which the economy of certain countries is conditioned by development and expansion of another economy to which the former is subjected".

In this dependency paradigm, an analysis at the world level is conducted in terms of two categories—centre and periphery. Amin contends that a world level analysis is necessary, because the social structure of the periphery is a truncated structure that can only be understood when it is situated as an element in a world social structure. The centre refers to the developed nations (self-centred nations) which, neo-Marxists argue, through colonization and past colonial domination, have transformed the backward areas into peripheral economies (outward-looking economies). The periphery is that portion of economic space which is characterised by backward technology with consequent low levels of renumeration of the labour force and/or by advanced technology with little capacity to absorb the mass of the population into the modern sector. Lenin did not examine the peripheral economies but the concepts produced by his work on imperialism, constitute a perspective for the analysis of the class struggle in the world economy.

Amin's study of the origins of underdevelopment is conducted in terms of two major and interrelated themes. First he analyses the transition from pre-capitalist formation to the social formations of peripheral capitalism. Amin tries to demonstrate that neoclassical economic theory is unable to explain the causes of underdevelopment. Secondly, he presents the general features of peripheral economies and how these structures will lead to stagnation.

(a) *Transition from pre-capitalist formations to the peripheral capitalism*: Neoclassical economic theory of transition from subsistence economies to market economies is presented by Amin as "doubly superficial and inadequate" because the results of such work always suffer from the inadequacies of a 'science' that isolates the economic field from that of sociology. Amin rejects not only the methodology of neoclassical economic theory but also the terminology: "transition from subsistence economies to market economies". He argues that the problem is not one of transition from subsistence economies (i.e., economies without commodity exchanges) to market economies (which would imply that what is meant is a simple commodity economy, or that all market economies are similar), but a problem of transition from economic formations which are non-capitalist (but not necessarily non-commodity) economies to capitalist economic formations. Thus, Amin asserts that the only scientific concept is that of transition from pre-capitalist social formations to the social formations of peripheral capitalism. This analysis of transition is an extension of the theory of the transition from feudalism to capitalism (from the European feudalism to capitalism) developed by Marx.

Amin believes that aggression by the capitalist mode of production, from outside, against these formations (pre-capitalist formations), constitutes the essence of the problem of their transition to formations of peripheral capitalism. Amin contends that pre-capitalist formations are transformed by colonial trade, foreign investment, import-substituting industrialisation and the international division of labour within multinational firms. The instruments are used by the capitalist mode of production to combat the tendency of the rate of profit to fall.

For colonial trade, Amin observes that the colonial authority concerns itself with stimulating monetarisation of the primitive economy, as the conventional expression has it. What is meant here is the use of methods that are purely and simply methods of violence, and therefore methods of primitive accumulation. The obligation to pay taxes in money form is the most widespread device employed.

With foreign investment, the conditions for unequal exchange, i.e., for the reproduction of underdevelopment are gradually assembled. But amin believes that foreign capital is the symptom not the cause of the problem. The real problem is that foreign capital was invested not in local production designed for the local market but in producing for the external market. Moreover, it is impossible for local capital to find investment freely. Amin explains the role of foreign investment as, "The penetration by foreign capital speeds up the formation of native capital. The latter cannot find investment, for the general reason that commercial exchange still goes on, parallel with the penetration of foreign capital, and that local capital, weak because newly formed (and therefore small in amount) is incapable of competing with the advanced industry of the centre. The foreign capital that flows in makes the crisis still more intense."

The development which will result from this influx of foreign capital will become increasingly external to the local economy. Dualism in the crudest form, the juxtaposition of two independent sectors, may sometimes make its appearance. Amin recognises, however, that a steady accumulation of capital which increases total demand, will take place as a result of foreign capital penetration. But he notes that, although accumulation occurs, the rate of development is slower, because craftsmen return to agriculture and the tertiary sector which offers substantial resistance to subsequent development; the specific direction taken by foreign investment; and finally, the limited possibilities for the newly formed native capital to be invested.

Industrialisation by import-substitution is viewed by Amin as the third form of aggression by the capitalist mode of production against subsistence economies because the industrial monopolies endeavoured "to maximise their profit on the whole of their activities, at the centre and in the periphery, and this led them to prefer investing in the periphery in production for export". The industries that were created employed modern techniques "that were too capital-using to absorb the unemployment caused by the aggression of the capitalist mode of production, and so reproduced the conditions of a market in which abundant labour supply kept wages low". It is Amin's opinion that the import substitution model of capital accumulation and development will simply increase the inequality within the system and impoverish the major part of the population. Using the reproduction model of Karl Marx, he explains why this strategy fails to bring about desired changes.

In this reproduction model, the economic system is divided into four sectors—(a) exports, (b) mass consumption, (c) consumption of luxury goods, and (d) capital goods. In a self-centred system there exists a determining relationship between sectors (b) and (d) which characterised the historical development of capitalism at the centre. Whereas, the periphery model of capital accumulation and economic and social development is characterised by a specific interconnection which is expressed by the link between the export sector and luxury goods consumption. Therefore, industrialisation through import substitution will start from the end, i.e., the manufacture of products corresponding to the more advanced stages of development of the centre, in other words, consumer durables.

The international division of labour within the multinational firms according to Amin leads to a new form of inequality between nations. Amin contends that wages at the centre are much higher even if the productivity is the same in the centre and periphery. Therefore, this division of labour deepens unequal exchange by internalising this in the firm. This new inequality has several effects—in the first place, the international division of labour deprives the periphery of any initiative of its own development, and thereby reduces to nil all chances not merely of 'catching up' in terms of consumption but even of aspiration to some sort of autonomy, if only of a cultural and political order. Then, it adds to the transfer of values from the periphery to the centre.

The peripheral formations have different origins and were integrated into the world system in different forms and epochs. But, despite their different origins the peripheral formations tend to converge toward a pattern that is essentially the same. Amin presents the essential features shared by all the peripheral formations beginning with the first one , i.e., the predominance of agrarian and commercial capitalism in the national sector of the economy. As a result of the predominance of agrarian capitalism, a large number of agricultural labours are thrown out of employment, and the proportion of landless peasants increases.

The second features shared by all peripheral formations is the creation of a local bourgeoisie in the wake of dominant foreign capital. Amin contends that in such case the mechanisms of primitive accumulation will function in favour of colonial capital. The third feature is the tendency to increase the role of state enterprises and a bureaucratic form of development. The rise of petty-bourgeois strata (officials, office workers, in some cases old-style craftsmen, small traders, middle peasants, etc.) which assume major importance in local affairs is a manifestation of the phenomenon of state capitalism.

(b) *Development of underdevelopment*: In his endeavours to prove that growth is blocked in the periphery, Amin uses central capitalism as a standard against which the experience of the underdeveloped countries is evaluated. Underdevelopment, however, can be understood only at world level because the underdeveloped economy "is a piece of a single machine, the capitalist world economy". The world level analysis is further justified as capitalism has become a world system, and not just a juxtaposition of 'national capitalism'. The social contradictions characteristic of capitalism are thus on a world scale, that is, the contradiction is not between the bourgeoisie and the proletariat of each country considered in isolation, but between the world bourgeoisie and the world proletariat.

Thus, the periphery is a structure that can only be understood when it is situated as an element in a world social structure. Moreover, that structure is truncated because the leading nucleus, the essential driving force, is at the centre of centres in the monopolies, and the bourgeoisie of the periphery has been formed in the context of a world market created, moved, and dominated by the centre.

The primary objective of Amin's world level analysis is to show that the integration of the periphery into the world capitalist system has led to unequal international specialisation which is manifested in three kinds of distortions in the development of the periphery. The distortions are the deviations from the "standard", "correct", "true", and "pure" capitalism, the central capitalism. The first distortion is the orientation of the periphery toward export activities. This distortion, "the decisive one", is said to result from the superior productivity of the centre in all fields, which compels the periphery to confine itself to the role of complementary supplier of products for the production of which it possesses a natural advantage—exotic agricultural produce and minerals. Therefore, that distortion does not result from inadequacy of home market.

The second distortion is the enlargement of the tertiary sector in the peripheral economies, which neither the evolution of the structure of demand nor that of productivities can explain. Amin explains that at the centre, hypertrophy of the tertiary sector reflects the difficulties in realising surplus value that are inherent in the advanced monopoly phase, whereas in the periphery it is from the beginning a result of the limitations and contradictions characteristic of peripheral development—inadequate industrialisation and increasing unemployment, strengthening of the position of ground rent, etc.

The third distortion, the orientation toward light branches of activity which use modern production techniques, is the source of special problems that dictate development policies in the periphery that are different from those on which the development of the West was based. In fact, we cannot confuse the underdeveloped countries with the now advanced countries as they were at an earlier stage of their development, because underdevelopment is manifested not in level of production per head, but in certain characteristic structural features. These characteristic features are the extreme unevenness in the distribution of productivities in the peripheral economies and in the system of prices transmitted to them from the centre; the disarticulation due to the adjustment of the peripheral economies to the need of the centre; and the economic domination of the centre which is expressed in the forms of international specialisation and in the dependence of the structures whereby growth in the periphery is financed.

Amin points out that the development of peripheral capitalism is neither regular nor cumulative. On the contrary, it is jerky and made up of phases of extremely rapid economic growth followed by sudden blockages and failures to take-off. These blockages are manifested in a double crisis of external payments and public finances, which is a chronic phenomenon in the history of the Third World.

Transforming the Agricultural Sector

Unlike W. Arthur Lewis, Amin does not believe that growth in the capitalist (industrial) sector would somehow drag the non-capitalist (agriculture) sector along the path of growth and development. Neither does he contend like Mellor, that increases in technology and appropriate government pricing policy for food grain, would solve unemployment and food problems in the poverty-stricken areas of the globe. Instead Amin considers a coordinated expansion on the agricultural and industrial fronts, as the only path toward development.

Amin's version of the "Walk on Two Legs" theory is organised around three major agricultural revolutions—(a) the expansion of the use of draft animals, (b) building up a machinery industry to produce investment goods, and (c) change fiscal policy.

Amin contends that the transformation of the traditional agriculture requires first of all a widespread adoption of animal traction which implies the replacement of the present extensive farming methods to more intensive methods which mixed farming will offer. Amin expects the productivity and returns from crop production to increase as a result of shifting from hand cultivation to animal traction. In fact he argues that agricultural productivity will increase three to four times as a result of animal traction. However, the success of this program calls for the mass mobilization of the rural people to create an awareness of animal traction technology.

This effort must be accompanied by a real effort at diversification of crops, the development of industrially important crops, high value plantation crops, and improvement of livestock and increased quality control. Amin predicted that the animal draft revolution would permit the construction of a solid agricultural base, on which large scale industry will rest. The second agricultural revolution consists of large investments in industrial plants and facilities that produce investment goods needed by industry and agriculture. Amin rejected the creation of import-substitution industries, because these industries will require capital and scarce resources (skilled labour), and they will increase inequility, and unemployment and thereby impoverish the major portion of the population. The third agriculture revolution presented by Amin relates to the reform of the fiscal system in order to mobilise local resources for development. The financing of animal traction and large-scale industry requires curtailing consumption of the high income groups in order to channel savings into productive investments. The state cannot rely on foreign aid, it must be strong enough to extract surplus purchasing power. Because, if investment is left to private firms, the needed structural change will never occur.

In 1975, Amin asserted that the underdeveloped nations did not need the advanced technologies of the West because it was the origin of their underdevelopment and the flourishing exploitation of the peripheral period. Hence, progress must pass through the stage of developing an independent technology. Otherwise, developing countries will have to wait until discoveries have been worked out in and for the developed world to be asked to pay in gold for "dross" which does not cover their needs. However, in 1970, Amin was saying that the problem of the choice of techniques is largely an artificial one which provides food for discussion in university circles, however there are really no efficient labour-intensive techniques.

The third revolution is the reform of the fiscal policy. Indeed, the majority of high income receivers in underdeveloped countries continue to maintain the feudal style of life and investment in luxury goods leaving little margin for savings. Nevertheless, it is possible that the members of the "strong government" that Amin recommends will transform themselves into a bureaucratic bourgeoisie that will use taxpayers' money for its own private purposes. Moreover, it is not evident that the government will be capable of engaging in economic activities more efficiently than the private businessman.

The Development Road for the Third World

Indeed, Amin's theory is an excellent source to reorient Marx's and Luxemburg's theories of accumulation. Amin's attempt provides a clear understanding of the process of development and underdevelopment within the global system in which capital accumulation prevents (or blocks) the peripheries from taking the development road necessary to eradicate underdevelopment. This proposition is also inconsistent with Marx's and Luxemburg's analysis arguing that capital penetration in pre-capitalist areas would develop these underdeveloped areas. Sica rightly points out, "Certainly it is clear that competent discussions and studies of the world economy must begin with [Amin's] Unequal Development." This statement refutes Schiffer's argument that Amin's theory does not fit reality, because capitalist penetration in the peripheries does hinder the development process, as the American occupation has done in Iraq.

The third stage (1880-present) is called monopoly capitalism (or imperialism), which is the most important stage for Amin's analysis, characterised by unequal exchange—the exchange of products whose prices of production, in the Marxist sense, are unequal—between the centre and periphery. Other characteristics of this period were stagnation, mobility of capital on a world scale, and the integration of the world market. For Amin, the export of capital to the periphery, where rates of exploitation were higher due to low wage-costs, prevented the fall in the rate of profit during the monopoly period by the mechanism of unequal exchange. Marx (1967) does suggest that one of the counteracting elements for the falling rate of profit is to move production operations to the underdeveloped area of the world because labour cost is very low and the rate of exploitation is very high. In fact, Amin argues that global capitalism is driven by the globalized law of value, which generates distortion by virtue of the fact that workers in the peripheral countries are paid at a lower rate than equally productive workers in the metropolitan centres. This is an unequal exchange because one hour of productive work in the advanced countries is exchanged for many hours of productive work in the Third World.

It is indeed unequal exchange, which explains the basic reason behind outsourcing of productive tasks to foreign countries. It also explains why the globalised law of value does not integrate labour market to capital and commodity markets through free international movement.

Amin criticises the non-capitalist road for development, because it is actually a form of capitalist development, which is integrated into new globalization. The failure of agricultural development in the peripheries is manifested in increasing food dependency. Without a genuine delinking of internal relative prices from those of world market, the rewards for peasant labour remained lower than those for urban labour. Industrialisation of the peripheries was dependent on external outmoded technology, and was not delinked. This non-capitalist development, Amin contends, brought increasing vulnerability through food shortages, technological dependency, and foreign debt.

Amin rejects the monopoly capitalist road of converting peasant-based subsistence agriculture to agribusiness, because it reintegrates the periphery into the global system and abandons delinking. This situation reinforces peripherization according to Amin and creates polarization, inequality, and underdevelopment. Amin demonstrates clearly that many Third World countries in Africa and elsewhere, which he actually calls the Fourth World, have been in economic stagnation for a long period of time and have not been able to establish genuine development, because multinational corporations have exploited and looted their economic surpluses. Amin contends that productivity differential is about 2000 to 1 between advanced and non-advanced capitalist agriculture. This reduces the relative prices of food to industrial prices to one fifth of what they were fifty years ago. This is a basic result of unequal development—industrial and agricultural societies in the centre and the Third World that could not replicate the pattern of the advanced countries. The monopoly capitalist (or imperialist) model of development serves the financiers and has disintegrated the social and economic fabric of the peripheries, an outcome that has created many political and ethnic problems.

Amin rejects the old Soviet road of creating cooperatives controlled and exploited by the state, and delinking deployed for this purpose produced a Soviet bourgeoisie. One should note that Amin did not consider the Soviet society as socialist. Socialism for him "means more than the abolition of private property... [it] has a positive meaning of alternative labour relations other than those defining wage status, alternative social relations allowing society as a whole...to control its social future. This in turn means a democracy far more advanced than the best bourgeois democracy."[13] Sovietism had no such a system. Nor was the Soviet system a capitalist system although the ruling class was a bourgeoisie. Capitalism for Amin means the dispersal of the property of capital on the basis of competition, whereas the USSR had state centralisation of property. Amin calls it "the Soviet mode of production".

Having rejected these existing roads, Amin formulates his own road based on a vision of a region delinked, modernised, autocentric, embarked on agricultural development, and in the early stages of successful industrialisation, based on an income distribution that wiped out the intolerable inequalities inherited from peripheral capitalism. This vision is based on "drawing on the inspiration of the Chinese communes", and builds around peasant revolution in the Third World. It implied, therefore, industrialisation at the service of agricultural development, which left behind the spurious bourgeois debate—import substitution or export industries. This vision can be implemented under the leadership of the working people. It follows that Amin is not committed to the national bourgeoisie of the peripheral countries, as Gerstein thinks. Nor can Amin's vision be considered as technical prescriptions that would presumably be useful to the national bourgeoisie in its struggle for independent development, as Gerstein incorrectly argues.

Amin's vision reflects world class struggle, pointing toward rebuilding of popular democratic societies based on the foundations of an internationalism of peoples, a proposition refuting Gerstein's argument that Amin "does not emphasize the class struggle". This popular transition on a global scale begins with the liberation of the periphery and the adoption of a local model of accumulation. Amin points out that a development that is not merely development of underdevelopment will therefore be national, popular-democratic, and socialist. And in Dunn's words, "The socialist mode of production is not possible on a national scale, but can only come about through the transformation of the world system as a whole."

EXPLOITATION

A common conception of exploitation is that it consists in the "unfair use" of other human beings. In Alan Wertheimer's words, then, "An exploitative transaction is one in which *A* takes unfair advantage of *B*". While Wertheimer acknowledges that exploitation can be employed in a nonmoral sense or in a nonpejorative sense, he works with what he calls a "moralised concept" of exploitation according to which exploitation "is, by definition, wrong because unfair". He points to two vital questions concerning exploitation in its various forms— its "moral weight", that is, how wrong it is, and its "moral force", that is, what its moral "upshots" are for those involved and for society as a whole.

For more than a century, one of the most popular economic doctrines in the world has been the exploitation theory. According to this theory, capitalism is a system of virtual slavery, serving the narrow interests of a comparative handful of businessmen and capitalists, who, driven by insatiable greed and power lust, exist as parasites upon the labour of the masses. Exploitation in itself denotes no more than utilisation or beneficial use. It is a form of social power (of effective capacity in human relations) which involves the capacity of party *A* (the exploiter) (i) to benefit from some characteristic of party *B* (the exploited), and (ii) to do so at party *B's* expense. There are three features of exploitation:

(a) *The characteristics of B from which A might benefit*: It include those 'positives' which might be exploited, such as productivity, talent, and attractiveness, as well as a number of 'negatives' which might be similarly exploited, such as poverty, physical or psychological dependence, and ignorance. Thus, in positive terms, the employer might exploit a productive employee, while, in negative terms, the rich might exploit the desperately poor.

(b) *The benefits to A*: The benefit in question is usually material, though it is conceivable in other terms—psychological, spiritual, and so on. Hence, the psychologically or spiritually "strong" might exploit the psychologically or spiritually "weak". In general terms, the exploiter benefits in the way of power, whether this power consists in possessions and wealth or psychological or spiritual dominance. Indeed, it is arguable that exploitation is premised on unequal relations of power: that to exploit, one must occupy a position of greater relative power in the first place (however localised this power might be). If this is so, inequality of power might generate greater inequality of power. Accordingly, we observe that money begets money, for instance.

(c) *The losses to B*: What *A* gains in an exploitative relationship represents a loss of some kind to *B*. (Were *B* to lose nothing, it would be senseless to claim that *B* was being exploited.) We should consider this loss in both material and non-material terms. Two cases spring to mind—the loss of "the full fruit of one's labour", and the loss of one's "dignity".

In material production, understood as the production of 'wealth' in accordance with (real or apparent) 'human needs', *A* might benefit (say, make a profit) through the labour of *B*. In such a situation, *B* might be held to lose either the product of his labour or the full value of his labour (receiving either a subsistence or more substantial wage in return). As such, *B* would be exploited by *A*. This remains the case even when we maintain that *B* receives a "fair day's wages for a fair day's work". The difference here would merely be that the degree of exploitation is smaller and perhaps more obviously 'fair' or justifiable. Moreover, the exploitative relation between *A* and *B* holds whether the mode of production is capitalist or communist (leaving slave, feudal, and other economies aside). The difference between capitalist and communist exploitation is that *B's* loss is private gain ('profit' in the ordinary sense) in the former case and public gain (for the 'common weal') in the latter.

Non-material or cultural aspects of exploitation are more difficult to analyse than material or economic aspects. Moreover, the attempt to prioritize one aspect over the other (usually the latter over the former, in accordance with the 'materialist conception of history', for instance) is fraught with difficulties. But, what *B* appears to lose when non-materially exploited is his or her 'dignity', a loss that is entailed by a process of 'humiliation'. (What *A* appears to gain from *B's* loss is simply power of some kind. For example, *B's* humiliation might lend *A* a sense of superiority or of prowess.) Of course, labour might be humiliating in itself, even when it is well rewarded in material terms.

In evaluating exploitative practices and institutions, at least three kinds of moral argument can be called upon. The first kind leads to the conclusion that exploitation is unjustifiable. The second kind indicates that certain forms of exploitation are justifiable. And the third kind can lead in both directions. The three kinds of argument are:

(a) *Deontological*: It is always wrong to treat human beings (or rational agents) as means to an end, or, specifically here, as instruments of power or profit. The advantageous use of *B* by *A* is wrong, irrespective of the consequences, that is, the losses that *B* may incur. While this argument has some appeal—especially with respect to issues of dignity and the more extreme cases of exploitation (such as slavery)—it may be held to preclude too much in the way of real human practice. It seems to preclude all forms of employment (other than self-employment) and even any kind of division of labour. Every division of labour may be said to be exploitative—to benefit some at the expense of others, even if such a situation is mutually beneficial. Indeed, this would seem to point to an instance of mutual exploitation. Thus, in a case where parties *A* and *B* cooperate and apply their respective skills in the pursuit of a goal, A may be said to exploit a positive characteristic of *B* while *B* simultaneously exploits another (or conceivably the same) positive characteristic of *A*. What *A* and *B* gain in this situation may be a superior product of labour, a lessening of the effort required to produce it, and greater leisure time. What they lose is arguably the full fruit of their own individual labour.

(b) *Voluntaristic*: Voluntaristic arguments concerning exploitation maintain that it is justifiable if and only if it is consented to (again, irrespective of the consequences or losses incurred). That is to say, if one freely and knowingly chooses to enter into an exploitative relationship, then that relationship is legitimate. We argued, above, that coercion is not a necessary element of exploitation and that exploitative relationships could, in principle, be voluntarily entered into. Thus, on voluntaristic terms, exploitation is justifiable in some instances. However, it is clear that not all exploitation is consented to—the slave has no choice, the child may not know any better, and so on.

(c) *Consequentialist*: We might evaluate exploitation solely with reference to its consequences, some of which (like 'social utility') might be held to be justifying. Thus, irrespective of issues of 'dignity' and consent, exploitation might or might not be justified. There are, of course, problems with this line of reasoning. Firstly, quite how we assess these matters (making, for example, 'interpersonal comparisons of utility') is questionable. And, secondly, this approach would seem to conflict with certain cherished moral intuitions (about the rights of individuals, for instance). Are we really to accept the sacrifice of the individual (say, the exploitation of the worker) to social well-being (expressed, say, in terms of 'economic growth')? And if we are not, according to the utilitarian, why not? These are complex issues that have bedevilled utilitarians, at least, for many years.

The Conceptual Framework

There are three aspects of classical economics which contribute to the exploitation theory. The two best known are—the labour theory of value and the iron law of wages. And the third is the conceptual framework within which the exploitation theory is advanced. Under this framework, wages are the original and primary form of income, from which profits and all other non-wage incomes emerge as a deduction with the coming of capitalism and capitalists. The framework easily leads to the assertion of the wage earner's right to the whole produce or to its full value. It itself is based on the further belief that all income which is due to the performance of labour is wages and that all who work are wage earners. According to Adam Smith, the produce of labour constitutes the natural recompense or wages of labour. In that original state of things, which precedes both the appropriation of land and the accumulation of stock, the whole produce of labour belongs to the labourer. He has neither landlord nor master to share with him. But, this original state of things, in which the labourer enjoyed the whole produce of his own labour, could not last beyond the first introduction of the appropriation of land and the accumulation of stock. It was at an end, therefore, long before the most considerable improvements were made in the productive powers of labour, and it would be to no purpose to trace further what might have been its effects upon the recompense or wages of labour.

When land becomes private property, the landlord demands a share of almost all the produce which the labourer can either raise or collect from it. His rent makes the first deduction from the produce of the labour which is employed upon the land. It seldom happens that the person who tills the ground has the wherewithal to maintain himself till he reaps the harvest. His maintenance is generally advanced to him from the stock of a master, the farmer who employs him and who would have no interest to employ him, unless he was to share in the produce of his labour, or unless his stock was to be replaced to him with a profit. This profit makes a second deduction from the produce of the labour which is employed upon land. The produce of almost all other labour is liable to the like deduction of profit. In all arts and manufactures the greater part of the workmen stand in need of a master to advance them the materials of their work, and their wages and maintenance till it be completed. He shares in the produce of their labour, or in the value which it adds to the materials on which it is bestowed; and in this share consists his profit.[14] Here Smith clearly advances the primacy of wages doctrine, i.e., the doctrine that in a pre-capitalist economy—the early and rude state of society—in which workers simply produce and sell commodities and do not buy in order to sell, the incomes the workers receive are wages. According to Smith wages are the original income. All income in the pre-capitalist society is supposed to be wages, and no income is supposed to be profit because workers are the only recipients of income. At the same time, Smith advances the corollary doctrine that profit emerges only with the coming of capitalism and is a deduction from what is naturally and, by implication, rightfully wages.

In a pre-capitalist economy, production, says Marx, is characterised by the sequence $C - M - C'$. In this state of affairs, a worker produces a commodity C, sells it for money M, and then buys other commodities C'. In this state of affairs, there is no exploitation, for there are no profits, no "surplus value"; all income is, presumably, wages. Surplus value, profit, emerges only with the development of capitalism, according to Marx. Here the sequence $M - C - M'$ applies. Under this sequence, the capitalist expends a sum of money M in buying materials and machinery and in paying wages. A commodity C is produced, which is then sold for a larger sum of money, M', than was expended in producing it. The difference between the money the capitalist expends and the money he receives for the product is his profit or surplus value.[15]

Thus, according to Smith and Marx, profits come into existence only with capitalism, and are a deduction from what naturally and rightfully belongs to the wage earners. This is not yet the exploitation theory itself, only the conceptual framework of the exploitation theory. It is a framework broad enough to include Marx, the leading proponent of the exploitation theory, and Böhm-Bawerk, its leading critic. Within this framework, Marx applies the *labour theory of value* and the *iron law of wages*, and arrives at the exploitation theory. Within this same framework, Böhm-Bawerk applies the *discounting approach*, and arrives at a critique of the exploitation theory.[16]

Böhm-Bawerk's explanation is that present goods are more valuable than future goods, and that the wage earner is justly treated in being given a smaller sum of present money than his future product will be worth. Marx's explanation is that the capitalist arbitrarily pays the wage earner a wage corresponding to the number of hours required to produce the wage earner's necessities and sells the wage earner's product at a price corresponding to the larger number of hours for which the wage earner works.

In the pre-capitalist economy, if such an economy ever in fact existed, all income recipients in the process of production are workers. But the incomes of those workers are not wages. They are, in fact, profits. Indeed, all income earned in producing products for sale in the pre-capitalist economy is profit or "surplus value"; no income earned in producing products for sale in such an economy is wages. For what the workers of a pre-capitalist economy receive are receipts from the sale of products. But they have no money costs of production to deduct from those sales receipts, for they have not acted as capitalists. They have not bought anything for the purpose of making possible their sales receipts, and therefore they have no money costs. The difference between receipts from the sale of products and zero money costs of production is the full magnitude of the sales receipts.

Thus, in the pre-capitalist economy, only workers receive incomes and there is no money capital. But all the incomes which the workers receive are profits, and none are wages. In the sequence $C - M - C'$, everything is surplus value. In the sequence $M - C - M'$, a smaller proportion of the incomes is surplus value—in degree that M' is large relative to M. The same conclusion, that in the pre-capitalist economy all income is profit, and no income is wages, can be arrived at by way of Ricardo's badly misunderstood proposition that "profits rise as wages fall and fall as wages rise". The wages paid in production, according to Ricardo, are paid by capitalists, not by consumers. If, as in the pre-capitalist economy, there are no capitalists, then there are no wages paid in production, and if there are no wages paid in production, the full income earned must be profits. Smith and Marx are wrong. Wages are not the primary form of income in production. Profits are. In order for wages to exist in production, it is first necessary that there be capitalists. The emergence of capitalists does not bring into existence the phenomenon of profit. Profit exists prior to their emergence. The emergence of capitalists brings into existence the phenomena of wages and money costs of production. Accordingly, the profits which exist in a capitalist society are not a deduction from what was originally wages. On the contrary, the wages and the other money costs are a deduction from sales receipts—from what was originally all profit. The effect of capitalism is to create wages and to reduce profits relative to sales receipts. The more economically capitalistic the economy, the more the buying in order to sell relative to the sales receipts, the higher are wages and the lower are profits relative to sales receipts.

Thus, capitalists do not impoverish wage earners, but make it possible for people to be wage earners. For they are responsible not for the phenomenon of profits, but for the phenomenon of wages. They are responsible for the very existence of wages in the production of products for sale. Without capitalists, the only way in which one could survive would be by means of producing and selling one's own products, namely, as a profit earner. But to produce and sell one's own products, one would have to own one's own land, and produce or have inherited one's own tools and materials. Relatively few people could survive in this way. The existence of capitalists makes it possible for people to live by selling their labour rather than attempting to sell the products of their labour. Thus, between wage earners and capitalists there is in fact the closest possible harmony of interests, for capitalists create wages and the ability of people to survive and prosper as wage earners. And if wage earners want a larger relative share for wages and a smaller relative share for profits, they should want a higher economic degree of capitalism—they should want more and bigger capitalists.

Socialism and Exploitation

As a final irony it turns out not only that capitalism is not a system of the exploitation of labour, but that the actual system of the exploitation of labour is socialism. Socialism establishes the very kind of exploitation for the alleged existence of which people seek to overthrow capitalism. The socialist state holds a universal monopoly on employment and production. Its citizens are economically powerless in their capacity both as workers and as consumers. No economic factor compels the socialist state to take account of their wishes. From an economic point of view, the rulers of the socialist state need be concerned with the values of the citizens only insofar as it needs them to have the health and strength required to work.

The leading moral-political principle of the socialist state is that the citizen is not an end in himself, as he is acknowledged to be under capitalism, but is a means to the ends of society. Since society does not inhabit any known mountain top, and cannot be communicated with in any direct way, its ends can be made known only through the rulers of the socialist state. Thus, the principle that the individual is the means to the ends of society necessarily means, in practice, that he is the means to the ends of society as divined, interpreted, and determined by the rulers of the socialist state. And what this means is that he is the means to the ends of the rulers. A more servile arrangement can hardly be imagined.

The position of the individual under socialism is that he must spend his life in toil for the ends of the rulers, who have no reason voluntarily to supply him with anything more than minimum physical subsistence. They will provide more (assuming they have the ability to do so) only if it is necessary to prevent riots or revolution or as a means of providing special incentives for the achievement of their own values, such as, above all, the power and prestige of the regime. Thus, they will provide a relatively high standard of living for rocket scientists, secret police agents, and such intellectuals and athletes whose accomplishments help to reflect glory on the regime. The average citizen, however, is fortunate if they provide him with subsistence. He is fortunate, because, the economic discoordination and chaos of socialism is so great that in the absence of an outside capitalist world to turn to for aid, socialism would lead to the destruction of the division of labour and hence to a reversion to the primitive economic conditions of feudalism. To borrow some of the platitudes of Marxism and use them truthfully for once, socialism "cannot even maintain its slaves in their slavery"; left to its own devices, it causes the average worker "to sink deeper and deeper into poverty", until mass depopulation occurs.

Marxian Exploitation Theory

One of the most important theories to make the rounds in 20th century world politics was the 'exploitation theory' proposed by the German Political theorist Karl Marx. Leftists all over the world have found it to their political convenience to blindly accept this theory, and to convince themselves of the morality of the workers' hours of toil.

Marx shouted that the source of the profits gained by the Capitalists is the exploitation of labour's productive effort. He accused scornfully, the capitalists of looting the workers of their rightful share of the returns of their productive labour. So according to Marx, profits are nothing but the 'surplus value' that the capitalist withholds from the labourer.

Marx, like other Classical economists, recognised the two kinds of values of any commodity—use value and exchange value. Use value being the personal utility that the commodity used as a consumer good yields to the consumer; while exchange value being the value that the commodity commands in a trade exchange in the market. He believed that if two commodities were exchanged for each other, they had something in common and propounded that to be the amount of labour hours required to produce the commodities. Thus, he proposed that people exchange commodities which had equal number of labour hours spent in producing them.

Marx in his preconceived mindset to arrive at an 'objective' theory of value, tried to find similarities in the properties of commodities that traded at the same exchange value at some particular point of time. He finally concluded that commodities with the same exchange value had the same amount (hours) of labour involved in producing them, and hence exchanged on equal terms. Thus was born Marx's version of the Labour Theory of Value.

According to Marx, capitalists are able to make profits only by exploiting their workers. Profits are made by the capitalist's appropriation of the surplus value created by the labour of his workers. In other words, profits are made by the workers producing for their capitalist employers sums of value greater than they are paid in wages. That sum of value which the workers receive in wages they pay back to the capitalist by working for the period of necessary labour. The sums of value that are created by workers during the period of surplus labour represent for the capitalist pure gain. It is a return for which they make no equivalent outlay. Marx called the rate of surplus value, therefore, 'an exact expression for the degree of exploitation of labour-power by capital, or of the worker by the capitalist'.

There are two schools of opinion on the question of what Marx meant by the term exploitation. Both schools agree that exploitation, for Marx, involves non-reciprocal benefit, i.e., one person benefits another without the second benefiting the first in return. Further, both schools agree that non-reciprocal benefit is not a sufficient condition of exploitation for Marx. This is because both schools agree that Marx recognises there to be cases of non-exploitative, non-reciprocal benefit of one party by another. The paradigm case of such non-exploitative non-reciprocal benefit is the deductions to earnings of the able-bodied that are to be made in socialism for provision of welfare for the disabled. As a result of these deductions, the disabled are benefited by the able-bodied without benefiting the able-bodied in return. Yet such welfare deductions to earnings are not regarded by Marx as instances of the disabled exploiting the able-bodied. Granted that such welfare provision will be present in socialism and that welfare provisions involves the able-bodied benefiting the disabled, it follows that non-reciprocal benefit is not a sufficient condition of exploitation for Marx.

According to the interpretation of one school, which we will call the justice interpretation, as well as there being non-reciprocal benefit, it must be unjust that the benefited party gain their benefit without reciprocating the benefit. In other words, proponents of the justice interpretation advance the following understanding of exploitation: *A* exploits *B* if and only if—(i) *B* benefits *A* in some way without *A* benefiting *B* in return, and (ii) *A's* failure to benefit *B* in return for *B's* benefiting *A* is unjust.

According to proponents of the justice interpretation, Marx believed that capitalism involves exploitation because he believed it was unjust that the capitalist appropriates the surplus value created by the worker without making a reciprocal return to the worker. On this view, Marx believed that a person was morally entitled to the full product of his labour, minus certain deductions that are necessary for replenishing and expanding means of production and for providing public goods and welfare for the disabled. Workers in socialism will receive such a product of their labour. In capitalism, workers receive less than this. Some surplus value that the worker produces which rightly ought to go to the worker goes to the capitalist. On this view, the deductions made from the product of the labour of the able-bodied for the provision of welfare for the disabled are not instances of exploitation because such deductions are not unjust. The disabled are morally entitled to them.

The other school denies that injustice is part of or even implied by exploitation as Marx understands it. According to this interpretation, which we will call the coercion interpretation, what makes non-reciprocal benefit exploitation is that the unreciprocated benefit is forced from the benefactors by the beneficiaries.[17]

The coercion interpretation of exploitation gives us the following understanding of it: *A* exploits *B* if and only if—(i) *B* benefits *A* in some way without *A* benefiting *B* in return, and (ii) *A* forces *B* to benefit *A*. According to the coercion interpretation, the provision of welfare for the disabled by deductions from the product of the labour of the able-bodied is not exploitation because it is not the case that the disabled force the able-bodied to make such provision. Such contributions are either made voluntarily or, if forced, are forced by the state. In the case of capitalism, the provision of surplus value for the capitalist is a non-reciprocal benefit forced from the worker by the capitalist. It is, therefore, a case of exploitation. The worker in capitalism is not forced to engage in surplus labour in the same way that slaves and serfs were. In the case of the latter it was threat of punishment if they refused. Rather, what forces the wage-labourer in capitalism to engage in surplus labour is the fact that the capitalist owns the means of production. Lacking means of production of their own, the wage-labourers are forced to accept the wage offers of the capitalists to procure means of subsistence, and the wage contracts to which they are forced to agree bind them to perform surplus labour.

According to the coercion interpretation of exploitation, not only is injustice not part of the notion of exploitation, it is not implied by it. The foremost proponent of this interpretation, Allen Wood, claims that Marx did not regard exploitation as unjust. Wood's coercion interpretation is based upon a number of remarks of Marx's which are *prima facie* difficult to reconcile with the view that he took exploitation to be unjust. Wood takes these remarks to establish conclusively that Marx regards capitalist exploitation to be just. However, according to Wood, the fact that exploitation is just, for Marx, does not constitute any defence of it. According to Wood, justice, for Marx, is simply whatever conforms to and harmonises with the prevailing mode of production. That an act or institution is just, therefore, does not justify or commend the act or institution in any way.

Such an account of Marx's view of morality as Wood offers squares with Marx's assertion that talk of 'fair distribution' by socialists constitute 'obsolete verbal rubbish'. It also squares with the fact that Marx nowhere says that capitalist exploitation is unjust, nor even says that socialism and communism will establish justice. Despite the impressive *prima facie* case in support of the coercion interpretation of exploitation made out by Wood, the case is by no means conclusive. There is, in fact, considerable reason for preferring the justice interpretation to it. First, as Cohen has pointed out, coercion seems to be neither a necessary condition, nor—together with non-reciprocal benefit—a sufficient condition, of exploitation as Marx understands the term. That coercion is not a necessary condition of exploitation, for Marx, becomes evident from the following case. Imagine a rich capitalist *B* who has no need to work but who—for a bet or for amusement—finds employment as a wage-labourer with capitalist *A*. In this case, *A* would obtain surplus value through *B's* labour and *B* would accordingly be exploited by *A*. Yet, in the case as presented, *B* is not forced to work as therefore is not forced to provide surplus value for *A*. Accordingly, since he is exploited but not coerced, it follows that coercion is not a necessary condition of exploitation. As Cohen has pointed out, coercion seems also not to be, together with non-reciprocal benefit, a sufficient condition of exploitation. Cohen asks us to imagine involuntarily unemployed adults with many dependants who threaten violence in the streets unless welfare payments are made to them by those able to provide them. On Wood's definition, these people would be exploiters. Yet it is difficult to believe that would have been Marx's view of them. Accordingly, coercion and non-reciprocal benefit are not jointly a sufficient condition of exploitation. The role that coercion plays in capitalist exploitation is that the workers' lack of means of production forces them to suffer exploitation. So, coercion is a cause of exploitation but is not itself part of what exploitation consists in.

A second reason for preferring the justice interpretation of exploitation to the coercion interpretation is that Marx makes many assertions which are otherwise difficult to understand if he did not think exploitation to be a form of injustice. Thus, for instance, Marx talks of 'the theft of alien labour-time on which the present wealth is based'. He also speaks of 'the learned dispute between the industrial capitalist and the wealthy landowning idler as to how the booty pumped out of the workers may most advantageously be divided for the purposes of accumulation'.

Finally, it is possible to reconcile the justice interpretation of exploitation with Marx's assertion that talk of 'just distribution' is obsolete verbal rubbish. Allen Buchanan has argued that Marx thought capitalism unjust but did not wish to emphasise its injustice because he thought that the very need for justice was a shortcoming in society. A virtue of communism would be that it would dispense with the need for justice. Justice is necessary only where there is scarcity and an opposition of interests between members of society. In full communism, scarcity will have been abolished on Marx's view and there will be complete identification between people. The circumstances giving rise to the need for justice will thus no longer obtain. This view leads to a very interesting interpretation of Marx.

It is Buchanan's view that Marx refrained from calling capitalism unjust (despite his speaking of the appropriation of surplus value as theft) because he believed that communism would be a society 'beyond justice'. The principle "From each according to his abilities, to each according to his need" is not, says Buchanan, a communist principle of distributive justice. Rather it is a description of how things will in fact be in communism. Thus, Marx refrained from calling the capitalist's exploitation unjust, because this would have obscured the fact that what Marx thought special about communism was not that it would be a just society, but that it would dispense with the need for justice by abolishing the circumstances that give rise to it.[18]

What is wrong with Marx theory of exploitation, is that he does not understand the phenomenon of time preference as universal category of human action.[19] That labour does not receive his "full worth" has nothing to do with exploitation but merely reflects the fact that it is impossible for man to exchange future goods against present ones except at a discount. Unlike the case of slave and slave master, where the latter benefits at the expense of the former, the relationship between the free labourer and the capitalist is a mutually beneficial one. The labourer enters the agreement because, given his time preference, he prefers a smaller amount of present goods over a larger future one; and the capitalist enters it because, given his time preference, he has a reverse preference order and ranks a larger future amount of goods more highly than a smaller present one. Their interests are not antagonistic but harmonious. Without the capitalist's expectation of an interest return, the labourer would be worse off because he would have to wait longer than he wishes to wait; and without the labour's preference for present goods the capitalist would be worse off because he would have to resort to less roundabout and less efficient production methods than those he desires to adopt. Nor can the capitalist wage system be regarded as an impediment to the further development of the forces of production, as Marx claims. If the labours were not permitted to sell their labour services and the capitalist to buy them, output would not be higher but lower because production would have to take place with relatively reduced levels of capital accumulation.

Austrian Exploitation Theory

A second-generation Austrian economist, Eugen von Böhm-Bawerk refuted the Marxian theory that the employer-employee relationship is intrinsically exploitative. He expressed his exploitation theory in his 1889 masterpiece, *The Positive Theory of Capital and its Critics*.

In focusing on the exploitation question, Böhm-Bawerk took the legitimacy of the "distribution" of the means of production for granted, and he rejected the labour theory of value, or of price formation. According to him, historically governments arranged for the few to control the means of the production at the expense of the many, forcing them onto the labour market. To the extent that is true, the wage system is exploitative, but the culprit is the State, not the market.

Böhm-Bawerk responded to the exploitation theorists that the difference between what a worker is paid and the market price of his product can be explained without resort to exploitation theory. One component of the employer's profit is interest on the money he advances workers as wages while the product is being readied for sale. Making and marketing products take time. Typically, Böhm-Bawerk said, workers cannot afford to wait until the product is sold before they are paid. They want a check every week. But how can they be paid before their products have been sold? Their employers pay them out of money accumulated previously. Thus, wages are in effect a loan, which like all loans is repaid with interest. This is so because of time preference. We value present goods more highly than future goods, meaning present goods are discounted from their future value.

Böhm-Bawerk was writing pure theory, as if he were saying, "In a free market here is what would happen." He was not implying that the theory would describe a particular time and place where the market was less than free "The essence of an institution is one thing, and the circumstances which may accidentally accompany it in its practical working out are another", he wrote. In fact, Böhm-Bawerk noted, exploitation can occur when competition among employers is suppressed, raising the employer's rate of interest to a level higher than it would have been under free competition and thus lowering wages. That, he said, was usury. He writes, "It is undeniable that, in this exchange of present commodities against future, the circumstances are of such a nature as to threaten the poor with exploitation of monopolists."

Böhm-Bawerk was merely applying the more general exploitation theory held by free-market thinkers at least back to Adam Smith—monopolies and oligopolies (suppressed competition) harm consumers and workers through higher prices and lower wages. For Smith monopoly was essentially the result of government privilege. This largely has been the view of later Austrians, also. (Mises allowed for the theoretical possibility of a resource monopoly without government privilege.) However, Böhm-Bawerk did not explicitly attribute monopolistic exploitation to the State in this discussion. He wrote, "something will suspend the capitalists' competition, and then those unfortunates, whom fate has thrown on a local market ruled by monopoly, are delivered over to the discretion of the adversary. Hence, the low wages forcibly exploited from the workers—sometimes the workers of individual factories, sometimes of individual branches of production, sometimes—though happily not often, and only under peculiarly unfavourable circumstances of whole nations."

Böhm-Bawerk doesn't say what that "something" might be. May be he means private collusion; may be he means government protection from competition. He gives only this clue, "Like every other human institution, interest is exposed to the danger of exaggeration, degeneration, abuse; and, perhaps, to a greater extent than most institutions." He cautions that "what we might stigmatise as 'usury' does not consist in the obtaining of a gain out of the loan, or out of the buying of labour, but in the immoderate extent of that gain. Some gain or profit on capital there would be if there were no compulsion on the poor, and no monopolising of property. It is only the height of this gain where, in particular cases, it reaches an excess, that is open to criticism, and, of course, the very unequal conditions of wealth in our modern communities bring us unpleasantly near the danger of exploitation and of usurious rates of interest."

Böhm-Bawerk emphasised that he is not condemning interest *per se*, but owing to accessory circumstances, interest may be associated with a usurious exploitation and with bad social conditions, in its innermost essence, it is rotten. Yet he asks, "What if these abuses are so inseparably connected with interest that they cannot be eradicated, or cannot be quite eradicated?" His response is, "Even then it is by no means certain that the institution should be abolished. Arrangements absolutely free from drawback are never allotted to us in human affairs. Instead of the absolute good, which is beyond reach, we must choose what, on the whole, is the relative best, where the balance, between attainable advantage and the drawbacks that must be taken into the bargain, is the most favourable possible for us. In the end he doesn't believe abuse is inseparably connected to interest, "There is no inherent blot in the essential nature of interest. Those, then, who demand its abolition may base their demand on certain considerations of expediency, but not, as the Socialists do at present, on the assertion that this kind of income is essentially unjustifiable."

Böhm-Bawerk claimed that economic theory necessarily needs to make a distinction between "the labourer's share of consumable goods", or "earnings", on the one hand, and "wages", on the other. This may be considered analogous to the distinction made by Adolf Wagner between capital as a "purely economic category" and capital "in a juridico-historical sense". Adolph Wagner (1835-1917) was a German economist and social reformer whose work prepared the development of the monetary and credit system in Germany and substantially influenced the central bank policy and financial practice before World War I.

Wages, in Böhm-Bawerk's this stricter definition, and private capital are both facts of usage, while the labourer's income, or earnings, and social capital both are facts intrinsic and fundamental to any theory of industrial society. The labourer, from the point of view of consumption of products, is no longer "labourer", he is simply a member of society, and his share of the product of industry is the share of an individual member of society. As a consumer, he is not a "labourer", and his share of consumable goods is not "wages", in the strict technical sense of the term.

Based on Böhm-Bawerk's analysis, wages may coincide with the labourer's share of the product—with earnings—but wages is a category having a different significance for economic theory from that of earnings or of goods consumed. While the labourer's earnings, or share of consumable goods, is his share of public capital, his wages are paid out of private capital. It is only then that the term "wages", in the strict technical sense, can properly be employed.

Classical-Liberal Exploitation Theory

There are two theories of the state (as well as correspondingly, two theories of exploitation) within Marxism—there is the customarily discussed and very familiar one, of the state as the instrument of the ruling class (and the concomitant theory which locates exploitation within the production process); and there is the theory of the state which pits it against "society" and "nation" (two surprising and significant terms to find in this context in writers who were supremely conscious of the class divisions within society and the nation). Moreover, it would seem suggestive that it is the second theory that predominates in those writings of Marx which, because of their nuanced and sophisticated treatment of concrete and immediate political reality, many commentators have found to be the best expositions of the Marxist historical analysis.

Although it would be difficult to demonstrate, it appears highly probable that the second theory of the state (linking it with parasitism and exploitation), must surely have been influenced by the classical liberal writers. The view that exploitation of and parasitism upon society were attributes of the non-market classes, of the classes that stood outside of the production process, was a very widespread one in the early and middle 19th century. It is the basis of Saint-Simon's famous parable (itself a residue from earlier liberal influences on that writer); it is the real meaning of the celebrated typology of "military" vs. "industrial" societies—a typology founded on the distinction between market and non-market forces.

Society had created its own organs to look after its common interests. But, these organs, at whose head was the state power, had in the course of time, in pursuance of their own special interests, transformed themselves from the servants of society into the masters of society. Politicians form a separate and powerful section of the nation. The major party which rules the country, is itself in turn controlled by people who make a business of politics. For instance, it is in America that we see best how there takes place this process of the state power making itself independent in relation to society. We find two great gangs of political parties, who alternately take possession of the state power and exploit it by the most corrupt means and for the most corrupt ends—the nation is powerless against these two great cartels of politicians who are ostensibly its servants, but in reality dominate and plunder it. We may in passing take note of the beautiful irony of the fact that, unlike a libertarian analysis of the period of American history under discussion, Engels's analysis here completely ignores the massive use of state power by segments of the capitalist class, and limits itself to the exploitative activities of those directly in control of the state apparatus.

Marx did not originate class analysis or the idea of class conflict. These things have their roots in radical liberalism, or libertarianism, predating Marx's writings. Indeed, Marx himself paid homage to the originators, a group of historians in post–Napoleonic France who have been neglected by all but a handful of modern-day libertarians. The names of the key 19th-century French historians are Charles Comte, Charles Dunoyer, and Augustin Thierry, whose publication, *Le Censeur européen*, was a hotbed of radical liberal thought. As related by Raico, Grinder, and Hart, Comte and Dunoyer were influenced by the important, but underappreciated, French liberal economist J.B. Say, whom Murray Rothbard lauded as brilliantly innovative, the superior of Adam Smith. Indeed, the seeds of a radical liberal class theory were to be found in the second and subsequent editions of Say's *Treatise on Political Economy* (first published in 1803), which reflected his response to Napoleon's military spending and economic manipulation.

The huge rewards and the advantages which are generally attached to public employment greatly excite ambition and cupidity. They create a violent struggle between those who possess positions and those who want them. According to Hart, Comte and Dunoyer were struck by Say's view that services provided in the marketplace are productive—that is, useful—"immaterial goods" and that the entrepreneur, like the labourer, is a producer. Hart writes, "A consequence of Say's view is that there were many productive contributors to the new industrialism, including factory owners, entrepreneurs, engineers and other technologists as well as those in the knowledge industry such as teachers, scientists and other "savants" or intellectuals.

This is important to the issue of class, the purpose of which is to identify the exploiters and exploited. As everyone knows, Marx, at least in some of his writings, thought only workers were industrious, with owners of capital belonging to the exploiting class (with the state as its "executive committee"). He placed owners of capital among the exploiters because of his labour theory of value (inherited from Adam Smith and David Ricardo). Since, the value of goods was equivalent to the socially necessary labour required to produce them, the profit and interest collected by "capitalists" must be extracted from workers' just rewards—hence their exploitation. If the labour theory of value fails and if exchange is fully voluntary, void of state privilege, then no exploitation occurs.

Thus, it is crucial to see that the thinkers from whom Marx apparently learned about class analysis put in the productive class all who create utility through voluntary exchange. The "capitalist" (meaning in this context the owner of capital goods who is unconnected to the state) belongs in the industrious class along with workers.

The theorists of industrialism concluded from their theory of production that it was the state and the privileged classes allied to or making up the state, rather than all non-agricultural activity, which were essentially nonproductive. They also believed that throughout history there had been conflict between these two antagonistic classes which could only be brought to end with the radical separation of peaceful and productive civil society from the inefficiencies and privileges of the state and its favourites. Thus, political and economic history is the record of conflict between producers, no matter their station, and the parasitic political classes, both inside and outside the formal state. Or to use terms of a later subscriber to this view, John Bright, it was a clash between the tax-payers and tax-eaters.

Say regarded economics and politics as separate disciplines, with the latter having little effect on the former, the liberal class analysts saw that Say's own work had more radical implications. The science of political economy was 'value laden' as we might say and implied quite specific policies on property, government intervention in the economy and individual liberty, something Say did not appreciate but which Dunoyer and Comte incorporated into their work.

As both Hart and Raico point out, Comte and Dunoyer also absorbed much from another great liberal, Benjamin Constant, who had penned important essays showing that an "era of commerce" had replaced the "era of war" and that the modern notion of liberty was poles apart from the ancient notion of liberty—participation in politics. As Hart puts it, Dunoyer was interested in the sentence "the unique end of modern nations is peace, and with peace comes comfort, and the source of comfort is industry", which nicely summed up his own thoughts on the true aim of social organisation.

These concepts, in particular, permeate the writings of Richard Cobden and John Bright, who conceived of themselves as waging a struggle on behalf of the producing classes of Britain against the aristocracy, which supported expansive government. Of the Anti-Corn Law agitation, Bright said, "I doubt that it can have any other character [than that of]...a war of classes. I believe this to be a movement of the commercial and industrial classes against the Lords and the great proprietors of the soil."[20] The "tax-eating" vs. the "tax-paying" class was a contrast which Bright especially was fond of using. Both men saw class-conflict everywhere in the Britain and Ireland of their time—in protectionism and monopolization of land, of course, but also in such policies as heavy taxes on newsprint, Church tithes, and limitation of the franchise, and most particularly in expenditures for war preparation and in a belligerent foreign policy and imperialism.

Later in the century, Bright identified other classes as the promoters of imperialism. In the case of the British occupation of Egypt in 1882, Bright (who resigned from the cabinet on account of it) believed that the City of London (i.e., financial interests) were at work, and, according to his biographer, "he did not think that we ought to involve ourselves in a series of wars to collect the debts of bondholders or find new lands for commercial exploitation". He agreed with his friend Goldwin Smith, the classical-liberal historian and anti-imperialist, who wrote him that it was simply a "stock-jobbers' war". This was long after Cobden had died, but the latter would doubtless have agreed. He once wrote, "We shall offer no excuses for so frequently resolving questions of state policy into matters of pecuniary calculation. Nearly all the revolutions and great changes in the modern world have a financial origin."[21]

One wonders how the contemporary social scientist—bereft of the libertarian theory of class conflict—would have to interpret such views. The analysis would have to be that there are "unexpected Marxian elements" present even in the thought of leading liberals. Or, more probably, in view of the Manchesterites having looked askance at the influence of financial interest on government policy, there would be an analysis along the lines of "early petty-bourgeois proto-Fascism". In this connection we should consider the changeover of certain French liberals, such as Charles Dunoyer, from Anglomania to Anglophobia. This transformation, mentioned by Liggio, is very interesting when counterposed to the Manchester School's perception of British society, foreign policy, and imperialism. Cobden and Bright were harping critics of the status quo in Britain and Ireland, constant naggers, especially of those who ran the foreign affairs of the country.

Classical liberalism is often contrasted with a new social liberalism, which is supposed to have developed out of the classical variety around 1900. But social liberalism deviates fundamentally from its namesake at its theoretical root in that it denies the self-regulatory capacity of society—the state is called on to redress social imbalance in increasingly ramified ways. The plea that it intends to preserve the end of individual freedom, modifying only the means, is to classical liberals hardly to the point—as much could be claimed for most varieties of socialism. In fact, social liberalism can scarcely be distinguished, theoretically and practically, from revisionist socialism. Furthermore, it can be argued that this school of thought did not develop out of classical liberalism around the turn of the century—when, for instance, the alleged fraudulence of freedom of contract in the labour market is supposed to have been discovered.

Rise of Direct Exploitation

Financialisation is part of the epochal change that followed the first oil shock of 1973-74, which signalled the end of the long post-war boom and ushered in a long downturn punctuated by repeated economic crises. During this period there has been a technological revolution in information processing and telecommunications. The impact of technological changes on the sphere of circulation has been great. Furthermore, neo-liberalism has replaced the Keynesianism of the long boom, drawing on profound institutional and political changes, above all, deregulation of labour markets and the financial system. Three aspects of these processes are particularly relevant to financialisation. First, productivity growth has been problematic from the middle of the 1970s to the middle of the 1990s, most significantly in the USA. The new technology failed to generate the expected gains. It took two decades for productivity growth to begin to recover, and that mostly due to the microprocessor industry. After 1995, a broad foundation was gradually created for faster productivity growth to across several economic activities in the USA. Productivity growth picked up even in the services sector, including on financial trading (though not in banking). Nonetheless, other major capitalist countries, including the UK, have not registered similar gains. The relationship between new technology and productivity growth, therefore, remains open to debate.

Second, the process of work has been transformed, partly due to technological and regulatory change, and partly due to bouts of unemployment at key junctures of the period. Casual labour and entry of women into the labour force have had a strong impact on work practices. It is likely that there has been a rebalancing of paid and unpaid labour, while information technology has encouraged the invasion of private time by work, as well as growth in piece work and putting out practices. In Marxist terms, it is probable that labour has been intensified, and unpaid labour stretched. From the extensive literature on job satisfaction, for instance, it transpires that work intensification associated with new technology is a key reason for dissatisfaction with work in developed countries, together with loss of discretion over work choices.

Third, global production and trade have become dominated by multinational enterprises created through successive waves of mergers and acquisitions. The bulk of Foreign Direct Investment takes place among developed countries, but there have also been substantial flows to developing countries since the mid-1990s, rising significantly after 2000. Competition has intensified globally, but without formal cartels or zones of exclusive trading and investment rights. The rise of the multinationals has been accompanied by a shift in the most dynamic sites of production growth away from the West—above all, toward China. There have even appeared sizable South-South flows of FDI (UNCTAD 2006). To be sure, Germany and Japan continue to earn large manufacturing surpluses. Nonetheless, there has been a general shift of capitalist activity toward financial and other services in the West, typified by the USA and the UK.

Financialisation should be understood against the background of hesitant productivity growth, altered work practices, and global shifts in productive capacity. Since the late 1970s, real accumulation has witnessed mediocre and precarious growth, but finance has grown extraordinarily in terms of employment, profits, size of institutions and markets. There has been deregulation, technological and institutional change, innovation, and global expansion. Finance now penetrates every aspect of society in developed countries while its presence has grown strongly in the developing world. Perhaps the most significant development, however, has been the rise of direct exploitation of workers and others. While real accumulation has been performing indifferently, the capitalist class has found new sources of profits through the revamped mechanisms of finance.

Banking as mechanism of direct exploitation: Commercial banking during the post-war boom involved straightforward financial intermediation—banks mobilised cheap (or even free) deposits to finance loans to industrial and commercial corporations. Financial controls regulated interest rates and circumscribed lending activities. However, since the late 1960s, there has been deregulation of interest rates and lending activities. Captive deposits are no longer available and banks have been obliged to create other liabilities in order to engage in lending. The result has been rapid financial innovation and a host of new financial assets. At the same time, large corporations have tended to obtain funds directly in open markets, thus relying less on banks for loans. Increasing reliance of large corporations on open markets rather than banks for external finance is a characteristic feature of financialisation. There are differences among US, German and Japanese corporations in this respect, for instance, US corporations rely more heavily on bonds. These reflect the bank-based character of the German and Japanese financial systems as opposed to the market-based character of the US system (briefly discussed in section 6). But the trend is not in doubt. Equally important is that large corporations across the developed world rely heavily on retained profits, rather than external funds, to finance industrial investment on a net basis.[22] The response of banks to shrinking traditional lending outlets to corporations has been, first, to turn toward the personal revenue of workers and others, and second, to focus on financial market mediation. The former includes lending for mortgages, consumer loans, credit cards, and so on. The latter refers to transactions of securities, derivatives, money trusts, insurance, as well as a variety of other services related to open markets. There are significant variations among leading countries according to their own historical and institutional development, but the general trend is not in doubt.

This represents a major transformation of capitalist finance. Economics typically treats banks as financial intermediaries that derive profit from the spread between interest on their assets and liabilities. Thus, bank profits ultimately derive from industrial and commercial enterprises, who are the main borrowers of banks. But financialisation has turned the personal income of workers and others into a major source of profits for banks. A precondition for this has been increasing involvement of individuals in the operations of the financial system, in terms of both assets and liabilities. Once again, there are significant differences among leading countries, reflecting history, institutions, and plain custom with regard to housing, pensions, insurance, consumption and so on. But the trend is not in doubt. Individual workers and others have become increasingly implicated in the workings of the financial system—they have become 'financialised'. The result has been accrual of an increasing proportion of individual income to banks and other financial institutions as payment for loans and other financial obligations.

In Marxist terms the extraction of financial profit out of personal income can be called *direct exploitation*. It is direct in the sense that it by-passes production—the normal venue of exploitation—and occurs in circulation. It is also exploitation, though the reasons are more complex. Commodity trading in the sphere of circulation is not natural terrain for exploitation since, typically, *quid pro quo* prevails. Only if traders were systematically misinformed about values, or extra-economic force was applied, could exploitation arise. But finance is about dealing in money or loanable money capital, rather than produced commodities. It involves the exchange of promises and obligations, based on trust, instead of direct application of *quid pro quo*. The final transfer of value between counterparties depends on institutional framework, legal arrangements, information flows and, even, social power. It is possible, in principle, to squeeze the borrower and extract usurious returns. Moreover, finance directed at personal revenue is advanced to cover basic needs of workers and others—housing, pensions, consumption, and so on. This is in contrast to finance that is advanced to cover investment or circulation needs of capitalists. Specifically, recipients of the former focus on obtaining use values, while recipients of the latter aim at the expansion of value. Consequently, they have sharply different objectives, purposes, information, access to alternatives, and ability to 'economise'. Industrial and commercial capitalists are ultimately capable of bypassing or replacing the mechanisms of finance, if these prove too expensive. This is not easily available to individual workers and others, who have thus become objects of direct exploitation by finance.

The shift toward direct exploitation has had major implications for the operations of banks, while creating fresh sources of instability and crisis. To analyse those it is important to mention that, for Marxist political economy, banking capital emerges out of merchants' capital and specialises in handling money as well as making loans. Banks operate in the sphere of circulation, but also mobilise idle money lying outside circulation. Consequently, banks have an ambivalent attitude toward the turnover of the total social capital: they are necessary for advanced capitalist production, but retain a detached and even predatory stance toward it. To be more specific, banks offer both money-dealing and money-lending services, which raise the profitability of productive capital by reducing costs of circulation, accelerating turnover, lessening money reserves, and making available fresh capital to expand surplus value creation. But banks are peculiar capitalist enterprises that produce neither value nor surplus value. Essentially, banks acquire assets (promises of others to pay them) by creating liabilities (promises of banks to pay others). Thus, they are vulnerable to anything that disturbs the flow of liabilities. Banks also invest their own capital, but this is typically a small proportion of their assets, i.e. they are highly indebted enterprises.

Securitisation poses profound questions about the broader social and economic role of banks in financialised capitalism. The classics of Marxism stressed that banks played an integrating role in the capitalist economy by collecting information on borrowers and transferring available resources.[23] But financialisation has wrought significant changes in this respect as the banks have shifted toward direct exploitation and financial market mediation. Some insight can be obtained from mainstream economics, according to which banks acquire information in qualitative ('soft') and quantitative ('hard') ways. The former involves regular contact with borrowers, personal relations, visiting the site of borrower operations, and placing staff on company boards. The latter involves analysis of quantitative data on companies, the stock market, other markets, and the economy as a whole.

Direct exploitation has changed the focus of banks from 'soft', 'relational' methods towards 'hard', statistically-driven techniques. To operate the latter, banks require computer power and huge databases on individuals, enterprises, and the economy as a whole. Thus, banks have become memory stores of economy and society, reaching far into personal, social and economic life. In financialised capitalism, private capital has arrogated to itself the right to collect huge volumes of personal information, subsequently to use it for the purposes of profit-making.

The turn toward direct exploitation has produced systemic banking failure to collect information and assess risk. Banks are certainly capable of acting as the nerve system of the capitalist economy when their focus is on collecting idle funds to lend to productive capitalists. But when it comes to meeting the financial needs of large numbers of individuals, banks appear to be ill-equipped and badly disposed to dealing with the informational requirements. They approach the task from the narrow standpoint of their profit-making, which encourages them to seek computationally-intensive, pseudo-scientific techniques. However, housing, private consumption, and so on, are social needs. The recipients are not 'economising' capitalists and the knowledge that is required to make funds available to them has strongly social and 'relational' aspects. It would be impossible for banks to acquire such knowledge on the requisite scale, even if they were disposed so to do. This is an inherent limitation of direct exploitation—social needs can be met only very partially through private finance and require social answers.

Open financial markets and direct exploitation: The counterpart to the transformation of banks, and a hallmark of financialisation, is growth of open financial markets (in shares, bonds, derivatives, and so on). These mobilise idle money in parallel with the structured credit system that mostly comprises banks. But they operate on different principles and give rise to different financial intermediaries. They also offer fresh opportunities to banks to make profits through financial market mediation and direct exploitation.

Stock markets are markets for equity, i.e. for property rights over corporations that give a legal claim to future profits. Share prices represent the discounted value of future profits and the benchmark discount rate is the rate of interest (adjusted for risk). This process was called by Marx (1894, ch. 29) the formation of 'fictitious capital'. Share prices, in other words, are formed at considerable distance from value creation in production; they reflect rational estimation of enterprise prospects, but also expectations, rumours and plain manipulation of buyers. Consequently they allow for capital gains and offer natural scope for speculation.

Bond markets, on the other hand, are markets for long-term debt by enterprises, banks, and the state. They generally carry less risk than the shares issued by an enterprise. The fictitious aspect of their prices allows for capital gains but, since they are debt, less than for shares. Financialisation has turned bond markets into major sources of funds for corporations. In recent years bond markets have also surged in developing countries as international reserves increased in recent years, thus providing foreign capital with the opportunity to extract large profits (Painceira, 2008).

Derivatives markets have grown enormously during the last three decades, but they do not involve transfer of loanable capital (or idle money) to those who intend to employ it. Rather, derivatives are essentially bets that allow for the management of risk, of for outright speculation. They can be simple, as in forward contracts in foreign exchange, or complex, as in various Interest Rate Swaps. All have an underlying asset, which can be real or financial (or even imaginary, such as the weather). The complexity and size of derivatives markets is in inverse proportion to their broader economic significance. Industrial and other enterprises, facing risks associated with production and trade, make limited use of derivatives. The heaviest users are financial institutions aiming to cover themselves from the risks of other financial transactions, or to speculate.

Stock markets have been fundamental to financialisation, but not due to providing capital for investment by industrial enterprises (Corbett and Jenkinson 1996, 1997). Rather, equity has been the main lever for the centralisation of capital, the stuff of mergers and acquisitions (M&A). Equity creates distance and opposition between shareholders (capital as property) and managers (capital as function). The governance of large joint-stock enterprises has become a major issue in financialised capitalism.

Open market profits, institutional investors and direct exploitation: Open financial markets have provided banks with fresh fields of profitability associated with financial market mediation (for which banks earn fees) and with trading on own account. Typical are investment banking services, which involve collecting information about counterparties, placing securities with buyers, reducing transactions costs, underwriting securities, and so on. Of decisive importance has been the abolition of the Glass-Steagall Act in the USA in 1999, and of similar regulations in other countries (such as Article 65 in Japan), which prevented commercial banks from engaging in investment banking. In the course of such activities banks often advance loanable capital, but that is aimed at securities transactions and the receivers frequently are other financial institutions.

The source of profits made by financial institutions in open financial markets poses difficult problems for political economy. Hilferding (1981, pp. 128-29) suggested that banks appropriate a part of 'promoter's' or 'founder's' profits, that is, the value of shares discounted at the rate of interest minus their value discounted at the (higher) rate of profit. This difference is the future profit of enterprise accruing in a lump sum to the seller of equities at the time of an IPO. But this is not very persuasive since different rates of discount could not be systematically applied to the same flow of expected returns without financial markets becoming segmented. Moreover, the future profits of enterprise would accrue to those who continue to run the enterprise, not the sellers of shares. It is more plausible that the source of such profits is to be found in the redivision of loanable money capital (and plain money) that is mobilised through open financial markets. To stock of idle money formed as the total social capital goes through its turnover is mobilised either indirectly through banks, or directly through open financial markets. Direct mobilisation is still facilitated by banks and other financial institutions, remunerated through a share of the sums traded. Since this process takes place on the basis of fictitious prices, it is susceptible to sentiment, rumours, and manipulation, thus creating a further field of direct exploitation.

The growth of open financial markets, contrary to what might have been expected, has led to a proliferation of financial intermediaries. Dominant among them are institutional investors—insurance companies, money trusts, unit trusts, money funds, hedge funds and, above all, pension funds. There are significant differences among them. Insurance companies, for instance, collect premia and seek relative secure returns on assets, while pension funds collect long-term savings and seek growing returns on assets. However, they all intermediaries since they concentrate idle money across capitalist society and make it available for investment in open financial markets.

The remarkable growth of institutional investors during the last three decades is a further hallmark of financialisation, and integral to direct exploitation. Two factors are fundamental to it. First, there has been partial withdrawal of the state from welfare provision, particularly pensions, forcing workers and others to plan for retirement through private placement of savings. This has been exacerbated by the gradual ageing of the population and longer periods of survival after retirement. Second, deregulation of interest rates that has encouraged savings to flow away from banks in search of higher returns. State policy has promoted and encouraged the placement of savings with institutional investors.

NOTES

1. Gunnar Myrdal—*Prospects for an International Economy* (New York, 1956), p. 464.
2. Everett E. Hagen—*An Analytical Model of the Transition to Economic Growth*, M.I.T., CIS (Document C/57-12), p. 1.
3. Need-achievement may dominate behaviour of business leaders only in some aspects of their life. Sr. John Rockefeller was an extremely

conventional man in his home and religious life, and Henry Ford's intense life-long interest in collecting and preserving things of the past suggests a constant fear of venturing too boldly into the new.

4. $\frac{dK}{Y} = \frac{dK'}{Y} + \frac{dL}{P} \cdot \frac{P}{Y}$. Since both $\frac{dK'}{Y}$ and $\frac{dL}{P}$ approach a constant as $\frac{Y}{P}$ increases, if dL is large relative to dK', $\frac{dK}{Y}$ may fall as $\frac{Y}{P}$ gets large.
5. Osvaldo Sunkel, "National Development Policy and External Dependence in Latin America", *The Journal of Development Studies*, Vol. 6, no. 1, October 1969, p. 23.
6. Theotonio Dos Santos, "The Structure of Dependence", in K.T. Fann and Donald C. Hodges, eds., *Readings in U.S. Imperialism*. Boston: Porter Sargent, 1971, p. 226.
7. Andre Gunder Frank, "The Development of Underdevelopment", in James D. Cockcroft, Andre Gunder Frank, and Dale Johnson, eds., *Dependence and Underdevelopment*. Garden City, New York: Anchor Books, 1972, p. 3.
8. Karl Marx, "The Future Results of the British Rule in India", *New York Daily Tribune*, No. 3840, August 8, 1853.
9. CEPAL—Comisión Económica para América Latina, it is the Spanish acronym of United Nations Economic Commission for Latin America (UNECLA).
10. In its most noticed version, see Frank (1967). For Furtado's view on underdevelopment, Furtado (1975).
11. Furtado (1961), p. 20.
12. See Tavares and Serra 1973.
13. Amin 1994:173.
14. Adam Smith, *The Wealth of Nations*, Cannan Edition, Bk. I, Chap. VIII.
15. Karl Marx, *Das Kapital*, Vol. I. Pt. II, Chap. IV.
16. Böhm-Bawerk, *Capital and Interest*, Vol. I, pp. 263-71; Vol. II, pp. 259-89.
17. The leading proponent of the coercion interpretation is A.W. Wood, 'The Marxian Critique of Justice.' In M. Cohen, T. Nagel and T. Scanlon (eds.), op. cit., pp. 3-41; and 'Marx on Right and Justice: A Reply to Husami', in *ibid*., pp. 107-35; and A.W. Wood, Karl Marx, London, 1981.
18. See A.E. Buchanan, *Marx and Justice*, London, 1982, Ch. 5, esp. p. 59.

19. F. Fetter, *Capital, Interest and Rent* (Kansas City: Sheed Andrews and McMeel, 1977).
20. George Macaulay Trevelyan, *The Life of John Bright* (London: Constable, 1913), p. 141.
21. *The Political Writings of Richard Cobden* (New York: Garland, 1973) I, p. 238.
22. See Corbett and Jenkinson (1996, 1997).
23. Lenin (1964, p. 223) thought that banks had become institutions of a truly 'universal character' in capitalist society, while Hilferding (1981, p. 368) imagined that the German economy could be controlled through 'six large Berlin banks'.

4

Social Capital

After going through this chapter, you will better understand:

- ➤ bridging, bonding and linking social capital
- ➤ regeneration of social capital
- ➤ problems in the regeneration of social capital
- ➤ benefits of social capital
- ➤ measurement of social capital
- ➤ the downside of social capital
- ➤ the gender aspect of social capital
- ➤ social capital and time resources
- ➤ community heterogeneity and social capital

The term social capital is believed to have been first used by an American school reformer, L.J. Hanifan, who in 1916, saw regular contact between neighbours as an accumulation of social capital. In the 1950s, the concept was applied within Canadian urban sociology in connection with studies of club memberships. About a decade later, the term was used by a sociologist, Jane Jacobs, in connection with neighbourhood as a resource for individuals and groups. Thus, the first applications of the term social capital were mostly sociological in scope, linked to neighbourhood networking and education, often unequally distributed among groups.

The term social capital was subsequently rediscovered and reinvented several times during the course of the century before being popularised by the work of Robert Putnam in the mid-

1990s. His write-up "Bowling Alone: America's Declining Social Capital" which appeared in *Journal of Democracy*, presented a compelling account of America's dramatically declining social capital over the latter half of the 20th Century.

Social capital is an empirically elusive concept and has been subject to much discussion and debate with reference to its social regeneration, economic benefits, positive and negative aspects, indicators of measurement, gender insensitivity, and its implications for development policy. Various erudite scholars and research scientists have tried to define social capital in their own way accentuating its specific aspects as per the focus of their study.

According to Robert Putnam[1] social capital refers to the connections among individuals, social networks and other forms of reciprocity and trust which arise from them. Cooperation and collective well-being are other qualities attributed to social capital in Putnam's definition. He transforms social capital from a simple social process which benefits individuals and groups to an entity that can be consolidated for society's benefit as a whole. Although Putnam has been criticized for imbuing community with highly positive connotations and ignoring the downside of social capital, his view is considered relevant to economic regeneration.

Bourdieu[2] describes social capital as a potential source linked to networks and relationships of mutual acquaintance and recognition, giving members the collectively owned capital. Bourdieu's definition is rooted in Marxist tradition as it highlights the structural constraints that exist on individuals and unequal access that people have, to resources, due to distinctions of class, race and gender. For Bourdieu, access to resources and issues of power within society are key to social capital. Effectively viewed as connections and social obligations in Bourdieu's understanding, social capital can, under certain conditions, be converted into economic capital. Although the critics have pointed out that the nation fails to focus on the complexity of the conditions under which such a process takes shape, yet it is being used as an important tool in formulating policies. For Bourdieu the network of relationships is the product of investment strategies aimed at establishing or reproducing social relationships that are directly usable in the short- or long-term. His definition of social capital is considered all-inclusive as it links actual or potential resources to a durable network of more or less institutionalized relationships and provides the community with the backing of collectively owned capital.

Coleman[3] defines social capital by its function, viewing it as a resource to be drawn upon. According to him, "...social relations constitute useful capital resources for actors through processes such as obligations, expectations, trust and information channel norms". Here, social capital takes three forms: (i) the obligations and expectations which rely upon the trustworthiness of the social environment; (ii) the capacity of information to flow through the social structure in order to provide a basis for action; and (iii) the presence of norms accompanied by effective sanctions. Coleman also differentiates social capital from other forms of capital in that it does not necessarily bring benefits only to the individual, but rather to all of those who are part of the social structure. He finds social capital necessary for social integration and social control, and this notion highlights the importance of closer and denser ties within the social structure.

Fukuyama[4] defines social capital as a set of informal values or norms shared among members of a group that permits cooperation between them. The most important value for him is trust as it leads to cooperation, thus making both groups and networks operate smoothly. The radius of this conceptualization is trust, and further it expands outside of the family, the more likely it is to be based upon moral resources and ethical behaviour. Where groups have a narrow radius of trust, their in-group solidarity reduces their ability to cooperate with outsiders, because, it is difficult for people to trust those outside of narrow circles. Scholars like Ritzen have used the term 'social cohesion' instead of social capital and defined it as "...a state of affairs in which a group of people—delineated by a geographical region like a country—demonstrates an aptitude for collaboration that produces a climate for change".[5] They also hold that the norms, networks and other related forms of social connection are important bases for this aptitude.

While there has been much debate about its definition, social capital can be understood as networks of social relations which are characterized by norms of trust and reciprocity, and which facilitate coordination and cooperation for mutual benefit. Social capital demonstrates how the presence of dense networks within society and accompanying norms of generalized trust and reciprocity allow people to overcome their common problems where collective action is required, more efficiently. It has been accepted as the concept capable of linking together economy and culture and, as such, the disciplines within human sciences. As a result, the concept has been embraced as a panacea for a plethora of social problems. For example, social capital has been included in World Bank's policy discourse for the Third World.

BRIDGING, BONDING, AND LINKING SOCIAL CAPITAL

Different combinations of network characteristics affect the overall capability of social capital. In the social capital theory and research, distinctions have been made on the basis of different combinations of network characteristics, between 'bonding', 'bridging' and 'linking' social capital. Bonding social capital is generated when we reinforce our associational activities with already known or related people. Thus, it refers to the trust and reciprocity in dense or closed networks. Bonding refers to the interactions between people who are on a more level playing field. It refers to the vertical links between a person and other outside groups. In contexts of collective socio-economic disadvantage, bonding networks can provide members of a local community with crucial resources especially through material aid, service, work and emotional support that family and close friends supply.

Bridging social capital is generated when we connect with people who are outside the circle of our natural or instinctive acquaintances. Such people are in sufficiently different circumstances from ourselves. The differences might be of class, ethnicity, religion, education, or income. Bridging social capital involves overlapping networks which may give access to resources and opportunities which exist in one network to a member belonging to another. Heterogeneity of network members is said to enhance the bridging capabilities of social capital. The distinction between these two forms of social capital is important from the point of view of studying the different functions they tend to serve. Xavier Briggs has stated that the bonding social capital is good for 'getting by' and the bridging social capital for 'getting ahead'.

The linking social capital is a relatively newer concept and involves social relations with those in authority, which may be used to garner resources or power. Some scholars have identified private and public social capital, viz. those aspects which impact an individual and those which affect the community at large, respectively.

REGENERATION OF SOCIAL CAPITAL

According to Coleman, the creation of social capital is largely an unintentional process. Though it is productive in nature it can get depleted if it is not renewed.

If social capital is something intangible how can it be created? If it is "largely an unintentional process", as Coleman puts it, how can it be encouraged? Despite these tricky questions, social scientists have talked about the regeneration of social capital. Some go to the extent of saying that although it is productive in nature, yet it can get depleted if it is not renewed. It is pertinent to mention here, that the states do not have many obvious levers by which to create social capital. It has also been suggested in some studies on social capital that the states may negatively impact the development of social capital if they undertake certain activities that are better left to the private section or to the society at large. The state may unwillingly create conditions in which people may become dependent on it and stop taking their own initiatives. According to this interpretation, grassroots level regeneration has more to contribute to social capital development than top down governmental approaches. Societies need to share the same language, norms and moral values to avoid disintegration. Developing these factors may, therefore, be the moot point of regeneration practice. The development work needs to create a wider radius of trust which is more achievable through grassroots approaches.

The economic aspect cannot be segregated from the regeneration of social capital. Communities in which high levels of poverty exist may remain insular and have increased level of in-group trust, which serves to exclude others and hinder the extension of social capital to other sections of society. It is here that the government can play a significant role in the creation of social capital by making the policy decision whereby there is a broadbased economic growth, alleviation of poverty, and the social aspect of development work is effectively taken case of. The strengthening of local community network can be directed by social policy and related interventions.

The tribals and other isolated groups in the eastern parts of India are a case in example. They may be having a strong trust within their communications but feel excluded from the mainstream Indian society, because living in abject poverty and destitution, they feel neglected and insecure. In order to bring them within the ambit of social capital, the government must frame policies and provide means to improve their economic condition. Social and economic inequalities manifest themselves in community relationships in complex and subtle ways, though on the surface they may seem to be based upon trust and reciprocity. For example, inclusion and exclusion occur in society based upon gender, ethnicity, age, religious affiliations and access to resources, etc. Therefore, the policymakers and regeneration drivers need to know which aspects to target in which sections of community with the orientation of overall policy for development.

Complementarities between institutions and social capital have been found, and it has been established that trust and civic norms are stronger in countries which have more formal institutions which protect people's rights. When we treat social capital as a by-product of religion, tradition, shared historical experience and cultural norms, we also accept the importance of various institutions that are directly or indirectly attached to these aspects in the regeneration of social capital.

Problems in the Regeneration of Social Capital

As seen above, the scope of social capital is wide and encompasses a number of aspects. The range of general issues associated with it have a direct bearing on the social regeneration settings. Besides, there are particular issues related to regeneration which prove problematic in forming and fostering social capital. Some such issues are briefly discussed below.

Social capital thrives on trust, but the same is not guaranteed within any neighbourhood. The impact of historical divisions within areas and intense deprivation amidst plenty can undermine levels of trust between individuals and groups within neighbourhoods. The recent incident of death due to hunger, of one of the three sisters living together in southern part of New Delhi, bears testimony to the fact that there can be a lack of trust within neighbourhoods. Suicides by farmers due to abject poverty perpetuated by crop failure in some parts of Andhra Pradesh and elsewhere also point to the same lack of trust.

It has been argued that social capital is highly context-dependent. Although the literature on social capital recognizes that integrated responses are necessary in addressing neighbourhood problems, yet social capital regeneration may not be possible in some context. Different neighbourhoods may have different combinations of factors that influence their activities. Different factors or combinations thereof bring success in different places. External factors such as demography and geography are most determining at the level of neighbourhood. The socio-economic situation and the institutional environment within the area become predominant in the creation of social capital in many other contexts. Identifying the key factors and finding the core combinations to suit particular areas often prove to be difficult tasks.

Some social scientists feel that the sustainability of social capital depends on the ability of certain individuals to mobilize their own cultural and economic capitals along with those of others. Such individuals—also called 'community leaders or regeneration professionals' by Purdue[6]—are better placed to bring others forward in developing social capital. They play a crucial role in building social capital through their work at the grassroots level and through partnerships with outside elite groups. The problem in this regard is that many of these regeneration professionals are temporary and migratory and hence, do not hold the type of commitment to the neighbourhood that the residents do. As such, they do not constitute the fabric of neighbourhood social capital, but at best, only a fleeting source thereof.

Voluntary organisations are often said to play a crucial role in the creation of social capital. The apprehensions in this regard are that they invariably rely heavily on a small number of people. This creates two problems: one, a concern about their dependency and sustainability, and second, it inhibits inclusiveness and diversity. It has been pointed out that the volunteers mostly mix up with high levels of in-groups—which proves counter-productive to the regeneration of social capital because of exclusivity of the common people.

The above problems notwithstanding, area-based regeneration initiatives have been taken in many societies and yielded positive outcomes. It has been widely accepted now that the social capital can be developed through effective regeneration. It can serve as a useful tool in development work. The enhancement of different forms of skills through creation of human capital by social capital, particularly within deprived areas is the goal of regeneration work.

BENEFITS OF SOCIAL CAPITAL

Social capital has a number of benefits for the individual as well as for society at large. It has, therefore, been called a resource comprising beneficial social connections and relationships. The individual is helpless socially if left to himself, but if he comes into contact with his neighbourhood, there will be an accumulation of social capital which may immediately satisfy his societal needs. Norms of reciprocity create a willingness to help others, generating goodwill, fellowship and sympathy among individuals of a social unit. Social capital is said to improve the quality of life via psychological and biological processes. Individuals rich in social capital can cope better with traumas and even fight illnesses better. Social capital is also said to improve individual awareness of ways in which the human fate is linked, allowing people to become more tolerant, less cynical and more empathetic to the needs of others. Without these opportunities facilitated by networking and social relationship, people are more likely to be governed by their worst impulses creating chaos in society.

The role of social capital as a harbinger of regional development has been well recognized. According to Putnam, in high social capital areas public spaces are cleaner, people are friendlier and streets are safer. As such, social capital is a great source to be harnessed and used in development. The local volunteers can play a role in greasing the wheel because they put time into service delivery, empower themselves and others, motivate paid workers to carry out additional tasks, enhancing their utility and capability. This is akin to creating self-help groups in society for durable and sustainable regional development.

Social capital also has economic benefits. Civic values created by it influence socio-economic performance and thereby reduce transaction cost in the market, increase trust, minimize burdens of enforcing agreements and hold down the diseconomies of fraud and theft. Both Putnam and Coleman give equal weight to economic and social aspects of social capital and believe that these pave the way for the acquisition of other forms of capital. As stated earlier, social capital under certain conditions can be converted into economic capital. As a regeneration driver, social capital effectively meets the socio-economic aspect of development work accelerating growth and alleviating poverty. Social capital positively impacts output through its effect on human capital and access to credit. A low social capital is said to reduce investment and slow down economic growth.

According to Amartya Sen's capability approach, the capabilities are ends while income, infrastructure and rights are resources; without access to these resources the so-called capabilities cannot be acquired. The norms of cooperation and reciprocity, trust and civic involvement which are the ingredients of social capital contribute to providing access to resources. Thus, social capital becomes a means of acquiring capabilities, and participates in the economic development and well-being of the region. As such, vital links to Sen's idea of social development through capability approach can be traced to social capital.

Social capital can also be an important factor in coping with economic shocks. The fact that in South Africa, households in communities with greater social capital have been able to come safely through the difficult period of economic shocks has been established by M. Carter and A. John.[7] In Indonesia, local industrialization caused social capital to increase and tide over the economic depression during the late 1990s. Social capital acts as a buffer against economic disadvantages by mitigating the effect of deficiency of economic sources.

Social capital as a concept has provided a wide scope for research and study and offered ground for sustained interaction and future theoretical development within the arena of social science. Being a multidisciplinary and interdisciplinary concept, it has created research ties and opened the way for networking opportunities between disciplines. The concept has enriched social science by adding to its core values through terms such as norms of cooperation, reciprocity, trust, shared networks, relationships of mutual acquaintance, neighbourliness and economic regeneration, etc. Another key merit of social capital as a concept is that it shifts the focus of analysis from the behaviour of individual agents to the webs of relations between agents, social units and institutions acting as a link between micro, meso and macro levels of analysis and facilitating wider research.

Social capital contributes to research participation. Such participation not only requires knowledge and trust between individuals, groups and committees, but also motivation and cooperation which are provided by social networks. Potential participants and researchers often exist in different social systems. There can be barriers in creating interest, sharing knowledge, collecting samples and conducting self-contained and complete studies and reaching a consensus about the results of the research. Social capital helps remove these barriers through building a trust between participants, researchers and respondents.

The impact of social capital on education has also been highlighted in some studies. Some scholars find a significant positive association between social capital and schooling. Similarly, the influence of social capital on the general standard of health of people in the community has also been recognized. If health and knowledge are examples of capabilities, social capital again supports Amartya Sen's capability theory, and becomes an important instrument of social development.

MEASUREMENT OF SOCIAL CAPITAL

Just as there is no clear definition and causal relationships of social capital, there is a lack of measurement tools for it. Since it is something intangible, it cannot be properly gauged. However, some scholars have tried to measure it through associational activities the people engage themselves in. The number and diversity of functions of social organisations in each area such as neighbourhood committees, clubs, welfare associations, sports promotion agencies and local branches of national or international associations for retired people and women, and other bodies promoting civil and human rights determine the density of associational activities of that area which can form the basis of measurement of social capital.

Voter turnout in the elections is also an indicator of social capital. Viewing from the angle of individual vote, the probability of his/her vote affecting the outcome of elections is extremely small. People still cast their vote because they are driven by a sense of civic duty and an engagement towards the common good. Thus, higher the voter turnout in the elections, higher the level of social capital.

Crime rate within a region is also used to measure social capital. This method is based on the belief that distrust accompanies conflict. The areas having high level of distrust are generally the high conflict areas and are plagued by high rate of crime, violence and subversive activities. Low crime rates are indicative of a high level of social capital.

The wide gap between theoretical understanding of social capital and the ways social capital has been measured in the empirical work so far has led to several problems. The following four ways have been suggested for avoiding these problems:

(a) Social capital measurement and practice needs to be theoretically established. Failing this, anything and everything will be labeled as social capital, and old, redundant ideas may be represented in a new guise.

(b) Social capital should be perceived as a source to collective action. We may wish to determine whether social capital produces many social and economic outcomes such as cooperative and active communities. However, we must not equate other social actions or outcomes with social capital.

(c) It is a multi-dimensional concept. We must, therefore, understand how its various dimensions relate to the concept as a whole.

(d) Social capital varies by network type and social scale. Its dimension and outcome in one network may not correspond with those in another network.

These four principles are extremely helpful in making social capital a useful theoretical, empirical and policy tool.

Measurement Framework

A convenient and all-inclusive measurement framework of social capital is based on of its hypothesized determinants, networks and outcomes. The hypothesized determinants of social capital include the following:

(a) Family characteristics such as age, sex, health and endurance level.

(b) Other characteristics like marital status, presence of children, their number, age groups, etc. and other dependents.

(c) Resources like income level, ownership or tenancy of residence, education level and other skills, and knowledge of local area.

(d) Attitudes and values like shared objectives and tolerance of other ethic groups in the community.

(e) Characteristics of the area such as urban/rural, level of socio-economic advantage, presence of networks and institutions in the area, and safety and security in the local area.

The measurement of social capital in an area is a direct function of the presence or absence of these key determinants. We have to see them in totality to arrive at the level of social capital present in the community.

Networks, considered to be the key players in the formation of social capital include the following:

(a) Informal ties including those with in-laws, neighbours, friends, co-workers, and kinship ties with family members and relatives. Informal ties are characterized by natural or personal forms of negotiated trust and reciprocity.

(b) General relationships such as with local people, general people and with those in civic groups. These relationships are governed by a generalized trust and reciprocity.

(c) Institutional relationships like allegiance to institutional systems. They are characterized by trust in institutions including customs and traditions.

These are the networks in which trust and reciprocity operate. They may be termed three sets of social relations belonging to informal, general and institutional realm respectively. They are further governed by certain factors. For example, the informal ties are governed by the number of neighbours known personally. Similarly, the number of work contracts influences the informal ties with workmates. Density and closeness in informal ties are governed by the facts whether family members know each other's close friends and whether friends know one another. Similarly, general relationships are impacted by the fact whether local people know one another. Ethnic diversity of friends, educational diversity of groups a person is a member of, and the cultural mix of people of a local area are other key factors that have a direct bearing on the general as well as institutional relationships. In the social capital framework, the hypothesized determinants and the networks in which trust, reciprocity and cooperation operate lead to certain desired outcomes. Some such outcomes are enumerated below:

(a) Individual and family well-being. This includes both, capacity to get by and get ahead—the first exemplified by meeting child care needs and—the second, by gaining opportunities for positive change.

(b) Public well-being which includes public health. This may be characterized by low incidence of disease and higher efficiency.

(c) Neighbourhood area well-being, characterized by reduced crime, and tolerance of diversity in the community.

(d) Political well-being, brought by upholding the values of democracy, and by better governance.

(e) Economic well-being, characterized by higher growth rate, prosperity and poverty alleviation.

(f) Vibrant civil life shown by higher volunteering and community cooperation.

These outcomes of social capital are the most important in measurement framework. They are the indication that the determinants and networks have resulted in the desired positive change in the individual, the neighbourhood and the country.

The measurement of the concept social capital is at present in the nascent stage. As the empirical research is going on, some common themes are developing and new realities are coming to light. Consensus about measurement is being achieved gradually. However, it remains an emergency field where it is necessary to test and validate various approaches. Refinement and firm establishment of the core concepts shall come over a period of time through research, application and re-testing.

THE DOWNSIDE OF SOCIAL CAPITAL

American sociologist Alejandro Portes[8] has pointed out the downside of social capital saying that it does not always work as an important factor to enhance growth. There are negative types including isolated groups webbed together by specific trust. The small sections that exist in some societies attempt to monopolise cooperative relations which may prove dangerous for the surrounding society. The often mentioned examples in this regard are al-Queda, Hell's Angels and other terrorist groups. This dark side of social capital which is also called excessive bonding social capital is destroying the common good. Individuals between groups which are excessively bonded with one another are at times highly destructive towards non-members.

It has also been suggested that social capital is like a double edged sword which can cut both ways. The ties developed by it can bring about greater control over wayward behaviour and provide beneficial access to resources, but at the same time, it can restrict individual freedoms and stop outsiders from gaining access to same resources.

There are also some disadvantages of indulging in social acts. For example, an attempt to save someone in an extremely difficult situation, trapped in fire, flood or an attack by hooligans may put us in grave personal danger. These negative aspects of social capital have been ignored in most of the studies of social capital. The researchers must study these aspects deeply so that there is more clarity on the concept and better ways are found for the regeneration and measurement of social capital. More importantly, effective steps can be taken for the dilution of the dangerous excessive bonding in right earnest, and weak ties are allowed to exist side by side strong ties so that the tolerance level of superglued groups and fundamentalists towards other ethnic groups within society is built.

THE GENDER ASPECT OF SOCIAL CAPITAL

It has been stated that the gender relations and inequalities have been overlooked in many explanations of social capital. Davies[9] go to the extent of calling the concept gender blind. Even theorists like Bourdieu who do not completely ignore the gender aspect treat it as a secondary social aspect.

Those who criticize social capital theories for being male-biased argue that women are most closely tied to their communities. Their domestic responsibilities keep women closer to provide spaces such as their homes and local community groups which mostly constitute the primary sites of local, social community networks. The local community schemes and groups which are related to childcare and not to employment and work do not attract men. Under such circumstances, women prove to be more effective in building social capital through local networks. In several sections of society, women are known to have provided informal childcare, emotional and material support to their neighbours and friends. Ignoring all these factors, the process of social capital is not operated to the benefit of women. The supposed decline or lack of social capital within poorer communities is even attributed to women. The rise of women's employment is viewed as a major contributing factor to the decline of social capital. This, however, overlooks the fact that the women who venture out of their traditional vicinities to go to their workplace build the 'bridging' social capital by interacting with people outside their pool of acquaintances.

Studies have found that women's and men's experiences of social and economic life differ from each other's in significant ways. They are exposed to different durations and intensities of poverty risks and general exploitation. The research must, therefore, highlight gender differences. We need a theoretical and policy understanding of social capital that recognizes the distinction between women's and men's social relationships. Mainstreaming the gender issues has now started to gain momentum in social capital research and will soon start to make a real impact on the social losses of women.

The approach of treating men and women as separate entities has, however, been criticized for unwillingly creating an unnecessary dichotomy between them. This approach gives a false impression that men and women are two separate groups, and denies the fact that it is interdependence that governs gender dynamics. Moreover, social capital as a network of trust, cooperation and reciprocity cannot be segregated for men and women. If it benefits men it benefits women equally well. The argument that it is women who build social capital and men who spend it also does not hold much water. In Indian Society, mostly, the men venture out for work daily. When they interact with their colleagues and other acquaintances they generate 'bonding' social capital. When they converse with new people they create 'bridging' social capital. Thus, men are equally involved in the regeneration of social capital as women. It is only that men are able to capitalize more on their networks whereas women are inhibited and constrained in their pursuits.

SOCIAL CAPITAL AND TIME RESOURCES

Another question that has caught the attention of researchers is: How does time, generally considered as a personal and social resource, influence the development and maintenance of social capital? Unpaid work done for the benefit of persons outside of one's own household can be considered a gift of time. It may be reciprocated by a gift of another's time though variable in scale and form. The study of gifts of time is of great significance to the theory of social capital as it indicates the culture of helpfulness. Social workers, non-government organisations (NGOs) which work for the welfare of society, and volunteers engaged in serving particular groups like old, neglected persons, orphans, physically challenged people and children give a gift of time to these disadvantaged groups with or without financial support. Their efforts may be called an input to social capital.

COMMUNITY HETEROGENEITY AND SOCIAL CAPITAL

It is believed that the community heterogeneity hinders the creation of social capital. This belief is based on the "us versus them" theory. In a community comprised of several heterogeneous groups, people generally feel threatened by other groups in a fight for resources, cultural dominance and political control. Moreover, individuals from different groups are not likely to have common norms and values. In such communities the behaviour of people is difficult to predict. There are hurdles to trust, and the agreements are self-enforcing rather than by consensus. It has been widely accepted that the social capital formation is significantly lower in ethnically and economically heterogeneous communities.

There have been attempts to define or measure community heterogeneity. It is principally marked by ethnic and social divisions but other differences such as in income, language, customs and local identity are also important indicators. However, differences in age groups do not constitute community heterogeneity as it is a universal phenomena and exists in every community though in varying degrees.

The level of party system fragmentation is also considered a measure of community heterogeneity because it indicates the number of socio-economic divisions in the electorate. Further, there are certain factors that promote or block the emergence of community heterogeneity. The socio-economic context of the community plays an important role in this regard. The policymakers must, therefore, aim to make the progress broadbased so that the differences in society are reduced and bonds of solidarity, trust and reciprocity are created.

CONCLUSION

Social capital has been called an enigmatic and elusive concept because it defies any all-inclusive definition and deals with the non-material form of capital invisible to the eye. As a conceptual entity it is highly debated within sociological literature, wider academic fields and policy discussions. Much of the criticism of the concept is based on the untested assumptions about the ways social capital is manifested, generated and distributed empirically. Despite several studies, relatively little is known about social capital in practice and about how the true value of the concept might be imbued in policy.

In recent years, however, social capital has been the focus of community research and policy. It is increasingly being recognized as a constructive force that leads to improved performance on a vast array of social, political and economic phenomena. Initiatives are being taken to develop social capital, perceiving its productive outcomes, and it is becoming more visible in the policies of some countries. Evidence is growing that social capital has enormous effects on socio-economic growth, health, crime and even the effectiveness and functioning of the governments. Discourses on development have shifted their attention from being purely economic to more holistic that encompasses quality of life, equitable distribution and sustainable development.

The idea of social capital has allowed scholars to assess the quality of relationships among people within a particular community and depict how that quality impacts their ability to achieve shared goals. However, social capital is valuable only to the extent that community members recognize and sustain its utility. We must, therefore, improve our understanding of social capital and appreciate its contribution towards poverty alleviation, social stability and broadbased economic development. The policymakers must focus on the programs, designs and methods for operationalising the concept of social capital in a diverse range of interventions. The government must facilitate cutting edge research on the concept so that it could be made an effective tool of socio-economic development.

NOTES

1. R.D. Putnam (1995), Bowling Alone: America's Declining Social Capital, *Journal of Democracy*, 6 (1): 65-78.
2. P. Bourdieu (1999), *The Forms of Capital*, in Richardson, J. (ed.) *Handbook of Theory and Research for Sociology of Education*, Greenwood Press, New York.
3. J.S. Coleman (1984), Introducing Social Structure into Economic Analysis, in *The American Economic Review,* 74 (2): 84-88.
4. F. Fukuyama (2000), Social Capital, Civil Society and Development, *Third World Quarterly*, (31): 215-31.
5. J. Ritzen et al. (2000), *On 'Good' Politicians and 'Bad' Policies: Social Cohesion, Institutions and Growth*, World Bank Working Paper No. 2448.
6. D. Purdue (2001), Neighbourhood Governance: Leadership, Trust and Social Capital, *Urban Studies,* 38 (12): 211-24.
7. M.R. Carter and J.A. Maluccio (1996), *Participation, Social Capital, and Intersectoral Problem-solving: African and Asian Cases*, World Development, 31 (7): 1147-63.
8. A. Portes (1998), Social Capital: Origins and Applications, *Annual Review of Sociology*, Vol. 24, 1-24.
9. R. Davies (2002), *Monitoring and Evaluating* NGO *Achievements*, in V. Desai and R.B. Potter (eds.) *The Comparison to Development Studies*, Arnold, UK.

5

Poverty

After going through this chapter, you will better understand:

- conceptual issues
- alternative measures of poverty—head count ratio, income gap ratio, and poverty gap ratio
- Sen measures of poverty, FGT measure
- Mollie Orshansky's strategy to poverty measurement
- impact of poverty
- strategies for poverty eradication

A person is said to be in poverty when he is deprived of income and other resources needed to obtain the conditions of life—the diets, material goods, amenities, standards and services—that enable him to play the roles, meet the obligations and participate in the relationships and customs of his society. There are various meanings of poverty which depend on who asks the question, how it is understood, and who responds.

(a) The first cluster of meanings is related to income-poverty or consumption poverty. Usually economists use these measures to refer poverty.

(b) The second cluster of meanings is related to the lack of material or want. Besides income, this includes lack of or little wealth and lack or low quality of other assets such as shelter, clothing, furniture, personal means of transport, radios or television, and so on. This also tends to include no or poor access to services.

(c) The third cluster of meanings derives from Amartya Sen, and is expressed as capability deprivation, referring to what we can or cannot do, can or cannot be. This includes but goes beyond material lack or want to include human capabilities, for example skills and physical abilities, and also self-respect in society.

(d) The fourth cluster takes a more broadly multi-dimensional view of deprivation, with material lack or want as only one of several mutually reinforcing dimensions.

(e) The above four clusters of the meanings of poverty tend to overlook and ignore the analysis and views of the objects of the definition and description—"the poor", that is people who are in bad condition variously described as poor, marginalised, vulnerable, excluded or deprived. Then there arise a fifth cluster, which is the multiplicity of their meanings.

These five clusters of the meanings of poverty are the expressions of our education, training, mindsets, experiences and reflections. The interrelation between the various dimensions of the poverty can be described by the following web.

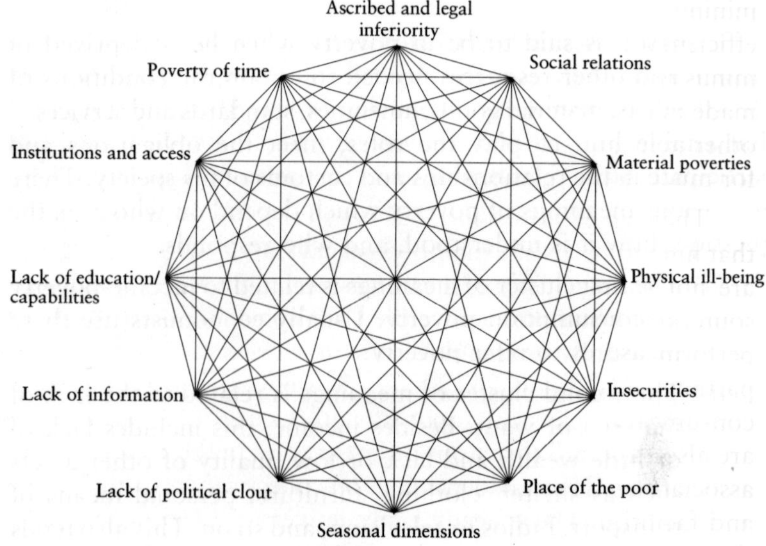

Fig. 5.1

The historical definition of poverty focuses on income, the economic resources available to a family, rather than on outcome measures of consumption or well-being. Living in poverty implies that a family has so little income that they are unable to purchase the things that we as a society think they need for a minimally decent life. Definition of the poverty varies from place to place. For example, poverty in United States means serious economic need or economic deprivation and typically implies more than merely escaping starvation; it means being able to purchase the goods and services that are necessary to afford adequate and stable housing, find and hold a job (if physically able), participate as a citizen in the community, keep oneself and one's family reasonably healthy, and provide the things that one's children need to participate effectively in school.

The concept of poverty is very old. Since the 1880s, three alternative conceptions of poverty have evolved as a basis for international and comparative work, which depend principally on the ideas of subsistence, basic needs and relative deprivation. According to the subsistence idea, a result of work prompted by nutritionists in Victorian England, families were defined to be in poverty when their incomes were not sufficient to obtain the minimum necessaries for the maintenance of merely physical efficiency. A family was treated as being in poverty if its income minus rent fell short of the poverty line. Although allowance was made in calculating the income level for clothing, fuel and some other items, this allowance was very small, and food accounted for much of the greatest share of subsistence.

The idea of subsistence has been criticised because it implies that human needs are mainly physical rather than social. People are not simply individual organisms requiring replacement of sources of physical energy; they are social beings expected to perform socially demanding roles as workers, citizens, parents, partners, neighbours and friends. Moreover, they are not simply consumers of physical goods but producers of those goods and are also expected to act out different roles in their various social associations. They are dependent on collectively provided utilities and facilities. These needs apply universally and not merely in the rich industrial societies. The lack of elaborate social institutions and services in developing countries and their scant resources raise the question whether or not the most basic material subsistence needs can be met in those countries. Meeting such needs as the satisfaction of hunger is widely accepted as a priority. Such needs have been included in the categorisation of 'absolute' poverty, which can also be labelled 'extreme' or 'severe'.

From an analytical perspective, history of poverty can be traced back at least to the codification of poor laws in medieval England, through to the pioneering empirical studies, at the turn of the century, by Booth in London and by Rowntree in York. Rowntree's finding, which was published in 1901, was the first to develop a poverty standard for individual families, based on estimates of nutritional and other requirements. During the 1960s, the main focus was on the level of income, reflected in macro-economic indicators like GNP per head, which was associated with an emphasis on growth.

By the 1970s the concept of 'basic needs' approach began to exert wide influence, supported strongly by the International Labour Organisation. This approach has two elements:

(a) minimum consumption needs of a family—adequate food, shelter and clothing, as well as certain household furniture and equipment; and

(b) essential services provided by and for the community at large, such as safe water, sanitation, public transport and health care, education and cultural facilities; and in rural areas it also includes land, agricultural tools and access to farming.

The basic needs approach is an extension of the subsistence approach of poverty, since in addition to material needs for individual physical survival and efficiency, there are the facilities and services, such as, health care, sanitation and education, required by local communities and population as a whole. As a result of Robert MacNamara's celebrated speech to the World Bank Board of Governors in Nairobi in 1973, and the subsequent publication of *Redistribution with Growth*, poverty became a prominent matter of study. There are two other factors which brought the attention towards the poverty.

(a) Emphasis on relative deprivation, inspired by the work of Runciman and Townsend of UK—Townsend, in particular, helped in redefining the poverty not just as a failure to meet minimum nutrition or subsistence levels, but rather as a failure to keep up with the standards prevalent in a given society.

(b) Broading the concept of income poverty to a wider set of 'basic needs', including those provided socially.

Following the pioneering work in mid-1970s of International Labour Organisation, poverty came to be defined not just as lack of income, but also as lack of access to health, education and other services. The concept of basic needs inspired policies like integrated rural development and aimed at establishing at least some of the preconditions for community development, and it played a prominent part in national development plans fostered by the international community, especially UN.

In the 1980s, new concepts were added to the definition of poverty. Some of the concepts were related to:

(a) the incorporation of nonmonetary aspects, particularly as a result of Robert Chambers' work on powerlessness and isolation, which helped to inspire greater attention to participation.

(b) a new interest in vulnerability, and its counterpart, security, associated with better understanding of seasonality and of the impact of shocks, notably drought. This pointed to the importance of assets as buffers, and also to social relations. It led to new work on coping strategies.

(c) broadening of the concept of poverty to a wider construct, livelihood. This was adopted by the Brundtland Commission on Sustainability and the Environment, which popularised the term sustainable livelihood.

(d) theoretical work by Amartya Sen, who had earlier contributed the notion of food entitlement, or access, emphasised that income was only valuable in so far as it increased the capabilities of individuals and thereby permitted 'functionings' in society.

(e) the study of gender—the focus moved from women alone (women in development) to wider gender relations (gender and development).

There was further development of the poverty concept in the 1990s. The idea of well-being came to act as a metaphor for absence of poverty, with concomitant emphasis on how poor people themselves view their situation. Inspired by Amartya Sen, United Nations Development Program developed the idea of human development as, 'the denial of opportunities and choices most basic to human development—to lead a long, healthy, creative life and to enjoy a decent standard of living, freedom, dignity, self-esteem and the respect of others'.[1]

The third social formulation of the meaning of poverty—relative deprivation—was developed in the late 20th century. Relativity applies to both income and other resources and also to material and social conditions. In the current century, societies are passing through such rapid change that a poverty standard devised at some historical date in the past is difficult to justify under new conditions. Today's societies cannot be subjected to the same laws, obligations and customs that applied to a previous era. Globalisation has connected the people and their standards of living, while inequalities within and between countries have widened. Therefore, merely updating any historical benchmark of poverty on the basis of some index of prices cannot be useful all the times. Over many years the 'relativity' of meanings of poverty has come to be recognised, in part if not comprehensively. Adam Smith, for example, recognised the ways in which 'necessities' were defined by custom in the early part of the 19th century, citing the labourer's need to wear a shirt as an example. It is not enough to describe poverty as a condition applying to those whose disposable income is low relative to that of others. This is to fail to distinguish conceptually between inequality and poverty. Poor people are not just the victims of a maldistribution of resources but, more exactly, they lack, or are denied, the resources to fulfil social demands and observe the customs as well as the unfolding laws, of society. This criterion lends itself to scientific observation, measurement and analysis of multiple deprivations.

Poverty Line

Poverty line refers to a critical threshold of income, consumption, or, more generally, access to goods and services below which individuals are declared to be poor. It, thus, represents a minimum level of acceptable economic participation in a given society at a given point in time. We can find out the poverty line for a particular society simply by collecting data on minimum nutrient levels that make up an adequate diet, on the prices of foodstuffs that contain such nutrients, and on the costs of shelter and clothing, and then adding up the consumption expenditures needed to obtain these basic requirements. The prevailing legally decreed minimum wage in a country can be used to estimate the poverty line of that country.

The poverty line used in the United States is nutrition-based, based on Orshansky's estimates, which take into consideration a minimum-budget estimates for food requirements, scaled by three (the scaling proxies for other requirements such as rent and clothing).[2] On the other hand in India, poverty line is determined by using estimates of expenditure necessary to guarantee a minimum consumption of calories. In determining such poverty lines one point should be noted that the poorer the country, the better the nutrition-based approximation and the scaling become more problematic as the average standard of living rises.

The Millennium Development Goal and World Bank define poverty as $1-a-day poverty line, which is a solely monetary measure and is monodimensional. The basis for this poverty line is the median of 10 of the lowest national poverty lines in the world. It has not been derived from any consideration of well-being or basic needs. According to the World Bank economists, this measure is frugal and must be deemed a conservative estimate whereby aggregate poverty in the developing world is defined by the perceptions of poverty found in the poorest countries. This implies that the $1-a-day poverty line is unreasonably low and is lower than developed world populations would consider morally justifiable. However, World Bank is now using poverty indices for a $2-a-day line which seems to be based simply on a doubling of the $1-a-day poverty line. If we follow this concept of poverty line, the highest population lies between the \$1-a-day to \$2-a-day poverty lines.

The another measure of poverty line is the ethical poverty line (EPL) which has been derived from globally standardised and ethically justifiable well-being outcomes for which sufficient data already exist in the World Development Indicators (WDI). This measure does not overcome the inherent problem of all income poverty lines, namely that they oversimplify and reduce the complexity of global poverty to a monodimensional monetary measure. However, it at least provides a morally defensible basis for setting the line and the intellectual background to it draws on two specific areas of research:

(a) on well-being measures and their determinants; and

(b) on public health, relating individual life-expectancy to individual income levels.

The above mentioned two areas can be combined to derive an international poverty line directly from aggregate life expectancy outcomes. If poverty is best defined in terms of low levels of well-being rather than income, and life-expectancy at birth is the indicator of well-being, then an ethical poverty line can be developed by modelling the relation between national average life-expectancy outcomes and their underlying source in individual absolute poverty levels. The model assumes the observed fact of a 'kink' in the correlation curve indicating the critical consumption level. Applying the model to national populations disaggregated by consumption level, the statistical correlation was established between modelled life-expectancies and the actual ones published in World Development Indicators. Similar correlations were achieved from the best of the functions investigated for the model. Collectively, these results set the kink consumption at between \$2.7-a-day and \$3.9-a-day, and probably around \$3-a-day. Raising the poverty line to the ethical poverty line both puts many more people in poverty and raises the threshold that each poor person has to climb over to get out of poverty.

Nanak Kakwani introduced a new method for determining the poverty line using utility theory. He used the Hicksian concept of income as the maximum that can be spent from a stock of capital while leaving the value of the stock intact. Thus, he has linked income generation and consumption to define the poverty line. He has defined the poverty line as that level of expected income which allows the individual to consume enough food while maintaining his labour power intact. Thus, to prevent any deterioration in health, enough food should be purchased. Then the poverty level will crucially depend on the availability of work and the wage rate. If the individual cannot earn enough to be able to eat so as to prevent deterioration in health, and, in general, labour power, then he is poor.

Nanak Kakwani's[3] definition of poverty line has several advantages when compared to the standard definition which relies on calories. It is dynamic since availability of work or wages change, e.g., due to seasonal changes or because the individual's health may deteriorate, he will move in and out of poverty. It also relates the consumption of food to income generation while avoiding imposing any specific calorific requirements. It is firmly based in an economic theoretic definition of income. The definition connects in an obvious way to issues of health and nutrition and thus builds a bridge between monetary measures and the human poverty index. In principle, though data demanding in practice, we can define this critical food intake at individual level allowing for age, gender, health status. Thus, this approach presents a way of connecting consumption and income generation via the notion of labour capacity to work; and allows for different levels of required food consumption for different individuals breaking away from any uniform dollar-a-day notion.

ALTERNATIVE MEASURES OF POVERTY

Poverty is a multidimensional problem which reflects failures in many dimensions of human life—hunger, unemployment, homelessness and victimisation, and social injustice. Therefore, the determination of a poverty line cannot be based on an arbitrary selection of a low level of income. Only scientific criteria independent of income can justify where the poverty line should be drawn. The multiplicity and severity of different types of deprivation can constitute those criteria. The key is therefore to define a threshold of income below which people are found to be thus deprived. The measure of multiple deprivations must be decided on the basis of evidence about each and every sphere of the range of social and individual activities people perform in fulfilment of individual and family needs, and social obligations. The degree of material and social deprivation relative to income is the basis for ascertaining the threshold amount of income ordinarily required by households of different compositions to surmount poverty.

If $y = (y_1, y_2, ..., y_n)$ is a vector whose components are the incomes of N households, arranged in ascending order, and if z is the poverty line, then a household is poor if $y_i \leq z$. Let M households ($i = 1, 2, ..., M$) are poor, then a poverty measure, denoted $P(y; z)$, is a real valued function which associates a level of poverty with y and z. In this section we shall consider two alternative measures of poverty—head count ratio, income gap ratio and poverty gap ratio.

Head Count Ratio

One natural measure of poverty is simply to count the number of people below the poverty line. This measure is known as head count and if we divide this by total population of the country or region under consideration, we get the head-count ratio. Thus,

$$Head\ Count\ Ratio\ (HCR) = \frac{Head\ Count\ (M)}{Total\ Population\ (N)}$$

where,

Head Count = number of people below the poverty line.

The problem with this method is that it does not show the extent to which individual income (or expenditure) falls below the poverty line. It is also insensitive towards the fact that people further below the poverty line are poorer than people closer to it. The problem with *HCR* in the multidimensional case is in part parallel to the problem in the unidimensional case. If one poor person becomes poorer in any given dimension, the headcount remains unchanged. Further, if one poor person becomes poor in a dimension in which that poor person had previously been non-poor, *HCR* remains unchanged. This violates what we will call dimensional monotonicity. Intuitively speaking, this is the property that if the position of person *i* who is deprived with respect to the set of dimensions declines—the person becomes deprived in a greater number of dimensions—then overall poverty should increase.

Income Gap Ratio

Income gap ratio (IGR) is defined as the difference between the poverty line and the average income (or consumption) of the population living under the poverty line, expressed as a fraction of the poverty line and it measures the depth of poverty. It is the measure of total shortfall of the poor from the poverty line divided by the total income required to bring all the poor people to the poverty line. Thus, the income gap ratio is the mean distance of the incomes of the poor from the poverty line, expressed as a proportion of the poverty line as

$$\textit{Income Gap Ratio}\ (IGR) = \frac{\sum_{i=1}^{M}(z - y_i)}{Mz} = 1 - \frac{\mu^P}{z}$$

where,

μ^P = mean income of the poor.

Income gap ratio in itself is not a good measure of poverty. Suppose that some households or individuals who are poor but close to the poverty line are improving their standards of living over time, and thereby become non-poor. In this case IGR will increase because the mean distance separating the poor from the poverty line will increase (this happens because some of those who were less poor have emerged from poverty so that those still in poverty are on average further away from the poverty line), suggesting a deterioration in welfare, while nobody is worst off and some people are actually better off.

Poverty Gap Ratio

Poverty gap ratio (PGR) is defined as the ratio of the average of income (or extra consumption) needed to get all poor people to the poverty line, divided by the mean income (or consumption) of the society. Thus, PGR is the mean distance of the incomes of the entire population—the non-poor being assigned a distance of zero—from the poverty line, expressed as a proportion of the poverty line as,

$$\textit{Poverty Gap Ratio (PGR)} = \frac{\sum_{i=1}^{M}(z-y_i)}{Nz} = \frac{\sum_{i=1}^{M}(z-y_i)}{Mz}\cdot\frac{M}{N} = IGR{\cdot}HCR$$

The reason for dividing by the average for society as a whole is that this gives us an idea of how large the gap is relative to resources that potentially may be used to close the gap. In this way, the PGR is not really a measure of poverty itself, but a measure of resources required to eradicate it. It is a measure of the poverty deficit of the entire population, where the notion of poverty deficit captures the resources that would be needed to lift all the poor out of poverty through perfectly targeted cash transfers. When IGR will increase, the PGR will decrease, because the head count ratio of poverty will decrease, suggesting an improvement towards poverty reduction. The problem with IGR is that it is defined only on the population that is poor, while the poverty gap is defined over the population as a whole.

The severity of poverty can be described by the squared poverty gap ratio measure. While the poverty gap ratio takes into account the distance separating the poor from the poverty line, the squared poverty gap ratio takes the square of that distance into account. When using the squared poverty gap ratio, the poverty gap is weighted by itself, so as to give more weight to the very poor. Squared poverty gap ratio is given by

$$\textit{Squared Poverty Gap Ratio (SPGR)} = \frac{1}{N}\sum_{i-1}^{M}\left(\frac{z-y_i}{z}\right)^2$$

The SPGR takes into account the inequality among the poor. A transfer from a poor to an even poorer would reduce the ratio; a transfer from a very poor to a less poor would increase the ratio.

SEN'S MEASURES OF POVERTY

Amartya Sen[4] (1976) pioneered the axiomatic approach to the measurement of poverty by explicitly setting out the axioms against which a poverty measure should be judged. His poverty measure makes use of three poverty indicators—the proportion of poor, the income gap ratio, and the distribution of income among the poor. Two problems are faced in the measurement of poverty—(i) identifying the poor among the total population, and (ii) constructing an index of poverty using the available information on the poor. The first problem involves the choice of a criterion of poverty—selection of a poverty line in terms of real income per head—and then ascertaining those who satisfy that criterion, i.e., fall below the poverty line. The simple solution of the second problem is to count the number of the poor and check the percentage of the total population belonging to this category, which is known as the head-count ratio (HCR). This measure of poverty is completely insensitive to the distribution of income among the poor—a transfer of income from the poorest poor to those who are better off will either keep HCR unchanged, or make it go down. Thus, according to Sen, HCR violates the following two axioms:

(a) *Axiom of Monotonicity*: Given other things, a reduction in income of a person below the poverty line must increase the poverty measure.

(b) *Axiom of Transfer*: Given other things, a pure transfer of income from a person below the poverty line to anyone who is richer must increase the poverty measure.[5]

Another measure, which is used by the United States Social Security Administration, is the poverty gap ratio (PGR), which is the aggregate shortfall of the income of all the poor taken together from the poverty line. PGR is also completely insensitive to the number of people or the percentage of people who are poor, sharing a given poverty gap. This measure satisfies the axiom of monotonicity but violates the axiom of transfer. Thus, there is a need of such a poverty measure which can satisfied the above two axioms.

Let us consider a community S consisting n people and $S(x)$ denotes the set of people with income less than or equal to x. Now, suppose z represents the poverty line and $S(z)$, the set of the poor people. $S(\infty)$ is the set of all that belongs to S. If g_i

represents the income gap of an individual i, then it can be given by the difference between the poverty line z and his income y_i as

$$g_i = z - y_i \qquad \text{... (5.1)}$$

Here one point should be mentioned that the poor has non-negative g_i while others have negative. The aggregate gap $Q(x)$, for any income configuration represented by an n-vector $\vec{y}$, of the set $S(x)$ of people with income less than or equal to x is a normalised weighted sum of the income gaps g_i of everyone in $S(x)$, using non-negative weights $v_i(z, \vec{y})$ is given by

$$Q(x) = A(z, \vec{y}) \sum_{i \in S(x)} g_i v_i(z, \vec{y}) \qquad \text{... (5.2)}$$

From equation (5.2) we see that v_i has been defined as a function of the vector $\vec{y}$ along with z, not of y_i alone, implying that no requirement of additive separability has been imposed. In this condition, the index of poverty P of a given income configuration $\vec{y}$ will be the maximum value of the aggregate gap $Q(x)$ for all x represented by

$$P = \max_x Q(x) \qquad \text{... (5.3)}$$

Since, the weights v_i are all non-negative, therefore from (5.1) and (5.2) we have

$$P = Q(z) \qquad \text{... (5.4)}$$

Equation (5.4) states that the index of poverty P of a community is given by the value of the weighted aggregate gap of the poor in that community.

Following the *Axiom of Transfer*, if person i is accepted to be worse-off than person j in a given income configuration $\vec{y}$, then the weight v_i on the income shortfall g_i of the worse-off person i should be greater than the weight v_j on the income shortfall g_j. Now, suppose that $W_i(\vec{y})$ and $W_j(\vec{y})$ be the welfare levels of i and j under configuration $\vec{y}$ leading the *Axiom of Relative Equity*.

(c) *Axiom of Relative Equity*: If $W_i(\vec{y}) < W_j(\vec{y})$ then $v_i(z, \vec{y}) > v_j(z, \vec{y})$ for any pair (i, j).

Axiom of Relative Equity gives expression to a very mild requirement of equity. Therefore, another axiom is proposed, which incorporates *Axiom of Relative Equity*.

(d) *Axiom of Ordinal Rank Weights*: The weight $v_i(z, \vec{y})$ on the income gap of person i equals the rank order of i in the interpersonal welfare ordering of the poor.

Axiom of Ordinal Rank Weights can be easily made a theorem derived from more primitive axioms by two ways. The first is to follow the equidistanced cardinalisation of an ordering, i.e., if *A*, *B*, and *C* are ranked in that order in terms of their weights, and if there is no intermediate alternative between *A* and *B*, and none between *B* and *C*, then we can say that the degree of superiority that an individual has given to *A* over *B* should be considered the same as the degree of superiority that he has accorded to *B* over *C*. Using *Axiom of Relative Equity* we find that if *i* is worse-off than *j*, then the weight on *i's* income gap should be greater than on *j's* income gap. Combining this with the appropriate normalisation of the origin and the unit, we arrive at the *Axiom of Ordinal Rank Weights*.

The second way is to consider a relativist view of poverty, viewing deprivation as an essentially relative concept. A person has greater sense of poverty if he occupy a lower position in the welfare scale, and his welfare rank among others may be taken to indicate the weight to be placed on his income gap. From this approach also we can derive the *Axiom of Ordinal Rank Weights*.

Since, the *Axiom of Relative Equity* and the *Axiom of Ordinal Rank Weights* are in terms of welfare rankings, and the observed data are given on income rankings, we shall consider the relation between income and welfare. It may be possible that a richer person may have lower welfare than a poorer person. It is not possible to consider such details while dealing with a general measure of poverty for the whole community. The following *Axiom of Monotonic Welfare* has been constructed on the cruder assumption that a richer person is also better off and the individual welfare relation follows a strict complete ordering.

(e) *Axiom of Monotonic Welfare*: The relation 'greater than' is defined on the set of individual welfare numbers $\{W_i(\vec{y})\}$ for any income configuration $\vec{y}$ is a strict complete ordering, and the relation > defined on the corresponding set of individual incomes $\{y_i\}$ is a sub-relation of the former, i.e., if $y_i > y_j$, then $W_i(\vec{y}) > W_j(\vec{y})$ for any pair of (i, j).

Now, once again we consider the two measures of poverty which are generally used. The *HCR* is the ratio of the number of people with income $y_i \leq z$, to the total population size n and is written as

$$HCR = q/n \qquad \dots (5.5)$$

And the other measure is *PGR* which is silent on the number of people who share the gap, but can be easily normalised into a per-person *IGR* as

$$IGR = \sum_{i \in S(z)} g_i \,/\, qz \qquad \dots (5.6)$$

Both *HCR* and *IGR* are not informative because neither gives adequate information on the exact income distribution among the poor. Neither measure satisfies the transfer axiom, or the requirement of putting a greater weight on the income gap of the poorer person. In the case where all the poor have exactly the same income level $y^* < z$, *HCR* and *IGR* together will give adequate information on the level of poverty, because the two measures together can tell us all about the proportion of people who are below the poverty line and the extent of the income shortfall of each. To obtain a simple normalisation, we consider the following axiom.

(f) *Axiom of Normalised Poverty Value*: If all the poor have the same income, then $P = HCR \cdot IGR$.

All the above mentioned axioms taken together determine unique poverty index which can be stated easily if the persons can be arranged in a non-decreasing order of income satisfying:

$$y_1 \leq y_2 \leq y_3 \leq \dots < y_n \qquad \dots (5.7)$$

Thus, for a large numbers of the poor, the only poverty index satisfying *Axioms of Ordinal Rank Weights, Monotonic Welfare and Normalised Poverty Value* is given by

$$P = HCR\ [IGR + (1 - IGR)\ G] \qquad \dots (5.8)$$

where, G is the Gini coefficient of the income distribution of the poor.

Let us prove the equation (5.8).

Using *Axiom of Monotonic Welfare*, there is a way of numbering the individuals satisfying equation (5.7), such that

$$W_1(\vec{y}) < W_2(\vec{y}) < \dots < W_n(\vec{y}) \qquad \dots (5.9)$$

For any person $i \leq q$, there are exactly $(q + 1 - i)$ people among the poor with at least as high a welfare level as person i. Then, by using *Axiom of Ordinal Rank Weights* we have

$$v_i(z, \vec{y}) = q + 1 - i \qquad \dots (5.10)$$

Therefore, from equations (5.2) and (5.4) we have

$$P = A(z,\vec{y})\sum_{i=1}^{q} g_i(q+1-i) \qquad \dots (5.11)$$

Let us consider a case when all the poor have the same income y^* and the same income gap $g^* = z - y^*$, then the equation (5.11) becomes

$$P = A(z,\vec{y})g^*\frac{q(q+1)}{2} \qquad \dots (5.12)$$

Following the *Axiom of Normalised Poverty Value* we get

$$P = \left(\frac{q}{n}\right).\left(\frac{g^*}{z}\right) \qquad \dots (5.13)$$

Solving equations (5.12) and (5.13) we get

$$A(z,\vec{y}) = \frac{2}{(q+1)nz} \qquad \dots (5.14)$$

From equations (5.11) and (5.14) we get

$$P = \frac{2}{(q+1)nz}\sum_{i=1}^{q}(z - y_i)(q+1-i) \qquad \dots (5.15)$$

The Lorenz distribution of incomes of the poor is given by the Gini coefficient G as

$$G = \frac{1}{2q^2m}\sum_{i=1}^{q}\sum_{j=1}^{q} |y_i - y_j| \qquad \text{... (5.16)}$$

where, m is the mean income of the poor.

Since, $|y_i - y_j| = y_i + y_j - 2\min(y_i, y_j)$, equation (5.16) becomes

$$G = 1 - \frac{1}{q^2m}\sum_{i=1}^{q}\sum_{j=1}^{q} \min(y_i, y_j)$$

$$= 1 + \frac{1}{q} - \frac{2}{q^2m}\sum_{i=1}^{q} y_i(q+1-i) \qquad \text{... (5.17)}$$

From equations (5.15) and (5.17) we have

$$P = \frac{1}{(q+1)nz}\left[zq(q+1) + q^2m\left(G - \frac{q+1}{q}\right)\right] \qquad \text{... (5.18)}$$

Using equations (5.5) and (5.6), equation (5.18) reduces to

$$P = HCR\left[1 - (1 - IGR)\left(1 - G\left(\frac{q}{q+1}\right)\right)\right] \qquad \text{... (5.19)}$$

If q is very large, equation (5.19) reduces to equation (5.8). Hence, equation (5.8) is proved.

Thus, Sen's poverty measure represented by equation (5.8) takes account of:

(a) the number of poor persons, relative to the population, through head count ratio (HCR);

(b) the depth of their poverty through income gap ratio (IGR); and

(c) the relative deprivation through Gini coefficient (G) calculated on incomes of the poor.

Poverty and Inequality

We have derived the poverty index by using the more primitive concept of the aggregate gap $Q(x)$. Here, one point should be noted that given the weighting system precipitated by *Axioms of Ordinal Rank Weights and Monotonic Welfare*, the value of $Q(x)$ is the same for all $x \geq z$, so that P defined by equation (5.3) as $\max_x Q(x)$ can be taken to be $Q(x)$ for any $x \geq z$ and not merely $x = z$. This is because, due to the *Axiom of Ordinal Rank Weights* the weight on the income gap g_i of person i equal to the number of people among the poor who are at least as well off as person i.

Following the *Axiom of Monotonic Welfare*, the inclusion of people above the poverty line z does not affect the value of Q since the weight on their income gap g_i is zero. But, while measuring the inequality the income gaps of people above the poverty line is also considered. Also, income gaps should be calculated not from the exogenously given poverty line z, but from some internal characteristic of the income configuration $\vec{y}$, possibly the mean income. The variation from poverty line to mean income will transform an absolute measure of poverty into a relative measure of inequality. For this z is replaced by the mean income m^* of $\vec{y}$. To incorporate all these changes we modify the *Axiom of Ordinal Rank Weights* as follows:

(d*) *Modified Axiom of Ordinal Rank Weights*: The weight $v_i(z, \vec{y})$ on the income gap of person i equals the number of people in S who are at least as well off as person i.

For the *Modified Axiom of Ordinal Rank Weights*, the weight v_i on the income gap of person i should be $(n + 1 - i)$. The measure of inequality η corresponding to the measure of poverty index P as specified in the equation (5.8) is the value obtained in place of P by replacing the number of poor, q, by the total number of people in the community, n, and replacing the poverty level, z, by the mean income of the community, m^*. Thus, we get the following statement:

> The measure of inequality, η, corresponding to the poverty index approximates the Gini coefficient for large n.

We can prove the above statement by replacing q by n, and z and m by m^* in the equations (5.15) and (5.17), in the formulations of P and G. Thus, the poverty measure, P, obtained in the equation (5.8) is essentially a transformation of the Gini coefficient from the measurement of inequality to that of poverty. Following figure provides a diagrammatic representation of P and G.

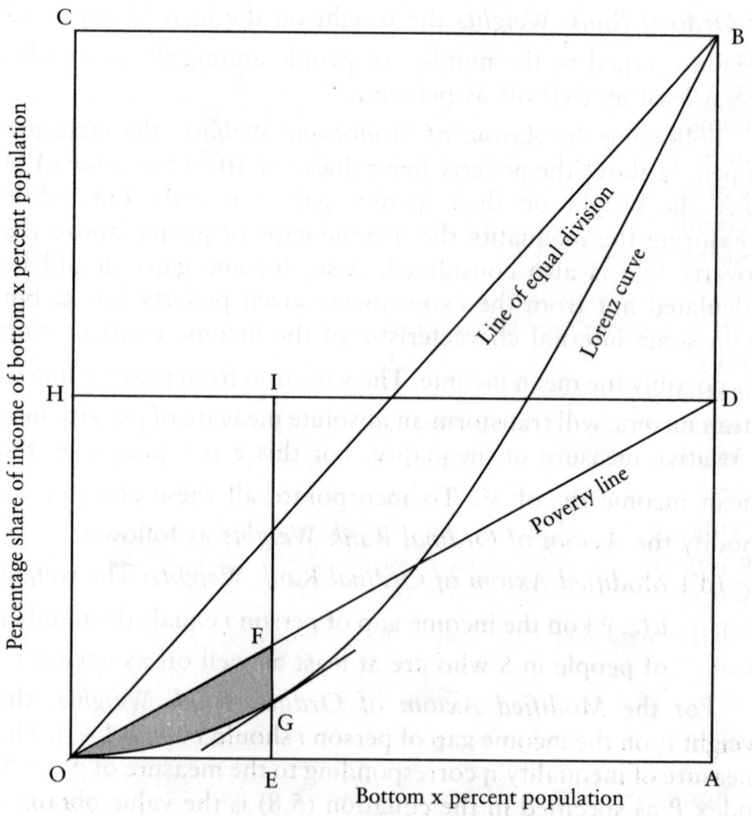

Fig. 5.2

In the Fig. 5.2, the line OGB represents the Lorenz curve and the line OB is the line of equal division. The Gini coefficient G is given by area OGB divided by area OAB. The poverty line is given by the slope of the line OD and OE represents the number of the poor. The poverty measure P is determined by the area OGF divided by area OEI. The difference between the two lies in

(a) the slope of the poverty line OD being different from the slope of the normalised mean income line OB, and

(b) counting only the poor, i.e., OE, in the poverty measure, as opposed to all, i.e., OA.

We can uderstand the rank-order weighting form of the Gini coefficient G and the poverty measure P intuitively by considering the area under the curve OGB, which the Gini numerator leaves out, i.e., area included by $(1 - G)$. At every point poor man's income is included and if there are n persons his income comes in n times. On the other hand, the highest income is included in the area under OGB exactly once at the point A when everyone is counted in. The *ith* poorest man comes in at the ith point of observation and has his income included for the remaining $(n - i)$ observations as well, thereby having his income counted in $(n + 1 - i)$ times. This produces the rank order weighting through the mechanism of the Lorenz curve, and it is this remarkable coincidence of weighting according to ordial ranks satisfying *Modified Axiom of Ordial Rank Weights* given *Axiom of Monotonic Welfare*. The same way of intuitively understanding the result regarding the poverty measure can be easily suggested by considering the number of times the gap between the slope of the poverty line OD and the slope of the income of the poor OGB gets counted in.

Differentiating equation (5.8) with respect to IGR and G, gives

$$\frac{\partial}{\partial G}\left(\frac{\partial P}{\partial IGR}\right) = -HCR < 0 \qquad \text{... (5.20)}$$

Equation (5.20) implies that the larger the inequality of income among the poor the smaller the increase in poverty will be when IGR increases. On the other way round, the larger the income inequality, the greater the increase in poverty should be when the poverty-gap ratio increases. Thus, the derivation in equation (5.20) should be strictly positive instead of being negative. Therefore, an alternative poverty measure which gives positive sign to the derivatives in equation (5.20) and at the same time satisfies all Sen's basic axioms can be written as

$$P^* = HCR \cdot IGR\ (1 + G) \qquad \text{... (5.21)}$$

The poverty measures represented by equation (5.20) requires an axiomatic justification similar to that of Sen's measure.

Modified Sen's Measure of Poverty

A stronger version of the *Axiom of Transfer*, known as the *Axiom of Strong Transfer* states that a regressive transfer from a poor person to a rich person must always cause the value of the poverty index to fall even if, in the process, the beneficiary crosses the poverty line. Sen's measure of poverty satisfies the *Axiom of Transfer*, but it does not necessarily satisfy the *Axiom of Strong Transfer*. Sen's measure gives too much importance to the poverty line and in the presence of measurement errors in income this importance may be largely spurious.[6]

Violation of the *Axiom of Strong Transfer* implies that Sen's measure is not continuous at the poverty line. To overcome this problem, define the censored income distribution $y^* = (y_1, y_2, ..., y_M, z, z, ..., z)$ obtained from y by replacing all non-poor incomes with the poverty line income, z.[7] The continuous version $P^*(y; z)$ of a non-continuous poverty measure $P(y; z)$ is given by:

$$P^*(y; z) = P(y^*; z) \qquad \text{... (5.22)}$$

Using the equation (5.22), the continuous version of Sen's measure of poverty is given by

$$P^* = HCR \cdot IGR + (1 - HCR \cdot IGR)G^* \qquad \text{... (5.23)}$$

where, G^* represents the Gini coefficient computed over the censored distribution, y^*. This version of Sen's measure of poverty satisfies the *Axiom of Strong Transfer*.

Limitations in the Axiomatisations of Sen's Measure

Following are some of the limitations in the axiomatisations suggested by Sen in the derivation of poverty index.

(a) In Sen's measure of poverty index, poverty has been defined as a normalised weighted sum of the income shortfalls of the poor from the poverty line. This definition, together with an axiom specifying the weights by the rank order (*Axiom of Ordinal Rank Weights*) of the poor in terms of their incomes, and a normalisation axiom (*Axiom of Normalised Poverty Value*), leads to the unique functional form for the poverty measure. This measure has four main properties—(i) monotonicity in the incomes of the poor, (ii) strict S-convexity in these incomes which lends the measure its inequality-sensitivity, and (iii) two technical but convenient properties of continuity in the incomes of the poor and a normalisation in the unit interval.

The use of the *a priori* definition of poverty leaves the linear form of Sen's poverty measure unjustified. None of the properties stated above are implied by the axioms themselves in the absence of the definition of poverty used. Thus, the use of this definition of poverty obscures the role of Sen's central axioms in the derivation of the poverty measure, because it does not permit it to be made clear as to what extent the axioms are responsible in inducing the above mentioned properties for the measure.

(b) Sen has used a normalisation axiom in deriving his poverty index, which specifies that in a situation where all the poors have equal incomes, the proverty value is given by the product of the head-count ratio and the income-gap ratio. The multiplicative form chosen for the axiom is arbitrary. Also, apart from the particular form that normalisation axiom takes, there is a prior problem in the intuitive motivation for the axiom. However, Sen has justified this axiom on the ground that "in the special case in which all the poor have exactly the same income level, $y^* < z$, it can be argued that *HCR* and *IGR* together should give us adequate information on the level of poverty, since in this special case the two together can tell us all about the proportion of people who are below the poverty line and the extent of the income shortfall of each".[8] But, defining poverty in terms of *HCR* and *IGR* is neither necessary nor sufficient for deriving an appropriate measure of poverty for the special case of equal incomes of the poor.[9]

Sen's measure of poverty has the virtue of taking the income distribution among the poor into account. But his index has never been used outside the academic literature because it lacks the intuitive appeal of some of the simpler measures of poverty.

Also, because it "cannot be used to decompose poverty into contributions from different subgroups".[10]

FOSTER-GREER-THORBECKE (FGT) MEASURE OF POVERTY

Foster, Greer and Thorbecke[11] proposed a generalised class of decomposable poverty measures, known as FGT family of poverty measures which combines information on the extent of poverty as measured by the head count ratio, the intensity of poverty as poverty gap ratio, and inequality among the poor as measured by the Gini coefficient. FGT family of poverty measures:

(a) is additively decomposable with population-share weights,

(b) satisfies the basic properties proposed by Sen,

(c) is justified by a relative deprivation concept of poverty, and

(d) consists of parameter which can be interpreted as an indicator of aversion to poverty.

FGT measure is referred to as decomposable poverty measure. A poverty measure is said to be decomposable if the poverty measure of a group is weighted average of the poverty measures of the individuals in a group.[12]

Let y_i be a measure of income, n the size of the population, and z the poverty line. Now ranking the households according to their measure of income and defining households $i = 1, ..., q$ as poor and $i = (q + 1), ..., n$ as non-poor, the Foster-Greer Thorbecke poverty measure can be given by

$$P_\alpha = \frac{1}{n}\sum_{i=1}^{q}\left(\frac{z - y_i}{z}\right)^\alpha, \quad \forall\, \alpha \geq 0 \qquad \text{... (5.24)}$$

The larger the value of α, the more sensitive the measure is to the well-being of the poorest household. Therefore, here we consider the values for $\alpha = 0, 1,$ or 2 only. Here one point should be noted that $(z - y_i)$ is by definition positive for all poor households $(i = 1, ..., q)$ since all poor households earn less than the poverty cut-off point.

When $\alpha = 0$, P_α reduces to $P_0 = q/n$ which is the head count ratio and is totally insensitive to the depth of poverty.

When $\alpha = 1$, we get P_1 as the summation of the relative poverty gap over all poor households and dividing by the total number of households, which is known as the poverty gap ratio and measures the depth of poverty because it is a function of both the distance of each poor household from the poverty line and the number of poor.

When $\alpha = 2$, we get P_2 as the average of squared normalised shortfalls, which is also a measure of the depth of poverty and is an improvement on P_0 and P_1 because it also takes into account the inequality amongst the poor. P_2 is made up of two components—(i) an amount due to the poverty gap, and (ii) an amount due to the inequality among the poor, measured in terms of the coefficient of variation. P_2 can be given by the equation:

$$P_2 = \frac{(P_1)^2}{P_0} + \frac{(P_0 - P_1)^2}{P_0} \cdot (C_q)^2 \qquad \text{... (5.25)}$$

where, C_q is the coefficient of variation of the income among the poor.

We can calculate the measure of inequality, P_2, in two ways—either using equation (5.24) for $\alpha = 2$ or equation (5.25). Before using equation (5.25) we shall have to use equation (5.24) to calculate P_0 and P_1, i.e., for $\alpha = 0$ and $\alpha = 1$ respectively. One advantage of using P_2 in terms of P_0 and P_1 is that it provides a breakdown of the two components of poverty measure.

The mean and the variance level of income of the poor households are given by

$$\text{Mean income, } \mu = \frac{1}{n}\sum_{i=1}^{n} y_i \qquad \text{... (5.26)}$$

$$\text{Variance, } V = \frac{1}{n}\sum_{i=1}^{n} (y_i - \mu)^2 \qquad \text{... (5.27)}$$

Let q be the number of poor households. Then the mean and variance of income of the poor households can be calculated by substituting q for n in equations (5.26) and (5.27). An expression for $(C_q)^2$ is given as

$$(C_q)^2 = \frac{\frac{1}{q}\sum_{i=1}^{q}(y_i - \mu)^2}{\mu^2} = \frac{\frac{1}{q}\sum_{i=1}^{q}(y_i)^2 - \mu^2}{\mu^2} = \frac{1}{q\mu^2}\sum_{i=1}^{q}(y_i)^2 - 1 \qquad \text{... (5.28)}$$

Expressions for P_0 and P_1 can be given as

$$P_0 = q/n \text{ and } P_1 = q/n - q\mu/nz \qquad \text{... (5.29)}$$

Using equation (5.29) in (5.25) we get

$$(P_1)^2 = \left(\frac{q}{n}\right)^2 - \frac{2q^2\mu}{n^2 z} + \left(\frac{q\mu}{nz}\right)^2$$

$$\therefore \quad \frac{(P_1)^2}{P_0} = \left(\frac{q}{n}\right) - \frac{2q\mu}{nz} + \frac{q\mu^2}{nz^2} \qquad \text{... (5.30)}$$

$$P_0 - P_1 = \frac{q\mu}{nz}$$

$$\therefore \quad \frac{(P_0 - P_1)^2}{P_0}\cdot(C_q)^2 = \frac{q\mu^2}{nz^2}\cdot(C_q)^2 \qquad \text{... (5.31)}$$

P_2 is determined by summing equations (5.30) and (5.31). Substituting $(C_q)^2$ in equation (5.31) with equation (5.28) and simplifying gives

$$P_2 = \frac{q}{n} - \frac{2q\mu}{nz} + \frac{1}{nz^2}\sum_{i=1}^{q}(y_i)^2 \qquad \text{... (5.32)}$$

P_2 can also be calculated directly from equation (5.24) as

$$P_2 = \frac{1}{n}\sum_{i=1}^{q}\left(\frac{z - y_i}{z}\right)^2 = \frac{1}{n}\sum_{i=1}^{q}\left(1 - \frac{2y_i}{z} + \frac{(y_i)^2}{z^2}\right)$$

$$= \frac{q}{n} - \frac{2q\mu}{nz} + \frac{1}{nz^2}\sum_{i=1}^{q}(y_i)^2 \qquad \text{... (5.33)}$$

Equations (5.32) and (5.33) give the same result.

Sen's measure takes the poverty as a normalised weighted sum of the income shortfalls of the poor. In contrast to the rank order weighting scheme of Sen, *FGT* measure takes the weights to be the shortfalls themselves and the deprivation depends on the distance between a poor household's actual income and the poverty line, not the number of households that lie between a given household and the poverty line. Despite this basic difference in weighting, several of the arguments advanced in support of Sen's measure are also true for the *FGT* measure. For example, in Sen's measure poorer households have been given higher weights. *FGT* measure also satisfies this requirement. According to Sen weights should be based on a notion of relative deprivation experienced by the poor households. *FGT* measure also takes into account several different aspects of relative deprivation including the magnitude of relative deprivation, or the extent of the difference between the desired situation and that of the person desiring it. Where the desired situation is to receive enough income to be able to meet the accepted conventions of minimum needs and the existing situation is given by the poor household's income, the magnitude of relative deprivation is precisely the income shortfall of that household. This aspect of relative deprivation is taken into account in the weighting scheme of *FGT*.

FGT measure satisfies following two axioms:

(a) *Axiom of Transfer Sensitivity*: If a transfer $t > 0$ of income takes place from a poor household with income y_i to a poor household with income $y_i + d$, $(d > 0)$, then the magnitude of the increase in poverty must be smaller for larger y_i.

FGT measure does not satisfy this axiom directly, but it can be generalised to a class which contains poverty measures that do. For each $\alpha \geq 0$, let P_α be defined as

$$P_a = \frac{1}{n}\sum_{i=1}^{q}\left(\frac{z - y_i}{z}\right)^{\alpha} = \frac{1}{n}\sum_{i=1}^{q}\left(\frac{g_i}{z}\right)^{\alpha} \qquad \ldots (5.34)$$

From the equation (5.34) we see that the measure P_0 is simply the head count ratio *HCR*, while P_1 is the *HCR·IGR*, a renormalisation of the income-gap measure. The measure *FGT* is obtained by setting $\alpha = 2$. The parameter α can be viewed as a measure of poverty aversion—a larger α gives greater emphasis to the poorest poor. As α becomes very large P_α approaches a measure which considers only the position of the poorest household. The properties of this family of measures can be summarised by the following proposition.

Proposition: The poverty measure P_α satisfies the *Axiom of Monotonicity* for $\alpha > 0$, the *Axiom of transfer* for $\alpha > 1$, and the *Axiom of Transfer Sensitivity* for $\alpha > 2$.

For $\alpha > 0$ the *Axiom of Monotonicity* holds because g_i increases as y_i falls. Any transfer from a poor household to a richer one may be viewed as some combination of the following two types of regressive transfers:

(a) from a poor household to another poor household that stays poor, or

(b) from a poor household to a household at or above the poverty line.

The strict convexity of P_α in the vector of poor incomes for $\alpha > 1$ satisfies form (a), while a transfer of the form (b) increases P_α by inspection. Following Kolm, P_α satisfies the *Axiom of Transfer Sensitivity* for $\alpha > 2$.

Now let us consider the case of decomposability. Let the population be divided into *m* collection of households $j = 1, 2, \ldots, m$ with ordered income vectors y_j and population sizes n_j. To analyse poverty by population subgroups we shall consider the following axiom:

(b) *Axiom of Subgroup Monotonicity*: Let $\vec{y}$ be a vector of incomes obtained from *y* by changing the incomes in subgroup *j* from y_j to $\vec{y}_j$, where n_j is unchanged. If $\vec{y}_j$ has more poverty than y_j, then $\vec{y}$ must also have a higher level of poverty than *y*.

When incomes in a given subgroup change and the rest remaining fixed, the above axiom requires subgroup and total poverty to move in the same direction. If we follow this criterion, the Sen's measure and its variants are not well-suited for poverty analysis by subgroup, since they violate this consistency requirement in certain cases. On the other hand it can be shown that *FGT* measure satisfies subgroup monotonicity, and satisfies the following proposition of decomposability.

Proposition: For any income vector y broken down into subgroup income vectors $y_1, y_2, ..., y_m$

$$P_\alpha(y; z) = \sum_{j=1}^{m} \frac{n_j}{n} P_\alpha(y_j; z) \qquad \text{... (5.35)}$$

and P_α is additively decomposable with population share weights.

Equation (5.35) permits a quantitative, as well as qualitative, assessment of the effect of changes in subgroup poverty on total poverty. Increase in poverty in a subgroup will increase total poverty at a rate given by the population share n_j/n; the larger the population share, the greater the impact. The quantity $T_j = (n_j/n)\ P_\alpha(y_j;\ z)$ can be interpreted as the total contribution of a subgroup to overall poverty while $100T_j/P_\alpha(y;\ z)$ is the percentage contribution of subgroup j.

MOLLIE ORSHANSKY'S MEASURE OF POVERTY

In USA two slightly different poverty measures are used—(i) poverty thresholds, based on the thrifty food plan by the U.S. Department of Agriculture, and (ii) poverty guidelines, a simplification of the poverty thresholds used to determine eligibility for a number of programs. The poverty thresholds are established after the year is over, based on the current population survey from March of the current year. They are used mainly for statistical purposes and research, such as preparing estimates of the number of Americans in poverty each year. On the other hand poverty guidelines are issued at the beginning of each year, generally in February or March, and are used to determine eligibility for poverty programs such as the Oregon Health Plan. In this section we shall discuss only poverty thresholds.

Poverty thresholds were developed by Mollie Orshansky of the Social Security Administration (SSA) of U.S. in 1963-1964. A research project at SSA was to use the current population survey to assess the economic well-being of children in the U.S. To do so, Orshansky developed a measure of income inadequacy (known as poverty thresholds) for families to compare the well-being of children in families of different size and composition. She based her poverty thresholds on the 'thrifty food plan', which was the cheapest of four food plans developed by the U.S. Department of Agriculture (USDA). According to the USDA, the food plan was designed for temporary or emergency use when funds are low.

Mollie presented the poverty thresholds as a measure of income inadequacy. In her words, "if it is not possible to state unequivocally how much is enough, it should be possible to assert with confidence how much, on an average, is too little", she goes on to note that such poverty thresholds may be "arbitrary, but not unreasonable".[13] She has built her poverty thresholds on two empirical findings from food consumption research at USDA.

(a) Findings of the 1962 Economy Food Plan that meets the nutritional requirements of a healthy diet at minimal cost (not minimum cost) for individuals of different age-gender groups and families of different size and composition. The cost of the food plan was treated as an adequate standard of food expenditures for a household with income at the poverty threshold.

(b) The 1955 Household Food Consumption Survey finding that for all households of two or more persons, the average dollar value of food used during a week (both at-home and away-from-home) accounted for one-third of after tax cash income. The inverse of the expenditure share was multiplied by the cost of the Economy Food Plan to calculate the poverty threshold of income.

The multiplier approach used by Mollie to specifying the poverty threshold is in contrast to a family budget approach or a relative income approach of Fisher. This approach is based on a standard of adequacy for food and a food expenditure share, but not other necessities purchased by households. Mollie noted that there was no generally accepted standard of adequacy for essentials of living except for food. She has made two key contributions in her use of the above mentioned findings to calculate the poverty thresholds:

(a) development of equivalence scales for families of different size and composition, and

(b) and use of the average food expenditure share for all households, and not just that of low income households.

Mollie differentiated her thresholds not only by family size, but also by farm/non-farm status, by the number of family members who were children, gender of the head of household, and by aged/non-aged status. The result was a detailed matrix of 124 poverty thresholds. Generally, the figures cited were weighted average thresholds for each family size.

Minimal Cost for Healthy Diet

The 1962 Economy Food Plan was a minimal cost food plan that met the nutritional requirements of a healthy diet for individuals distinguished by seventeen age-gender groups plus pregnant and lactating women, and for families distinguished by size and composition.[14] This plan was concerned with the quantity of food needed in one week from each of eleven food groups to provide three meals at home every day. The cost of the food plan varies by age-gender group. It was not designed to be a minimum cost food plan but a palatable food plan at minimal cost that met the 1958 recommended dietary allowances. It was designed for temporary or emergency use when funds are low and included foods that require a considerable amount of home preparation with little waste and required skill in food shopping and preparation.

Development of Economy Food Plan was an elaborate and complex process which required two distinguished steps:

(a) determination of the food plan for the individual age-gender groups, and

(b) using the individual food plans to create family food plans where family types were distinguished by size and composition.

The first step involves development of a minimal cost food plan for each individual age-gender group, starting with historical average consumption by food group for low-income individuals. For the 1962 Economy Food Plan, average consumption was from the 1955 Household Food Consumption Survey. The amount of food by food group in the food plan was selected to meet nutrient requirements while maintaining minimal costs and diet palatability. One means of maintaining palatability in the food plan was to minimize the change in food consumption from historical average consumption while adjusting the amount of foods in the food plan to meet the nutritional requirements of a healthy diet.

The second step involves development of a family food plan and estimation of its cost from the individual age-gender food plans. This step is started by summing the food amounts and cost of the individual food plans into a family food plan, where even for families of the same size the summed family food plan cost varies due to the composition of age-gender members in the family. Then the sum of the family food plan cost is multiplied by the family-size adjustment factor for economies of scale in family food costs. The adjustments increase the summed food plan cost for families smaller than four persons and decreases the cost for larger families. A four-person family is a reference family, so its Economy Food Plan cost is the sum of individual food plan costs.

The food expenditure share used to derive the multiplier for estimating the poverty thresholds was a key decision on the part of Mollie. One choice would be to use the food expenditure share for low-income families, but she found reason to use the average food expenditure share of all families instead. The reason was related to Engel's law, which states that as the income of a family increases it spends a smaller percentage on food. In setting the poverty thresholds, a goal was to set the cost of food as a percentage of income that permits adequate expenditure on nonfood necessities. If an average food expenditure share of low-income families was used, other expenditures may not be adequate because they may be sacrificing other necessities in life to have enough to eat. A more conservative choice was to use the food expenditure share for families of higher income. What level of income is arbitrary, and a reasonable choice was average income for all families. Essentially, she adapted Engel's law by assuming that equivalent levels of an adequate diet was reached only when the proportion of income required to purchase an adequate diet was identical, that is, equal to that of the average family.

Mollie's Poverty Thresholds and Equivalence Scales

Except for unrelated individuals, i.e., single member families, Mollie estimated the poverty thresholds for families of different size and composition by summing the cost of individual food plans, adjusting the cost for family size, and multiplying the adjusted cost of the family food plan by the inverse of the food expenditure share. For families of three members or more, a one-third average food expenditure share of after-tax income for all families of two members or more was inverted for a multiplier of three used with the cost of the Economy Food Plan to calculate the poverty thresholds. For families with two members, a food expenditure share of 0.27 was inverted for a multiplier of 3.7. A larger multiplier was justified for smaller families due to economies of scale in non-food expenditures for larger households. For one member families the poverty threshold was set at 80 percent of the poverty threshold for two members families.

The number of nonfarm family types was simplified to sixty-two types, varying in size from one to six, plus seven or more members. Weighted average poverty thresholds by family size were calculated as weighted for the distribution of family types within each family size.[15] The equivalence scales for the poverty thresholds are the ratio of the per person poverty threshold relative to the per person poverty threshold for a family of four. Equivalence scales adjust the poverty threshold for household size and composition.

Mollie's equivalence scales and the family-size adjustment factors for economies of scale in food expenditures are both anchored at one for a family of four. For families of three, five and six persons, the difference between the Mollie equivalence scale and the family-size adjustment factor are small and due to differences in the food plan costs of individuals making up the families, which affect the weighted average poverty thresholds for a family size. For a family of seven persons or more, the value would be 0.87 if we assume an average of 7.5 family members rather than the value of seven used in the calculations for the table, which is more consistent with the family-size adjustment factor of 0.9. The equivalence scale of 1.27 for a family of two-member is larger than the 1.10 family-size adjustment factor due to the larger multiplier (3.7 compared to three) applied to the cost of the Economy Food Plan. For the one member family, the equivalence scale of 1.97 reflects the fact that the poverty threshold is set at 80 percent of the two-member family.

Mollie noted that, as the general standard of living moves upward, the standard of what constitutes an appropriate measure of income inadequacy also changes. Later, she wrote, “There must be a framework for adjusting a poverty line for changes over time in the level of economic activity and the resultant rise in wages and general standard of living.”

Thrifty Food Plan

Subsequent development of the food plans has not affected the poverty thresholds, which remain tied to the 1962 Economy Food Plans, but are annually revised by inflating them with the Consumer Price Index. Still, the 1975 food plan update offers some insight into the relevance of the Economy Food Plan as a basis for estimating poverty thresholds. More recent updates for 1983, 1999, and 2006 have maintained procedural consistency with the 1975 update, though the consumption data and dietary standards for each revision were more up-to-date, and the model more elaborate.

In the 1975 food plan update by Peterkin, Chassy, and Kerr, the Economy Food Plan was replaced by the Thrifty Food Plan, which was designed for more long-term use. The cost of the Thrifty Food Plan was set equal to the cost of the 1962 Economy Food Plan inflated to 1975 prices. The cost equivalency is a key feature of all updates in that the cost of a new food plan is set equal to the cost of the previous food plan adjusted for inflation with a food plan price index. The price adjusted Economy or

Thrifty Food Plan cost remains a reasonable minimal cost of food for poverty threshold calculations so long as the food plan price index has not been significantly altered by a change in the food shares in the food plans by the updates. For the 1975 food plans, Kerr and Peterkin econometrically estimated new family-size adjustment factors for economies of scale in family food costs, with data from the 1965 Household Food Consumption Survey. The only change with the new adjustment factors from those derived for the 1962 food plans using 1955 survey data is a refinement in the treatment of larger households. Subsequently, Nelson, Beebout, and Skidmore reviewed alternative estimates of family-size adjustment factors and found that there was not sufficient evidence that alternative values would be an improvement over those being used.

In short, Mollie calculated poverty thresholds for families of various sizes by taking the dollar costs of the economy food plan for families of those sizes and multiplying the costs by a factor of three—the "multiplier". She has used somewhat different procedures to develop thresholds for two members and one member units. She differentiated her thresholds not only by family size, but by farm/nonfarm status, by the gender of the family head, by the number of family members who were children, and (for one and two members units only) by aged/non-aged status. The result was a detailed matrix of 124 poverty thresholds, later reduced to 48. Actually, Mollie developed and discussed two sets of poverty thresholds—one derived from the economy food plan, and the other derived from the somewhat less stringent low-cost food plan. It was the lower of the two sets of poverty thresholds—the set derived from the economy food plan—that the Office of Economic Opportunity adopted as a working definition of poverty in May 1965. One of the most important reason for the adoption of the lower set of thresholds was that the lower set yielded approximately the same number of persons in poverty as the Council of Economic Advisers' $3,000 or $1,500 poverty line.

IMPACT OF POVERTY

Poverty is a global problem of huge proportions. Of the world's 6.0 billion people, 2.8 billion live on less than $2-a-day and 1.2 billion on less than $1-a-day.[16] On of the most fundamental feature of poverty is that it affects the access of the poor to markets, which in turn has repercussions for the entire economy affecting all markets—the ability to obtain credit, to sell labour, to rent land for cultivation, etc. In this section we shall discuss some of these effects.

Poor have no access to credit market. They are not able to get loans which they can use to improve their living conditions by investing in a productive activity. Following are reasons for the failure of credit market for the poor.

First, the poor have no collateral which can be used for repayment of loan. Collateral is a means to prevent intentional default on the part of the borrower. The possibility of lost collateral reduces the incentive to walk away without repaying the loan. The poor lack the wherewithal to put up adequate collateral and therefore are denied loans.[17] Also, collateral may be charged as a way of ensuring the self-selection of low-risk borrowers, or to motivate borrowers to work harder on their projects. Thus, inability of the poor to provide necessary collateral keep them away from the formal credit market and in this situation informal credit sources step in to fill the gap, because they accept collateral in forms, such as labour, that the formal sector does not.

Second, the incentives to repay for the poor are limited, independent of their inability to put up collateral. This can be explained using the principle of diminishing marginal utility. Each additional unit of money for the poor has greater value than the rich, which implies that when the time to repay loans comes around, the calculus of whether or not to default on the loan is naturally goes in favour of default. This can be shown with the help of a diagram.

In Fig. 5.3, Y_p and Y_r are the incomes of the poor and the rich respectively. Now suppose that both the individuals, poor and rich, have taken the same amount of loan C. Since the utility function exhibits diminishing marginal utility, we find from the Fig. 5.3 that utility loss to the poor from repayment, given by the segment of length *A*, exceeds the corresponding utility loss to the rich, given by the segment of length *B*. Here one point should be noted that the poor have much more to lose from default, which supports the argument that initial poverty reduces access to the credit market.

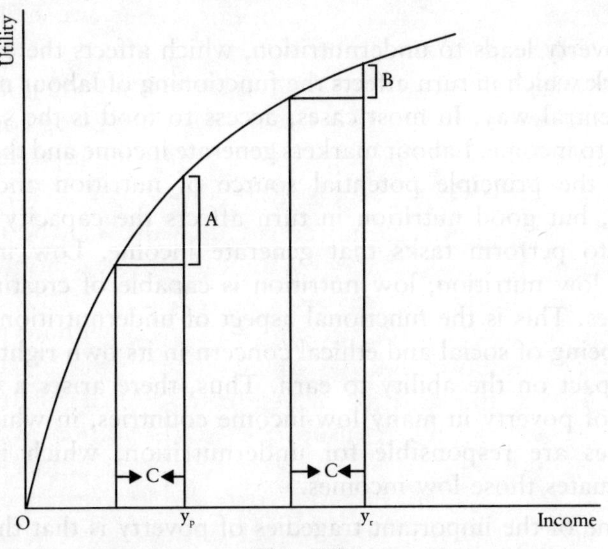

Fig. 5.3

On the other hand insurance market works better under conditions of poverty. The reason is that the future holds risks that we are unwilling to take. To insure against such uncertainties, we typically pay a sum of money, say every year, to an insurance company which plays no role in our life until any bad incidents occurs, when the insurance company pay the amount for which we have insured.

The opportunity cost of labour for the poor is lower than that of richer people. Therefore, they are likely to earn lower wages when they are employed and, in general, the cost of their time is lower. This feature allow them to credibly supply more effort to the task at hand without necessitating a large cutback in the degree of insurance that they receive. This low opportunity cost of effort is helped along by the fact that their marginal utility of consumption is very high. Thus, even if they are participating in schemes that insure them to a high degree, they will rarely freeload on such schemes. Therefore, when the people involved are poor rather than rich, it is far easier to have informal schemes that involve a large amount of shared labour and effort, as well as transfers of money or gain, to tide over bad times.

Poverty leads to undernutrition, which affects the capacity to work which in turn affects the functioning of labour markets in a central way. In most cases, access to food is the same as access to income. Labour markets generate income and therefore create the principle potential source of nutrition and good health, but good nutrition in turn affects the capacity of the body to perform tasks that generate income. Low incomes create low nutrition, low nutrition is capable of creating low incomes. This is the functional aspect of undernutrition, apart from being of social and ethical concern in its own right, it has an impact on the ability to earn. Thus, there arises a vicious circle of poverty in many low-income countries, in which low incomes are responsible for undernutrition, which in turn perpetuates those low incomes.

One of the important tragedies of poverty is that the poor may not afford to share their poverty equally. Unequal sharing arises fundamentally from the fact that certain minimum amounts of nutrition, care, and economic resources have to be devoted to each person in order for that person's life to be productive and healthy. In the case of extreme poverty, equal division of household resources might help no one, because the average amounts are far too small. The merit of unequal division is that it helps some individuals in the household to be minimally productive under extreme circumstances. Thus, due to poverty certain individuals may be systematically denied nourishment and medical care, so that scarce resources can be better focused on some remaining subset of family members. The denied individuals are typically females, both adults and children, and the old and the infirm.

STRATEGIES FOR POVERTY ERADICATION

There are a number of poverty reducing strategies depending upon the imagination and creativity of the policymakers. Generally, the poverty eradication policies are based on sustained growth, social development, environmental protection and social justice. Social justice requires the involvement of women in economic and social development, equal opportunities and the full and equal participation of women and men as agents and beneficiaries of people-centred development.

There are only few poverty reducing strategies, which are actually put to use, and most of those are incomplete in the sense that they are put only to partial use. There are many reasons for this, such as:

(a) lack of resources,

(b) lack of knowledge,

(c) inaccurate use, or misuse of knowledge, and

(d) administrative inadequacy in organising and implementing a poverty reducing strategy.

Thus, if knowledge, resources and administrative expertise increase, then poverty reduction would also increase. However, there may be some stronger forces that intervene to prevent poverty reduction. There may be some direct forces which have interest in neglecting poverty reduction or even trying to stop it from being implemented and carried out in an efficient manner. The reason for this may be the dislike of poor people, the dislike of sharing resources or the fear of changing a social structure in favour of the poor. There may be some indirect forces that keep on producing poverty at a rate that no poverty reduction program can keep up with. There are some unintentional poverty producing forces which have a larger impact on poverty formation than direct poverty production forces.

To understand the poverty reducing strategies we shall have to take into account also the forces that work against poverty reduction. Here one point should be kept in mind that all poverty reducing strategies are accompanied by a counter-strategy that attempts to reduce the effect of the initial poverty reducing strategy. The negative forces built into a counter-strategy can be political, cultural, economic or symbolic.

Thus, poverty reducing strategies need to be analysed and understood not only in terms of intended positive effects but also in terms of counterforces that come into play when a new poverty reducing strategy is introduced. Before discussing the poverty reducing strategies further, following points should be noted:

(a) The knowledge policymakers have about poverty and the poor will structure their way of thinking and their proposals for poverty reducing strategies.

(b) The way poverty is defined and the strategy chosen to reduce it, are closely linked. Any definition tends to narrow down the perspective, focus on a certain cause, or a limited set of causes. This eliminates or makes invisible other causes.

(c) There are several dimensions of poverty reduction process, and without a theory tailored to the phenomenon in question there is no known methodology that can be used to claim that poverty reduction on one dimension is more useful than poverty reduction on some other dimension.

(d) The process of poverty reduction lies in the distribution and redistribution of a whole range of resources—material as well as immaterial.

(e) Any change in established distribution create conflicts of interest. Thus, changes created by a poverty reducing strategy will develop counter-strategies that may hamper or stop poverty reduction. Therefore, for every poverty reducing strategy a counter-strategy should be identified.

(f) All the poverty reducing strategies does not aim in the same direction. They might have opposing goals. There may be direct conflicts among different strategies so that one cannot be implemented unless the other fails.

Classifying Poverty Eradicating Strategies

Poverty eradicating strategies can be classified in several ways. But, there is no system that provides a classification according to how successful or unsuccessful they have been. Some of the poverty eradicating strategies are classified according to which methodology they use, for example a participatory approach, cash transfers, community work and measurements through social indicators. Much of the present poverty eradicating strategies are built around such methodologies.

Some other methods characterise the poverty eradicating strategies according to which group they are directed at. Through this approach we can better understand the context in which the poverty eradicating strategies have to function and the relationship between the various poverty eradicating strategies. It also makes visible the fact that the impacts of poverty eradicating strategies are very different for the various groups. whether this is intended or not. The range of poverty eradicating strategies highlight different causes of poverty, concepts used are often different, strategies are organised and financed in different ways, and variations are found in the ideological reasons for poverty eradication.

Poverty Eradicating Strategies According Targets

Following are six major targets, ranging from organisational levels to the international community, and the strategies directed towards these targets for the poverty eradication.

(a) *Individual and household*: The most common poverty eradicating strategy has always been to transfer resources directly to the individual or the household. Basic food and shelter have dominated such transfers, and globally this is still the preferred strategy. The criteria for transfer vary, but some kind of deservedness has invariably been formulated, whether the criteria have been set by the government or any organisation working in the field of poverty eradication.

(b) *Community*: The poverty eradicating strategies through the community use the fact that the poor are part of a social context that can be utilised to eradicate poverty. This may be due to following reasons:

(i) the poor need to organise to get out of poverty,

(ii) the poor need the support of the community to manage their individual resources,

(iii) resources are better controlled in the community than when distributed directly to the individual and household,

(iv) a synergy is created in the community to utilise the resources better,

(v) a long-term engagement is more likely in case of institutionalised resources, and

(vi) there is a built-in learning effect in communal participation that can be used for other purposes.

The community approach of poverty eradication is promoted both as methodology and as a goal in itself. However, it is necessary to distinguish between the participation of the poor in the creation of certain activity, and the use they make of an activity already established. For example, it is widely accepted that the initial organisation of a health care unit needs to be done within a professional framework, while a trade-off between professional standards and the need to integrate the poor is necessary to make them use the unit.

(c) *Sectors*: According to the different functions that are considered important for the working of society, it can be divided into different sectors. Some of the most successful poverty eradicating strategies have been channelled through these sectors. For example, investments in the health care sector have provided tangible results such as increased life expectancy among poor populations, decreased infant and child mortality, and improved access to health care. Other example is the investments in the educational sector which have cut down illiteracy and improved vocational skills, while investments in the waterworks have increased access to safe water and proper disposal of wastewater.

Certain characteristics of the sector make the sectoral approach a useful method for poverty eradication. A sector is based on a certain kind of expertise, and the success of the experts lies mainly within that sector. The expertise is international in scope, i.e., a medical doctor can carry his trade in any cultural setting, and the organisation around the trade has to conform to certain professional standards. In principle, medical treatment should be given to the poor at the same standard as to any other population, and life should be saved at any price. The shared frame of reference between local medical expertise and medical expertise on the donor side increases the likelihood of a two-way communication. Given the still stricter regulations on medical practice, it may be added that unprotected poor populations provide a useful testing ground for medical experts, a situation which has yielded both negative and positive results.

On the other hand the educational sector is based on a more diffuse kind of expertise, and the international component is not very present in primary and secondary education. That gives larger scope for local variations that may or may not benefit the poorest groups. One of the positive outcomes stems from schools in rural areas where the curriculum has been tailored to local needs in agricultural production. One of the negative outcomes can be observed in the lower school attendance for girls. Whereas the water sector has many of the same characteristics as the health sector. It is guided by a strong expertise, uniform requirements for technology and a professional organisation, and shared norms across the international arena. However, the education of the experts does not include ethical norms that give the poorest populations the same preferences as the non-poor when water is scarce.

(d) *Processes and social institutions*: This area of poverty eradicating efforts is the most difficult to penetrate. It is also the area where poverty reducing strategies are more likely to succeed on implementation. Poverty is static, in the sense that some people will experience deprivations throughout their lives. Poverty is also dynamic, in the sense that the causes of poverty change, the consequences of poverty change, and the lives of poor people change throughout their lifespan with new opportunities and the development of new coping strategies.[18] For the outsider, the lives of the poor may look the same. For the poor, their lives are as dynamic as those of the non-poor. A whole set of processes are at play that move the poor in and out of poverty. Some of those processes are initiated by the poor themselves, as part of their coping strategies. Other processes are beyond their control.

One example of such mixed processes that has been happening for a long time is the move of poor rural populations into urban areas. One route is to leave the rural area that offers few or no opportunities, go to a smaller town as the first move, then continue to a larger town or city, before finally ending up in the mega-city with the hope of getting out of poverty. From the outside we can say that the already existing massive scale of city-poverty offers little relief for the newcomers and the steady stream of rural migrants ought to be reversed. At what stage in this process is a poverty eradicating strategy the most effective? It is not uncommon that a scout is sent out to clear a path before the other follows. In the past this was commonly a man. Now it is often more often a women, since unskilled female labour is more in demand than unskilled male labour. This implies that effective poverty reducing strategies ought to be gender sensitive and should be coordinated on several administrative levels.

Following are different kinds of processes that affects the poverty eradication:

(i) One of the poverty producing strategies is the tax on consumer goods and flat rate taxes—tax on consumer goods forces the poor to pay a higher percentage of their income on necessary consumption such as food, while a flat rate of tax makes them pay a relatively large part on the remainder of their income once basic expenditures have been paid.

(ii) Tax exemptions and lower taxes can be seen as examples of poverty sustaining strategies—the poor neither profit from tax exempts, nor lower taxes, because they have none of the traditional items to exempt and too little of a formal income, if any, to benefit from lower taxes.

(iii) Negative income tax is an example of a direct measure to compensate poor people for lack of income, and can be seen as an explicit poverty reducing strategy.

The migration and taxation examples shows that there are at least two problems involved in intervening in such processes:

(i) identifying the process so precisely that a poverty reducing strategy becomes effective, and

(ii) to obtain a consensus amongst the many actors involved in the poverty discussion about how intervention should be carried out and which processes should be targeted.

The vested interests of the many actors and the different cultural and intellectual background of policymakers and others, are likely to interfere seriously with all attempts to efficient, or make poverty reduction more effective.

Once a process with an impact on poverty is identified, the next step forward is to create institution building around viable and effective poverty eradicating strategies. Since poverty eradication is a conflictual issue, the continued success of an effective poverty reducing strategy depends on a firm organisational structure to carry it through over time. Many of the poverty eradicating strategies in foreign aid programs and NGO activities are too short-lived to make an impact. But organising on foreign ground is often seen as interference in internal affairs, and external actors are expected to keep a low profile. Small-scale operations with a limited time span are more likely to be accepted by regional and national authorities. However, it is a paradox, that such operations are exactly the kinds of poverty eradicating strategies that are the least effective.

(e) *The nation*: Most developing countries cannot at present afford a welfare state, and also they do not have the necessary infrastructure to implement it. This touches upon a major discussion as to whether views on poverty eradication should be based on the present situation or on a more positive vision for the future. In case of poor countries it is taken for granted that once a surplus from expected economic growth is in place, then welfare measures and poverty reducing strategies will follow. This may be a doubtful supposition. So far much of the surplus coming from national economic growth, has been absorbed by the upper and middle classes in the developing countries. It is an open question whether poor countries experiencing economic growth are politically willing to prioritise welfare investment that are substantial enough to be labelled poverty eradication. The so-called 20/20 compact presented at the UN World Social Summit in Copenhagen in 1995, was developed to put pressure on national governments to prioritise poverty reducing strategies in basic education and health care.

Another strategy to pressure for improvements is the UNDP Human Poverty Index (HPI) used by the Human Development Report (1997). This index of poverty performance sets the poorest performing countries in the stocks. On the one hand, it can be used by the countries to call for more foreign aid. On the other hand, it can also be used to monitor change over time and improve performance. The major weakness with this index, and any other poverty statistics, is that the database is weak. Unfortunately, the poorer the country, the poorer is its statistics on poverty.

(f) *The international community*: Internationalised markets, multi-national corporations working outside national legislation, the migration of labour, price setting of commodities far from the local producers, all influence the formation of poverty, one way or the other. There are few accepted poverty reducing strategies available to meet this kind of poverty producing forces, and there is no arena waiting for international decisions on anti-poverty strategies. The UNDP has made itself the major player for an ambitious poverty eradication scheme, and different agencies in the UN family have followed up within their specific areas. Several years ago the World Bank moved into the vacuum left by a weak UN and developed a policy for poverty reduction that has dominated political ways of thinking about poverty in all corners of the world. Its major publication *Attacking Poverty*[19] drew up a range of strategies to combat poverty worldwide. On the face of it economic growth is still the major strategy. Good governance, increased democracy, more responsiveness to the needs of the poor, risk management, social capital formation are some of the other poverty reducing strategies put forward. While there is general agreement that the bulk of the ideas are necessary to further poverty reduction, strong criticism has been raised because the ideas are tainted by ideological underpinnings and too loose to be turned into concrete strategies for poverty eradication.

The endurance of poverty is a violation of human rights. The earlier conventions on economic, social and cultural rights (1966/1976) that 135 countries have ratified, as well as the 1948 UN Universal Declaration of Human Rights lie ready to be used. The UN Secretary General, Kofi Annan, had stressed that the notion of human rights should penetrate all organs within the UN. UN High Commissioner for Human Rights (UNHCHR) has written an important document on the relation between human rights and poverty (2002). United Nations Educational, Scientific and Cultural Organisation (UNESCO) is trying to move one step further and see human rights as a tool for 'the abolition of poverty'. United Nations International Children's Emergency Fund (UNICEF) has a long tradition for using human rights as a moral foundation for their activities. Part of the International Labour Organisation (ILO) conventions take their support from the human rights framework. But at present, no sanctions are available to secure that such rights be enforced, and the legal instruments available are too diffuse for concerted action.[20]

NOTES

1. UNDP Human Development Report 1997.
2. Orshansky 1963, 1965.
3. Nanak Kakwani, *Poverty and Well-being* in *Poverty in Focus*, UNDP, 2006, p. 20.
4. Amartya Sen, Poverty: An Ordinal Approach to Measurement, *Econometrica*, 1976.
5. Cf. Dalton's "principle of transfers" in measuring inequality; see Atkinson [2, pp. 247-49]. See also Dasgupta, Sen and Starrett, and Rothschild and Stiglitz.
6. Shorrocks 1995.
7. Takayama 1979.
8. Sen 1976, p. 223.
9. Pattanaik and Sengupta 1993.
10. Deaton 1997, p. 147.
11. James Foster, Joel Greer, and Erik Thorbecke, A Class of Decomposable Poverty Measures, *Econometrica*, 1984.
12. Aguirregabiria 2003.
13. Orshansky 1965.
14. Cofer, Grossman, and Clark.
15. Orshansky 1965, p. 28.
16. World Bank 2000.
17. Banerjee and Newman 1994.
18. Chambers 1997.
19. World Bank, 2000/2001.
20. Else Oyen, *Poverty Reducing Strategies*.

6

Resource Allocation and Economic Development

After going through this chapter, you will better understand:

- classical approach, general vs partial analysis
- demand criterion, social marginal productivity criterion
- Chenery's model, Polak criterion
- rate of turnover criterion
- employment absorption criterion
- growing points criterion, leading sectors criterion
- reinvestment criterion, application of investment criteria
- shadow prices, agriculture vs industry
- heavy industry vs manufacturing industry
- cottage and small scale industries
- human investment and material investment

An appropriate allocation of available productive resources is the most important problem in Economics. Lionel Robbins goes to the extent of defining Economics as a study of the allocation of scarce means, capable of alternative uses, among competing ends so as to maximise the achievement of these ends.

THE CLASSICAL APPROACH

The classical economists held that the free and unhampered working of the price mechanism would lead to an ideal allocation of resources and consequently to the maximisation of national income. Any interference with the volume and composition of investment would result in a non-optimum national income. Actually, this is not true. In fact, it is possible to raise the rate of economic growth and to increase national income by a judicious interference with the volume and allocation of investment.

The contention of the classical economists is based on the colossal assumption of perfect competition which does not exist in the real world. In a world of imperfect competition, the uncoordinated investment decisions of the individuals may lead to non-optimum allocation of resources owing to a number of reasons. Individual investors take into consideration the private and not social marginal product. Industries offering considerable external economies may not attract enough resources because these do not enter into the calculation of private investors. Each individual investor controls a small part of the total production. While deciding his production, he is unaware of the production plans of other producers. This often leads to underproduction or overproduction and consequently to wastage of productive resources. In a world of imperfect competition, individual investors are handicapped by a lack of knowledge about the most profitable opportunities for investment. Price mechanism functions well under the assumption of small changes. Actually, large changes may be involved because of the existence of indivisibilities. Private investors are, often, shortsighted. Projects requiring long-term finance may fail to attract enough resources even if they would have contributed comparatively more towards the economic development and towards an increase in national income.

The prevailing prices of inputs and products do not reflect the value of these factors to society. Foreign exchange rates, wage rates, interest rates, land rents and product prices are affected by a number of factors, *viz.*, tariffs, subsidies and taxes applied by the government to achieve objectives unrelated to the allocation of resources. Prices are affected also by traditions, institutions and other non-economic factors. Once it is accepted that allocation of resources is to be decided by some central planning authority and not to be left at the mercy of the freely working forces of demand and supply, there immediately arises the question as to what would be the criteria for determining the allocation.

Objectives

Before we examine the criteria for the allocation of resources, we have got to be clear as to the objectives to be achieved. The objectives to be achieved depend partly on values that come from outside economic analysis and are, therefore, arbitrary to some extent. This has been the main cause of confusion in the discussions on the criteria for the allocation of resources. Different authors put forward different criteria, mainly, not because they held different opinions but because they had different goals in mind. Following may be mentioned among the economic goals which seem to be widely accepted:

(a) Maximisation of per capita output either overtime or at some time in future. Ordering of income magnitudes over time or the determination of the precise future time at which the maximum output is to be achieved is a very complicated problem.

(b) Minimisation of inequalities in the distribution of income and wealth.

(c) Achievement of equilibrium in the balance of payments with the outside world.

GENERAL VS PARTIAL ANALYSIS

The problem of allocation of resources can be approached in two ways: *viz.*, (i) general analysis, and (ii) partial analysis. Both approaches take some resources and relationships in the economy as given and try to determine the composition of the development program which would lead to maximum economic welfare. For determining the composition of a development program, general analysis involves a simultaneous consideration of all the relevant factors in an economy.

> After determining what resources are available, what projects can be carried out using these resources, how the projects are related, and what demand need to be satisfied, this approach uses some of the recently developed

> mathematically-based techniques to determine simultaneously what prices should be assigned to various resources (for example, wage rates), what types of investment should be undertaken to use the resources, and what results can be expected.[1]

This approach, however, requires a good deal of factual information about the various magnitudes and relationships. It is not easy to obtain all this information, at least, at present. It is not possible, therefore, to follow this approach in actual practice.

The alternative partial analysis approach takes into account the costs and benefits of individual projects. It does not, however, neglect the relationship of individual projects to the development program as a whole. As far as possible the costs and benefits of individual projects are appraised in the light of the development as a whole.

> The first step is to estimate the wage, interest and foreign exchange rates that would prevail if there were no distortions, due to tradition, government regulation, and the like. A guess is then made about the general nature of the development program likely to be carried out and the changes in the rates that will result from the program. The resulting shadow rates reflect the future value of the various factors to society. They, rather than the actual rates prevailing at the time, are then used to estimate the costs and returns of a particular proposal.[2]

Estimation of shadow prices involves a number of difficulties. Further difficulties are involved in making the private entrepreneurs act in accordance with shadow prices rather than the prevailing market prices; this would require a complicated system of taxes and subsidies or direct interferences by the state.

Both the general and partial analysis techniques have, of course, limitations. They cannot take into account all important magnitudes and interrelations. This is more true of partial analysis. The indirect effects of a project on the economy are so numerous and diffused that it is not possible to take all these into consideration. Failure to take into account small and remote indirect effects may not materially affect the efficiency and consistency of a development program. But inability to take into consideration important indirect effects will result into a loss of the efficiency and consistency of the development program. Further, economic cost-benefit calculation cannot take into consideration social effects. Different projects have different effects on population growth, human attitudes and motives, values and institutions which cost-benefit calculations cannot take into consideration.

A number of criteria have been put forward by different authors for determining the allocation of resources. Let us briefly examine some of the important criteria.

DEMAND CRITERION

According to the traditional economists approach, investible resources should be allocated in accordance with the anticipated pattern of the expanding effective demand. The incremental value of various demands indicates the need for additional productive capacities which must be built through investment allocations. If the pattern of income distribution does not significantly change with growth, the incremental values of various demands resulting from an increase in income can be estimated from the estimates of income elasticities of demand. The required amount of investment for any sector can be estimated by multiplying the volume of incremental demand by the capital coefficient of the sector concerned. The required total amount of investment can be obtained by adding the investments required in various sectors. The thus obtained required total investment will have to be adjusted to accommodate indivisibilities of processes and specificity of resources in order to meet the specific requirements of production.

The demand for intermediate goods and capital goods is derived from the demand for consumer goods. If the technological interrelationship coefficients of the productive system are known, the required amount of intermediate and capital goods can be estimated from the growth of demand for consumables. This approach leads to the development of an interdependent demand structure. Different productive units provide demand for each other and support each other by their outputs and employments.

This approach of resource allocation fully respects the sovereignty of consumers in determining the pattern of their consumption. Consumer's choice weighted by his anticipated expenditure is the primary consideration in determining the allocation of productive resources. Some interference with the consumers' sovereignty may be essential because of anticipated scarcities like the foreign exchange scarcity. Interference may also be necessary to bring desirable changes in the pattern of income distribution on welfare considerations.

The approach to development by leading from finished goods to capital goods, however, is likely to be very slow. Because of technological indivisibilities, intermediate and capital goods industries cannot be developed in piecemeal manner along with the slowly growing demand for finished goods. Establishment of capital goods industries will have to be delayed till the additional demand for finished goods is sufficient to justify the establishment of these industries. For achieving rapid economic development, infringement on consumers' sovereignty is very essential. Historically, inventions have played an important part in shaping consumers' pattern of demand.

> ...consumer preferences have been continually tempered with and altered to accommodate newer products of innovations. There was no demand for motor cars before the automobile industry was established. There was no economic need for chemical fertilisers before the farmer was educated to its use. Innovations have thus always preceded consumers' known wants.[3]

In most of the underdeveloped countries, the general standard of living being near subsistence, the marginal propensity to consume is very high. Unless consumers' choices are infringed upon, the rate of saving and hence that of capital formation will remain very low. Rapid economic development can be achieved only by restricting consumption and increasing the volume of savings available for investment.

SOCIAL MARGINAL PRODUCTIVITY CRITERION

The criterion was first put forward by A.E. Kahn.[4] It is the most popular of all the criteria of resource allocation. It states that the allocation of resources will be optimum when the social marginal productivity of such resources is the same in all its uses. Application of this criterion raises a number of difficulties. The concept of social marginal productivity is a very vague one. It is not clear as to what is precisely meant by the word 'social'. In determining the social marginal productivity of an investment, consideration has to be paid to the present value of the output stream connected with the investment. In evaluating costs, consideration has to be paid not only to private costs but also to social costs for which no payment is made by the private investor, e.g., smoke nuisance, water pollution, etc. Similarly in evaluating output, consideration has to be paid not only to the product accruing to the private investor but also to the indirect benefits accruing to the society for which it makes no payment to the private investor, e.g., external economies.

Social marginal productivity criterion emphasizes the maximisation of aggregate output from current investment effort. It does not seem to take into consideration the effect of the allocation of resources on the rate of growth of the agent of production. To be more concrete it does not take into consideration:

(a) the indirect effect of allocation on the expansion of entrepreneurship, on the improvement in quality and increase in quantity of labour force and on the expansion of skill;

(b) the effect of the investment allocation on future saving habits which constitute an important factor in determining the future rate of investment;

(c) the effect of investment allocation on future consumption pattern which is an important factor determining as to whether the consumption is simply on population maintenance or on the expansion of growth agents;

(d) the indirect effect of the investment allocation on the rate of population growth which is an important factor determining, the per capita output.[5]

In an underdeveloped country, consideration needs to be paid not only to the maximisation of current output but also to the rate of growth of the economy. "Suppose that in every period 110 percent of the GNP is consumed, would we then say that development is taking place even if in period after period the GNP is the maximum it could possibly be under the circumstances."[6]

Even when transfer of marginal units from one use to another cannot increase aggregate output, it may be possible to increase it by large movement of resources from one use to another. Structural adjustments are needed much more in underdeveloped countries than in developed countries. The marginal principle, therefore, is not so important in underdeveloped countries. The United Nations experts proposed that for ensuring maximum output from a given volume of resources, the planning authority should satisfy itself that it is not possible to increase aggregate output by either marginal or large shifts of resources from one use to another.[7] The actual application of the structural principle is more difficult than that of the marginal principle. The cost and productivity of marginal changes can be calculated much more easily because many such changes are occurring at all times. For appraising the cost and productivity of structural changes, one has to depend mostly on qualitative judgments which can be tested only by actual affecting such adjustments.

The social marginal productivity criterion assumes a closed economy. It does not take into consideration international relations. For achieving an equilibrium in the balance of payments, deviations might be essential from the allocation of resources determined on the basis of the social marginal productivity criterion.

The criterion assumes that the production is subject to the law of decreasing returns. Actually, certain industries might be subject to the law of increasing returns up to a certain scale of production.

It neglects the effect of resource allocation on the distribution of income. Distribution of income is important not only on social considerations but also because it considerably affects development in a number of ways. It, for instance, affects the volume of savings and thereby the rate of investment.

The social marginal productivity criterion assumes that production techniques remain constant. This may be true in case of minor changes in investment. When changes in investment are large, it may be profitable to shift to certain different techniques. With the change in techniques, marginal productivity of a factor no longer remains a continuous function of inputs.[8]

The social marginal productivity criterion assumes that when investment is varied in a particular sector, economic conditions remain constant in other sectors, i.e., economic conditions in a particular sector are independent of those in other sectors. This may be true when the changes involved are very small. This assumption does not hold in case of fairly large changes. Economic variables in different sectors are interdependent and any significant change in economic variables in one sector acts and reacts on those in other sectors. Prevailing product and other prices play an important part in determining marginal productivity. Change in investment in a particular sector will cause changes in factor prices in all other sectors and in the prices of products which can be directly or indirectly substituted for the product concerned. Changes in factor and product prices change the relative profitability of different sectors of production. Investment in one sector may create certain external economies or diseconomies for other sectors. Marginal productivities in different sectors, therefore, are interdependent and not independent.[9]

The criterion implies that, in an underdeveloped economy in which capital is scarce and labour relatively abundant, capital investment in any one direction should be discontinued at a point at which the marginal productivity of capital is higher, and that of labour lower than would be appropriate if the country had more capital and less labour. To this extent the principle favours spreading capital rather widely and thinly throughout the economy and employing labour-intensive rather than capital-intensive techniques of production.

Some economists, however, are of the opinion that if underdeveloped countries spread their capital widely and thinly and use labour-intensive techniques, new investment will not make a sufficient impact in any one sector of the economy to bring about any substantial transformation in the economic structure or to achieve a 'take-off into self-sustained growth'. They think that it would be more advantageous to concentrate the available capital on the establishment of industrial nuclei or islands of advanced and relative capital intensive technology even by starving the rest of the economy of capital in the hope that these industrial nuclei or 'development blocks', consisting of a number of mutually sustaining projects, will constitute strategic growing points from which the impulse towards growth will spread to the rest of the economy.

The marginal productivity of investment in different lines would differ over different periods of time. The marginal productivity of investment in the production of a new commodity, for instance, may be low in the beginning because few people know about or want the commodity. But gradually more and more people may start desiring it and after some time the investment might become highly productive. Further, cost conditions may also change over a period of time. As the management and workers acquire knowledge, skill and experience, it may be possible to reduce the cost of production.

CHENERY'S MODEL

Hollis B. Chenery developed a measure of social productivity in terms of a social welfare function which takes into consideration not only gross national product but also employment, income distribution, balance of payments, etc.[10] He expresses the function algebraically as $U = U(Y, B, D)$, where U stands for the social welfare, Y for the national income, B for the balance of payments effects, D for the effect on distribution of income. The increment in social welfare, U, corresponding to an increase in investment (measuring U in national income units) can be written as

$$\Delta U = \Delta Y + \frac{dY}{dB}\Delta B + \frac{dY}{dD}\Delta D + \ldots$$

There arises the question as to how the values of the parameters $\Delta Y, \Delta B, \Delta D$, etc. and $\frac{dY}{dB}, \frac{dY}{dD}$, etc. are to be calculated by applying a set of corrections (*viz.*, the tariffs, taxes, subsidies, external economies and unused resources) to the businessman's calculations of annual rate of profit.[11] The balance of payments effect includes both direct and indirect investment effects (i.e., imports of machinery, etc. for the project and multiplier effect of investment on income and imports), and also direct and indirect effects on imports of operating project.[12] Chenery has not given any method or principle for determining the value of $\frac{dY}{dB}, \frac{dY}{dD}$, etc.

POLAK CRITERION

Polak[13] and Buchanan[14], the formulators of this criterion, were mainly concerned with determining a correct pattern of investment for economies reconstructing or developing with the help of foreign loans.

Financing reconstruction or development with the help of foreign funds gives rise to the problem of repayment of the loans and interest thereupon. To avoid strain on balance of payments at the time of repayment, funds should be appropriately allocated between different industries. Polak distinguished between the following three types of industries:

(a) 'Export promoting' or 'import substituting' industries, i.e., industries producing goods which are exported or which replace imported goods in the domestic market. Such industries ease the strain on the balance of payments.

(b) Industries producing goods which replace similar domestic goods in the home market or which replace certain exported goods in the foreign market. The effect of such industries on the balance of payments is neutral.

(c) Industries producing goods which are sold in the domestic market in addition to those previously sold to meet the increased demand caused by a rise in incomes. The effects of such industries on the balance of payments may be either neutral or unfavourable. The likelihood of the later possibility is larger because of two considerations, *viz.*, (i) investment in these industries may require some imported equipment and (ii) derived demand for imports operating through the multiplier and the marginal propensity to import. To avoid strain on the balance of payments, sufficient investment should be made in the first type of industries.

RATE OF TURNOVER CRITERION

This criterion was put forward by Polak and Buchanan. It states that in a development program the topmost priority should be given to those investments which yield the highest value of output compared to the amount of investment. Generally, the rate of capital turnover is higher in consumer goods industries than in producer goods industries. If investment is made according to this criterion, consumer goods industries will get a higher priority than the producer goods industries. Concentration of investment in consumer goods industries may initially maximise output but will slow the rate of growth in future.

A lower capital-output ratio in case of individual projects may not always lead to a lower aggregate capital-output ratio. Similarly, a higher capital-output ratio in certain industries may not lead to a higher aggregate capital-output ratio. Let us illustrate this by taking a concrete example. Capital-output ratio is very high in industries like railways, roads, electricity and irrigation schemes. But investment in these may considerably lower the capital-output ratio in other industries by creating external economies. Thus investment in industries with a high capital-output ratio may lower the aggregate capital-output ratio.

Sometimes, the high turnover may be owing to a high rate of depreciation, and the rate of net output may not be high. This defect of the criterion can, of course, be removed by expressing the criterion, in terms of the net rate of turnover.[15] The contribution to output from an increment of investment should be considered over the whole fruition period and not only during the initial period. The rate of capital-turnover may be lower for more durable equipment but it may turn out to be cheaper or more productive if the contribution to output is considered over the whole fruition period. In the long run, industries subject to the law of increasing returns having a lower capital-turnover rate may contribute more to the national product than those subject to the law of constant or decreasing returns and having a higher capital-turnover rate.[16]

Regarding the application of this criterion for choosing between different techniques, the techniques chosen according to this criterion will be efficient only if the additional cost of labour is zero because under such conditions the rate of return over capital cost will be maximised. If the additional labour cost is positive, such techniques may not be the most efficient ones. In such cases, the additional cost of labour will have to be taken into account.[17]

EMPLOYMENT ABSORPTION CRITERION

The underdeveloped countries are characterised by surplus labour and shortage of capital. The vast unemployment and underemployment of labour force offers considerable scope for increasing output by utilising the surpuls manpower. This has led to the proposal that underdeveloped countries should apply techniques which require more labour and less capital.

This criterion, however, may not invariably maximise output. Sometimes a technique requiring the same amount of capital and a larger amount of labour may lead to a smaller output than that which can be obtained by using certain other techniques requiring the same amount of capital but a smaller amount of labour. The employment absorption criterion will be alright if the objective is simply to maximise employment irrespective of the output. Actually, increase in employment is desired not for its own sake but for increasing output. Techniques using larger amount of labour should be applied only if combined with the same amount of capital yield larger output. Adherence to capital-saving and labour-intensive investments may lead to perpetuation of low labour productivity. Further, maximisation of the rate of investment may not in the very distant future create more employment for labour than the capital saving and labour-intensive use of the existing investment potential can do in the immediate future.

GROWING POINTS CRITERION

This criterion lays emphasis not merely on breaking bottlenecks but on concentrating on investments which provide a forward impetus to growth. The growing points in an economy are determined by a number of factors like location of resources, historical sequences, transport costs, distribution of population and incomes, and other social and economic factors.

LEADING SECTORS CRITERION

W.W. Rostow divides the sectors of an economy into the following three categories[18]:

(a) Primary growth sectors, where possibilities for innovation or for the exploitation of newly profitable or hitherto unemployed resources yield a high growth-rate and set in motion expansionary forces elsewhere in the economy.

(b) Supplementary growth sectors, where rapid advance occurs in direct response to—or as a requirement of—advance in primary growth sectors.

(c) Derived growth sectors, where advance occurs in some fairly steady relation to the growth of total real income, population industrial production or some other overall, modestly increasing variable.

Overall growth is based on the direct and indirect consequences of rapid growth in certain key sectors during some periods. Historically, the leading sectors have ranged from cotton textiles, through heavy industrial complexes, to a wide variety of consumer goods industries. The basic conditions for qualifying as key sectors are that there must be enlarged effective demand for their products; they should have production functions of high productivity, thus leading to rise in output per head; they should generate maximum of reinvestible surplus which can be ploughed back into productive investments; they should set up a chain of effective demand for other products and generate external economies which will turn industrialization into an automatic and cumulative process. If investment is concentrated in a limited and number of such leading sectors which generate growth in a multiple ways, it can be a powerful engine of transformation and progress.

It is, however, very difficult to identify the key sectors in an underdeveloped economy. This is because there is no automatic equivalence between the concept of profitability as determined by the cost-price relationships in the free market and the concept of maximum real rate of return in terms of full consequences of an investment because several elements (e.g. external economies, impact on skills and attitudes, etc.) involved in it are not amendable to measurement by our present tools of analysis.

REINVESTMENT CRITERION

Walter Galenson and Harvey Leibenstein suggested the 'marginal per capita reinvestment quotient' criterion. They aimed at maximising the per capita output potential at some future point of time. According to this criterion, the allocation of resources will be optimum when the marginal per capita reinvestment quotient of capital is equalised in its various alternative uses. Marginal per capita investment quotient is determined by the following basic factors[19]:

(a) gross productivity per worker;

(b) "wage" goods consumed per worker;

(c) replacement and repair of capital;

(d) increments in output as a result of non-capital using innovations, such as improvements in skills, health, energy, discipline and malleability of the labour force;

(e) decline in mortality;

(f) decline in fertility; and

(g) direction of investment.

The first six factors determine the per capita investment available period after period and the seventh factor concerns its allocation.

The gross productivity per worker minus the consumption per worker determines the gross amount available for reinvestment per worker. Net amount available for reinvestment during any period can be obtained by deducting replacement and repairs per worker. Over a certain period, productivity may increase because of factors other than increment of capital, *viz.*, improvement in skills, health, energy, or discipline of labour force, improvement in the organisation of production. Increase in productivity owing to such like factors has to be taken into account. Capital per worker is affected by changes in labour force which is determined in turn, leaving aside the question of labour participation, by the morality and fertility rates of population.

Algebraically, the rate of investment is given by

$$r = \frac{p - ew}{c}$$

where,

p = net output per machine;

e = number of workers per machine;

w = real wage rate; and

c = cost per machine.

The authors assume that the whole of the profit is reinvested and whole of the wages consumed. The reinvestment rate is not very different from the well-known rate of surplus.

The authors held that the maximum rate of reinvestment would be attained by the maximisation of capital-labour ratio. Wage rate is a critical variable and the amount of employment provided in any future year by a unit of investment considerably depends upon the wage, deduction from the product of industry. The higher the real wage rate, the larger is the potential employment that can be obtained by the use of capital-intensive machinery. The authors concluded that the criterion of the marginal per capita reinvestment quotient and the corollary of high capital-labour ratio are the appropriate guides in formulating the program for economic development.

Increase in capital-labour ratio may not always lead to an increase in investment rate.[20] It is not necessary that the most capital-intensive techniques will yield the highest rate of profit. Increase in capital-labour ratio would raise not only labour productivity but also cost of capital. Increase in capital-labour ratio will increase the rate of growth only if the resultant rise in labour productivity exceeds the additional capital cost.

The assumption that all wages are consumed and all profits reinvested is not true in actual practice. This, of course, does not invalidate the criterion so long as the marginal propensity to spend of the wage-earners is higher than that of the profit recipients.

A more rational way of raising the reinvestment rate would be to prevent an increase in the expenditure of wage earners rather than using capital-intensive techniques. Subscription of capital for labour for increasing profit-wage ratio in countries having vast amounts of unemployed and underemployed would be a sheer waste of productive resources.

Galenson-Leibenstein criterion does not take into consideration the international relations. In case the import-content is higher for capital-intensive techniques, it may not be practicable to use these techniques because of a shortage of foreign exchange.

This criterion appears to put a higher value on future income than on present income. Social marginal productivity criterion was criticised for concentrating on present and neglecting future. The criterion errs on the other extreme. In fact, an appropriate balance should be maintained between the present and the future output. One generation should not be overstrained to provide comforts to some other generation. The appropriate time-pattern of growth is determined by social, political and economic considerations of community. One solution of the time-pattern of growth is to attempt to maximise the present value of the output stream by applying some discounting procedure.

Intensification of capital may render some labour surplus. Unemployed labour has got to be fed. The authors have neglected the social cost of unemployment.[21]

Galenson and Leibenstein propose that the consumption of the labour should be minimised and investment maximised. But investment in labour is not less important than the investment in capital goods. At certain stages investment in labour may accelerate the rate of investment more than investment in capital goods.

APPLICATION OF INVESTMENT CRITERIA

In actual practice, the planning bodies in most of the countries pay little heed to the vast literature existing on the investment criteria and, for determining the allocation of resources, rely primarily on 'common sense' and political considerations.[22] There are a number of reasons for this. There is a lack of agreement on the appropriate criteria for the allocation of resources. A number of criteria have been put forward by different authors. There exists a good deal of confusion. Practitioners in planning agencies or ministries of finance, often, do not have the time, the inclination, and the training to study the vast literature on the subject for determining for themselves the most appropriate criteria. Many criteria have been framed in technical terms, expressed in mathematical form and discussed at a highly abstract level. These are beyond the comprehension of the practitioners. Often, the formulators of the criteria have not paid sufficient attention to the feasibility of applying the criteria to actual situations.

Cost-benefit calculations cannot be applied to projects whose output is not marketed and cannot be adequately measured in monetary terms. This is particularly the case with projects which contribute directly to human well-being and effectiveness and do not produce tangible goods, e.g., expenditure on health, education, housing, etc. It is not possible to calculate the comparative contribution to economic growth of an expenditure of one million dollars on education and on malaria control. Expenditure on malaria control improves the health and thereby the efficiency of labour. But it is impossible to calculate the contribution to production resulting from a certain amount of expenditure on malaria control. Cost-benefit calculations cannot be applied to fields like agriculture, transport, small industry and certain private investments because of the non-availability or inadequacy of data. The problem of the non-adequate and reliable data is particularly acute in underdeveloped countries. The International Labour Organisation observes:

> It may be felt that the many pages of economic journals and other literature devoted in recent years to controversy over investment criteria in underdeveloped countries yield

disappointingly little in the way of practical guidance.... Moreover, not all of the considerations on which sound investment decisions must be based are economic in character. There are important sociological and psychological considerations concerning which economic analysis, as such, can have little to say.[23]

SHADOW PRICES

Whatever the criteria for resource allocation, difficulties arise in the measurement of present and future benefits from a given project and of the costs that are incurred obtaining such benefits. Market prices, particularly those of production, form a very imperfect guide to resource allocation in underdeveloped countries because of the existence of fundamental disequilibria which are reflected in the existence of massive underemployment at the prevailing wage rates, deficiency of funds at current interest rates, and the shortage of foreign exchange at the existing exchanges rates. The equilibrium level of wage rates will be considerably lower than market wages while the equilibrium interest rates will probably be much higher than market rates.

If the criterion is to be based on the concept of social product, it will be essential to remedy this defect. To do this, J. Tinbergen[24], and H.B. Chenery and K.S. Kretschmer[25] suggest the use of "accounting prices" or "shadow prices" which truly reflect intrinsic values of factors of production.

In the practical application of this theory, however, a certain amount of arbitrariness may enter into the assessment of these intrinsic values. It is difficult to predict the shifts in accounting prices resulting from the realisation of investment programs. Moreover, the application of accounting prices might result in favouring, more than long-term consideration would warrant, those projects which are labour-intensive, which create or save foreign exchange and which promise a quick yield on the capital employed.

The concept of accounting prices has to be given precision before it can be applied in the actual preparation of economic plans. A recent attempt at greater precision defines accounting prices as "the values of the marginal productivity of factors when a selection of techniques has been made which produces the maximum possible volume of output, given the availability of resources, the pattern of final demand and the technological possibilities of production".[26] After this the government has to calculate the marginal productivity of factors and operate the system of subsidy and taxation in such a way that the supply prices of factors to the producers become equal to the value of their marginal productivity.

The allocation of resources between agriculture and industry, between heavy industry and manufacturing, between cottage industries and large scale industry and between human investment and material investment has, often, been a matter of great controversy. Let us briefly examine this controversy.

AGRICULTURE VS INDUSTRY

Case for agriculture: Underdeveloped countries are marked by an acute shortage of capital. The best suited lines for such countries, therefore, are those which require more labour and less capital. Industry is comparatively more capital-intensive and, therefore, not very suitable to underdeveloped countries. Agriculture, on the other hand, requires more labour and less capital and, therefore, better suits underdeveloped countries.

Underdeveloped countries are often characterised by a shortage of foreign exchange. These should, therefore, put greater emphasis on sectors which require lesser imported goods and contribute more to foreign exchange earning. Investment in industry requires more imported goods than investment in agriculture. Investment in agriculture is likely to add more to foreign exchange earnings. In the world market, competition is less stiff for agricultural products than for industrial products. Further agricultural countries have got established markets for agricultural products but will have to create new markets for industrial products which is not very easy. Industry, of course, will economise foreign exchange to the extent domestic inputs replace imported goods.

Gestation period is far smaller in agriculture than in industry. This consideration is very important in underdeveloped countries, often suffering from strong inflationary pressures.

Distribution of wealth is more even in an agricultural than in an industrial economy. Industrialisation leads to a marked inequality in the distribution of wealth and income. It divides the society into two antagonistic classes, *viz.*, the capitalists and the labourers, which is highly inimical to the stability of the society. Industrialisation distorts regional distribution, too. Industry is not so widely scattered as agriculture over the whole country. Industry tends to be concentrated at certain places because of a number of advantages arising from concentration.

Agriculture is the backbone of industrialisation. Prosperous agriculture will provide market for manufactured products and thereby offer incentives for industry. Surplus for capital formation in the industrial sector has to come primarily from agriculture. In the initial stages of development, underdeveloped countries require large amounts of foreign exchange for the importation of capital goods, technical know-how, essential raw materials, etc. For earning this badly needed foreign exchange, they will have to depend primarily on the export of primary products. Increase in incomes caused by development program will increase the demand for food. Income elasticity of demand for food is very high in underdeveloped countries. Demand for food will increase also because of the rapid growth of population. Technical improvements in agriculture relieve workers from agriculture which can be diverted to growing industries. In the absence of this, growth of industries may lead to a rise in wages which would be a factor hindering industrialisation. Thus the development of agriculture is very essential for a smooth development of the economy. This has been well emphasised by a number of economists:

> If agriculture stagnates, the capitalist sector cannot grow; capitalist profits remain a small part of the national income, and saving and investment are correspondingly small. Smooth economic development requires that industry and agriculture should grow together.[27]

> Industrialisation...can be expected to follow, almost automatically, upon the growth of the food surplus of the agricultural sector—whereas it is certainly not the case

> that a rise in industrial production in itself induces agricultural supplies.[28]
>
> As food happens to be the most important category of wage-goods and as most of the incomes of workers are spent on purchases of foodgrains, it is the extent of increase in marketable surplus of foodgrains that in its expansion of employment in investment.... A determined persistence in expansion of the fixed capital to the neglect of expansion of wage-goods will land the economy in a ridiculous situation, in which there would tend to be unemployment both of labour as well as of equipment, with no possible escape out of the situation.[29]

The economic history of the leading industrialised countries also shows that in the initial stages of development, prosperous and expanding agriculture formed the basis of industrialisation. Japan provides a good example of this. In Japan, a typical farm is yet of two or three acres. But productivity per acre is two or three times of that in other parts of Asia. There was a fifty per cent increase in productivity during the thirty years before the First World War and the productivity doubled by the thirties. The secret of this increase in productivity was the Japan Government's investment of about three-quarters and one per cent of the national income on agricultural research, extension services and education. But agricultural sector was not permitted to retain the increased productivity beyond what was needed for its improvement. A large portion of the increased productivity was mopped up through higher rents and taxes and utilised in constructing industry and social overhead capital.

The erstwhile U.S.S.R. provides another example where the industrialisation was financed from increased productivity in agriculture. The Gold Coast, Myanmar and Uganda are also mopping up a large portion of the increased agricultural production for financing non-agricultural sectors.

Industrialisation requires huge amounts of capital and starts yielding after a long period of time. Large scale industrialisation is precluded also by a lack of sufficiently widespread managerial and entrepreneurial ability and economic and social overhead facilities like transportation, communications and power. Provision of such basic facilities for large-scale expansion of industry requires a considerably long period. In contrast, the production in agriculture can be raised quickly with a little capital and minor changes in techniques which, given suitable government policies, most of the farmers are able and willing to effect. Development of agriculture is also capital-saving to the extent it requires minimum expenditure on overheads like housing, roads and social and health facilities and obviates large-scale population movements.

Case for industry: The traditional case for industrialization rests on the fact that the per capita income is higher in industrial than in agricultural countries. Even in the same country industrial workers are generally more prosperous than the agricultural workers. Industry is considered to be more profitable than agriculture. Jacob Viner, however, does not agree with this view. "The agriculture is not necessarily associated with poverty, becomes obvious when one considers Australia, New Zealand, Denmark, or Iowa and Nebraska. That industrialisation is not necessarily associated with prosperity becomes obvious when one considers Italy or Spain."[30] A similar observation has been made by Dr. Loeb:

> Countries with a low percentage of economically active population in agriculture and a high percentage of economically active population in industry are generally countries having a high per capita income. But the relationship is not an absolute one. For instance, the proportion of the population of Canada, New Zealand, and Sweden occupied in agriculture is about four times that of the United Kingdom, yet their real income per head is greater. The United Kingdom has an appreciably larger proportion of its population occupied in industry than the United States, but a considerably lower real income per head. The same applies to Belgium as compared with Switzerland, Australia compared with New Zealand, Sweden compared with Western Germany....[31]

Sometimes it is argued that industrialisation is not the cause of higher per capita income and both industrialisation and higher incomes are the result of certain common factors like rich natural resources, enterprising, skilled and energetic people, topography and climate favourable to production, a higher land-labour ratio, etc. Generally, industry is more capital-intensive than agriculture. The larger per capita income in industry is partly because of a larger amount of capital associated with a worker in industry. If the same amount of the capital is associated with a worker in agriculture, productivity in agriculture will rise considerably.

The case for industrialisation is stronger from a long-term than from a short-term view of economic development. Because the amount of arable land is limited, it is not possible to absorb the whole population in agriculture. Ultimately, a large portion of the population will have to find employment outside agriculture and mining. With the introduction of mechanisation, the number of workers required in agriculture will decline considerably. Industry, on the other hand, requires very little land. If sufficient capital is available, industry can absorb a far larger number of workers. Law of diminishing returns starts operating earlier in agriculture. On the other hand, although ultimately subject to diminishing returns, the limits within which the industry operates under increasing returns are very wide. Marginal productivity, distinct from average productivity, is likely to be higher in industry than in agriculture because of the existence of far larger resources in agriculture than in industry. During business cycles fluctuations in the prices of agricultural products are larger than those in the prices of manufactured goods. Agricultural economies, therefore, are more unstable than the industrial economies. Fertility rates are higher among the rural population than among the urban industrial classes. The possibility of the increase in production being dissipated by an increase in population, therefore, is larger in agriculture than in industry.

Past experience shows that technological progress has been more rapid in manufacturing than in agriculture. Comparatively slower technological progress in agriculture won't make specialisation in agriculture unprofitable if the rapid technological progress in industry is reflected in lower prices and not in higher profits because, under these conditions, terms of trade will move in favour of agricultural countries and thus they would obtain the full benefit of rapid technological progress in industry. Actual experience, however, shows that rapid technological progress in industry has not fully reflected itself into lower prices and, therefore, the benefit obtained by industrial countries has been larger than that obtained by the agricultural countries.

It is held by the proponents of industrialisation that in the coming years, the terms of trade are likely to move against the primary-producing countries because of a number of factors, *viz.*, rapid increase in the production of foodstuffs and agricultural raw materials in all countries, particularly in developed countries; increased use of synthetic substitutes for raw materials, i.e., synthetic rubber, synthetic fibres, plastic, aluminium, etc.; recent inventions drastically decreasing the required amount of raw materials and fuel per unit of manufacturing output; vast increase in the demand for capital goods in exchange for primary products from developing countries; low income-elasticity of demand for foodstuffs. Singer states that

> it is a matter of historical fact that ever since the seventies the trend of prices has been heavily against sellers of food and raw materials and in favour of the sellers of manufactured articles. The statistics are open to doubt and to objection in detail, but the general story which they tell is unmistakable.[32]

A similar view is held by the experts of the Economic Commission for Latin America under the direction of Prebisch.

> Had the rise in income, in the industrial centres and the periphery, been proportionate to the increase in their respective productivity, the price relation between primary and manufactured products would have been the same as if prices had fallen in strict proportion to productivity. Given the higher productivity of industry, the price relation would have moved in favour of the primary products.[33]

But because of changes in actual money income, "while the centres kept the whole benefit of the technical development of their industries, the peripheral countries transferred to them a share of the fruits of their own technical progress".[34] On the other hand there are some who hold that the terms of trade are likely to move in favour of primary-producing countries. A number of reasons are put forward in support of this prediction, *viz.,* increase in population, increase in demand for and decline in supply of primary products owing to the implementation of industrialisation programs in almost all underdeveloped countries, production of primary products is subject to the law of increasing costs, etc. In fact, it is difficult to say anything definite about the future course of the terms of trade between the primary and manufactured products.

Industrialisation is a pre-requisite for improvements in agriculture. Improvements in agriculture are possible only when employment opportunities can be found for the workers who will be rendered surplus by such improvements.

Conclusion: In fact, development in agriculture and industry must go hand in hand. Development in one sector will be checked if the other sector is not correspondingly developed.

> If manufacturing is to continue its expansion it must be accompanied by an expansion of either agriculture or production for exports, or by import substitution. In the same way, an expansion of agriculture must be accompanied by an expansion of either manufacturing or production of export goods or by import substitution, although about this case there are no differences of opinion.[35]

HEAVY INDUSTRY VS MANUFACTURING INDUSTRY

The traditional course of development in advanced countries has been from manufacturing to heavy industry. Russia, of course, provides an important exception to this traditional pattern of development. She first concentrated on heavy industry and later on developed manufacturing and agriculture. This, of course, was made possible by a number of favourable factors. She did not suffer from an overall shortage of food. Shortage was mostly of marketable surplus and this problem was successfully solved by the introduction of collective farming. It did not lack assured supplies of water for agriculture and, therefore, the need for investment in irrigation projects was not very urgent. In Russia, the rate of population growth is not very high. Above all, it has a type of government which made possible inflicting hardships on people which is not possible in a democratic country. Further, it had to develop heavy industry inflicting great hardships on consumers because it was either unwilling or unable to import the required equipment. She did not obtain enough foreign capital.

It is contended by the proponents of heavy industry that it is not necessary that the presently developing countries should follow the course of advanced countries. Advanced countries had to follow this, course out of necessity because the techniques of heavy industry were not known in the beginning. Rate of economic development can be considerably accelerated by first building heavy industry. In these days of uncertain political conditions, it is safer to domestically develop the capital goods industries. In case of a world war, it may not be possible for the manufacturing industries to work if the machinery and spare parts cannot be imported. Heavy industry is very essential for defence.

The case against heavy industry rests mostly on the feasibility and not on the desirability of establishing it. Underdeveloped countries are characterised by an acute shortage of capital and skill and a surplus of manpower. Those industries best suit underdeveloped countries which require more labour and less capital and skill. But heavy industry requires more capital and skill and less manpower. Underdeveloped countries are generally short of foreign exchange while the foreign exchange intensity of heavy industry is far higher than of manufacturing industry. Manufacturing industry starts producing goods much earlier than the heavy industry. This consideration is very important in underdeveloped countries suffering from inflationary pressure. Establishment of heavy industry without inflationary pressures requires a considerable rise in the rate of saving. A considerable increase in the rate of saving in underdeveloped countries characterised by an extremely low per capita income will inflict considerable hardships on masses.

Manufacturing industries create demand for the products of capital goods industries and thus offer incentives for the establishment of latter industries. In this way, investment in manufacturing industries induces investment in capital goods industries. Investment in heavy industry, on the other hand, is not likely to induce much investment in the manufacturing industry.

Establishment of heavy industry before the existence of manufacturing industry may lead to lack of demand for the products of heavy industry. One way of avoiding excess capacity in heavy industry will be to export capital goods abroad. This will also make possible the importation of consumer goods which will relieve inflationary pressures. It is, however, doubtful if the underdeveloped countries can compete with advanced countries in the world market for capital goods. Underdeveloped countries cannot keep pace with advanced countries in the field of technological developments in heavy industry. Advanced countries are spending vast amounts on research. Underdeveloped countries cannot afford to spend so much on research. Neither they possess the requisite talent for research. Underdeveloped countries, generally, adopt the techniques and process developed in advanced countries after a considerable time-lag. Advanced countries, therefore, are always ahead of the underdeveloped countries in the field of technological developments. Advanced countries can offer much better terms of sale than the underdeveloped countries. Availability of credit, for instance, is an important consideration for importers in case of durable goods like machinery which continue giving service over a long period. Advanced countries can give much larger credit than the underdeveloped countries which suffer from an acute shortage of capital.

Conclusion: Underdeveloped countries should concentrate neither exclusively on manufacturing industries nor exclusively on heavy industries. Both types of industries should be developed in a balanced manner.

COTTAGE AND SMALL SCALE INDUSTRIES

Cottage and small scale industries are best suited to the conditions prevailing in underdeveloped countries. They require more manpower and less capital and modern skills. They require lesser imported goods. They provide larger employment. They lead to a more equitable personal and regional distribution of income. Investment in cottage industries starts yielding fruit much earlier. These can be combined with agriculture and integrated with large scale industry. Japan offers the best example of an integration between the cottage industries and the large scale industries. In underdeveloped countries characterised by a shortage of capital and skill and vast unemployment and underemployment of manpower, the social cost of production of cottage industries is likely to be far lower than the private cost of the same products from modern industry. The main difficulties arise, however, from the fact that cottage industries cannot compete with modern large scale industries. To develop cottage industries, their efficiency should be improved by all means and they should be protected from competition from modern industry.

A higher rate of development can be achieved by concentrating resources on heavy industry and cottage industries. The available capital, skill and foreign exchange should be used for building heavy industry and consumer goods should be produced in cottage industries requiring lesser amounts of capital, skill and foreign exchange. Modern large-scale manufacturing industry should be permitted to produce consumer goods for export because cottage industries cannot compete in foreign markets. Cottage industries will supply consumer goods to meet the increased demand for these resulting from investment in heavy industry which starts yielding production after a long time-lag and, thus, prevent inflationary pressures generally associated with large investment in heavy industry. Cottage industries will provide employment to the surplus manpower which cannot be utilised if investment is concentrated on heavy industry. On the other hand, investment in heavy industry will generate demand for the products of cottage industries which generally suffer from a shortage of demand. Once the heavy industry is built, cottage industries can generally be replaced by modern manufacturing industry which can provide a higher per capita income than cottage industries. Ultimately, economic development consists in associating more and more capital with labour. Cottage industries should be used only during the transitional period for economising capital, skill and foreign exchange and to provide employment to surplus manpower.

HUMAN INVESTMENT AND MATERIAL INVESTMENT

The term "human capital formation" is the process of acquiring skills, education and experience which are crucial for economic development. It means investment in man and his development as a creative and productive resource. It includes investment by society in education, investment by employers in training, as well as investment by individuals of time and money in their own development.

An important cause of the low productivity in the underdeveloped countries lies in the utterly inadequate investment in human beings. The United Nations experts observe "most development programs accord too low a priority to investment in human beings, and provide correspondingly too high a priority to investment in material capital.[36] Expansion of social services weakens obstacles to development by improving the productive efficiency of labour, by increasing its mobility and by encouraging innovations. To quote again the United Nations experts, "In our opinion most underdeveloped countries are in the situation that investment in people is likely to prove as productive, in the purely material sense, as any investment in material resources, and in many cases investment in people would lead to a greater increase of the flow of goods and services than would follow upon any comparable investment in material capital."[37]

It is important to note that all expansion of social services is not at the expense of alternative use of resources. A large part of the expenditure on social services results merely in transfer of power to consume from one class of community to another—from rich to poor, from employed to unemployed, from healthy to sick, or from unmarried to married.

There are two ways in which expansion of social services may be at the cost of capital formation.[38] The first way is where the persons who are taxed to obtain resources for the provision of social services react by reducing their saving rather than their expenditure. The other way in which provision of these services may reduce capital formation is when those who are taxed to obtain the requisite resources succeed in shifting the tax. A large part of the social service payments to industrial workers, for example, is intended to be financed from deductions in their wages. But because of their organisational strength, they are able to resist this social service levy or manage to offset the levy by securing an increase in the level of their real wages. Thus, taxes are shifted to other classes or the government may have to shoulder the responsibility by reducing its investment in capital-formation projects.

The above analysis of the ways in which the expansion of social services may be at the cost of capital formation should not be interpreted as a judgement against social services. It merely points out that any substantial expansion of social services must be supported by effective measures to increase the propensity to save. Even if social services are expanded at the cost of material capital, it need not lead to adverse effects on productivity. It merely means that investment is being made in people rather than in material capital. Expansion of social services improves the productive capacity of people and thereby creates conditions for a higher rate of capital formation. Sometimes social service funds (e.g., insurance fund, provident fund) prove rich sources of saving and investible funds.

As the underdeveloped countries have limited resources, they should adopt a selective policy in expanding social services. Top priority should be given to those services which have a direct bearing on productivity or weaken the obstacles to development. In any program of development, education and public health services deserve a high priority. In a community where the majority of people work as small farmers, agricultural extension should be accorded the high priority. Observations made by the U.N. experts may be quoted with benefit:

> We believe that an increase of 50 percent in two decades or less would be possible even without any substantial increase in capital or any substantial reorganisation of the agricultural system, if farmers were taught modern techniques—mainly the use of fertilisers and of seed control.... We can think of no other investment that is likely to yield bigger return in the immediate future.[39]

Public health measures have two opposite types of effects. On the one hand, they facilitate development by improving the productive capacity of the people. But on the other hand, they reduce the mortality rate leading to overpopulation which is a great obstacle to economic development. The most productive expenditure on public health is that which reduces the incidence of debilitating diseases like malaria, yaws, hookworm, or bilharzia and which improves dietary standards, which increase the capacity to work. In a public health program, particularly in densely populated areas population control measures should be given a very high place.

NOTES

1. Gustab F. Papanek, *Framing a Development Programme*, International Conciliation (March, 1960), p. 352.
2. *Ibid.*, p. 326.
3. S.S. Wagle, *Technique of Planning* (Bombay, 1961), p. 85.
4. A.E. Kahn, Investment Criteria in Development Programme, *Quarterly Journal of Economics* (February, 1951), pp. 38-61.
5. Harvey Leibenstein, *Economic Backwardness and Economic Growth*, (New York, 1957), pp. 258-59.
6. Walter Galenson and Harvey Leibenstein, Investment Criteria, Productivity, and Economic Development, *Quarterly Journal of Economics* (August, 1955), p. 345.
7. United Nations, *Measures for the Economic Development of Underdeveloped Countries*, (Geneva, 1951), pp. 49-50.
8. Siro Lombardini, Quantitative Analysis in the Determination of the Efficiency of Investment in Underdeveloped Areas, Alant T. Peacock (ed.) *International Economic Papers* (London, 1959), p. 132.
9. *Ibid.*, p. 132.
10. Hollis B. Chenery, Application of Investment Criteria, *Quarterly Journal of Economics* (August, 1953), pp. 76-96.
11. *Ibid.*, p. 82.
12. *Ibid.*, pp. 88-93.
13. J.J. Polak, Balance of Payments Problems of Countries, Reconstructing with the Aid of Foreign Loans, *Quarterly Journal of Economics* (February, 1953), pp. 208-40.
14. F.S. Buchanan, *International Investment and Domestic Welfare*, (New York, 1941), pp. 95-108.

15. A.K. Sen, Some Notes on the Choice of Capital-Intensity in Development Planning, *Quarterly Journal of Economics* (November, 1957), p. 562.
16. Galenson and Leibenstein, n. 6, p. 347.
17. Sen, n. 15, p. 562.
18. W.W. Rostow, *The Stages of Economic Growth,* (London, 1960), p. 52.
19. Galenson and Leibenstein, n. 6, p. 352.
20. D.R. Khatkhate, Investment Pattern, Techniques and Growth, *Economia Internazionale* (February, 1961), p. 26.
21. Hans Neisser, Investment Criteria, Productivity, and Economic Development: Comment, *Quarterly Journal of Economics* (November, 1955), pp. 644-55.
22. Papanek, n. 1, p. 307.
23. International Labour Office, Some Aspects of Investment Policy in Underdeveloped Countries, *International Labour Review* (May, 1958); Reprinted in Gerald M. Meier, *Leading Issues in Development Economics,* (New York, 1954), p. 243.
24. J. Tinbergen, *The Design of Development* (Baltimore, 1958).
25. H.B. Chenery and K.S. Kretschmer, Resources Allocation for Economic Development, *Econometrica* (October, 1956), pp. 365-99.
26. A. Quayyum, *Theory and Policy of Accounting Prices* (Amsterdam, 1959).
27. W. Arthur Lewis, *The Theory of Economic Growth* (London, 1955), p. 7.
28. Nicholas Kaldor, *Characteristics of Economic Development*, mimeograhed contribution at a conference in Milan, 1954, p. 10, *Cf.* G.F. Loeb, *Industrialisation and Balanced Growth* (Netherlands), p. 57.
29. C.N. Vakil and R.P. Brahmanand, *Planning for an Expanding Economy* (Bombay, 1955), pp. 214-18.
30. Jacob Viner, *International Trade and Economic Development* (Oxford, 1953), p. 45.
31. G.F. Loeb, *Industrialisation and Balanced Growth* (Netherlands, 1957), p. 15.
32. H.W. Singer, The Distribution of Gains Between Investing and Borrowing Countries, *American Economic Review,* Papers and Proceedings (May, 1950), p. 477.

33. United Nations Economic Commission for Latin America, *The Economic Development of Latin America and its Principal Problems* (New York, 1950), p. 10.
34. *Ibid.*, p. 10.
35. G.F. Loeb, *Industrialisation and Balanced Growth* (Netherlands, 1957), p. 57.
36. United Nations, n. 7, p. 53.
37. *Ibid.*, p. 52.
38. United Nations, n. 7, pp. 51-52.
39. United Nations, n. 7, p. 53.

7

Occupation Structure and Economic Development

After going through this chapter, you will better understand:

- classification of production—general principles, optimum occupation pattern
- productivity in tertiary occupation
- occupation choice and human capital formation
- inefficiency of inequality
- Alesina and Rodrik—economic growth, tax policy, and distributive politics
- Deininger and Squire—inequality and growth

Economic development is associated with a relative shift in the structure of the workforce away from agriculture, towards industry and services. This is the case not only for primary product importers like Great Britain, where agriculture's share has declined to less than four percent, but also for specialized primary producers like Australia, Denmark and New Zealand, where agriculture's share has declined to ten or fifteen percent. According to Simon Kuznets, who restricts himself to twenty-five countries for the comparison of long-term trends in the structure of the labour force for which reasonably comparable information is available, India is the only case of a virtually unchanged employment structure, which makes the Indian experience an important one in the history of economic development.

Since the 1970s there has been witnessed a fast increase in the change in occupational structure and a marked increase in the demand for skilled workers in developing as well as developed countries. The most common explanation for these developments has been skill-biased technological change stemming from progress in, for example, information and communication technologies.[1] There exist positive relations between demand for skills and research and development expenditures, innovation or other technology proxy variable. Alternative explanations for the changes in occupational structure have been globalisation via foreign trade[2], including outsourcing[3], and organisational change.[4] The empirical literature investigating skill-biased technological change has mostly concentrated on high-income countries, but some recent contributions have investigated the issue for less developed countries.[5] The cross-country analysis of skills upgrading usually proceeds from shift-share analysis. The shift-share analysis disentangles a country's skills upgrading into between industry and within industry effects. Between industry effects capture changes in the skill structure due to shifts in the industry composition, while within industry effects capture changes due to shifts in individual industries' skill structure. The within industry developments in the demand for skills are mostly attributed to technological change, but organisational change and trade could also play a role. The cross-country comparative studies have also limited themselves to developed OECD countries[6] or added a scattered selection of developing countries around the world.[7]

Thus, under a straightforward decomposition, a country's skills structure is a combination of the developments between industries and within industries. Reallocation of labour between industries shows the level of economic development in a country. Raiser *et al.* (2004) have summarized the cross-country studies on the relationship between employment structures and economic development. They concluded that the richer the country, the smaller its employment share in agriculture and industry, and the larger its employment share in services. Elsewhere, developments in within-industry skill structures were found to be similar in high and middle income countries.[8] Continuing along this line of thought, countries at different levels of economic development should display similar developments in skill structures within industries, but independent developments between industries.

The amount and quality of the production factors are key elements behind the economic development of a country. Labour decomposition in a country provides a straightforward picture of where the country is standing in terms of its industry structure and within-industry skill use. The target of income convergence for countries cannot be achieved if some countries operate with less advantageous industry structures or production technology. Investigation of the dynamic developments in skill structures makes it possible to explain past developments and provide input for future developments. Expectancies about future developments in skill structures provide essential input for educational and labour market policies.

CLASSIFICATION OF PRODUCTION

For analytical purposes, production is, generally, divided into the following three main classes:

(a) primary production including agricultural and pastoral production, mining, fishing, forestry and hunting;

(b) secondary production including manufacturing, building construction and public works, and gas and electricity supply; and

(c) tertiary production covering the rest of the activities, the principal of which are distribution, transport, public administration, domestic services and all other activities producing non-material goods.

An analysis of the statistics of occupation structure of various countries leads to the following general principles[9]:

(a) Per capita, real income is low in which the percentage of total population employed in primary production is high.

(b) Barring a few exceptional cases (e.g., New Zealand, Australia, etc.), per capita value productivity is higher in secondary and tertiary occupations than in primary occupations.

(c) Agricultural productivity itself (both per acre and per capita) is higher in countries in which the percentage of total population employed in agriculture is lower than in those in which percentage of agricultural population is higher.

(d) In industrial countries, secondary employment tends to fall and tertiary employment tends to rise.

Optimum Occupation Pattern

An occupation pattern will be non-optimum if the national output can be increased by transferring workers from certain occupations to others. There are certain occupations, however, which may be less productive but are still very essential for the country. Take the case of defence services. If the workers employed in defence services are transferred to agriculture or industry, total national output will be increased. Transfer of workers from defence to other occupations, however, may not be very desirable for political reasons. To take another case, it is considered desirable for a country that it should, as far as possible, be self-sufficient in food and essential raw materials. Free trade and multilateral balancing permanently assured, no country need produce its own food and agricultural raw materials if the workers can be employed more productively in other occupations. In the actual world, a country may find it difficult to obtain the required quantity of food, and raw materials because of a number of reasons, *viz.*, export restrictions, payment difficulties, strained political relations with food-producing countries, overall shortage of food, war, transportation difficulties, etc. Thus while considering changes in occupation-structure, care should be taken that production of essential goods and services is not decreased.

A more appropriate and more realistic criterion for judging the desirability of a change in occupation-structure, therefore, is that total net output can be increased without any decrease in the output of goods and services considered essential for the country. According to this criterion, occupation structure in most of the underdeveloped countries is non-optimum. Marginal productivity of labour in agriculture is almost zero (sometimes even negative). If a portion of workers is transferred from agriculture to other occupations, production in agriculture, even with unchanged techniques, capital and skills, will remain unaffected. This was well demonstrated during the war when the transfer of a portion of workers from agriculture to war occupations left the agricultural output almost unaffected. In cases in which the marginal productivity of labour is negative in agriculture, transfer of workers from agriculture to other occupations will increase production not only in other occupations but also in agriculture itself. Experience in advanced countries shows that a decline in agricultural population has, generally, been associated with an increase in total net output, increase in agricultural output per worker, and increase in total agricultural output.

A change in occupation structure cannot be considered in isolation. It has to be considered along with the change in the stock of capital, technology and other resources. In most of the underdeveloped countries, there is little possibility of changing the occupation-structure without a vast amount of expenditure on the formation of capital and skills. The increase in output from a change in occupation-structure may be partly or wholly because of a change in the stock of capital and technology that is associated with the change in occupation-structure. Larger output per worker in secondary and tertiary occupations may simply be owing to a larger amount of capital associated with workers in these occupations. Desirability of a change in occupation-structure will be established only if it can be demonstrated that more output can be obtained by using a particular amount of productive resources combined with a particular number of workers from certain occupations than from others. Mere existence of surplus workers in agriculture is no proof of a non-optimum occupation structure. This demonstrates simply the existence of unemployment and tells nothing about the appropriateness of the occupation-structure. In underdeveloped countries, because of the existence of vast unemployment and underemployment, the marginal social cost of labour is almost zero. So long as marginal social cost of labour remains zero; optimum occupation-structure will be determined solely in reference to the marginal productivity of productive resources other than labour in different occupations. Case for a change in the occupation-structure will be established if it can be shown that the marginal productivity of productive resources other than labour is high in secondary and tertiary occupations than in primary occupations.

PRODUCTIVITY IN TERTIARY OCCUPATIONS

It is widely believed that income per capita is the highest in the tertiary occupations and a transfer of workers from primary and secondary occupations to tertiary occupations constitutes economic progress.

> ...in every progressive economy there has been a steady shift of employment and investment from the essential 'primary' activities, without whose products life in even its most primitive forms would be impossible, to secondary activities of all kinds, and to a still greater extent into tertiary production.... The shifts of employment towards secondary and tertiary production revealed by the census are the inescapable reflection of economic progress.[10]
>
> Studying economic progress in relation to the economic structure of different countries, we find a very firmly established generalisation that a high average level of real income per head as always associated with a high proportion of the working population engaged in tertiary industries.... Low real income per head is always associated with a low proportion of the working population engaged in tertiary production and a high percentage in primary production, culminating in China, where 75-80 percent of the population are primary producers. High average real income per head compels a large proportion of producers to engage in tertiary production.[11]

The proposition that per capita income is lowest in primary production, higher in secondary production and the highest in tertiary production does not hold good in all countries. In Australia and New Zealand, for instance, the *per capita* income is higher in primary occupations than in secondary and tertiary occupations. In several underdeveloped countries, the percentage of workers employed in tertiary occupations is fairly high. But this does not mean much. There is a marked difference between the tertiary occupations in developed and those in underdeveloped countries. In developed countries, tertiary occupations emerge out of a high level of incomes in other sectors. In underdeveloped countries, employment in tertiary occupations emerges out of a number of factors without the existence of high incomes in other occupations. Personal services form an important part of tertiary employment in underdeveloped countries. This is the result of gross inequalities in the distribution of wealth and income. Labour being very cheap, rich people have a tendency to keep a whole army of servants, often, just for prestige purpose. This kind of employment is not possible in developed countries because of very high wage rates. Distributive services form another important part of tertiary employment. Increase in primary and secondary production increases the demand for distributive services but the mere existence of a large number of persons in distributive services does not mean prosperity.

> Petty retail trading is...enormously expanded in over-populated economies; each trader makes only a few sales; markets are crowded with stalls, and if the number of stalls were greatly reduced the consumers would be no whit worse off....[12]

In developed countries, tertiary employment is mostly in occupations like commerce, transport, banking, entertainment and recreation, etc. which exist along with prosperity of the whole economy.

> We should thus distinguish between the 'low-income' type of tertiary employment and the high-income types, between service occupations, that are poverty induced and those that are prosperity induced. An overpopulated agricultural country requires not only a shift in its occupation structure from primary employment to secondary and tertiary, but also from low-income varieties of secondary and tertiary employment to high-income types.[13]

Tertiary occupations in advanced countries are highly capital-intensive, e.g., transportation, banking, commerce, etc. Tertiary occupations in underdeveloped countries, on the other hand, require very small amount of capital, e.g., personal services, retail trading, etc. Because of the requirement of lesser capital, it is easier for people to enter such occupations. Employment in such occupations, in fact, is a serious problem and there is need for shifting workers from such low-productivity occupations to high-productivity occupations.

OCCUPATION CHOICE AND HUMAN CAPITAL FORMATION

Let us consider a perfectly competitive economy where production of the final good is determined by a neoclassical production function that combines physical capital, human capital and unskilled labour. Individuals are considered to be identical regarding their preferences and cognitive abilities, but may differ on their endowments of the complementary factors to the schooling process, which is a composite index of parental level of education, child nourishment, neighbourhood and peer effects, and the degree of accessibility to the formal schooling system, among other things. The distribution of the complementary factors to the schooling process across individuals is assumed to be exogenously given, and the degree of inequality in this distribution of complementary factors is referred as the degree of 'inequality of opportunities'. Given the endowment of the complementary factors, each individual in the economy decides how much time he would invest in human capital formation, and then compares the income he would receive if he decides to work as a skilled worker, with the wage he would receive if he decides not to invest time in human capital formation and to work as an unskilled worker.

Unequal access to the complementary factors of the educational system can be partially linked to wealth or income inequality. However, there are some predetermined characteristics of individuals that cannot be modified and/or cannot be purchased in the market once the time to make investment decisions in education comes, e.g., pre- and post-natal care, neighbourhood effects, parental level of education and school quality. To analyse the effects of inequality of opportunities on human capital investment decisions, we shall assume that all individuals are endowed with an equal share of the total capital stock of the economy and the production of human capital uses only the individual's time. This implies that investment in human capital does not involve any monetary payment; and the negative relation between human capital and inequality will not rely on the existence of credit market imperfections to finance educational investments. However, we assume that the amount of time of labour force participation that an individual sacrifices per unit of time invested in education varies with the individual's endowment of the complementary factors to the educational process.

Now suppose that the technology of production for final goods consists of unskilled labour, skilled labour (human capital) and physical capital according to a neoclassical production function, which is characterised by aggregate constant returns to scale and diminishing marginal returns to each one of these factors represented by the following equation:

$$Y = f(L^u, H, K) = \left(L^u\right)^{\alpha} H^{\beta} K^{1-\alpha-\beta} \quad \text{... (7.1)}$$

and, $H = L^s \bar{h}^s$

where,

L^u = the number of individuals who work as unskilled labour,

H = total human capital in the economy,

L^s = number of individuals that acquire human capital,

$\bar{h}^s$ = average level of human capital across those individuals who invest a positive amount of their time in human capital formation and work as skilled workers, and

K = exogenously given aggregate capital stock.

For simplicity we assume that the total population consists of a continuum of individuals of size 1, i.e., $L^u + L^s = 1$. And we assume a perfectly competitive markets where firms choose the number of unskilled and skilled workers and also hire physical capital in order to maximise profits. The inverse demand for each one of the factors of production is given by the following equations:

$$w^u = \alpha(L^u)^{\alpha-1} H^{\beta} K^{1-\alpha-\beta} \quad \text{... (7.2)}$$

$$w^s = \beta(L^u)^{\alpha} H^{\beta-1} K^{1-\alpha-\beta} \quad \text{... (7.3)}$$

$$r = (1-\alpha-\beta)\left(L^u\right)^{\alpha} H^{\beta} K^{-\alpha-\beta} \quad \text{... (7.4)}$$

where,

w^u = unskilled wage rate,

w^s = wage rate per unit of human capital, and

r = rental rate of capital.

Individual's Human Capital Decision

We assume individuals with identical preferences and cognitive abilities; and having endowed with one unit of time which can be allocated between labour force participation and investment in human capital. We shall denote the fraction of time allocated by individual *i* to the accumulation of human capital as u_i, where $0 \le u_i \le 1$. Also, for each unit of time, u_i, that individual *i* devotes to human capital accumulation, he will acquire a level of human capital equal to $b(u_i)$, implying that human capital formation uses only individuals' time, and the function $b(u)$ captures the technology of human capital formation. We also assume that $b(u)$ is an increasing and concave function of the fraction of time invested in human capital formation, u, i.e., $b'(u) > 0$ and $b''(u) < 0$. Thus, we assume that there are decreasing returns to time investment in human capital formation and the functional form for the technology of human capital formation is

$$b(u_i) = u_i^{\gamma} \text{ with } 0 < \gamma < 1 \quad \text{... (7.5)}$$

where, γ = elasticity of human capital with respect to time devoted to its accumulation.

We also make an assumption, in addition to an endowment of one unit of time, that each individual in the economy has a given endowment of the complementary factors to the educational process. Let us denote the individual *i's* endowment of the complementary factors by θ_i with $\theta_i \geq 0$, and also θ_i is distributed across individuals according to the distribution function $F(\theta, \phi)$, that is $\theta \sim F(\theta, \phi)$ with the support of θ being $\left[\underline{\theta},\overline{\theta}\right]$ and $\underline{\theta} \geq 0$. The parameter ϕ captures the degree of equality in the distribution of endowments of the complementary factors to the schooling process across individuals.

In terms of labour force participation, each individual *i's* endowment of the complementary factors to the schooling process, θ_i determines the effective time cost per unit of time devoted to human capital formation. We can state this in a simple manner as, for each unit of time that individual *i* allocates to the accumulation of human capital, he sacrifices a fraction of time of labour force participation equal to $1/(1 + \theta_i)$. This assumption implies that different individuals face different costs of acquiring human capital. Thus, the larger the endowment of complementary factor that individual *i* has, the lower the fraction of time of labour force participation that he sacrifices per unit of time invested in the formation of human capital. The total effective time of labour force participation sacrificed by an individual *i*, who invests a fraction u_i of his time in human capital accumulation, is given by $u_i/(1 + \theta_i)$. The remaining fraction of time, $1 - u_i/(1 + \theta_i)$, is devoted to skilled labour force participation. Individual *i's* supply of human capital in the labour market is given by

$$h_i = \left(1 - \frac{u_i}{1 + \theta_i}\right) u_i^{\gamma} \qquad \text{... (7.6)}$$

In the equation (16.6), the term in parenthesis in the right hand side represents the amount of time devoted to skilled labour force participation and the second term is the amount of human capital acquired by the individual. Individual takes the skilled wage rate, w^s, as given, and chooses the fraction of time investment in human capital accumulation, u_i, in order to maximise his total wage income. Thus, the problem for the individual i is given by

$$\max_{u_i} w^s h_i = \max_{u_i} w^s \left(1 - \frac{u_i}{1+\theta_i}\right) u_i^\gamma \quad \text{... (7.7)}$$

subject to $0 \le u_i \le 1$.

The solution of the constrained maximisation problem (7.7) is given by

$$u_i^* = \frac{\gamma}{(1+\gamma)} \cdot (1+\theta_i) \quad \text{... (7.8)}$$

From the equation (7.8) we find that the higher the endowment of complementary factors to the schooling system for individual i is, the larger is his time investment in human capital formation.

Substituting equation (7.8) into (7.6), individual *i's* supply of human capital in the labour market is given by

$$h(\theta_i) = \frac{\gamma^\gamma}{(1+\gamma)^{1+\gamma}} \cdot (1+\theta_i)^\gamma \quad \text{... (7.9)}$$

Thus, from equation (7.9) we find that the higher is the individual *i's* endowments of the complementary factors to the schooling system, the greater is his supply of human capital in the labour market.

Choice of Occupation

Given individual *i's* endowment of the complementary factors, and the corresponding optimal time investment in human capital accumulation, the individual compares the income he would receive under the two alternative occupations—skilled or unskilled. One choice for the individual is to become an unskilled worker implying that no time has been invested in human capital formation. In this case, he would supply one unit of unskilled labour in the market and his income would be given by the unskilled wage rate. Thus,

Income of an unskilled worker = w^u ... (7.10)

If the individual chooses to become a skilled worker, he would optimally invest a fraction u_i^* of his time in the accumulation of human capital, and his total wage income would be given by the skilled wage rate multiplied by the amount of human capital he supplies in the labour market.

$$\text{Income of a skilled worker} = w^s \cdot \frac{\gamma^\gamma}{(1+\gamma)^{1+\gamma}} \cdot (1+\theta_i)^\gamma \quad \text{... (7.11)}$$

Thus, from equations (7.10) and (7.11) we can conclude that an individual will choose the occupation that yields the highest income. Comparing the incomes under the two alternatives occupations, skilled and unskilled, there exists a threshold value of the endowment, θ^*, that determines the choice of an individual to remain as an unskilled worker, devoting no time to human capital formation or become a skilled worker, investing time in human capital formation. However individuals with an endowment $\theta_i = \theta^*$ are indifferent between investing a fraction of time u_i^* in human capital formation and working as skilled workers, and devoting all their time to working as unskilled workers. Equating equations (7.10) and (7.11), the threshold endowment of the complementary factors to the schooling process can be written as

$$\theta^* = \left(\frac{(1+\gamma)^{1+\gamma}}{\gamma^\gamma} \cdot \frac{w^u}{w^s} \right)^{1/\gamma} - 1 \quad \text{... (7.12)}$$

Thus, individuals having endowment lower than the threshold endowment θ^* will not invest any time in human capital formation and will work as unskilled labour. On the other hand, individuals having endowment of the complementary factors larger than the threshold endowment will invest a fraction u_i^* of their time in human capital formation and will work as skilled labour. We can summarise the optimal occupational choice by an individual by the following two expressions:

(a) If $\theta_i < \theta^*$, individual will work as unskilled worker and will receive income = w^u.

(b) If $\theta_i \geq \theta^*$, individual will invest, u_i^* in the acquisition of human capital, and will work as skilled worker receiving

$$\text{income} = w^s \frac{\gamma^\gamma}{(1+\gamma)^{1+\gamma}} (1+\theta_i)^\gamma .$$

Given the occupational choice of each individual, and the assumption that the endowments of the complementary factors to the schooling process are distributed across the population according to the distribution function $F(\theta, \phi)$, the number of unskilled individuals, L^u, is given by the fraction of the population with an endowment of the complementary factors lower than the threshold endowment. In the same way, the number of skilled individuals, L^s, is given by the fraction of individuals with an endowment of the complementary factors larger than the threshold endowment. Thus, the number of unskilled and skilled individuals can be given by the following expression:

$$L^u = F(\theta^*, \phi) \text{ and } L^s - F(\theta^*, \phi) \qquad \text{... (7.13)}$$

where,

$F(\theta^*, \phi)$ = fraction of individuals with an endowment of the complementary factors lower than the threshold endowment.

Human Capital

The sum of individual's human capital supplied in the labour market gives the total amount of human capital, H, supplied in the labour market. The total amount of human capital, H, can be obtained by integrating equation (7.9) over those endowments larger than the threshold endowment because these are the endowments for which individuals acquire positive levels of human capital. Since the size of the population has been normalised to one, total human capital in the economy, H, is equal to the average human capital across all individuals, $\bar{h}$. Consequently, the expression for both, total H and average human capital $\bar{h}$ can be written as:

$$H = \bar{h} = \frac{\gamma^{\gamma}}{(1+\gamma)^{1+\gamma}} \int_{\theta^*}^{\bar{\theta}} (1+\theta)^{\gamma} \, dF(\theta, \phi) \qquad \dots (7.14)$$

From the equation (7.14), we see that the total level of human capital in the economy depends, among other things, on the distribution of endowments of the complementary factors to the educational process across individuals. Here one point should be noted that the average level of human capital depends on the parameter ϕ, which is a measure of the degree of equality in the distribution of endowments.

The average level of human capital among the skilled individuals is given by the total human capital in the economy, represented by equation (7.14), divided by the number of skilled individuals. That is, average human capital among the skilled individuals is given by:

$$\bar{h}^s = \frac{\dfrac{\gamma^{\gamma}}{(1+\gamma)^{1+\gamma}} \displaystyle\int_{\theta^*}^{\bar{\theta}} (1+\theta)^{\gamma} \, dF(\theta, \phi)}{1 - F(\theta^*, \phi)} \qquad \dots (7.15)$$

Equilibrium in Labour Market

Equilibrium in the labour market is given by the pair of wages, (w^u, w^s) for which both labour markets, skilled and unskilled, get cleared. To determine the equilibrium wages we shall have to solve for the equilibrium threshold endowment of the complementary factors, θ^*, as a function of the parameters of the model.

Using equations (7.2) and (7.3), the ratio of unskilled to skilled wages can be written as

$$\frac{w^u}{w^s} = \frac{\alpha}{\beta} \cdot \frac{H}{L^u} \qquad \dots (7.16)$$

Using equations (7.13) and (7.14), equation (7.16) can be written as

$$\frac{w^u}{w^s} = \frac{\alpha}{\beta} \cdot \frac{\dfrac{\gamma^{\gamma}}{(1+\gamma)^{1+\gamma}} \displaystyle\int_{\theta^*}^{\bar{\theta}} (1+\theta)^{\gamma} \, dF(\theta, \phi)}{F(\theta^*, \phi)} \qquad \dots (7.17)$$

The labour market equilibrium can be determined using equations (7.12) and (7.17). Replacing the ratio of unskilled to skilled wages from equation (7.17) into equation (7.12), the equilibrium threshold endowment of the complementary factors to the educational process, θ*, can be implicitly determined by the following equation:

$$\theta^* = \left[\frac{\alpha}{\beta} \cdot \frac{\int_{\theta^*}^{\bar{\theta}} (1+\theta)^\gamma \, dF(\theta,\phi)}{F(\theta^*,\phi)} \right]^{1/\gamma} - 1 \quad \text{... (7.18)}$$

With the information gathered in the previous paragraphs, we can construct a measure of human capital inequality which is known as the human capital Gini coefficient. Human capital Lorenz curve can be depicted as follows:

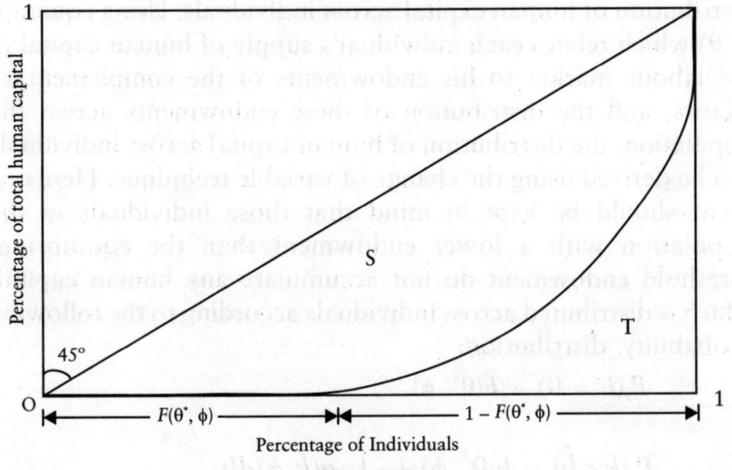

Fig. 7.1

For computing the human capital Lorenz curve, first individuals' human capitals are ordered by magnitude, starting with the lowest. After that we draw the cumulative proportion of the population so ordered, from zero to one along the horizontal axis, against the cumulative proportion of total human capital, from zero to one along the vertical axis. Since a fraction $F(\theta^*, \phi)$

of individuals do not accumulate any human capital and as a result the human capital Lorenz curve is truncated at zero for a cumulative proportion of the population equal to $F(\theta^*, \phi)$. Individuals whose endowments of the complementary factors are equal to the equilibrium threshold endowment, i.e., the individuals with $\theta_i = \theta^*$, supply positive amounts of human capital in the labour market. Due to this, after the individual with $\theta_i = \theta^*$, the cumulative proportion of total human capital is greater than zero and increasing in θ_i, and therefore increasing as we move to the right in the Fig. 16.1. Using Fig. 16.1, the human capital Gini coefficient can be defined as:

$$Gini_h = \frac{S}{S+T} \qquad \text{... (7.19)}$$

Thus, from equation (7.19) we find that the larger the human capital Gini coefficient is, the more unequal is the distribution of human capital across individuals. Using equation (7.9) which relates each individual's supply of human capital in the labour market to his endowments of the complementary factors, and the distribution of these endowments across the population, the distribution of human capital across individuals can be derived using the change of variable technique. Here one point should be kept in mind that those individuals in the population with a lower endowment than the equilibrium threshold endowment do not accumulate any human capital, which is distributed across individuals according to the following probability distribution:

$$P_r(h = 0) = F(\theta^*, \phi)$$

$$P_r(h < \hat{h}) = F(\theta^*, \phi) + \int_{h(\theta^*)}^{\hat{h}} g(h, \phi)\, dh$$

$$\text{for } \hat{h} \in \left[h(\theta^*),\, h(\bar{\theta})\right] \qquad \text{... (7.20)}$$

where,

$$g(h, \phi) = f\left[\theta(h), \phi\right] \left|\frac{d\theta}{dh}\right|$$

$h(\theta^*)$ = human capital supplied in the labour market by an individual with an endowment of the complementary factors equal to the equilibrium threshold endowment, i.e., individual with $\theta_i = \theta^*$;

$h(\bar{\theta})$ = human capital supplied in the labour market by an individual with the highest endowment of the complementary factors in the population, i.e., individual with $\theta_i = \bar{\theta}$; and

$f(.)$ = density function associated with the cumulative distribution function $F(.)$.

Using equation (7.9) we can obtain the values of $\theta(h)$ and $\frac{d\theta}{dh}$. The human capital Gini coefficient can be determined by:[14]

$$Gini_h = 2\int_{h(\theta^*)}^{h(\bar{\theta})} hG(h,\phi)g(h,\phi)dh - 1 \quad \dots (7.21)$$

where,

$$G(\hat{h},\phi) = \int_{h(\theta^*)}^{\hat{h}} g(h,\phi)dh.$$

Wage Income Distribution

The wage income Lorenz curve can be constructed by replacing the equilibrium threshold endowment, θ^*, and using the distribution of human capital across individuals given in equation (7.20). We get the following wage income Lorenz curve.

From Fig. 7.2 we find that a fraction $F(\theta^*, \phi)$ of individuals work as unskilled labour and all receive the same wage income, given by the unskilled wage rate W_u. On the other hand individuals with an endowment of the complementary factors larger than the equilibrium threshold endowment receive wage income equat to $w^s \cdot \frac{\gamma^\gamma}{(1+\gamma)^{1+\gamma}} \cdot (1+\theta_i)^\gamma$. And the wage income

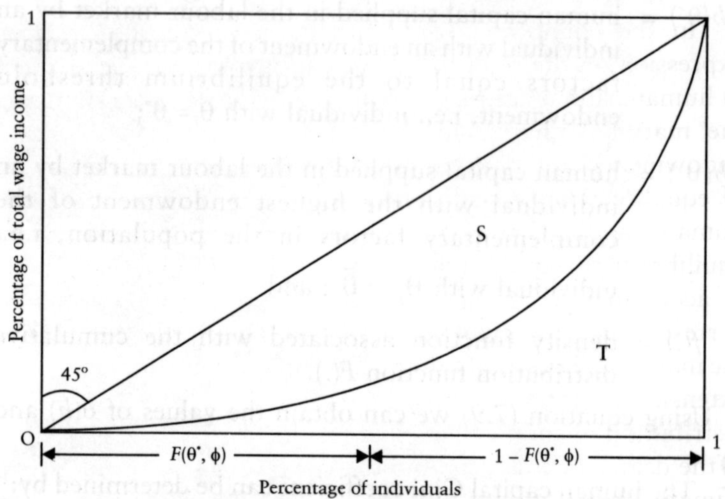

Fig. 7.2

Gini coefficient is given by $Gini_w = S/(S+T)$. In the following paragraph we shall examine the relation between average human capital in the economy and the inequality of opportunities.

Average Human Capital and Inequality of Opportunities

The distribution of the complementary factors to the educational process is determined by the cumulative distribution function $F(\theta, \phi)$ and the parameter ϕ measures the degree of equality in the distribution of endowments. Replacing the equilibrium threshold endowment, θ^*, in equation (7.14), the marginal change in average human capital that results from a marginal change in the degree of equality of opportunity is given by

$$\frac{dh}{d\phi} = \psi\left[\int_{\theta^*(\phi)}^{\bar{\theta}(\phi)} (1+\theta)^{\gamma} \frac{\partial f(\theta,\phi)}{\partial \phi} d\theta - (1+\theta^*)^{\gamma} f(\theta^*,\phi)\frac{d\theta^*}{d\phi} + (1+\bar{\theta})^{\gamma} f(\bar{\theta},\phi)\frac{d\bar{\theta}}{d\phi}\right] \quad \ldots (7.22)$$

where, $\psi = \dfrac{\gamma^{\gamma}}{(1+\gamma)^{1+\gamma}}$ and $\dfrac{d\theta^*}{d\phi}$ can be obtained using implicit function theorem from equation (7.18).

In the equation (7.22), the first term of the bracketed expression on the right hand side captures the marginal change in human capital across the skilled individuals that results from the marginal change in the density of the distribution of endowments caused, in turn, by a marginal change in the degree of equality. The second term captures the marginal change in human capital that results from a marginal change in the equilibrium threshold endowment, i.e., how much human capital is accumulated by the individuals with $\theta_i = \theta^*$, times the corresponding marginal change in θ^*. The third term captures the marginal change in human capital that results from a marginal extension/contraction of the upper bound of the support of the distribution of endowments that results from a marginal change in the degree of equality. And the last term measures how much human capital is accumulated by those individuals with the highest endowment, times the corresponding change in this endowment level that results from a marginal change in degree of equality in the distribution of endowments.

INEFFICIENCY OF INEQUALITY

The competitive equilibrium is assumed to be Pareto optimal in the neoclassical theory. On the other hand, consumption externalities potentially break the link between Pareto optimality and competitive equilibria and open the door for beneficial government intervention.[15] The idea that individual well-being depends on the consumption of others has been used in the analyses of government policy and of stock market behaviour. We shall use this idea to show that welfare declines as inequality rises, that equilibrium inequality is inefficient, and that some redistribution is optimal.[16]

Let us define 'concern' as an increase and 'jealousy' as a decrease in individual utility when other people's consumption rises. In other words, an increase in other people's consumption generates a positive externality in the case of concern and a negative externality in the case of jealousy. It has been found that as general consumption grows, preferences gradually evolve from being dominated by concern to being dominated by jealousy.

The specifics of the situation determine whether individuals experience concern or jealousy with respect to other people's consumption. An individual preferences exhibit concern for the consumption of others when that consumption is very low, that the extent of concern diminishes as the consumption of others increases, and that concern eventually turns to jealousy as the consumption of others continues to increase. For example, a reduction in hunger in the country will make most people feel better. But individuals are likely to envy people who own a BMW.

Let us divide the society into two groups—X and Y. We assume the population to be fixed and normalised to unity, each having size equal to 1/2. We also assume per capita consumption to be x and y, respectively for each group. Welfare is given by $W = (U^X + U^Y)/2$. Let c_i, $(i = X, Y)$ be the individual consumption with the assumption $c_X = x$ and $c_Y = y$, i.e., there is symmetry within each of the two groups.

Externalities in consumption depends on the difference between individual and per capita consumption, $c_i - x$ and $c_i - y$.[17] Let the individual utility function be $U^i = U(c_i, c_i - x, c_i - y, n_i)$, $i = X, Y$, where n_i is individual labour, $c_i, x, y, n_i \geq 0$, and U is twice differentiable with $U_{c_i} > 0, U_{n_i} < 0, U_{n_i n_i} \leq 0$, $\forall\, c_i, n_i, x, y$. In order to abstract from redistribution based on differences in marginal utility, we assume $U_{c_i c_i} = 0$ with $U_{c_X} = U_{c_Y}$.

Let us assume that $U_{c_Y - x} = U_{c_X - y} = 0$ for $c_Y - x = c_X - y = 0$. Since, $c_X = x$ and $c_Y = y$, implying identical individuals within each group, externalities associated with consumption differences only occur across groups, and the utility function simplifies to

$$U^X = U(c_X, c_X - y, n_X) \text{ and } U^Y = U(c_Y, c_Y - x, n_Y) \quad \text{... (7.23)}$$

with $U_{c_X - y} = U_{c_Y - x}$ for $c_X - y = c_Y - x$ and $U_{c_X} + U_{c_X - y} > 0$, $U_{c_Y} + U_{c_Y - x} > 0$, i.e., individual utility in a group increases when everyone's consumption in that group increases. Taking $y(x)$ as given, individuals in group $X(Y)$ chose $c_X(c_Y)$ in order to maximise $U^X(U^Y)$ subject to the constraint $c_i = f^i(n_i), f^i_{n_i} > 0, f^i_{n_i n_i} < 0$, where f^i is the twice differentiable production function of individuals in group i, $i = X, Y$. Suppose that conditions for an interior solution are satisfied, then the first-order condition is given by

$$U_{c_X} + U_{c_X - y} + \frac{U_{n_X}}{f^X_{n_X}} = 0; U_{c_Y} + U_{c_Y - x} + \frac{U_{n_Y}}{f^Y_{n_Y}} = 0 \quad \text{... (7.24)}$$

The social optimum is given by

$$U_{c_X} + U_{c_X - y} + \frac{U_{n_X}}{f^X_{n_X}} - U_{c_Y - x} = 0; U_{c_Y} + U_{c_Y - x}$$

$$+ \frac{U_{n_Y}}{f^Y_{n_Y}} - U_{c_x - y} = 0 \quad \text{... (7.25)}$$

Let, t_i be a proportional tax or subsidy rate. The private optimum is given by

$$U_{c_X} + U_{c_X - y} + \frac{U_{n_X}}{(1 - t_X) f^X_{n_X}} = 0; U_{c_Y} + U_{c_Y - x} + \frac{U_{n_Y}}{(1 - t_Y) f^Y_{n_Y}} = 0$$

$$\text{... (7.26)}$$

From equations (7.25) and (7.26), the optimum tax rates are

$$t^*_X = \frac{U_{c_Y - x}}{U_{c_X} + U_{c_X - y}}, \; t^*_Y = \frac{U_{c_X - y}}{U_{c_Y} + U_{c_Y - x}} \quad \text{... (7.27)}$$

If $U_{c_Y - x}, U_{c_X - y} < 0$ preferences exhibit concern and if $U_{c_Y - x}, U_{c_X - y} > 0$ preferences exhibit jealousy. For example, if x falls so that $c_Y - x$ increases, the externality $U_{c_Y - x} < 0$ if individuals in group Y feel concern for the fall in consumption in group X, and $U_{c_Y - x} > 0$ if the individuals feel jealousy.

Assuming that individuals are concerned (jealous) about those whose consumption is lower (higher) than their own, with $U_{c_x - y}(U_{c_y - x}) \lesseqgtr 0$ for $c_x - y(c_y - x) \gtreqless 0$ and $U_{c_X - y, c_X - y}$, $U_{c_Y - x, c_Y - x} < 0$, following two propositions arise.

Proposition 1: Equilibrium inequality is inefficient, and the optimal intervention entails a reduction in inequality.

Let us start with the conditions $f^Y = f^X$ and $c_Y - x = c_X - y = 0$. Then from equation (7.27) we have $U_{c_Y - x} = U_{c_X - y} = 0$ and $t_X^* = t_Y^* = 0$. Now suppose that f^Y increases and f^X decreases in such a way that y increases by τ and x decreases by τ, with $c_y - x = 2\tau$ and $c_x - y = -2\tau$. Then we have $U_{c_x - y} > 0 > U_{c_y - x}$ and $t_X^* < 0 < t_Y^*$.

This shows that equilibrium inequality is inefficient and the optimal policy reduces inequality by redistributing from the rich to the poor, i.e., from Y to X.

Proposition 2: An increase in inequality reduces welfare.

Since, inequality increases with τ, with $\partial U^X/\partial\tau = -U_{c_X} - U_{c_X - y} + U_{c_Y - x}$ and $\partial U^Y/\partial\tau = U_{c_Y} + U_{c_Y - x} - U_{c_X - y}$. Then, we get

$$\frac{\partial W}{\partial \tau} = \frac{U_{c_Y} - U_{c_X}}{2} + \left(U_{c_Y - x} - U_{c_X - y}\right) \quad \text{... (7.28)}$$

The first term of equation (7.28) is equal to zero and the second term is negative due to $U_{c_X - y} > 0 > U_{c_Y - x}$. Thus, we have $\partial W/\partial\tau < 0$. Hence, an increase in inequality reduces welfare.

Development institutions can contribute in the development of developing countries by supporting policy reform and investing in public projects with high social rates of return and thereby raising consumption for a given amount of work. Let us consider one group with the externality depending on per capita consumption x. The impact on utility of increased consumption for a given amount of work is $U_c + U_x$, where the first term denotes the impact of an increase in own consumption and the second term denotes the impact of an increase in the consumption of others. The externality U_x is likely to be positive at low levels of consumption. On the other hand, at high levels of consumption, U_x is likely to be negative and therefore the impact $U_c + U_x$ is likely to be small.

According to Inkeles, higher income is likely to raise utility in poorer countries, on the other hand he and Frank argued that higher income need not raise utility in rich societies.[18] Easterlin based his findings on time series studies and noted that higher income has little or no effect on happiness in developed countries. There are no time series studies for the developing countries. Frey and Stutzer finding, based on international cross-sectional analysis, is that "...higher income clearly raises happiness in developing countries, while the effect is small, if it exists at all, in rich countries".[19] Thus, the social return to increased income declines with the income level.

It has been found that $U_c + U_x$ is larger in developing countries than in developed ones, and is larger in least developing countries than in middle-income ones. Therefore, in order to maximise their impact, development institutions should allocate much of their efforts to helping the poorest develping countries and should focus on the poorest segments of the populations in middle-income countries. This is also true in the case where externalities depen on consumption differences. The first of these efforts would lower cross-country inequality while the second would lower within-country inequality. According to Bourguignon and Morrisson, there is difference between cross-country and within-country inequality.[20] They argued that world inequality is mainly due to within-country differences in the early part of the period and cross-country differences in the later part. Therefore, they believe that focusing on cross-country differences may be more effective in reducing world inequality.

ALESINA AND RODRIK MODEL OF DISTRIBUTIVE POLITICS AND ECONOMIC GROWTH

In this section we shall examine the relationship between economic growth, tax policy, and distribution of wealth and income in Alesina and Rodrik model.[21] Alesina and Rodrik showed that in a one-sector endogenous growth model with productive government spending and distributive conflict among agents, the more unequal is the distribution of wealth and income, the higher the rate of taxation, and the lower is the economy's growth rate. They have presented a cross-country evidence to support the negative relationship between inequality in income and land distribution and subsequent growth.

In this model we make following assumptions:

(a) Individuals differ in their relative factor endowments.

(b) There are two types of factors—an accumulated factor, capital and a nonaccumulated factor, labour.

(c) Growth is due to expansion of the capital stock, which is in turn determined by individual saving decisions.

(d) Long-run growth is endogenous, as the aggregate production function is taken to be linearly homogenous in capital and (productive) government services taken together.

(e) The provision of government services is financed by a tax on capital.

(f) A small tax on capital benefits everyone.

(g) There is heterogeneity in the ownership of factors implying that individuals differ in their ideal rate of taxation.

(h) Since the tax on capital affects accumulation and growth, this difference also carries over to individuals' preferences over the ideal growth rate.

(i) An individual whose income derives entirely from capital prefers the tax rate that maximises the economy's growth rate.

(j) The lower an individual's share of capital income relative to his labour income, the higher is his ideal tax, and the lower his ideal growth rate.

Let us consider a simple endogenous growth model with labour and capital as the primary factors of production. In this model output is linear function of capital and public services taken together. Each firm produces output y with a Cobb-Douglas production function as

$$y = Ak^{\alpha} g^{1-\alpha} l^{1-\alpha}, \quad A > 0 \text{ and } 0 < \alpha < 1 \qquad \text{... (7.29)}$$

where,

A = technological parameter,

k = aggregate stock of capital,

l = aggregate stock of labour, and

g = aggregate level of government spending on productive services.

The economy produces a single good which can be used for either consumption or investment. The price of the good is fixed at unity. One of the important characteristics of this model is that it attributes a constructive role for government. The redistributive policies of the government interacts with growth-enhancing policies, which take place through various spending programs above and beyond direct cash transfers.

To finance spending on public services, the government generates revenue through a tax on capital income, τ. The budget is assumed to be balanced every instant, so that

$$g = \tau k \qquad \text{... (7.30)}$$

Under the assumption that factor markets are perfectly competitive, wages and rates of return on capital are determined by the usual marginal productivity conditions. Taking the partial derivatives of equation (7.29) and substituting from (7.30), we get

$$r = \frac{\partial y}{\partial k} = \alpha A \tau^{1-\alpha} = r\tau^{*} \qquad \text{... (7.31)}$$

$$w = \frac{\partial y}{\partial l} = (1-\alpha)A\tau^{1-\alpha}k = \omega\tau^{*}k \qquad \text{... (7.32)}$$

Due to inelastic supply of labour, the economy's aggregate labour endowment, l, is set equal to unity. Also, once the tax on capital that finances government spending is taken into account, the marginal productivity of capital, r, is independent of the capital stock, which prevents diminishing returns from setting in. Since higher taxes allow more government spending on productive services for any given level of k, the marginal productivities of labour and capital are both increasing in the tax rate on capital. Wage rate is also increasing in the capital stock. Therefore, net of taxes, capital and labour income are given by

$$y^k = [r(\tau) - \tau]k \qquad \text{... (7.33)}$$

$$y^l = \omega(\tau)k \qquad \text{... (7.34)}$$

The tax on capital plays two critical roles:

(a) it affects the net return to owners of capital, and hence will alter the incentive to accumulate; and

(b) it increases the instantaneous level of wage income while reducing its rate of growth insofar as it also induces a lower rate of capital accumulation.

Since, a higher rate of taxation allows the government to increase its spending on services that increase productivity, wage income is increasing function in τ.

Since, individuals are alike in all respects except for their initial ownership shares in the economy's aggregate stocks of capital and labour, therefore each individual can be indexed by his relative factor endowment, σ^i, as

$$\sigma^i = \frac{l^i}{k^i/k}, \qquad \sigma^i \in [0, \infty) \qquad \text{... (7.35)}$$

A high σ^i denotes that the individual is capital-poor, whereas a low σ^i represents a capital-rich individual. Individuals earn income from both capital and labour. Therefore, using equations (7.33) and (7.34), we have

$$y^i = \omega(\tau)kl^i + [r(\tau) - \tau]k^i = \omega(\tau)k^i\sigma^i + [r(\tau) - \tau]k^i \quad \text{... (7.36)}$$

Here one point should be noted that the income depends both on individual ownership of capital and on the aggregate stock of capital. Assuming that all individuals have the same logarithmic utility function, the consumption-saving decisions of the *i*th individual can be determined by solving the problem:

$$\max U^i = \int \log c^i \cdot e^{-\rho t}\, dt \quad \text{... (7.37)}$$

such that

$$\frac{dk^i}{dt} = \omega(\tau)k^i\sigma^i + [r(\tau) - \tau]k^i - c^i \quad \text{... (7.38)}$$

where,

c^i = consumption, and

ρ = discount rate.

The paths of r, k, and τ are assumed to be given for an individual consumer. The solution of the equation (7.37) can be given as

$$\hat{c}^i = \{r(\tau) - \tau\} - \rho, \qquad \forall i \quad \text{... (7.39)}$$

where,

$$\hat{c} = (dc/c)/dt$$

Let us assume that τ remains unchanged over time, then each individual accumulates along a steady-state path given by

$$\hat{k}^i = \hat{c}^i = r(\tau) - \tau - \rho = \gamma(\tau) \quad \text{... (7.40)}$$

Equation (7.40) implies that all individuals accumulate at the same rate, resulting in a common economy wide growth rate $\gamma(\tau)$, which is independent of the initial distribution of factor endowments. Also, the relative factor endowments σ^i remains constant over time, and the distribution of factor ownership is time-invariant. These results can be generalised to any time-separable, isoelastic utility function.

Let us consider a more general instantaneous utility of the form $(c^{1-\eta}-1)/(1-\eta)$, instead of $\log(c)$. Then, the corresponding accumulation rate (under constant τ) would be $\hat{k}^i = \hat{c}^i = \eta^{-1}(r - \tau - \rho)$, which is independent of initial factor ownership shares. The implication of such type of utility function is that the wealth (and income) distribution is constant over time. From equation (7.40) we find that the growth is linear in the difference between the after-tax return to capital and the discount rate, with the following properties:

$$\gamma_{\tau} = \frac{\partial \gamma}{\partial \tau} = \frac{\partial r}{\partial \tau} - 1 \gtrless 0, \text{ as } \tau \lessgtr \left[\alpha(1-\alpha)A\right]^{1/\alpha} \qquad \text{... (7.41)}$$

The higher is the after-tax return to capital, the higher the economy's growth rate. The tax on capital has a non-linear effect on growth. For small tax rates the productivity-enhancing effect of public spending dominates, and the after-tax return to capital increases in τ. On the other hand, for large tax rates, the after-tax return to capital falls as τ is raised further. Therefore, the relationship between the economy's growth rate and the tax on capital is represented by an inverse U-curve—the growth rate first increases, and then decreases, as τ is progressively raised. The growth-maximising tax rate can be given by

$$\tau^* = [\alpha(1-\alpha)A]^{1/\alpha} \qquad \text{... (7.42)}$$

where, τ^* is determined by technological parameters and is time invariant.

Case of Heterogeneity in Factor Ownership

Along the optimal path, the instantaneous level of consumption can be given, using equations (7.37) and (7.39), as

$$c^i = \left[\omega(\tau)\sigma^i + \rho\right]k^i \qquad \text{... (7.43)}$$

Equation (7.43) shows that individual i consumes his entire labour income $\{\omega(\tau)\sigma^i k^i\}$ plus a fraction of his capital stock

(ρk^i). Then the maximisation problem for the government becomes:

$$\max_{\tau} U^i = \int \log c^i \cdot e^{-\rho t} dt \qquad \text{... (7.44)}$$

such that

$$c^i = \left[\omega(\tau)\sigma^i + \rho\right]k^i$$

$$\hat{k}^i = \gamma(\tau)$$

$$\hat{k} = \gamma(\tau)$$

The constraints of the equation (7.44) shows that the choice of policy affects both the level of consumption and its growth rate. The economywide growth equation $\hat{k} = \gamma(\tau)$ belongs here as a constraint because k enters the definition of σ^i. This results in the following implicit characterisation of individual *i's* most preferred tax, τ^i.

$$\tau^i \left\{1 - \alpha A(1-\alpha)(\tau^i)^{-\alpha}\right\} = \rho(1-\alpha)\theta^i(\tau^i) \qquad \text{... (7.45)}$$

$$\text{where, } \theta^i(\tau^i) = \frac{\omega(\tau^i)\sigma^i}{\omega(\tau^i)\sigma^i + \rho} \qquad \text{... (7.46)}$$

In equation (7.45), $\theta^i(.)$ represents the share of the labour-income component in consumption expenditures of individual i, and it is increasing in σ^i. Since time does not enter in the equations (7.45) and (7.46), the government's optimal policy involves a constant tax rate over time. Hence, individual behaviour based on a fixed τ is fully consistent with the actual equilibrium outcome.

Equations (7.45) and (7.46) yield a unique τ^i which increases with σ^i, i.e., the more capital-poor is an individual, the higher is his ideal tax on capital. In case of a pure capitalist, individual has no labour income and $\sigma^k = 0$, where the superscript k represents this type of individual. Using equation (7.45), the pure capitalist's ideal tax is given by

$$\tau^k = [\alpha(1-\alpha)A]^{1/\alpha} = \tau^* \qquad \text{... (7.47)}$$

From the equation (7.47) it is clear that ideal tax for a capitalist is precisely the one that maximises the economy's growth, τ^*. Since, τ^i is increasing in σ^i, implying that an individual with some labour income (i.e., with $\sigma^i > 0$), no matter how small this income is, prefers a tax rate that exceeds τ^* and a growth rate that falls short of the maximum, $\gamma(\tau^*)$. In particular, if wealth were evenly distributed in the economy, the representative individual, with $\sigma^i = 1$, would pick $\tau^i > \tau^*$. This implies that a government that maximises the welfare of the representative individual will not want to maximise the economy's growth rate. This shows that growth and welfare are not the same. The intuition behind this result is best seen by distinguishing between level and growth effects of tax policy. Along the optimal consumption path a pure capitalist, with $\sigma^i = 0$, consumes a constant fraction of his capital stock, given by ρk^i, and the instantaneous level of his consumption is therefore independent of τ. Thus, the value of the consumption stream of an individual is maximised by simply selecting the level of τ that maximises the rate of capital accumulation. For anyone other than capitalist, the instantaneous level of consumption has a labour-income component also, which depends on τ. In the case of $\tau > \tau^*$, an increase in taxation has two distinct effects:

(a) it raises the level of consumption of any individual who receives labour income, and

(b) it reduces the rate of growth of aggregate income, including real wages and consumption.

Let us consider a situation where τ has been set at the growth maximising τ^*. A marginal increase in τ will have only a second-order effect on accumulation, since growth is at its maximum, and hence only a second-order effect on the growth rate of consumption. On the other hand, it will have a positive first-order effect on the instantaneous consumption level of any individual who receives labour income. An increase in τ must therefore be beneficial for anyone except a pure capitalist. Thus, trade-off will always result in a level of taxation that exceeds the growth-maximising one, except in the limiting case of a pure capitalist. Also, the larger is the share of labour income for an individual, the more significant is the level effect, and the higher the ideal tax.

Economic Growth and Wealth Distribution

The decision over the tax rate is reached by pairwise comparison under majority voting rule. Since voting takes on a single issue, household preferences are single-peaked, and there exists a monotonic relationship between a voter's relative factor endowments and his preferred tax policy. In such case the median-voter theorem can be applied. Since the ideal policies are constant over time and the distribution of factor endowments is also time invariant, it does not matter whether voting takes place only once at time zero or is repeated every period. Thus, the tax rate chosen by majority rule, τ^m, can be given by

$$\tau^m\left\{1-\alpha A(1-\alpha)(\tau^m)^{-\alpha}\right\}=\rho(1-\alpha)\theta^m(\tau^m) \quad \text{... (7.48)}$$

where,

$$\theta^m(\tau^m)=\frac{\omega(\tau^m)\sigma^m}{\left[\omega(\tau^m)\sigma^m+\rho\right]} \quad \text{... (7.49)}$$

and, σ^m = relative factor-endowment share of the median voter.

Notice that it does not matter when and how often voting takes place in that the optimal tax rate remains constant over time, and the distribution of factor endowment is also time-invariant. Under majority voting, the political equilibrium yields a tax rate that is the ideal tax rate of the median voter—the latter identified by his relative factor endowment σ^m. The equation (7.48) establishes a relationship between the distribution of factor ownership and growth.

In a perfectly egalitarian society everyone has the same labour/capital share, i.e., $\sigma^m=\sigma^i=1, \ \forall i$. In actual, real-world distributions, the labour/capital share of the median voter is above the average share, i.e., $\sigma^m-1>0$. Furthermore, the greater the inequality, the larger is the difference between median and average likely to be. Hence, σ^m-1 can be treated as the relevant indicator of inequality. This measure captures how much below the average share lies the median share of capital ownership.

Since, factor ownership is directly related to income, our results can be easily related in terms of income inequality. Rearranging equation (7.36) we can express individual *i's* income as

$$y^i = \left[\omega + (r - \tau)\cdot\left(\frac{1}{\sigma^i}\right)\right]\cdot l^i k \qquad \text{... (7.50)}$$

Since we have assumed unskilled labour, all individuals would have more or less a common value for l^i. A direct consequence of this is that y^i will be inversely related to σ^i. Consequently, the larger the gap between σ^m and unity, the larger the gap that will exist between median and average incomes. Therefore, from equation (7.48) we conclude that the higher is σ^m above unity, the lower is the rate of growth of the economy, or, in more practical terms, the more unequal is the distribution of income and wealth, the lower is the rate of growth.

DEININGER AND SQUIRE: INEQUALITY AND GROWTH

The link between economic growth and income distribution has been the matter of concern for the economists and policy-makers from very long time. Following are some of the issues, which have important policy implications for developing countries.

(a) For developing countries, does economic growth result in a more unequal distribution of income, and is it necessary for per capita income to reach a certain minimum level before income inequality begins to decrease?

(b) Do countries with unequal income distributions experience slower economic growth than more egalitarian countries?

(c) Should governments consider adopting redistributive policies to improve the situation of the poor?

Different assumptions about the links between growth and inequality produce different outcomes for the poor. The base scenario assumes an egalitarian economy where the poorest group's share of total income does not change over a 60-year period. In this case, economic growth would raise the incomes of the poor. The second scenario is based on the famous Kuznets hypothesis, first formulated by Kuznets more than 50 years ago. This hypothesis suggests that, at low levels of per capita income, inequality increases with rising per capita income and decreases only in the later stages of development—resulting in an inverted U-shaped relationship between per capita income and income inequality—based on a model where individuals migrate from a low-wage rural sector with little inequality to an urban sector characterised by high income inequality and high average income. In this scenario, the poorest group's share of total income would decrease as economic growth takes off and would not be restored to initial levels for 60 years; as a result, the poor's per capita incomes are lower by an average of 10 percent over two generations.

Deininger and Squire[22] have identified a negative relationship between initial inequality and subsequent growth. They have used the cross-country data on income and asset distribution to show that

(a) there exists a strong negative relationship between initial inequality in the wealth distribution and long-term growth;

(b) inequality reduces income growth for the poor, but not for the rich; and

(c) available longitudinal data provide little support for the Kuznets hypothesis.

They have used two data sets to examine the interactions between growth and inequality and how they in turn affect efforts to reduce poverty in the course of economic development. They have utilised data on the distribution of land as a proxy for the distribution of assets rather than measures of income distribution that have traditionally been used to substantiate a negative relationship between initial inequality and growth.

They have incorporated some intertemporal element into the analysis of the aggregate inequality—income relationship as summarised in Kuznets' hypothesis, in contrast to past efforts that have relied on cross-country information.

Deininger and Squire have used the data on income shares to measure the change in income of the bottom 20 or 40 percent of the population. This reveals the fact that growth and the distribution of income evolve simultaneously and, for example, examine directly the impact of growth—inequality interactions on the poorest groups in society. The results can be used to make more specific inferences regarding the effect of initial conditions on the poor, thus generating information that could be of greater policy relevance than analyses relying on aggregate relationships.

It is an essentially empirical question whether an aggregate relationship between growth and inequality exists, and, if so, through what channels it might materialise. To provide a valid basis for inferences on the issues of inequality and growth, data on income distribution need to satisfy three criteria:

(a) They should be based on household surveys, rather than estimates drawn from national accounts statistics and general assumptions regarding the distribution of income across occupations or in other countries at a similar stage of economic development. Such synthetic estimates, prevalent in early studies, are unacceptable, since they presuppose the existence of the relationships that are to be tested in subsequent empirical analysis.

(b) They should have comprehensive coverage of all sources of income or uses of expenditure, rather than covering, say, wages only. A tax records and labour force statistics are more commonly available than detailed data from household surveys, many of the figures used in the literature refer to wage or taxable income. This generally overstates the Gini coefficient by about 15 points and, to the degree that data on wage income in the early year are complemented with data on total income in later years, may give the appearance of a spurious decrease in inequality. Own production is particularly important for low-income groups in developing countries. Whether or not own consumption is included will, therefore, have considerable impact on the inequality measure obtained.

(c) They should be representative of the population at the national level, rather than dealing with only the rural or urban population, or with taxpayers. Partial coverage, which is often misleading, is particularly common in Latin America, where many countries collect information only for the urban population. In Peru, for example, the Gini coefficient for rural households is 32, compared with 42 for urban households. In South Africa, the Gini coefficient for the white population is 48, compared with 62 for the whole population.

Based on these criteria, Deininger and Squire assembled a data set on income inequality that contains at least one observation on the Gini index for 108 countries and information on shares received by different quintiles in the population for 103 countries. There are 54 countries with four or more observations and 32 countries with eight or more observations. After that they have compared their data with those used in the empirical literature. With few exceptions—for example, Fields and Jakubson (1995) and Ravallion (1995) that are based on 'growth spells', nearly all empirical investigations of the Kuznets curve, from Ahluwalia (1976) to Anand and Kanbur (1993) have been based on the data set assembled by Jain (1975) which, despite a relatively large number (405) of observations, contains only a modest number of data points (61) satisfying the above stated minimum criteria.

Their data on income inequality also offer a considerable improvement over the ones used in the literature testing for a negative relationship between initial inequality and growth. Application of minimum quality standards also leads to a considerable reduction in the number of data points—from 55 observations included in the analysis to only 18—that satisfy the minimum criteria outlined above. Compared to their data, the 69 observations utilized in the high-quality data set of Alesina and Rodrik (1994), and to some degree the data used by

Perotti (1995) are of better quality, especially insofar as developing countries are concerned. The inclusion of observations from developed countries—from the compilation of Jain (1975)—is, however, not without problems.

(a) Some of the data for developed countries refer to wage incomes, creating the impression of very high disparities in countries with low inequality of net or gross household income—for example, Sweden.

(b) The relatively limited number of observations from developing countries—36 countries in Alesina and Rodrik; and 50 out of 67 data points in Perotti—gives rise to the suspicion that the statistical analysis captures structural differences between developed and developing countries more than regularities that are equally valid for both groups. No sensitivity analysis is performed to dispel this concern.

(c) Even if data of adequate quality are available, the desire to utilize initial income inequality often leads to the use of non-representative surveys that had been conducted in early years. For 16 countries included in the Persson and Tabellini sample, the first measure of income inequality of acceptable quality is dated more than 10 years later than the data point reported by them.

It has long been recognised that it may be the distribution of assets, rather than income, that underlies a systematic effect of inequality on growth, for example, by restricting access to credit markets and thus the ability to finance productive, but indivisible investments. Nevertheless, data on the distribution of assets have rarely been used in empirical analysis. To partially remedy this shortcoming, Deininger and Squire have assembled data on the initial distribution of operational holdings of agricultural land from the decennial FAO World Census of Agriculture and other sources for 261 observations from 103 countries. The data suggest that—as is the case with other assets—the distribution of land is more concentrated and characterized by greater cross-country variation than that of income with mean Gini coefficients of 63 and 37, and standard deviations of 19 and 9, respectively. Data on landholdings are attractive for a number of reasons.

(a) Possession of land could be a major determinant of individuals' productive capacity and their ability to invest, especially in agrarian economies where land is a major asset.

(b) In contrast to income, the measurement of which is often associated with large errors, the distribution of land is relatively easily ascertained and does not require assumptions regarding the mapping from income flows into stocks of assets.

The available data, however, refer to the operational rather than the ownership distribution of land. Nevertheless, we note that these data constitute a lower bound for the latter in that the rental market generally seems to contribute to a more equal distribution of landholdings. Using these data we find that, indeed, the assumption of a one-to-one mapping from the distribution of income to the distribution of assets that has been used in much of the literature receives little empirical support—the correlation between the Gini coefficients for initial distribution of land and income is relatively low 0.39. Finally, coverage is more equal both geographically and over time than for data on income distribution. In most cases, observations on land distribution are available for earlier dates than estimates on income distribution and for countries in which no nationally representative data on income inequality are available.

Initial Inequality and Long-run Growth

In this section, we shall analyse whether the strong relationship between initial inequality and long-term growth holds up to the scrutiny of better data. Thereafter, we shall consider whether additional insights can be gained by using an asset-based measure of inequality and study some of the potential channels through which initial inequality might affect future growth. There are three main results:

(a) The effect of the initial income distribution on subsequent growth is not very robust.

(b) Inequality in the initial distribution of land is significantly associated with lower subsequent growth, an effect that is more robust than that of initial income inequality.

(c) The fact that a significant relationship between inequality and growth does not exist in democratic societies suggests that explanations other than democratic voting may be at work. Wealth constraints that prevent the poor from accessing credit markets and which may be important determinants of the poor's ability to invest in physical and human capital and to substitute for insurance, could provide an alternative explanation.

There is a relationships between the level of income and its distribution, and the forces shaping the latter. A negative relationship between inequality and growth could emerge if investments in human or physical capital are lumpy and have to be financed through credit. Where information is costly and imperfect, equilibrium credit rationing will arise—that is, agents will be able to obtain credit only if they own assets that can be used as collateral.[23] A more unequal distribution of assets would then imply that, for any given level of per capita income, a greater number of people are credit-constrained. In an economy where individuals make indivisible investments—for example, in schooling and education—that have to be financed through borrowing, this would imply lower aggregate growth.[24] Investment possibilities may be limited not only by individuals' stock of collateralisable assets collaterable, but also by neighbourhood effects and social capital with even more pronounced effects in an intertemporal context through the possible impact on societies' ability to take advantage of exogenous technological possibilities.[25] Under these conditions, inequality in the initial distribution of assets could be maintained over time through intergenerational bequests, a hypothesis that would be in line with the stylised fact of relatively high intertemporal stability of income inequality within countries, compared to great variation across countries.[26]

Inequality can possibly affect future growth through political channels also. The degree of inequality could affect the median voter's desired pattern of policies or it could determine individuals' ability to access political markets and participate in costly lobbying. Empirical models that have utilized this argument generally rely on some version of the median voter theorem, which in its simplest version relies on democratic determination of tax rates.[27] As the median voter's distance from the average capital endowment in the economy increases with the aggregate inequality of wealth, he will be led to approve a higher tax rate. This in turn could reduce incentives for productive investment, resulting in lower growth. If this is true, democratic societies with a more unequal distribution of wealth should be characterised by exploitation of the rich by the poor, i.e., high taxes and, consequently, low investment and growth, whereas undemocratic ones with similar characteristics would not.

Now, we shall test the robustness of the inequality-growth relationship. For this, let us consider the following regression:

$$Growth_{it} = \alpha + \beta\ IGDP_{it} + \gamma\ IGINI_{it} + \eta\ INV_{it} + \mu\ BMP_{it} + \psi\ EDU_{it} + error \qquad \text{... (7.51)}$$

where,

i = countries,

t = time,

$IGDP$ = initial GDP,

$IGINI$ = measure of initial income inequality,

INV = investment,

BMP = black market premium, and

EDU = education as measured by either average attainment in the population or enrollment rates.

Often only a subset of the right hand side variables is included to avoid simultaneity. In the regression results, Deininger and Squire had not included the black market premium, a variable that one would expect to affect investment. They also run separate regressions for investment and education to determine to what degree these variables might be affected by other right hand side variables. Based on the finding that initial inequality affects education, but not investment, they reported their results with investment, but not education included. However, the substantive conclusions are little affected if either investment is dropped or other variables such as different measures of education, the black market premium, or measures of financial market development are added.

Given the low intertemporal persistence of growth rates within countries, it is desirable to use growth over long periods as the dependent variable.[28] Based on the availability of data from the Summers–Heston data set, we choose the period 1960–1992. Unfortunately, as the length of period increases, the quality or availability of distributional data available at the beginning of the period decreases. Short of using only a very small sample of high-quality data, there are two ways to deal with this problem. One way—admittedly imperfect—is to utilise the average Gini coefficient of the income distribution for whatever high-quality observations are available during the whole period under concern. There is some justification for this procedure in that Gini coefficients are relatively stable within countries—for the 44 countries with more than four observations, the average coefficient of variation is about 0.03, suggesting that these coefficients vary only very little around their mean. A second and preferred way is to utilise data on the initial distribution of land because here, high-quality data are available prior to 1960.

Given that measures of inequality for income and land are only moderately correlated—a correlation of 0.39 for the 57 countries where both are available—it is possible to introduce them together as potential determinants of subsequent growth. Doing so confirms the earlier results—initial land inequality is more significant than income inequality and stays significant if regional dummies are introduced. This result is robust to the introduction of other variables often included in growth regressions which may also affect investment—black market premium, education, and various other financial variables.

NOTES

1. Autor, Katz, Krueger 1998; Kelly 2007.
2. Morrison Paul and Siegel 2001.
3. Geishecker, Minondo and Rubert 2006.
4. Caroli and Van Reenen 2001; Piva et al. 2005.

5. Kijima 2006 for India; Kang and Hong 2002 for Korea.
6. Berman et al. 1998.
7. Berman and Machin 2000.
8. *Ibid.*
9. Bhabatosh Datta, *The Economics of Industrialisation*, Calcutta, 1957, p. 68.
10. A.G.B. Fisher, *Economic, Progress and Social Security*, London, 1964, pp. 6-7.
11. Colin Clark, *The Conditions of Economic Progress*, London, 1940.
12. W. Arthur Lewis, *Economic Development with Unlimited Supplies of Labour*, A.N. Agarwala and S.P. Singh (ed.), *The Economics of Underdevelopment*, Bombay, 1958, p. 402.
13. Bhabatosh Datta, *The Economics of Industrialisation*, Calcutta, 1960, p. 129.
14. Lambert (2001), chap. 2.
15. Dupor and Liu 2003.
16. Fehr and Schmidt 1994; and Bolton and Ockenfels 2000.
17. Solnick and Hemenway 1998.
18. Inkeles 1993; Frank 1999.
19. Frey and Stutzer 2002, p. 90.
20. Bourguignon and Morrisson 2002.
21. Alberto Alesina and Dani Rodrik, Distributive Politics and Economic Growth, *The Quarterly Journal of Economics*, Vol. 109, No. 2, (May, 1994), pp. 465-90.
22. Klaus Deininger and Lyn Squire, New Ways of Looking at Old Issues: Inequality and Growth, *Journal of Development Economics*, Vol. 52 (1998), pp. 259-87.
23. Stiglitz and Weiss 1981.
24. Chatterjee 1991; Tsiddon 1992.
25. Galor and Zeira 1993.
26. Banerjee and Newman 1993.
27. Persson and Tabellini 1994; Bertola 1993.
28. Easterly et al. 1993.

8

Dualism

After going through this chapter, you will better understand:

- dualism—technical, behavioural and social
- advanced Lewis model
- Ranis-Fei model
- Jorgenson model

Dualism describes a condition in which two distinct and separate economies coexist in the same country at the same time. It assumes a split of economic and social structures of different sectors so that they differ in organisation, level of development, and goal structures. It has a number of possible definitions and interpretations, but mainly it refers to economic and social divisions in an economy, for instance differences in the level of technology between sectors or regions, differences in the degree of geographic development and difference in social customs and attitudes between an indigenous and an imported social system. Generally, the concept of economic dualism differentiates between two sectors of economy:

(a) the traditional rural subsistence sector consisting of small-scale agriculture, handicraft and petty trade which are characterised by low productivity, low utilisation of capital inputs, and are technologically stagnant, and governed by tradition; and

(b) the modern sector of capital-intensive industry which is characterised by the use of modern inputs, high productivity, technological dynamism, and organised along commercial lines.

Economic, technological, and regional dualism are often the consequences of a social dualism, the absence of relationships between people of different race, religion, and language, which, in many cases, is a legacy of colonialism. In its all forms, dualism is the result of the growth of a money economy, which may either arise naturally as a result of specialisation or be imposed from outside by the importation of an alien economic system, for instance capitalism. Thus, a dual economy is characterised by:

(a) a difference in social customs between the subsistence and exchange sectors of the economy,

(b) a gap between the levels of technology in the rural subsistence sector and the industrial monetised sector, and

(c) a gap in the level of per capita income between regions of a country if the money economy and industrial development are geographically concentrated.

Social, technological and geographical dualism may occur together, with each type of dualism tending to reinforce the other. One of the major cause of the persistence of dualism is that the more progressive sectors typically have favourable access to scarce factors of production. Also, urban bias plays an important part in the process of dualism.[1] Since, economic development entails increased output and modernisation of production technique, among other things, an easy and logical way to attain development in a dualistic economy is to transfer resources from the low productivity rural sector to the higher productivity modern urban sector.[2] Development in dualism concepts is the suppression of the traditional sector by concentrating on and expanding the modern sector. In time, it is assumed that the trickle down effects will reduce and abolish dualism. In this line of thinking, the main problem is capital formation because its degree determines the scope and speed of expansion of the modern sector. In general, agriculture has to provide the resources, labour as well as capital, for expanding the modern sector. In details, the strategies vary and there exist several variants of dualistic models, depending upon the assumptions one make about productive conditions in the low productivity sector and whether the economy engages in international trade or not. According to Lewis, and Ranis and Fei, the marginal product of labour in agriculture is zero while it is positive and high in the modern industrial sector. On the other hand, Jorgenson considers the marginal product of labour in agriculture to be positive but low, compared to that of labour in the industrial sector and therefore there is a net gain in output when labour is transferred from the agriculture to the industrial sector.

The dualistic development models of Lewis, Ranis and Fei, and Jorgenson assume that the economy does not trade with the outside world and therefore they are characterised as closed dualism. On the other hand Paauw and Fei assume an open economy and explicitly models the foreign sector into their version of dualistic development. When analysing development in dualistic economies not only one has to consider the interaction between the industrial and traditional sectors, one also has to consider the interaction between the domestic economy and the international economy.

The process of economic development, regardless of the type of dualism one considers, emerges from the same way, i.e., transfer of resources from the traditional sector to the modern sector which could be achieved through market forces, or through direct involvement of government in resource allocation. It leads to increase in employment and hence output in the industrial sector, which results in the increase in the profits of entrepreneurs in that sector. These profits are then plowed back into increased investment in the industrial sector to employ more labour and the process rejuvenates itself through a dynamic growth process. Though investment for continued growth in the industrial sector comes from profits generated in that sector, the initial investment to employ the transferred labour comes from the agricultural surplus transferred by dualistic landlords.[3] The dualistic approach of development theory advocates the transfer of resources from the low productivity sector to the high productivity industrial sector without analysing the cause of productivity differential between the two sectors. This approach of development accepts the productivity differential as immutable and does not make any attempt to formulate policies to increase productivity in either sector. The agriculture sector's role is a passive one of labour release while the industrial sector is seen as the active sector. In this regard, dualistic development models depart from the tradition of classical economics that looks for ways to increase efficiency in all sectors and hence the economy.

Assumptions of dualistic development model, both implicit and explicit, need to be analysed for their validity and hence their effects on any rational development policy. It assumes a low or zero marginal productivity of labour in agriculture, and has the implication that its transfer as well as that of other resources from the agriculture sector does not involve any opportunity cost. However, this assumption does not hold anywhere. Empirical findings of Southeast Asia in the 1950s shows that the marginal product of labour in agriculture is positive and significant.[4] In African countries, labour shortages during the sowing and harvesting seasons negatively affect agricultural output, indicating that the marginal product of labour in the traditional agriculture sector is positive. Using the example of the 'Green Revolution' in Southeast Asia, it can be proved that contrary to the assumption of labour surplus in the agricultural sector, there is labour shortage in that sector.

In the dualistic models, it has been assumed that the low productivity of labour in agriculture is due to labour surplus. However, it can be argued that low labour productivity is due to capital shortage in that sector. In such case, the solution to the low productivity problem in agriculture would be a transfer of capital to the agricultural sector rather than a transfer of labour from that sector. With labour surplus in the agricultural sector, the marginal product of capital in that sector will be higher than in other sectors. Therefore, the optimal allocation of resources in the economy will imply the transfer of capital to the agriculture sector. But, the dualistic models have avoided this possibility by assuming that no capital is used in the agriculture sector. This assumption makes it possible to transfer labour to the industrial sector but not capital to the agricultural sector. This asymmetry of input use cannot be justified either on theoretical or empirical grounds.

Dualistic approach implicitly assumes the full employment at all times in the modern sector, which has an infinite capacity to create jobs to absorb all labour that is transferred from the agricultural sector. This assumption would be a realistic one if more jobs are created in the urban sector than the rate of labour transfer from the rural sector or if there is a mechanism to ensure that the total number of labour transferred from the rural sector exactly matches the number of jobs created in the urban sector. According to Todaro, each job created in the urban sector brings more than one labour from the rural sector to the urban sector to compete for that job, and that is why not all labour moving from the rural to the urban sector will be successful in acquiring one of the small number of jobs created in the urban sector.

Dualistic approach assumes that agricultural surplus can be easily transferred to finance investment in the industrial sector. This assumption is based on the fact that there is a landed aristocracy that can and do squeeze some surplus out of subsistence farmers to finance investment in the industrial sector. While this assumption may be true in some parts of the developing world, it is generally not true in Africa where land is communally held. Even where there is an aristocracy to levy a share of agricultural output from farmers, there is no reason to be believe that such resources will be efficiently invested in the industrial sector. These resources may be spent on conspicuous consumption or put in foreign bank accounts.

In dualistic approach, it has been assumed that labour productivity in the agriculture sector increases as more resources are transferred from the agricultural sector. With less people to feed in the agricultural sector, increased productivity implies that there is more agricultural surplus to be transferred to the industrial sector. All this is supposed to happen without increased investment in the agricultural sector. Here, the productivity in the agriculture sector will increase just by withdrawing labour and other resources. This will only be possible if the marginal productivity of labour is negative in agriculture. If the young and productive rural dwellers migrate to the urban areas, productivity in agriculture sector will decrease with rural to urban migration, if there is not an infusion of capital to compensate for the labour loss.

If any of the above discussed assumptions is not fulfilled, there will emerge unemployment in the modern sector and the dynamic industrialisation process will come to a halt. This will result in increase in unemployment in the industrial sector and decreases in output in the rural agricultural sector. Therefore, economic development will come to a standstill.

Social Dualism

Generally the discussions on inequality in economics revolve around income or its proxy through a Gini ratio or similar measures. However, in discussing development we extend the notion of inequality to regions and increasingly to gender and to indicators beyond income especially on such dimensions of human development as education and health. If we take income as a proxy for class, then the dimensions often discussed are class, region and gender inequality. However, a relatively less discussed area in economics is that of social inequality based on social identity. While social structure that has a systematic relationship with social identity, such as caste and caste-like groups, has been a concern of sociology, it is insufficiently linked into the domain of the economic correlates so as to delineate the interface between economic and social dimensions of development.

The vast informal economy of developing countries emerges as the unprotected and vulnerable segment, both in the legal and social sense. In fact, the economy of a developing country can be characterised as one with a large number of small economic units. While half the income is generated within the informal economy, an overwhelming proportion of labours and their families are dependent on it for work and livelihood sustenance. This gives one dimension of the inequality as between formal and informal sectors of the economy. Underlying this overall inequality is the entrenched social inequality arising out of the hierarchical social structure of the developing countries. The groups who are at the lower layers of social inequality are also the ones who are disproportionately represented in the informal economy and are poor and vulnerable.

Thus, the social dualism creates obstacles similar to those presented by a traditional society with no modern exchange sector at all. In such a situation, the major task is to provide incentives in the subsistence sector and drawing the subsistence sector into the money economy. It can be found that the indigenous subsistence sector may be reluctant to alter its traditional way of life and respond to incentives is not peculiar to a dual economy. That is why underdevelopment tends to be associated with social dualism, but it is misleading to regard social dualism as an underlying cause of backwardness and poverty. It is difficult to argue that development will be more rapid in the absence of a monetary sector, from which the existence of dualism stems. Even if the growth of the exchange sector makes little impact on attitudes in the indigenous sector, it is bound to make some contribution to development by employing labour from the subsistence sector and disseminating knowledge. Without the growth of the money economy it is difficult to envisage any progress at all. Thus, social dualism can be regarded as an inevitable consequence of development rather than as a basic cause of underdevelopment.

Technological Dualism

Technology creates wealth in an economy. This very important feature of technology may be visible in the industrial sector but relatively not seen in the agricultural sectors of developing countries. There exists significant difference in the level of technology used in industrial and agriculture sectors—the former employs modern technology known for high efficiency of production and large outputs per unit time whereas the later is dominated by traditional technology characterised by high labour intensity and low productivity in terms of input-output relationships. This difference in industrial and agricultural sectors in terms of technology generates 'technological dualism'. According to Wolgin, developing countries are likely to be subjected to greater and greater technological dualism and the importation of modern efficient and large scale technologies is expected to exacerbate the dualistic problem, create unemployment, and lead to greater inequality in income distribution.[5]

There are several analytical views to technological dualism. Following are some of them[6]:

(a) *The surplus labour absorption approach*: This approach is based on the fact that the process of development involves the extraction and disposition of surplus labour from the agricultural sector, and is associated with economists such as Lewis, Fei, Ranis, Jorgenson, and Wharton. The dualistic structure is seen by an asymmetry in the production function, i.e., the industrial sector uses reproducible capital and labour to produce its products, and the agricultural sector does not utilise any reproducible capital. This is due to the different capital intensities of the production process for each of the two commodities and the relative expensiveness of capital and cheapness of labour.

(b) *Factor market imperfection approach*: This approach first used by H. Myint views technological dualism as the utilisation of two different techniques in producing the same commodity, which must be due to the distortions in the factor markets such that different entrepreneurs face the same production function.

(c) *Two production functions approach*: This approach views the technological dualism as the existence of two production functions for the same commodity facing the respective sectoral entrepreneurs.[7] The two entrepreneurs are assumed to face differing endowments of non-conventional inputs such as managerial or organisational skills, levels of technological know-how, information and social attitudes.

According to Thirlwall, if the agricultural sector production processes are characterised by labour intensive techniques and variable technical coefficients of production, while the production processes in the industrial sector are capital intensive and possess relatively fixed technical coefficients, the technology of the industrial sector may impede growth in the agricultural sector.[8] Relatively fixed technical coefficients, i.e., low elasticity of factor substitution, implies that labour can be absorbed into the industrial sector only as fast as capital growth. High capital intensity will restrict employment opportunities in the industrial sector and agricultural sector will have to absorb more labour, while land remains relatively fixed. This will slow down the agricultural productivity because at the long run all available land becomes cultivated by highly labour intensive techniques and the marginal productivity of labour falls to a low level. However, in the long run, technological progress in the industrial sector will not ease the situation. Instead it will favour more capital intensive techniques and it will be difficult to employ more labour as investments and outputs expand.

Adoption of different level of technologies makes the industrial sector entrepreneur to produce same commodity at a higher production function than the agricultural sector entrepreneur. Improvement in the subsistent farmer's technology will only cause his output to increase along his prevailing production function. He can only produce at the same level as his commercial counterpart in the long run when his endowments of non-conventional inputs must have changed positively, which requires a very piecewise process. Thus, the short-term implication is that aggregate agricultural outputs remain low, since majority of farmers in developing economies are in the subsistent sector. If not checked the low productivity is sustained in the long-term.

According to development economists, the unemployment problem of developing economies is due to the existence of technological dualism. They believed that technological dualism is associated with structural or technological unemployment, a situation in which employment is limited, not due to lack of effective demand, but due to resource and technological constraints in the two sectors.

ADVANCED LEWIS MODEL

Lewis's model of economic development with unlimited supplies of labour is based on classical school foundations, including two sectors—agriculture and non-agriculture—with different, i.e., asymmetric behaviour postulated for each. This model has retained the basic heritage notion of the classical model, but there are some substantial deviations also. This model depicts a two-sector world built on physiocratic as well as classical antecedents in which agriculture is the dominant non-capitalist, or subsistence sector with only two factors at play, landlords and labours, and wages set in a bargaining context.

Lewis took the relatively small non-agricultural commercialised sector as potentially dynamic and expanding. However, he was much more optimistic concerning the ability to mobilise the hidden rural savings of Nurkse and Rosenstein-Rodan in a static context as well as via productivity change in agriculture. In his model, landlords were considered as a saving class as well as potential commercial and industrial entrepreneurs, and non-agricultural growth were seen as vigorous and sustained and not, as in the classical system, a temporary deviation from basic agricultural pursuits.

The main concern of Lewis was on organisational dualism and much less explicitly on product dualism. He never concerned himself in detail with the analysis of intersectoral relations or the intersectoral terms of trade. His main focus was on the reallocation of labour until the turning point is reached, i.e., the time when labour reallocation has outstripped population growth long enough for dualism to atrophy and the economy to become fully commercialised. Thus, at the core of the Lewis model is the labour market dualism—one sector is called industrial or urban, and the other is called agricultural or rural. Lewis presented the difference between urban and rural employment in picturesque terms as[9]:

> What we have is not one island of expanding capitalist employment, surrounded by a vast sea of subsistence workers, but rather a number of such tiny islands.... We find a few industries highly capitalised, such as mining or electric power, side by side with the most primitive techniques; a few high class shops, surrounded by masses of old style traders; a few highly capitalized plantations, surrounded by a sea of peasants. But we find the same contrasts also outside their economic life.... There is the

> same contrast even between people; between the few highly westernised, trousered, natives, educated in western universities, speaking western languages, and glorying Beethoven, Mill, Marx, or Einstein, and the great mass of their countrymen who live in quite other worlds.

The essence of labour market dualism in the Lewis model is the fact that labours earn different wages depending on the sector of the economy in which they are able to find work. According to Lewis, earnings in the subsistence sector set a floor to wages in the capitalist sector, but in practice wages have to be higher than this, and there is usually a gap of 30 percent or more between capitalist wages and subsistence earnings.[10] A part of the gap in wages is illusory because of the higher cost of living in the urban sector. However, there remains a real wage gap due to:

(a) the psychological cost of movement from subsistence sector to the more regimented and urbanised environment of the capitalist sector,

(b) the payoff to experience in the capitalist sector,

(c) labours in the urban sector acquiring tastes and a social prestige which have conventionally to be recognised by higher real wages, and

(d) the role played by labour unions and minimum wages.[11]

The novel feature of Lewis's framework is that the industrial sector faces an unlimited supply of labour at wages only somewhat higher than subsistence levels. This characteristic makes the Lewis model 'classical', in contrast to a 'neoclassical' model in which labour is scarce and has to be bid away from other uses. In the Lewis model, when the industrial sector wage is above the agricultural sector wage, the potential quantity of labour supplied to the industrial sector is the entire labour force. Since the industrial sector employers do not wish to employ all the labours who would like to work there at that wage, the employers face an effectively unlimited supply of labour. This implies that no individual employer need to raise the wage to attract additional labour, nor do employers as a whole within a substantial range and the labour supply curve is horizontal, but it is the wage as a function of employment, not the amount of labour supplied as a function of the wage.

The mechanism of the dynamics of the Lewis model is that over time, savings, investment, and capital accumulation produce economic growth in the industrial sector of the economy. For Lewis, the source of growth is profits. According to him, practically all saving is done by people who receive profits or rents and the savings of the labours are very small. The middle-classes save a little, but in practically every community the savings of the middle-classes out of their salaries are of little consequence for productive investment. Thus, Lewis assumed that the link from savings through investment through capital formation through economic growth takes place only in the industrial sector and only via profits.

According to Lewis, employment in the industrial sector is determined in a very neoclassical way, i.e., given the wage and the capital stock, employment is set according to the marginal product of labour. The process of savings, investment, capital formation, and economic growth shifts the marginal product of labour curve rightward. Labours respond to the increased demand for labour in the formal sector by taking up employment there to the extent possible. Over time, throughout a long range, the wage in the formal sector remains unchanged, because employers do not need to raise the wage to attract more labour. However, a turning point is reached once the supply of labour to the industrial sector is no longer unlimited.

In the informal sector, the marginal product of labour is zero or low, in any case below the average product of labour. In the words of Lewis,[12]

> An unlimited supply of labour may be said to exist in those countries where population is so large relative to capital and natural resources, that there are large sectors of the economy where the marginal productivity of labour is negligible, zero, or even negative.... The phenomenon is not, however, by any means confined to the countryside. Another large sector to which it applies is the whole range of casual jobs—the workers on the

> docks, the young men who rush forward asking to carry your bag as you appear, the jobbing gardener, and the like. These occupations usually have a multiple of the number they need, each of them earning very small sums from occasional employment; frequently their number could be halved without reducing output in this sector.

Lewis then turned to wage determination in the agricultural sector. Income sharing is one of the prominent feature of his work. In the words of Lewis[13],

> Most businesses in underdeveloped countries employ a large number of 'messengers', whose contribution is almost negligible; you see them sitting outside office doors, or hanging around in the courtyard. And even in the severest slump the agricultural or commercial employer is expected to keep his labour force somehow or other—it would be immoral to turn them out, for how would they eat, in countries where the only form of unemployment assistance is the charity of relatives? So it comes about that even in the sectors where people are working for wages, and above all the domestic sector, marginal productivity may be negligible or even zero.

Lewis did not take the agricultural sector wage as the minimum needed for survival, rather he thought of the agricultural sector wage as a basic wage, lower than the real wage received by industrial sector labours. Also, he regarded production in the agricultural sector as subject to diminishing returns, a point that is explicit in Fei and Ranis's amplification of the Lewis model. Thus, when economic growth takes place and workers are drawn out of the agricultural sector into the industrial sector, those who remain in the agricultural sector each receive a higher income than before. The agricultural sector wage should not remain constant. Indeed, the rising wage in the agricultural sector is a reason for the unlimited supply of labour to the industrial sector td run out eventually—because the supply price of labour to the industrial sector will have risen due to improved wage opportunities in the agricultural sector. The rising real wage in the agriculture sector has two implications—one is for the turning point in that sector and the other is for welfare analysis.

Now, let us consider the intersectoral linkage in the Lewis model. Lewis has considered a particular kind of intersectoral linkage—all labours not employed in the modern sector are assumed to take up employment in the agriculture sector. The reason for this assumption is that the only form of assistance for the unemployed persons is the support of relatives, which is assumed to be available only to agricultural labours residing in the countryside. However, in the dynamic context, as employment in the industrial sector expands, the model assumes that additional labours will move from the agriculture to the industrial sector. Kuznet has termed this process as intersectoral shifts.

An important feature of the Lewis model is that there is no open unemployment, only underemployment. Lewis's characterization of intersectoral linkages generates two major predictions:

(a) As long as a labour surplus exists, economic growth will generate intersectoral shifts of employment but little or no increase in real wages in the formal sector.

(b) Once the unlimited supply of labour is exhausted and the turning point is reached, subsequent economic growth is marked by economy-wide rising real wages.

Lewis considered the total output and output growth for the analysis of welfare. For him, income distribution was of interest only to the extent that it affected the level and growth of aggregate output. Therefore, the functional distribution of income in the Lewis model plays an important role, because the larger is the profit share of national income, the greater the resources available for savings, investment, capital formation, and subsequent economic growth.[14] On the other hand, Lewis did not take interest in the size of the distribution of income, i.e., Lorenz curves, Gini coefficients, income shares of the richest persons and the poorest persons and the like. Although, he was deeply concerned about poverty, his writings manifested a certain inconsistency about whether economic growth with unlimited supplies of labour would or would not have a beneficial effect on poverty. He knew that real wages and utility were higher in the industrial sector than in the agricultural sector and therefore each time a labour moved from the agricultural to the industrial sector, the labour's economic well-being increased, which implies that poverty in the economy should go down. This point was illustrated by the Lewis as, 'All that the workers get out of the expansion is that more of them are employed at a wage above the subsistence earnings.'[15] He also wrote, 'capital formation and technical progress result, not in increasing wages, but in raising the share of profits in the national income'.[16]

Lewis had considered diminishing returns to labour in the agricultural sector, with the consequence that labour earnings rise within the agricultural sector as workers leave it. In today's context, the rise in wages has an impact on the extent of poverty. Modern poverty indices view the extent of poverty as depending not only on how many poor people there are but also on how poor the poor are. Since during the Lewis's time, such indices and approaches were not available, he would have been thinking of poverty in terms of the poverty headcount instead. Considering the previous arguments, it can be seen that the modern sector enlargement has two beneficial effects on poverty:

(a) poverty falls among those labours who are able to move from the agricultural sector to the industrial sector; and
(b) poverty falls among the workers who remain in the agricultural sector.

Thus, contrary to Lewis's findings, wages can rise in his model *via* the above mentioned two mechanisms, and poverty is correspondingly reduced as Lewis-type growth takes place.

Now, we shall consider the extensions of the Lewis model. Lewis considered mainly organisational dualism, intersectoral labour markets explicitly and intersectoral financial markets implicitly. He had nothing to say about intersectoral commodity markets and the intersectoral terms of trade. The importance of balanced growth between the two sectors, while implicit in his reasoning, could really only be pinned down by superimposing product dualism on his organic dualism so that food shortage could lead to a rise in the real agricultural and, consequently, the unskilled industrial real wage, before the Lewis turning point, signaling the exhaustion of labour surplus, could be reached. Harris-Todaro and Fields contributed to the extensions of the basic Lewis model. Harris-Todaro introduced the notion that intersectoral labour reallocation is affected not only by the intersectoral wage gap but also by the probability of obtaining a industrial sector job. They believed in the institutional interventions in determining the level of the non-agricultural urban unskilled real wage, arising from union, minimum wage, and government wage setting, consistent with Lewis's intersectoral 'hill' concept. However, they insisted on a competitive neoclassical agriculture wage, in contrast to Lewis.

According to Fields, there are three choices for migrants from the rural to urban sector—a formal sector job or open urban unemployment, plus a third possibility, a job in the urban informal sector, which Lewis had also pointed to, and very few urban residents can afford to be openly unemployed and rely on usually non-existent unemployment insurance. Instead, just as in agriculture, they fall back on family sharing, while working at low levels of productivity, i.e., they are the urban underemployed. The works of Ranis and Stewart differentiates among two urban informal sub-sectors—a V-goods sub-sector which is dynamic and tied by subcontract to the urban industrial sector, and an agricultural sponge sub-sector which was the focus of both Lewis and Fields.

For the income distribution, Lewis's model has the implications very much in line with Kuznets's early contribution to the subject, which implicitly adopted a dualistic model as the economy moves from agriculture to manufacturing to services. Kuznets's reasons for anticipating an initial worsening of income distribution was that, as labour shifts from an equally distributed agricultural to a less equally distributed non-agricultural sector, this leads to a worsening of the overall distribution until wages rise in a one-sector world. This reason is similar to Lewis's view, which also has distribution likely to be worsening as long as wages are depressed, i.e., before the Lewis turning point is reached. Both Lewis and Kuznets had not taken into account the possibility that the employment effects of low wages during the early reallocation process can, in fact, lead to an increase in the wage bill and a functional distribution favouring labour, which can lead to an improvement in the family distribution of income. However, Lewis model has substantial influence on subsequent work on the relationship between growth and equity. It has also been applied to labour movements across countries, along with movements among two sectors in the closed economy. For instance, Kindleberger had used the Lewis model to describe the migration of surplus labour from the Maghreb countries of Northern Africa and Turkey to Europe during the postwar boom of the European Community.

Criticism of Lewis Model

Lewis model has been widely praised, but it has also been criticised and is today less frequently quoted. This is because of the shift in the sub-discipline to an emphasis, on the one hand, on macro-economic cross-section analyses and, on the other, on micro-econometric analysis with firm adherence to the neoclassical mono-economics paradigm, accompanied by the steadfast rejection of any bargaining theory of wages. Some of these criticisms are due to the misunderstandings caused by Lewisians who were not clear and cautious and consequently opened up the model to what might justifiably be called 'red herring' attacks.

In the Lewis model labour surplus was interpreted as zero marginal productivity of agricultural labour, which is a highly unlikely event, statistically or conceptually. This was subjected to vigorous attack by Schultz who took the evidence from India to show that the withdrawal of a large portion of the agricultural population did not lead to a decline in agricultural output. According to Sen, as people leave agricultural sector those who remain may work harder to increase the agricultural output. In the broad sense, any withdrawal of labour from agriculture is likely to be accompanied by a reorganisation of production by those who are left behind, i.e., technology change. Lewis considered the labour surplus in terms of human beings rather than man-hours, and his labour surplus was really defined in terms of an excess supply of labour at the going wage—a concept consistent with the Fei-Ranis emphasis on wages in agriculture exceeding the marginal product, which might be quite low, even if not zero.

Among others, Ootsuka also criticised the Lewis model on the ground that there did not exists institutionally determined rigid wage rates in agrarian communities.[17] If the sharing of income, which is related to the average agricultural product, determines the agricultural wages, one would expect to see a gradually rising real wage as the bargaining solution takes into account rising levels of that average product. Consequently, one will get a step function with gently rising real wages, but still not keeping up with productivity which rises faster. Thus, the fundamental point is that it is the sharing rule which matters, not the level of wage which is likely to vary over time. Moreover, the dual economy model assumes that agricultural wages are related to, but not necessarily equal to, the average product of agricultural workers, with the head of the household or commune, or whoever else commands the agricultural surplus, retaining a certain portion for his or her reinvestment purposes. Following this, we find that the Lewis's supply curve in the real world is gently rising over time and, therefore, not horizontal, which it is only at a given point in time. Over longer periods, we shall find a step function made up of annual unlimited supply of labour segments, econometrically difficult to distinguish from a gently rising supply curve.

Lewis model has retained the classical assumption that all profits are saved and all wages are consumed. This is also one of the ground of criticism of the Lewis model. This assumption is not necessary for the basic model and is simply stipulated by Lewis and his followers as a convenient simplification. Similarly, the notion that there is no physical capital accumulation in agriculture, with all the investment going into non-agriculture, is neither essential nor empirically correct, again considered only for simplification.

Contemporary development economists, working inside the neoclassical paradigm, have not accepted the notion of an exogenous unskilled agricultural real wage instead of one that is determined endogenously by the intersection of demand and supply. This is the most serious objection to the Lewis model. When development economists do accept the notion of institutional interventions, it is not a wage set by bargaining but one having to do with insurance, either over space or time. This is the crux of the contemporary critique of the Lewis model, i.e., the rejection of an exogenous bargaining wage or consumption share, exceeding the marginal product of labour at any point in time. Lewis model considered that in the particular setting of a heavily populated agricultural sector, with an extended family or other communal institutional arrangements, the unfavourable ratio of people to collaborating factors is part of the initial condition which makes it impossible for decision-makers to simply fire low productivity group members in order to reach a neoclassical equilibrium or to somehow refuse to share the group's income with them. However, there is no acceptable model which yields a uniquely determined bargaining wage. This also holds in the context of union or management bargaining in the advanced economy, yielding ultimately to a marginal productivity solution, even if the time lag in that case is substantially shorter.

The basic sharing assumption has got the support from anthropologists like Geertz and Scott. Ishikawa forwarded the concept of a minimum subsistence level of existence, which is one version of the institutional real wage and is defined by him as a "community principle of employment and income distribution" which promises all families an income not less than a minimum subsistence level.[18] Hayami and Kikuchi found that, in Indonesia, wages do not adjust on the basis of labour's marginal product but according to the subsistence requirements of the time and social conventions.[19] Osmani developed a model of downward rigidity of the sharing rule as insisted on by the workers.[20] The current work in behavioural economics may prove to be helpful in developing a theoretical structure to rationalise cross worker subsidisation in the absence of assured reciprocity, especially if some members of the group are likely to be leaving agriculture over time.

The historical evidence of England (1780-1840), Japan (1870-1920), and Taiwan (1950-1970) shows that labour abundant agriculture exhibits large increases in average agricultural labour productivity while the agricultural and non-agricultural real wages rose only gently, i.e., lagging substantially behind, until the commercialisation or Lewis turning point is reached. According to Sen even a horizontal supply curve of labour can be made consistent with neoclassical explanations. All these facts are fully consistent with an institutional wage which is gently rising as a result of the step function, until the turning point is reached and wages begin to rise steeply in concert with rising marginal productivity. Before that point is reached, a rising gap between agricultural productivity and wage levels is certainly not consistent with neoclassical assumptions about labour market clearance.

Rosenzweig with his micro-econometric evidence of steeply rising labour supply curves in a cross-section of heavily populated agricultural economies has put the final nail in the coffin of the classical dualistic model. However, the Lewis supply curve is merely a facet of the operational interaction between two sectors of a dualistic economy. The time path of the industrial wage determines the labour absorption path which is the locus of various combinations of wage rates and the labour absorbed, associated with different levels of the industrial capital stock and the level of technology. The labour absorption path is based on the time path of the industrial real wage, with a gently rising and then a steeply rising portion.

RANIS-FEI MODEL OF ECONOMIC DEVELOPMENT

Lewis had developed his model on development in an economy with a large agriculture sector and a small modern sector. His model was subsequently developed by John Fei and Gus Ranis[21], who analysed the transition process through which an underdeveloped economy hopes to move from a condition of stagnation to one of self-sustained growth in an article entitled "A Theory of Economic Development", published in the *American Economic Review* in 1961.

Lewis model was based on a theory of dualistic economic development for overpopulated and underdeveloped economies with vast amounts of surplus agricultural labour. In such type of economy, economic growth can be achieved by rapid capital accumulation in the non-agricultural sector, facilitated by drawing surplus labour in the agricultural sector. The path of transition in the Lewis type of economy is from the first, labour-surplus stage to the second, labour-scarce stage of development. Ranis and Fei extended the Lewis theory and defined three phases of dualistic economic development by sub-dividing the first stage of Lewis model into two phases. The third phase of the Ranis-Fei model corresponds to the second labour-scarce stage of the Lewis model. All the three phases of the Ranis-Fei model are distinguished by the marginal productivity of agricultural labour. The three phases can be illustrated through the Fig. 8.1.

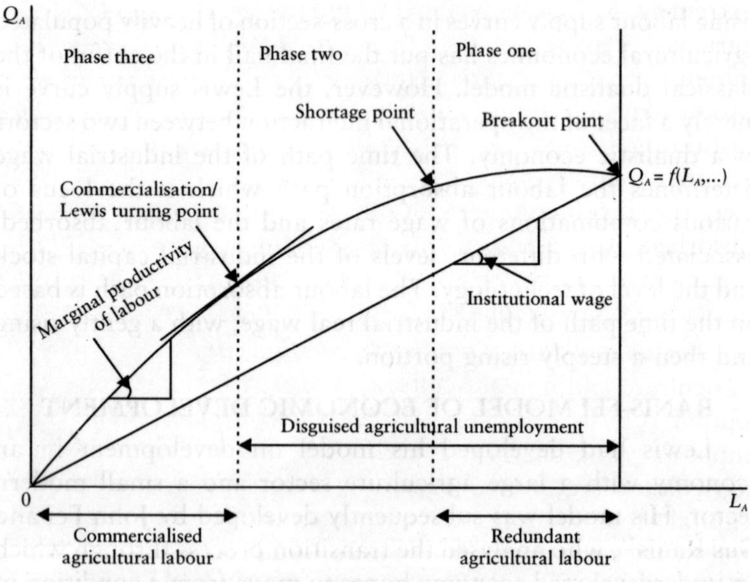

Fig. 8.1

The entry into each phase in the Ranis-Fei model of economic development is marked by a turning point:

(a) breakout point—leads to phase one growth with redundant agriculture labour,

(b) shortage point—leads to phase two growth with disguised agricultural unemployment, and

(c) commercialisation point—leads to phase three of self-sustaining economic growth with the commercialisation of the agriculture sector.

The Ranis-Fei model of dualistic economic development provides a suitable theoretical framework for studying the growth path of labour-surplus developing economies. It assumes the economy to be stagnant in its pre-conditioning stage. The breakout point marks the creation of an infant non-agricultural sector and the entry into phase one. Agricultural labour starts to be reallocated to the non-agricultural sector. Due to the abundance of surplus agricultural labour, its marginal productivity is extremely low and average labour productivity defines the agricultural institutional wage. When the redundant agricultural labour force has been reallocated, the agricultural marginal productivity of labour starts to rise but is still lower than the institutional wage. This marks the shortage point at which the economy enters phase two of development. During phase two the remaining agricultural unemployment is gradually absorbed. At the end of this process the economy reaches the commercialisation point and enters phase three where the agricultural labour market is fully commercialised.

Let us consider a dualistic economic framework with the agriculture and non-agricultural sectors, where the agricultural output (Q_A) is a function of cultivated hectares (H_A), labour input (L_A), agricultural capital (K_A), and output of the non-agricultural sector (Q_N) depends on employed labour (L_N) and capital stock (K_N). Production functions in both the sectors follow Hicks neutral technological progress [$f_A(T)$, $f_N(T)$], where T denotes time and the exact functional form of these contains trends that reflect socio-economic events and possibly dummies for structural shifts. Thus, the Cobb-Douglas production functions for both the sectors are given by:

$$Q_A = f(L_A, K_A, H_A, T_A) = \alpha_0 e^{f_A(T)} L_A^{\alpha_L} H_A^{\alpha_H} K_A^{\alpha_K} \quad \dots (8.1)$$

and $$Q_N = g(L_N, K_N, T_N) = \beta_0 e^{f_N(T)} L_N^{\beta_L} K_N^{\beta_K} \quad \text{... (8.2)}$$

The log-linear form of the equations (8.1) and (8.2) can be written as

$$\ln Q_A = \ln\hat{\alpha}_0 + f_A(T) + \hat{\alpha}_L \ln L_A + \hat{\alpha}_H \ln H_A + \hat{\alpha}_K \ln K_A + e_A \quad \text{... (8.3)}$$

$$\ln Q_N = \ln\hat{\beta}_0 + f_B(T) + \hat{\beta}_L \ln L_N + \beta_K \ln K_N + e_N \quad \text{... (8.4)}$$

where, the parameters with a hat are those to be estimated.

We shall test for constant returns to scale in each sector by the conditions $\alpha_L + \alpha_H + \alpha_K = 1$ and $\beta_L + \beta_K = 1$. Differentiating equations (8.3) and (8.4) with respect to time we obtain the following equations for decomposing sectoral economic growth rates as

$$g_{Q_A} = \frac{\partial f_A(T)}{\partial t} + \hat{\alpha}_L g_{L_A} + \hat{\alpha}_H g_{H_A} + \hat{\alpha}_K g_{K_A} \quad \text{... (8.5)}$$

$$g_{Q_N} = \frac{\partial f_N(T)}{\partial t} + \hat{\beta}_L g_{L_N} + \hat{\beta}_K g_{K_N} \quad \text{... (8.6)}$$

where the exponential growth rates for each factor X is calculated by either the instantaneous percentage growth rate in continuous time, $g_X = \frac{d \log X}{dt} \cdot 100$, e.g., $g_X = \frac{(\log X_{2011} - \log X_{1995})}{(2011 - 1995)} \cdot 100$ or the true annual (compounded) percentage growth rate in discrete time, $AGR = (\exp.\ g_X - 1) \cdot 100$.

AGR is used for representing the exponential growth rate and growth theory is usually expressed in continuous time and uses g_X. In the case of low growth rates, both AGR and g_X are close to each other. The time-derivatives with respect to the Hicks-neutral technological change $[f_A(T), f_N(T)]$ are the appropriate time-trend and time-dummy parameters in the estimated models.

Labour Reallocation Effect

Here we shall discuss two approaches to analyse the effects of labour reallocation away from the agricultural sector. First, a net impact of the sectoral labour reallocation is expected due to the relatively low productivity in the agricultural sector than the non-agricultural sector. Thus, the labour reallocation effect, *LRE*, can be represented by the product of the difference of labour productivity of the two sectors and the number of migrating labours. *LRE* is divided by real *GDP* to find out its contribution in the total output. The effect of labour reallocation can be derived using the average productivities of labour, *APL*, to proxy for labour productivity as:

$$LRE_{APL} = \frac{M}{Y}\left(APL_N - APL_A\right) \qquad \text{... (8.7)}$$

where,

M = net number of migrating labours, and

Y = real *GDP*.

Within this approach, alternatively we can compute the effect of labour migration using the marginal productivity of labour, *MPL*, which is the derivative of output to labour input, i.e., $MPL = dQ/dL$. Thus, the *MPL* in agricultural and non-agricultural sectors are given by:

$$MPL_A = \frac{dQ_A}{dL_A} = \hat{\alpha}_L \frac{Q_A}{L_A} = \hat{\alpha}_L\, APL_A \qquad \text{... (8.8)}$$

$$MPL_N = \frac{dQ_N}{dL_N} = \hat{\beta}_L \frac{Q_N}{L_N} = \hat{\beta}_L\, APL_N \qquad \text{... (8.9)}$$

where, $\hat{\alpha}_L$ and $\hat{\beta}_L$ are the estimated parameters in equations (8.3) and (8.4).

Thus, the effect of labour reallocation is given by

$$LRE_{MPL} = \frac{M}{Y}\left(MPL_N - MPL_A\right) \qquad \text{... (8.10)}$$

Here one point should be noted that the use of *MPL* which represents the slope of production function with respect to labour at the margin, may slightly underestimate *LRE*, while it may be overestimated using *APL*. However, *LRE* estimates using *MPL* and *APL* provide a reasonable range for the true value of the net impact of labour reallocation.

The World Bank proposed a second approach, specifically accounting for the labour reallocation effect as well as being valid for calculating the effect of labour reallocation away from the agricultural to non-agricultural sector.[22] This approach is also valid for computing the effect of labour reallocation from the state to non-state sector. In this approach, the agricultural labour reallocation effect is given by:

$$LRE_{WB} = \frac{L}{Y}\left(MPL_N - MPL_A\right)g_{l_N}\, l_N \qquad \text{... (8.11)}$$

where,

$$l_N = \frac{L_N}{L}$$

Equation (8.11) shows that a reallocation of labour away from agriculture will have a positive net effect on growth so long as the value of the marginal productivity of labour in the non-agricultural sector exceeds that in the agricultural sector. The size of this effect depends on the productivity and the share of labour, l_N, in the non-agricultural sector.[23]

In short, the first approach provides a reasonable band for the true value of the labour reallocation effect and the another one, independent of the actual number of migrants, gives a relatively accurate account for the contribution of sectoral labour reallocation to growth.

Agriculture Surplus and the Economic Development

There is disguised unemployment in the tradational sector and the wage rate is given by income sharing. Economic development takes place by the transfer of labour from agricultural sector to industrial sector and at the same time simultaneous transfer of surplus food-grain production, which sustains that part of the labour force engaged in nonagricultural activity. Figure 8.2 provides a schematic analysis of how the labour force and the corresponding agricultural surplus is transferred in the process of economic development.

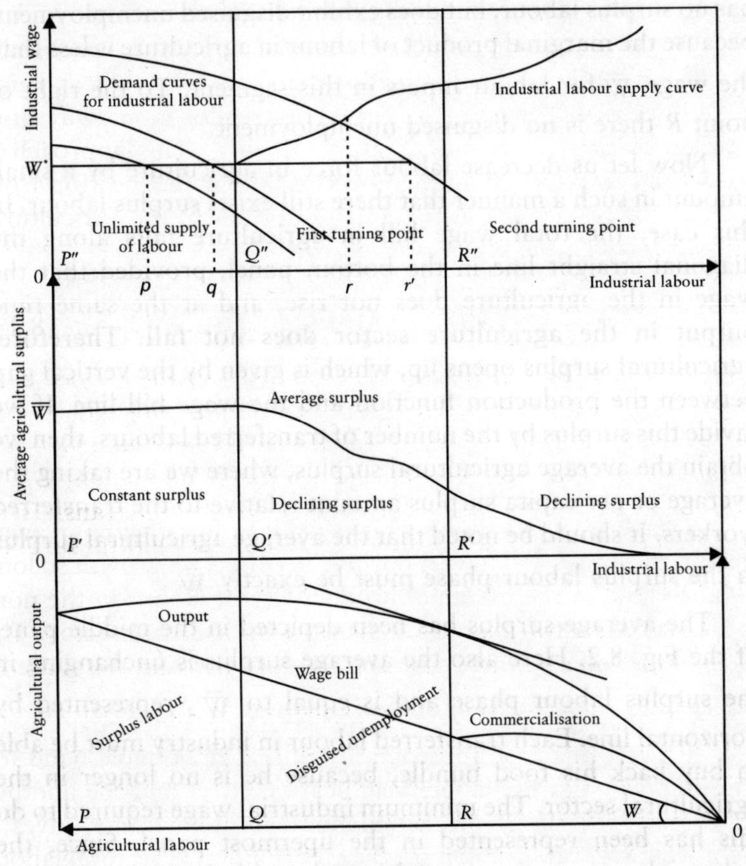

Fig. 8.2

In the Fig. 8.2, the industrial labour force is read from left to right and the agricultural labour force is read from right to left. Since the total labour force is divided between agriculture and industry, the width of the panels represents the entire labour force in the economy. Now, let us start with the bottom panel of the figure, which represents a typical agricultural production function. Since the entire labour force is in agricultural sector, there is a phase of surplus labour, which has been represented by segment *PQ*. If the income sharing decides the wages in this sector, then the average wage is just $\bar{W}$, which turns out to be the wage in the nascent industrial sector. Thus, the segment *QR* has no surplus labour, but does exhibit disguised unemployment, because the marginal product of labour in agriculture is less than the wage $\bar{W}$ for labour inputs in this segment. To the right of point *R* there is no disguised unemployment.

Now let us decrease labour force in agriculture by a small amount in such a manner that there still exists surplus labour. In this case, the total wage bill in agriculture falls along the diagonal straight line in the bottom panel, provided that the wage in the agriculture does not rise, and at the same time output in the agriculture sector does not fall. Therefore, agricultural surplus opens up, which is given by the vertical gap between the production function and the wage bill line. If we divide this surplus by the number of transferred labours, then we obtain the average agricultural surplus, where we are taking the average or per capita surplus amount relative to the transferred workers. It should be noted that the average agricultural surplus in the surplus labour phase must be exactly $\bar{W}$.

The average surplus has been depicted in the middle panel of the Fig. 8.2. Here also the average surplus is unchanging in the surplus labour phase and is equal to $\bar{W}$, represented by horizontal line. Each transferred labour in industry must be able to buy back his food bundle, because he is no longer in the agricultural sector. The minimum industrial wage required to do this has been represented in the upermost panel. Since, the industrial wage is represented in units of industrial goods, we must multiply $\bar{W}$ by the relative price, or the terms of trade between agriculture and industry to arrive at the required minimum industrial wage, which has been depicted by W^* in the uppermost panel. In the case of surplus labour, the minimum industrial wage required for compensation does not change, because the average agricultural surplus is not changing, leading to a perfectly elastic supply of labour, which has been depicted as a horizontal line emanating from the point W^* in the uppermost panel. In this zone, it is possible to have economic development with unlimited supplies of labour and an expansion in the industrial sector does not drive up the wage rate. However, as we move towards the phase of disguised unemployment, the average agricultural surplus begins to decline, because total output in the agricultural sector begins to fall, while those who are still there continue to consume the same amount per capita, which has been shown by the decreasing line in the zone $Q'R'$ of the middle panel.

Now if the wage is W^*, transferred labours will not be able to compensate themselves for the move, as it is physically not possible for each of them to buy $\bar{W}$ units of food due to decline in average agricultural surplus below $\bar{W}$. The immediate effect of this is that food prices start to rise and the terms of trade between rural and urban sectors begin to move against industry. Thus, to compensate for this price effect, the industrial wage must rise. But, the rising wage will not solve the problem because it is not possible for workers to buy their old food basket back, since there is not enough to go around. The only solution for this problem is that the industrial labours have to consume a mix of agricultural and industrial products, the latter compensating them for the loss of the former. This will depends on how close the traditional wage is to minimum subsistence. The closer is $\bar{W}$ to the minimum subsistence level, the larger is the compensation required and the steeper is the increase in the required industrial wage. This phase is referred as the first turning point.

At the point R, the phase of disguised unemployment comes to an end. At this point, the marginal product of labour begins to exceed the traditionally given wage rate and it becomes profitable to actively bid for labour, because the additional contribution of labour in agricultural production exceeds the cost of hiring labour. This implies that the wage in agricultural sector will rise.

To summarise, capital accumulation in the industrial sector is the engine of growth—more capital implies greater demand for labour which in turn induces greater rural-urban migration. As development proceeds, the terms of trade gradually turn in favour of agriculture and against industry—food prices rise because a smaller number of farmers have to support a greater number of nonagricultural labours. An increase in the price of food causes an increase in the industrial wage rate. The accumulation of capital drives the pace of development, but it is limited by the ability of the economy to produce a surplus of food.

JORGENSON MODEL

In the Jorgenson model[24] two sectors have been considered—modern (industrial) and backward (agricultural) sectors. Production in backward sector is determined by land and labour, and is subjected to diminishing returns. In modern sector, production is determined by labour and capital, and is subjected to the constant returns to scale. This model assumes a neutral technical progress. Population growth is determined by per capita food supply and the net rate of reproduction, i.e., birth rate minus the death rate.

Based on the above assumptions, Jorgenson forwarded his theory that surplus in agriculture, i.e., food production net of consumption, releases labour to be employed in industry and the growth rate of industrial employment is given by the growth of the surplus. After the initial investment, growth of accumulation is given by the growth of labour in the industrial sector and the terms of trade between the agricultural and the industrial sectors, though industrial real wages could be more than agricultural real wages to allow for labour migration. The gap is proportional to industrial wages and is stable in the long run. This gap also determines the terms of trade between the two sectors and the investment rate in the modern sector. Jorgenson has considered the closed economy. Now, let us consider a Cobb-Douglas type of production function:

$$Y = e^{\alpha t} L^{\beta} P^{1-\beta} \quad \text{... (8.12)}$$

where,

Y = agricultural production,

L = total land available,

P = total population, and

$e^{\alpha t}$ = change in output due to technical progress.

Since land is assumed to be fixed, equation (8.12) can be rewritten as

$$Y = e^{\alpha t} P^{1-\beta} \qquad \text{... (8.13)}$$

Now, per capita agricultural production is given by

$$y = \frac{Y}{P} = e^{\alpha t} P^{-\beta} \qquad \text{... (8.14)}$$

Differentiating equation (8.14) with respect to time and dividing by y, we get

$$\frac{dy}{dt} = \alpha e^{\alpha t} P^{-\beta} - \beta e^{\alpha t} P^{-\beta-1} \frac{dP}{dt}$$

$$= \alpha y - \beta \frac{y}{P} \cdot \frac{dP}{dt}$$

or, $$\dot{y} = \alpha y - \frac{\beta y \dot{P}}{P}$$

or, $$\frac{\dot{y}}{y} = \alpha - \beta \frac{\dot{P}}{P} \qquad \text{... (8.15)}$$

Now, suppose that $\dot{P}/P = \eta$, then we have

$$\frac{\dot{y}}{y} = \alpha - \beta\eta \qquad \text{... (8.16)}$$

or, $$\dot{y} = (\alpha - \beta\eta)y \qquad \text{... (8.17)}$$

Then, the general solution is given by

$$y(t) = e^{(\alpha - \beta\eta)t} \gamma(0) \qquad \text{... (8.18)}$$

Equation (8.18) specifies the situation where per capita income growth, $\alpha - \beta\eta > 0$, would be obtained for any positive level of output. In developing economy, the diminishing returns to labour in agriculture, β, is assumed to remain fixed.

Hence, public policy should be used to alter either the rate of technical progress, α, or the maximum growth rate of the population, η, or both. An increase in output per head would be assumed as long as $\alpha > \eta$. When $\alpha = \eta$, a low-level equilibrium is obtained.

The production function of the industrial sector is given by

$$Q = (C, L^i, t) \qquad \text{... (8.19)}$$

where,

Q = total industrial output,

C = capital,

L^i = industrial labour, and

t = time.

Since the technical progress is expected to be rapid in the industrial sector, we have

$$Q = A(t)C^{\gamma}L^{1-\gamma} \qquad \text{... (8.20)}$$

Now, let us consider that

$$\frac{\dot{A}}{A} = \lambda \text{, or } \dot{A} = A\lambda \qquad \text{... (8.21)}$$

By manipulation, we get

$$\dot{q} = e^{\lambda t}C^{\gamma} \qquad \text{... (8.22)}$$

where, q is output per head, Q/L.

Differentiating with respect to time and dividing through by q, we obtain

$$\frac{\dot{q}}{q} = \lambda + \gamma \cdot \frac{\dot{C}}{C} \qquad \text{... (8.23)}$$

Capital accumulation is required to promote and to escape stationary equilibrium in the developing economy, and to promote accumulation, it is imperative to extract positive agricultural surplus. The generation of surplus is vital for industrialisation and $\alpha - \beta\eta > 0$ is a necessary and sufficient condition for generating agricultural surplus. According to Jorgenson, the surplus in the agricultural sector should not only be extracted but it must persist to avoid any slipping back to the stationary state.

According to Lewis and Ranis-Fei models, the capital-output ratio falls at a given rate (λ/β). Considering that capitalists save all of their income, these models predict rising growth rates of output and employment as capital grows over time. However, the Jorgenson model predicts that growth rates of output and capital would be the same and employment in the modern sector would rise less rapidly than the rise in capital and output.

Criticisms of Jorgenson Model

On the following ground Jorgenson Model has been criticised:

(a) This model ignores the role of capital in the agricultural production function. However, empirical evidence does not always support this assumption. It has been seen that in some cases capital has played a significant role in raising agricultural output.

(b) Although the production relations between the modern and the backward sectors are considered to be different, no such difference in tastes is recognised. The spatial effects of structural change have also been ignored.

(c) It can be shown that once the assumptions regarding tastes and technology are altered the predictions of the model loses its generality.

(d) The neoclassical features of the model have their usual limitations.

(e) Although there may be some truth in the observations of Jorgenson that the marginal productivity of labour in agriculture is unlikely to be zero, particularly in the sowing and harvesting seasons, the point is not important for finding out the proper shadow price in a surplus labour economy.

NOTES

1. Lipton 1977.
2. Lewis 1954; Fei and Ranis 1964; Jorgenson 1961.
3. Fei and Ranis 1964; Lewis 1954.
4. Eicher and Witt 1964; Desai and Mazumdar 1970.
5. Wolgin 1978.
6. Ghandour and Muller 1977.
7. Meier 1995
8. Thirlwall 2003.
9. Lewis 1954, p. 147.
10. *Ibid.*, p. 150.
11. Lewis 1979.
12. Lewis 1954, p. 141.
13. *Ibid.*, p. 142.
14. *Ibid.*, pp. 156-60.
15. *Ibid.*, p. 158.
16. *Ibid.*, p. 190.
17. Ootsuka 2001.
18. Ishikawa 1975.
19. Hayami and Kikuchi 1982.
20. Osmani 1991.
21. G. Ranis and J. Fei (1961), A Theory of Economic Development, *American Economic Review*.
22. World Bank 1996.
23. *Ibid.*, pp. 67-68.
24. Dale Jorgenson, The Development of a Dual Economy, *Economic Journal*, June 1961.

9

Lewis and Myrdal on Economic Development

After going through this chapter, you will better understand:

- economic development with unlimited supplies of labour
- rural-urban migration and urban unemployment
- wage determination mechanisms in dual economy
- Ranis-Fei extension of Lewis theory
- Myrdal on economic development
- circular and cumulative causation
- backwash effects
- spread effects
- effects of trade, capital movements and migration

Arthur Lewis and Gunnar Myrdal are two most important pioneers of early development economics who have been awarded the Nobel Memorial Prize in Economic Science. Lewis formulated the *Theory of Economic Development with Unlimited Supplies of Labour* for which he received the Nobel Prize and with which he revolutionised contemporary thinking on development. On the other hand, Myrdal received the Nobel Prize for his pioneering work in the theory of money and economic fluctuations and penetrating analysis of the interdependence of economic, social and institutional phenomena.

In the early post-World War II era, Keynes's *General Theory* was supposed to help through the problems of countries with surplus labour because of its assumption of unlimited supply of labour at the current price and secular economic expansion. Keynes assumed that labour, capital, and land are unlimited in supply—both in the short-run sense that once the monetary trap is turned the real limit to expansion is not physical resources but the limited supply of labour, and in the long-run sense that secular expansion is embarrassed not by a shortage but by a superfluity of saving. From the point of view of countries with surplus labour, Keynesianism is only a partial explanation of development. On the other hand, Harrod-Domar model focuses on the steady state properties of the developed economy having little possibility for alternative technology choice. It gives less importance for the role of prices, relying heavily instead on savings-pushed growth competing with population growth. This model assumes full employment, market clearance, and perfect competition. According to Hirschman, Keynes deviated from the neoclassical mono-economics, full employment orthodoxy of the day, he focused on the temporary unemployment of both capital and labour in the advanced economy, not the secular unemployment of labour in the developing world.

At this juncture Lewis's theory of economic development with unlimited supplies of labour and Myrdal's theory of circular and cumulative causation came into great help in understanding the process of economic development in third world countries or developing economies. We shall discuss both the thories in this chapter.

ECONOMIC DEVELOPMENT WITH UNLIMITED SUPPLIES OF LABOUR

Arthur Lewis published his classic paper *Economic Development with Unlimited Supplies of Labour* in *The Manchester School* in May 1954. In this paper he has presented a model with an insight into the role of dualism in the process of economic transformation with the purpose of seeing what can be made of the classical framework in solving the problems of distribution, accumulation, and growth. Lewis based his model on the facts drawn from economic history rather than systematic quantitative evidence, which was not available for developing countries at that time. Through this paper, he has made two fundamental contributions to the subsequent emergence of development economics as an academic discipline:

(a) Develoment economics was presented as a policy science, concerned with the problems of economic underdevelopment and low standards of living for the vast majority of the world's population.

(b) The emphasis was given on development as a multidimensional process of economic, political, social and institutional change.

This model analyses the process of development through interactions between the traditional sector and the modern sector, i.e., agriculture-industry interaction. In agriculture sector, wage rate is considered to be institutionally determined at subsistence level along the tradition of classical economics, whereas that of modern sector is supposed to be established at the equation with marginal productivity of labour, along the tradition of neoclassical economics.

The starting points of Lewis model are dual economy and surplus labour. Dual economy implies existence of modern exchange sector and an indigenous subsistence sector. While surplus labour implies unlimited supplies of labour in the subsistence sector, i.e., the supply of labour exceeds the demand for labour at the subsistence wage implying the marginal product of workers in the subsistence sector is equal to, or less than, the subsistence or institutional wage so that a reduction in the number of workers would not lower the average product of labour and might even raise it. Movement of labour from subsistence to modern sectors is the centre stage of this model—subsistence sector supplies the labour and modern sector soaks up this supply.

Surplus labours are found in agriculture, petty trades and services, domestic services in the houses of wealthy people who keep retainers because their social position requires so, and in other areas. The labour whose marginal productivity is zero is not available to the industrial employers at a zero wage for the labourers as family members or retainers are provided a subsistence income on peasant farms or by their patrons. But it is available in unlimited quantities at a wage equal to the subsistence level of living plus a margin sufficient to overcome the friction of moving from the 'subsistence sector' to the 'capitalist sector', which may be called 'subsistence-plus' wage. As the supply of labour is unlimited, the new industries can be set-up and the existing ones can be expanded without limit at the ruling wage rate. The capitalistic sector also needs skilled workers. But Lewis maintains that skilled labour is only a temporary bottleneck and can be removed by providing training facilities to unskilled workers.

Since the marginal productivity of labour in the capitalist sector is higher than the ruling wage rate, there results a capitalist surplus. This surplus is used for capital formation which makes possible employment of more people from the subsistence sector. The increase in investment by the capitalists raises the marginal productivity of labour which induces capitalist-employers to increase their labour force till the marginal productivity of labour falls to equality with the ruling wage rate. This process goes on till the capital-labour ratio rises to the point where the supply of labour becomes inelastic.

Technical progress in the capitalist sector may also increase the share of profits in national income so long as there is surplus labour. It is much more likely to do so in a labour-surplus economy than in a full-employment economy because in the former, if the innovation increases the demand for labour, the labour can be obtained without bidding up the wage rates while under many conditions it may lead to a rise in wages in a full-employment economy.

Lewis was concerned with the process by which a community which was previously saving and investing 4 or 5 percent of its national income or less, converts itself into an economy where voluntary saving is about 12 to 15 percent of national income or more. To reach the answer, he dropped the assumption made by neoclassical macroeconomists that the supply of labour was fixed. Instead he assumed infinitely elastic labour supply and a capitalist sector develops by drawing labour from a subsistence sector. During an extended period wages in the capitalist sector remain constant because, due to existence of surplus labour in the subsistence sector the supply of labour to the capitalist sector exceeds demand at this wage rate. Profit of the capitalist is the surplus of output over wages. The ratio of profits to national income increases both because the profit ratio within a capitalist sector of a given size may increase through innovation and because the capitalist sector grows.

Let us consider the following Fig. 9.1.

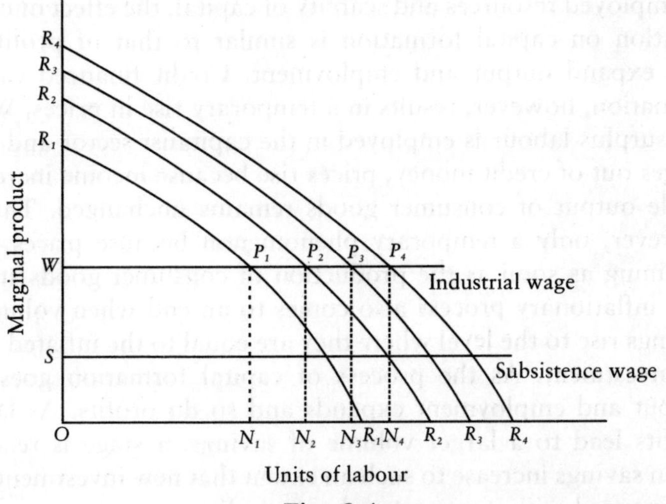

Fig. 9.1

In Fig. 9.1, the quantity of labour employed is measured along the X-axis and the marginal product along Y-axis. *S* is the subsistence wage and *W* is the capitalist wage. The curve *RR* represents the marginal product of labour in the capitalist sector. On the profit-maximising assumption, labour is employed in the capitalist sector up to the point where the marginal product of labour is equal to the wage rate, i.e., ON_1 will be employed. The marginal productivity of labour in the capitalist sector in the beginning is P_1N_1 for ON_1 labour. WP_1R_1 is the capitalist surplus at this stage. When this surplus is reinvested, the curve of marginal productivity shifts upwards to R_2R_2. The capitalist surplus and employment are now larger than before, being WP_2R_2 and ON_2 respectively. Further reinvestments raise the marginal productivity curve and the level of employment to R_3R_3 and ON_3 and so on, till no surplus labour is left. Thus, the essence of the development process is that the stimulus to investment in the capitalist sector comes from the rate of profit, which must rise over time because all the benefits of increased productivity accrue to capital if the real wage is constant.

Capital is created not only out of profits but also out of bank credit. In an underdeveloped country characterised by abundant unemployed resources and scarcity of capital, the effect of credit creation on capital formation is similar to that of profits. It will expand output and employment. Credit financed capital formation, however, results in a temporary rise in prices. When the surplus labour is employed in the capitalist sector and paid wages out of credit money, prices rise because income increases while output of consumer goods remains unchanged. This is, however, only a temporary phenomenon because prices start declining as soon as the production of consumer goods starts. The inflationary process also comes to an end when voluntary savings rise to the level where they are equal to the inflated level of investment. As the process of capital formation goes on, output and employment expands and so do profits. As larger profits lead to a larger volume of savings, a stage is reached when savings increase to such an extent that new investment can be financed without resort to bank credit.

The process of growth cannot continue indefinitely and must come to an end. According to Lewis, this can happen in the following ways:

(a) if the continuous process of capital formation leaves no surplus labour;

(b) if the expansion in the capitalist sector is so fast that it leads to an absolute decline in population in the subsistence sector which results in an increase in the average productivity of labour in the latter sector and thereby to a rise in the wage rate in the capitalist sector;

(c) if the expansion of the capitalist sector relatively to the subsistence sector turns the terms of trade against the former as a result of the rise in the prices of raw materials and food, the capitalists will have to pay higher wages to the workers;

(d) if the subsistence sector adopts improved techniques of production, real wages would rise in the capitalist sector which would lead to a reduction in the capitalist sector; and

(e) if the workers in the capitalist sector imitate the capitalist way of living and agitate for higher wages and if they succeed in getting a rise in wages, the capitalist surplus and the rate of capital formation will decline.

When the process of growth is adversely affected by any of the factors mentioned above, the process of capital formation can still be kept going by stimulating immigration or by encouraging export of capital to countries which possess abundant supplies of labour at the subsistence wage rate. Since immigration on a mass scale adversely affects the local labour, it is strongly opposed by the trade unions, and, therefore, is not a very practicable measure. The other best alternative is to export capital over which trade unions have hardly any control.

Rural-Urban Migration and Urban Unemployment

Due to high rural-urban wage differential in recent years, there has been rural-urban migration on an unprecedented scale. But, the expansion of the industrial sector has not generated sufficient employment for all the available workforce. Thus, the unemployment has been transferred from rural to urban sector. So long as the wage in urban sector is higher than the rural sector, the process of migration will continue.

Let S be the supply of labour to the urban sector which is a function of the expected urban-rural wage differential (d), and the expected urban-rural wage differential is equal to the actual urban wage times the probability of obtaining a job in the urban sector minus the average rural wage. Thus, we have

$$S = f(d) \qquad \text{... (9.1)}$$

and $d = wp - r$ ... (9.2)

where,

S = supply of labour,

d = rural-urban wage differential,

w = urban real wage,

p = probability of obtaining a job in the urban sector, and

r = average rural wage.

The probability of obtaining a job in the urban sector is given by

$$p = \frac{\lambda N}{W - N} = \frac{\lambda N}{U} \quad \text{... (9.3)}$$

where,

λ = net rate of new urban job creation,

N = level of urban employment,

W = total urban labour force, and

U = urban unemployment.

Substituting (9.3) into (9.2), we get

$$d = \frac{w \lambda N}{U} - r \quad \text{... (9.4)}$$

When expected urban wage equals the rural wage, i.e., $d = 0$, migration stops. Then equilibrium level of urban unemployment is given by

$$\frac{w \lambda N}{U} - r = 0$$

or, $$U^e = \frac{w \lambda N}{r} \quad \text{... (9.5)}$$

From the equation (9.5) we find that a reduction in the actual urban wage or a rise in the rural wage will reduce the equilibrium level of unemployment. An increase in the rate of new job creation will raise the equilibrium level of unemployment by increasing the probability of obtaining a job and encouraging migration.

Dividing both sides of equation (9.5) by N we get the equilibrium ratio of unemployment to employment as

$$\frac{U^e}{N}=\frac{w\lambda}{r} \quad \text{... (9.6)}$$

Now, let us consider the situation under what conditions the actual level of urban unemployment will rise. Suppose the rate of urban job creation is a function of the urban wage, w, and a policy parameter, α. Thus, we have

$$\lambda = f(w, \alpha); \qquad \frac{\partial\lambda}{\partial\alpha} > 0 \quad \text{... (9.7)}$$

In the case of increase in urban labour demand, the response of labour supply is given by

$$\frac{\partial S}{\partial\alpha}=\frac{\partial S}{\partial d}\cdot\frac{\partial d}{\partial\lambda}\cdot\frac{\partial\lambda}{\partial\alpha} \quad \text{... (9.8)}$$

Taking partial differentiation of equation (9.4) with respect to net rate of new urban job creation λ, we have

$$\frac{\partial d}{\partial\lambda}=\frac{wN}{U} \quad \text{... (9.9)}$$

Now from equations (9.8) and (9.9), we get

$$\frac{\partial S}{\partial\alpha}=\frac{\partial S}{\partial d}\cdot\frac{wN}{U}\cdot\frac{\partial\lambda}{\partial\alpha} \quad \text{... (9.10)}$$

Equation (9.10) reveals if an increase in supply in response to a policy change exceeds the increase in the absolute number of new jobs created then there will be an absolute level of urban unemployment. This condition can be written as

$$\frac{\partial S}{\partial d}\cdot\frac{wN}{U}\cdot\frac{\partial\lambda}{\partial\alpha} > N\cdot\frac{\partial\lambda}{\partial\alpha} \quad \text{... (9.11)}$$

or, $$\frac{\partial S}{\partial d}\cdot\frac{wN}{U} > N$$

or, $$\frac{\partial S}{\partial d}\cdot\frac{wN}{U}\cdot\frac{d}{w}\cdot\frac{U}{W} > N\cdot\frac{d}{w}\cdot\frac{U}{W}$$

or, $$\frac{\partial S}{\partial d}\cdot\frac{d}{W} > \frac{d}{w}\cdot\frac{U}{W}$$

or, $$\frac{\partial S/W}{\partial d/d} > \frac{d}{w}\cdot\frac{U}{W} \qquad \text{... (9.12)}$$

Substituting the value of d from equation (9.2) into equation (9.12), we have

$$\frac{\partial S/W}{\partial d/d} > \frac{wp-r}{w}\cdot\frac{U}{W} \qquad \text{... (9.13)}$$

Equation (9.13) is the condition for unemployment to increase in the urban sector. This condition implies that in the urban sector unemployment will increase as a result of a policy change to increase employment if the elasticity of the urban labour supply through migration with respect to the rural-urban wage differential exceeds the expected rural-urban wage differential as a proportion of the urban wage times the unemployment rate.

Here one point should be considered that the growth of total labour supply as a result of migration ($\partial S/W$) should not be considered the same thing as the rate of growth of migration ($\partial S/S$). Similarly, the elasticity of supply with respect to a change in job opportunities is not the same thing as the elasticity of migration with respect to a change in job opportunities. This can be shown by multiplying both sides of equation (9.11) by $\left[\frac{d}{w}\cdot\frac{U}{S}\right]$ instead of $\left[\frac{d}{w}\cdot\frac{U}{W}\right]$. Thus, we have

$$\frac{\partial S}{\partial d}\cdot\frac{wN}{U}\cdot\frac{\partial \lambda}{\partial \alpha}\cdot\frac{d}{w}\cdot\frac{U}{S} > N\cdot\frac{\partial \lambda}{\partial \alpha}\cdot\frac{d}{w}\cdot\frac{U}{S}$$

or, $$\frac{\partial S/S}{\partial d/d} > \frac{d}{w}\cdot\frac{U}{S}$$

or $$\frac{\partial S/S}{\partial d/d} > \frac{wp-r}{w}\cdot\frac{U}{S} \qquad \text{... (9.14)}$$

Since, $(U/S) > (U/W)$, for unemployment to increase following a job expansion program the elasticity of migration itself would have to be higher than the elasticity of labour supply.

Wage Determination Mechanisms

There are two types of surplus labour—first, the labours with positive but negligible marginal productivity, and second labours with zero or even negative marginal productivity. Both types of labours have different implications in the wage determination. If r is the real wage of labour then:

(a) Absolute surplus labour (ASL) or type I surplus labour exists when marginal productivity of labour is equal to or less than zero, i.e., $MPL \leq 0 < r_s \leq r$; r_s is the subsistence wage rate.

(b) Relative surplus labour (RSL) or type II surplus labour exists when marginal productivity of labour is greater than zero but lower than the actual wage received, i.e., $0 < MPL < r$.

Existence of type II surplus labour implies that, as long as $0 < MPL < r$ holds, it does not matter if MPL is lower or higher than the subsistence level (whether $MPL < r_s$ or $MPL > r_s$), though normally it is assumed to be lower than the subsistence level ($MPL < r_s$).

Wage determination in the rural sector: In the long run, wage in the rural sector is set to a constant low wage at the subsistence level as a result of the population adjustment dynamics. When economic development takes place, labours are drawn out of the rural sector into the urban sector. Since, wage in the rural sector is set in relation to the average productivity of that sector, in the absence of population growth, those who remain in the rural sector have higher average productivity and receive a higher income than before. Thus, the wage in the rural sector increases when type I and/or type II surplus labour moves out to the urban sector, although type I surplus labours in the rural sector make no marginal contribution.

Wage determination in the urban sector: There are two mutually contradictory mechanisms of wage determination in the urban sector. First, wage in the urban sector is set above the competitive wage level and is independent of the wage level in the rural subsistence sector. Second, the real wage in the urban sector is determined by the real wage in the rural sector and anything which raises the productivity of the rural sector will raise real wages in the urban sector.

According to second mechanism, the urban sector wage is determined by the wage in the rural sector. Following Todaro and Harris, let u be the urban unemployment rate and p be the probability of finding an urban job. The labour market equilibrium condition is

$$pw = r \qquad \dots (9.15)$$

where,

p = probability of obtaining a job in the urban sector,

w = wage in the urban sector, and

r = wage in the rural sector.

From equation (9.15) we see that an increase in rural wage will increase the urban wage too, provided urban unemployment rate remains constant. In this case, there is no real rural-urban wage difference. And if such is the situation there would not be an unlimited supply of labour to the urban sector at a constant wage rate. In absence of population growth, if surplus labour moves out of the rural sector, wages in that sector will increase and if wages in that sector increases, following equation (9.15), wages in the urban sector will also increase. Thus, according to second mechanism of wage determination in the urban sector, at a constant wage rate for a period of time, there is no unlimited supply of labour even in the circumstance that the rural sector has a stock of type I and type II surplus labour, given the population in the economy is constant. However, at a constant wage rate for a period of time, there can be an unlimited supply of labour if emigration to the urban sector happens slowly, which allows a dynamic population adjustment to take place. In the long run, when the average marginal productivity of labour in the rural sector is higher than the subsistence level, population in that sector will grow. The amount of new working population that adds to the rural sector would be equal to the number of people who moved out of this sector.

Now consider the first mechanism of wage determination in the urban sector. Equilibrium wage in the urban sector can be given by

$$w_e = \frac{wp - c_m}{(1+\kappa)}; \quad c_m \geq 0, \kappa \geq 0 \qquad \dots (9.16)$$

where,

w_e = equilibrium wage rate in the urban sector,

c_m = cost of migration, and

κ = proportionality of higher living costs in urban sector.

According to this mechanism, urban sector wage is institutionally set at a higher level than the rural sector. In the words of Lewis, "Earnings in the subsistence sector set a floor to wages in the capitalist sector, but in practice wages have to be higher than this",[1] and "different wages are paid to comparable workers".[2] Even after all cost adjustments, there are some real wage differences between the two sectors, i.e., $w_e > r$. An increase in the rural wage rate (r) will reduce the gap between the two sectors but not necessarily affect the urban wage rate (w_e) because the wage rate in the urban sector is not set as a fixed rate above the rural wage rate. Therefore, the urban sector faces an unlimited supply of labour, until the turning point is reached at $w_e = r$.

Ranis-Fei Extension of Lewis Theory

Lewis was not aware of the Ricardo-Schultz food problem that could stop the dual economic growth process before reaching the turning-point. Extended Lewis Model of Ranis-Fei indicates this problem.[3] Let us consider the Lewis-Ranis-Fei type of dual economy model.

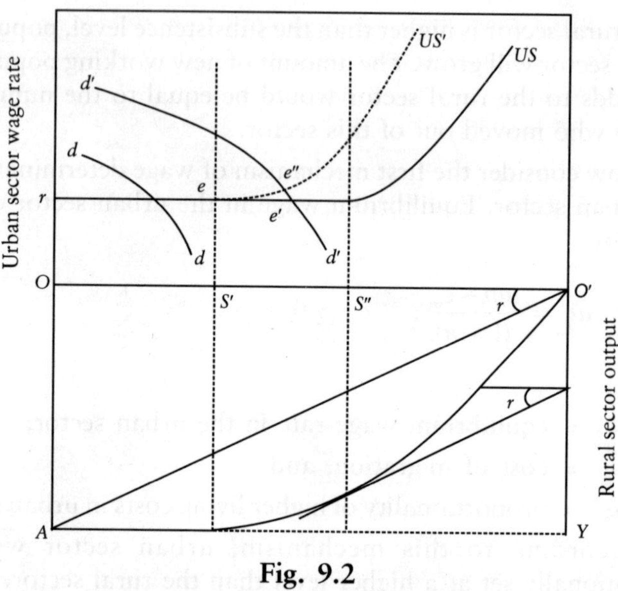

Fig. 9.2

Let *S* is the total labour force available for both rural and urban sectors. In Fig. 9.2 horizontal axis *OO′* represents *S* where urban sector labour force is measured from *O* to the right and that of rural sector from *O′* to the left. The upper half of the figure represents the market demand and supply relationships for urban sector labour force and lower half represents a production response to labour input in the rural sector in an inverted shape. Consider a point *S′* on the horizontal axis which implies distribution of labour force between *OS′* to urban sector and *O′S′* to rural sector. The curve *O′A* describes that rural output increases at a decreasing rate corresponding to increase in labour input from *O′* until point *S′*, beyond which labour's marginal product becomes zero. At point *O* all labours are utilised in the rural sector and marginal productivity of labours are zero. The tangent to the curve *O′*A determines the average productivity (*r*) of the labour in the rural sector which is the institutionally determined subsistence wage rate.

In the Fig. 9.2, *dd* is the demand curve for labour in the urban sector. Due to capital accumulation in the urban sector demands for labour shifts to *d′d′*. The wage rate in the urban sector remains constant upto the point S'' because the marginal product in the rural sector continues to be lower than the institutional wage rate of urban sector. The point S'' is known as the Lewis turning-point.

After urban employment crosses the point S', marginal product of labour in the rural sector becomes positive. In this case, migration of labour from rural to urban sector results in an absolute decline in total food production which in turn raises the food prices relative to urban product prices. Point S' is also known as shortage point. Beyond this point, the wage rate in the urban sector needs to be increased so that urban sector labours can afford same food basket for their subsistence as they used to get earlier.

From point S' onwards labour supply curve in the urban sector becomes upward-sloping. Rise in food prices in urban sector is high because of reduction in the food production in the rural sector, characterised by low demand elasticities. This will make the supply curve of labour in the urban sector sharp which will result in sharp decline in profit of the urban sector and the capital accumulation stops before reaching point S''.

In the surplus labour phase, the average surplus of rural sector does not change, therefore minimum urban sector wage required for compensation does not change. This creates a perfectly elastic supply of labour represented by horizontal line originating from point r in upper panel of Fig. 5.2. In this zone it is possible to have economic development with unlimited supplies of labour and an expansion in the urban sector does not drive up the wage rate.

At the point S'' the disguised unemployment phase come to an end and the marginal product of labour begins to exceed the traditionally given wage rate. Now it becomes profitable to hire labour, because the additional contribution of labour in the rural sector exceeds the cost of hiring. It will result in an increase in wage in rural sector. This phenomenon may be considered as the commercialisation of agriculture associated with a sharp decrease in the average surplus of rural production resulting in second turning point in the urban sector wage rate. Now, in the urban sector not only must the wage compensate for a declining rural surplus and a movement of the terms of trade against urban sector, it must compensate labours for a higher income foregone in the rural sector, and this creates a sharper upward movement in the urban sector wage rate.

Rural-urban migration increases with higher capital accumulation in the urban sector which is the engine of growth. As development proceeds, the terms of trade gradually turn against urban sector because food prices rise as a smaller number of farmers must support a greater number of non-agricultural labours. As a result of this urban sector wage rate rises. Thus, the development process is limited by the ability of the economy to produce a surplus food.

When developing economies try to achieve economic modernization by forcing resource reallocation from rural to urban sector without making any effort to increase in rural productivity, they fall in a trap represented by shortage point *S'* (also known as Ricardian trap). Jorgenson has analysed this problem in his two-sector model, which is similar to the Lewis-Ranis-Fei model only with difference that no surplus labour exists in the rural sector and the neoclassical marginal principle is used to determine the wage in the rural sector. To come out of this trap urban sector must be supported by technological progress in rural sector to prevent the sharp increase in food prices.

In short, Lewis-Ranis-Fei theory implies that development takes place via the joint transfer of labour and food surplus from the traditional rural sector to the modern urban sector.

Critical Appraisal

The model assumes existence of surplus labour not in a seasonal sense but over the entire production cycle. But actually surplus labour, by and large, is a seasonal phenomenon; during busy seasons in some countries there is even a shortage of labour in the agricultural sector. Transfer of workers from agricultural sector to the industrial sector may, therefore, be accompanied by a decline in the agricultural production.

Lewis considers shortage of skilled labour only a temporary bottleneck which can be removed by providing training facilities to unskilled labour. Skill formation is not so simple a problem as assumed by Lewis. It poses difficult problems and takes a fairly long time.

Lewis assumes the existence of a capitalist class in the underdeveloped countries. In fact, the underdeveloped countries are characterised by a conspicuous absence of this class.

Lewis does not pay attention to the problem of an adequate volume of aggregate demand. He assumes that the entire production of the capitalist sector is either consumed by itself or exported. In actual practice, the process of growth may come to a halt if there appears a shortage of demand for the products of the capitalist sectors.

Lewis assumes an unlimited supply of labour in underdeveloped countries but this assumption does not hold true in case of many countries of South America and Africa which are sparsely populated.

The model assumes that capital accumulation takes place when the capitalist class continues to invest profits. It, therefore, presupposes operation of the 'investment multiplier' which is not applicable to underdeveloped countries. If profits decline or the prices of wage goods rise the whole process of capital accumulation will halt before all the surplus is absorbed.

Higher capitalist wage may not lead to the movement of surplus labour from the subsistence sector to the capitalist sector. People are so intensely attached to their family and land that they do not like to leave their kith and kin. Further, differences in language and customs, the problems of congestion, housing and high cost of living in the capitalist sector hinder the mobility of labour to this sector. This is a great weakness of the model.

Schultz does not agree that the marginal productivity of labour in overpopulated underdeveloped countries is zero or negligible. If it were so, the subsistence wage would also be zero. The fact is that every worker receives the subsistence wage, may be in kind, if not in cash. It is, therefore, difficult to find out the exact number of surplus labourers who are to move to the capitalist sector.

The Lewis model assumes that when surplus labour is transferred from the subsistence sector to the capitalist sector, the agricultural production remains unaffected in the subsistence sector. But the fact is that withdrawal of workers from the farms will reduce output. Prof. Schultz points out that there is no evidence for any poor country anywhere that would suggest that a transfer of even some fraction, say, 5 percent of the existing labour force out of agriculture, other things remaining unchanged, could be made without reducing its production.

It is wrong to say that only 10 percent of the people save. In fact, as Lewis himself admits in the case of Japan, people with low income also save in underdeveloped countries.

Lewis' view that inflation for the purpose of capital formation is self-destructive is difficult to believe in the face of acute shortage of consumer goods. Production of consumer goods does not increase rapidly owing to structural regidities. On the other hand, the marginal propensity to consume of the people is very high so that all increases in income lead to inflationary rise in prices.

Lewis' view that taxation will mop up increasing income cannot be accepted because the tax administration in underdeveloped countries is not so efficient and developed as to collect taxes sufficient enough for capital accumulation.

In spite of the limitations mentioned above, the Lewis model has the outstanding merit of explaining in a clear manner the process of development. The two sector model has great analytical value. It explains how capital formation takes place in underdeveloped countries which have plethora of labour and scarcity of capital. His study of the problems of credit inflation, population growth, technological progress and international trade gives the model a touch of realism.

MYRDAL ON ECONOMIC DEVELOPMENT

Gunnar Myrdal (1898-1987), a Swedish-educated economist, established his reputation as a development specialist with his massive *Asian Drama* (1968), which began in 1957 with his *Economic Theory and Underdeveloped Regions*. His model of the process of *circular and cumulative causation* can be used to understand the perpetuation of the development gap and divergences between North and South or between the 'centre' and the 'periphery' countries. There are three main propositions of the Myrdal's development theories.[4]

(a) Inequalities will tend to increase both within a country and internationally in the absence of counteracting policies.
(b) A biased international trade theory against the poor regions, particularly in the contention that trade in commodities will tend to equalise factor prices, especially wages.
(c) Greater income equality, rather than inequality, is the correct basis on which to achieve enhanced economic growth.

A few countries are highly developed economically and have very high levels of average real income per head. In contrast more than two-thirds of the people in the non-Soviet world live in countries where real income per head is only a small fraction of what it is in highly developed countries and, in fact, in most cases is much smaller than it was in those countries before they started to develop rapidly a century or more ago. Not only that, the disparities between the developed and underdeveloped countries are increasing with the passage of time. It is on the whole the industrialised countries which are industrialising further. They account for a major portion of the non-Soviet world's total savings. Since new inventions constantly raise the demand for capital, almost the entire capital is invested there. In contrast, in underdeveloped countries, where incomes are much lower, capital formation and investment tend to be on a smaller scale, even relatively to their lower incomes. The relatively faster increase in population in these countries worsens the matters still further. The people in underdeveloped countries are becoming increasingly aware of these huge international inequalities and the danger that they will continue to grow. The people in underdeveloped countries have a tendency to blame for their poverty the rest of the world, particularly the better off countries; rather they hold the world economic system responsible for the increasing inequalities between the developed and the underdeveloped countries. We are going to examine the significance of each of the above mentioned three propositions.

Circular and Cumulative Causation

Prof. Myrdal believes that the theoretical approach which we have inherited is inadequate to grip with the problem of inequalities.[5] The theory is based on unrealistic assumptions, an important of which is the assumption of stable equilibrium. The concept of stable equilibrium implies that every disturbance provokes a reaction within the system, directed towards restoring a new state of equilibrium, and the action and reaction will meet in one and the same time-space. An economic system which is not in rest is for this reason always moving towards equilibrium, though not necessarily in the straight way. The concept of stable equilibrium embodies the idea that when a change calls forth other changes as reaction, these secondary changes are counter-directed to the primary change.

In Myrdal's opinion, in contrast, in the normal case there is no such tendency towards automatic self-stabilisation in the social system. The system is by itself not moving towards any sort of balance between forces, but is constantly on the move away from such a situation. In the normal case a change does not call forth countervailing changes but, instead supporting changes, which move the system in the same direction as the first change but much further. As a result of such circular causation a social process tends to become cumulative and often to gather speed at an accelerating rate.

A social process can, of course, be stopped. One possibility is that new exogenous changes may occur which have the direction and strength necessary to bring the system to rest. The position of balancing forces which thus become established is, however, not a natural outcome of the play of the forces within the system. Moreover, the position is unstable. Any new exogenous change will by the reactions in the system again start a cumulative process away from this position in the direction of the new change. Alternatively the position of the rest may have been attained by policy interferences, planned and applied with the intention of stopping the movement. This is, of course, the very opposite of a natural tendency towards equilibrium, endogenous to the system.

Myrdal illustrates the principle of circular and cumulative causation with the help of the Negro problem in the United States. In order to simplify the explanation, he reduces his model to two factors: 'white prejudices' causing discrimination against the Negroes in various respects, and the 'low plane of living' of the Negroes. The two factors are mutually inter-related. The Negroes' low standard of living is kept down by discrimination from the whites while, on the other hand, Negroes' poverty, ignorance, superstition, slum dwellings, health deficiencies, dirty appearance, bad odour, disorderly conduct, unstable family relations and criminality stimulate and feed the antipathy of the whites for Negroes.

White prejudices and low Negro standards thus mutually 'cause' each other. If at a point of time things tend to remain about as they are, this means that the two forces balance each other: white prejudices and the consequent discrimination against the Negroes block their efforts to raise their low plane of living; this, on the other hand, forms part of the causation of the prejudice on the side of the whites which leads them to discriminatory behaviour.

Such a static 'accommodation' is, however, entirely fortuitous and by no means a stable equilibrium position. If either of the two factors should change, this is bound to bring a change in the other factor, too, and start a cumulative process of mutual interaction in which the change in one factor would continuously be supported by the reaction of the other factor and so on in a circular way. The entire system would move in the direction of the primary change, but much further. Even if the original push or pull were to cease after a time, both factors would be permanently changed, or the process of interacting changes would even continue without any neutralisation in sight.

Backwash Effects

The free play of market forces normally tends to increase, rather than decrease, the inequalities between regions.[6] If the things were left to market forces unhindered by any policy interferences, industrial production, commerce, banking, insurance, shipping and, in fact, almost all those economic activities which in a developing economy tend to give a bigger than average return—and, in addition, science, art, literature, education and higher culture generally—would cluster in certain localities and regions, leaving the remaining country more or less in a backwater. It is easy to see how expansion in one locality has 'backwash' effects in other localities. To be more concrete the movements of labour, capital, goods and services by themselves do not counteract the natural tendency to regional inequality; they rather accentuate the inequalities.

The regions where economic activity is expanding will attract net immigration from other parts of the country. Since migration is always selective, at least in regard to migrant's age, this movement by itself tends to favour the rapidly growing communities and adversely affects the others.

Capital movements tend to have a similar effect of accentuating inequalities. In regions where expansion takes place, increased demand stimulates investment which in turn increases incomes and demand and causes a second round of investment, and so on. Saving increases as a result of higher incomes but tends to lag behind investment in the sense that the supply of capital steadily meets a brisk demand for it. In the other regions, the lack of new expansionary momentum has the implication that the demand for capital for investment remains relatively weak, even compared to the supply of savings which will be low as incomes are low and tending to fall. Studies in many countries show how the banking system, if not regulated to act differently, tends to become an instrument for siphoning off the savings from the poorer regions to the richer and more progressive ones: where returns on capital are high and secure.

In a similar manner, trade operates with a bias in favour of the richer and progressive regions and against the poor and backward regions. The freeing and widening of the markets often confers such competitive advantages on the industries in already established centres of expansion, which usually work under conditions of increasing returns, that even the handicrafts and industries existing earlier in the other regions are thwarted. In the latter regions, not only manufacturing industry and other non-agricultural pursuits but agriculture itself shows a much lower level of productivity than in the richer region. Let us illustrate the backwash effect with an example.

Suppose there are two regions, Kolkata (K) and Mumbai (M), and assume that wages are determined by supply and demand of labour as shown in Fig. 9.3.

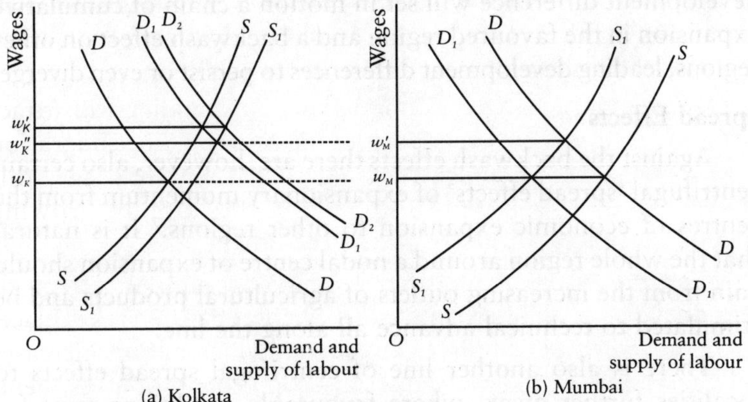

Fig. 9.3

Suppose in initial stage wage in both the regions are identical, i.e., $w_K = w_M$. Due to stimulus of some sort, the demand for labour, and therefore wage in region K relative to region M rises. This will shift the demand curve for labour in region K to D_1D_1, causing a rise in wage to w'_K. Now, the labours from region M will find better economic opportunities in region K, they will migrate to region K. According to equilibrium theory, there will be a tendency for wage levels to be equalised through a reduction in the labour supply in region M from SS to S_1S_1. The wage in region K will fall to w''_K equal to the wage in region M of w'_M, i.e., $w''_K = w'_M$.

However, movements of labours from region M to K will denudes the region M with human capital and entrepreneurs, and depresses the demand for goods and services and factors of production. On the other hand, movements of labours into region *K*, will stimulate enterprise and the demand for products, adding to the demand for factors of production. This implies that migration into region *K* will shift the demand curve for labour further to the right to D_2D_2, and migration from *M* will shift the demand curve for labour to the left to D_1D_1. These shifts in demand curve for labour will maintain the initial wage discrepancy at least to persist, if not widen. In short, an initial development difference will set in motion a chain of cumulative expansion in the favoured region and a backwash effect on other regions, leading development differences to persist or even diverge.

Spread Effects

Against the backwash effects there are, however, also certain centrifugal 'spread effects' of expansionary momentum from the centres of economic expansion to other regions.[7] It is natural that the whole region around a nodal centre of expansion should gain from the increasing outlets of agricultural products and be stimulated to technical advance all along the line.

There is also another line of centrifugal spread effects to localities further away, where favourable conditions exist for producing raw materials for the growing industries in the centres. If a sufficient number of workers get employment in these other localities, even the setting up of consumer industries will be stimulated. These, and also all other localities where new starts are being made and happen to succeed, become in their turn, if the expansionary momentum is strong enough to overcome the backwash effects from the older centres, new centres of self-sustained economic expansion.

The spread effects of momentum from a centre of industrial expansion to other localities and regions, operating through increased demands for their products and in many other ways, weave themselves into the cumulating social process by circular causation in the same fashion as the backwash effects in opposition to which they set up countervailing changes. They represent a complication of the main hypothesis that in the normal case the changes in other factors which are called forth as reactions by a change in one factor, always tend to move the system in the same directions as the first change.

Under no circumstances, however, do the spread effects establish the assumptions for an equilibrium analysis. In the marginal case the two kinds of effects will balance each other and a region will be stagnating. This balance, however, is not a stable equilibrium because any change in the forces will start a cumulative movement upwards or downwards.

Empirical evidence shows that while regional inequalities have been diminishing in the richer countries of the Western Europe, the opposite has been the tendency in the poorer countries. This phenomenon is explained by and large by the fact that the higher the level of economic development that a country has already reached, the stronger the spread effects will normally be. For a higher average level of development is accompanied by improved transportation and communications, higher levels of education, and a more dynamic communication of ideas and values, all of which tend to strengthen the forces for the centrifugal spread of economic expansion or to remove the obstacles for its operation.

The neutralisation of backwash effects, when a country reaches a high level of development where the spread effects are strong, will itself stimulate economic development and thus become an important factor in the cumulative process. The disappearance of poverty on a large scale is accompanied by a fuller utilisation of the potentialities of the human resources in a country. This is one of the reasons why rapid sustained progress becomes an almost automatic process when once a country has reached a high level of development. On the other hand, an important reason for the low rates of economic development in underdeveloped countries is the weak spread effects.

Effects of Trade, Capital Movements, and Migration

Trade by itself does not promote equality. On the contrary, it may have strong backwash effects on the underdeveloped countries. A widening of markets often strengthens the rich and progressive countries whose manufacturing industries have the lead and whose competitive position is strengthened by the external economies available to them, while whatever little industry, particularly small-scale industry and handicrafts, exists in underdeveloped countries is constantly threatened of being priced out by cheap imports from the industrial countries if it is not afforded protection. Examples can easily be cited of underdeveloped countries whose entire culture has been impoverished as a result of the establishment of trading contacts with the outside world. The main positive effect of international trade on the underdeveloped countries has in fact been to promote the production of primary products, which has come to form the bulk of their exports. The world demand for these products, however, is inelastic and, therefore, does not grow sufficiently fast.

Nor can the capital movements be relied upon to counteract international inequalities. As already seen, capital will tend to shun underdeveloped countries, particularly because the advanced countries themselves are rapidly developing further and can offer to owners of capital both good profits and security. Labour migration is not an important factor for international economic adjustment as between underdeveloped and developed countries.

At the international level, the backwash effects of trade and capital movements dominate the scene because the countervailing spread effects of expansionary momentum are very much weaker. Differences in legislation, administration and more generally, in language, in basic valuations and beliefs, in levels of living, production capacities and facilities, make national boundaries much more effective barriers to the spread of expansionary momentum than any demarcation lines within one country can be. Under these circumstances market forces will tend cumulatively to accentuate international inequalities.

NOTES

1. Lewis 1954: 150.
2. Lewis 1954: 148-49.
3. Ranis and Fei 1961.
4. Myrdal 1984: 152.
5. Gunnar Myrdal, *Economic Theory and Underdeveloped Region* (Bombay, 1966), pp. 23-34.
6. *Ibid.*, pp. 38-43.
7. *Ibid.*, pp. 43-45.

10

Population Growth and Development

After going through this chapter, you will better understand:

- natural and actual rate of population growth
- theory of demographic transition
- trends in population growth
- adjustment of birth and death rate
- Malthusian view on population growth
- cost-benefit analysis of having children
- growth impact—negative and positive
- population and environment
- surplus labour models—Nurkse and Sen models
- human resource as human capital
- role of human capital in development
- productivity of investment in human capital
- problems of human capital formation
- technological progress

The economic well-being of a country depends more than anything else on the quality of its inhabitants. Adam Smith wrote, in the opening words of *The Wealth of Nations,* "The annual labour of every nation is the fund which originally supplies it with all the necessaries and conveniences of life...." The past and present human effort and ability are the ultimate source of all economic goods and services.

As recently as ten or fifteen years ago, it was a matter of lively discussion and controversy as to whether or not the underdeveloped countries of South Asia were overpopulated and in what sense. But, now, it is generally accepted that these countries have entered a critical phase of sharply accelerated population growth, and that the prospects for successful economic development are crucially related to population trends.

The rapidly rising population is a phenomenon common to all underdeveloped countries. But as regards the anticipated increase in the size of the labour force in relation to natural resources, particularly, land resources, the emerging population crises are more specifically an Asian phenomenon so far as poor countries are concerned.[1] Outside the South Asia, only China, North Africa (including Egypt), and the Caribbean part of Latin America are confronted with a similar situation. Most parts of the continental Latin America are sparsely populated and possess substantial untapped natural resources which can be exploited at manageable costs by modern technology. In West Asia, the same is the case with Turkey, Syria, Iraq and probably, Iran. In most parts of Africa, a large labour force would not only be compatible with economic development but may be a pre-condition for it.

Population has a number of dimensions influencing economic development of which the following important may be mentioned:

(a) Quality of population referring to factors like level of education, quality of health, etc.

(b) Size of population, i.e., the number of persons occupying the country or any other specified territory.

(c) Rate of growth of population, i.e., the percentage by which the population is increasing or decreasing each year.

(d) Composition of population, i.e., the proportion of population which is male or female, the proportion of population falling into different age groups, etc.

(e) Distribution of population, i.e., the proportion of working force attached to different occupations of the economy, the proportion of population living in different regions—say rural and urban, etc.

(f) Growth differentials, i.e., differences in the rate of growth of different elements of population.

We shall briefly discuss below the first four dimensions which are more important.

Quality of population: It refers not only to racial or biological differences, which scientists have shown to be of minor importance, but also much more important differences arising from historical and cultural factors, from environments, quality of health, nutrition, and education, and from the quality of leadership provided by government and social elite. Quality of working population, including the rank-and-file of industrial and agricultural labour, the skilled engineers and technicians and the managerial and entrepreneurial elite, is an important factor determining the rate of development. For raising productivity of labour, it is very essential that masses are literate, healthy, and well fed, well clothed and well sheltered to be strong and energetic. In case labour force is inefficient, it will not be possible to take full advantage of rich natural resources, huge amounts of capital and superior technology.

Size of population: Given the total product, the larger the size of the population, the lower will be the per capita income. Thus given the total product, the smaller the size of the population, the better it is. Large population, however, helps production in a number of ways. It provides a large market and thereby offers incentive for investment. Large population and large market provide greater scope for the division of labour which brings in a number of economies. Large population makes possible the exploitation of indivisible resources which cannot be exploited by a small population.

'Working force' refers to that part of the population which is available for employment for productive purposes. The higher the proportion which the working population forms of the total population, the larger the possibilities for development. Size of the working population depends upon a number of factors, *viz.*, sex composition of the population, number of married women, distribution of population between different age groups, wants and tastes, degree of industrialisation or urbanisation, productivity, etc.

Change in age structure: The high fertility rates experienced in the South Asian countries have caused the age distribution of population to be skewed in the direction of high dependency burden. The populations of these countries contain a large number of children. A reduction in fertility rates would have the direct effect of decreasing the dependency burden. There would be fewer children to support.

A lower dependency burden would raise the per capita income. A rise in per capita income would mean a better standard of diet, clothing, housing, education and medical facilities which would be more pronounced in the poorest countries where particularly low levels of nutrition, health, and education depress the duration and efficiency of work. Further, at higher levels of per capita income, more can be saved and devoted to direct investment and the government can also squeeze out more in 'forced savings' through taxation and other means. Both forms of saving would, after some time, tend to increase per capita income still further, with cumulative effects similar to those of the initial rise in per capita income owing to a decline in the fertility rates. The decline in fertility rates would lower the costs and interruptions of work incidental to births. Lower fertility rates would also cause a decline in the mortality rate owing to a number of reasons, *viz.*, smaller number of maternal and infant deaths, better standards of living, and with progressively rising incomes, a broadened financial base for public health work. A fall in mortality rates, in turn, will raise incomes on account of the decline in illness associated therewith. There would also be a decrease in economic inconveniences and costs associated with every death, which are quite high in underdeveloped countries.

Rate of growth of population: It is an important factor determining the rate of economic development. History shows that growth in income has been followed by an increase in the rate of population growth. It is feared that, unless a comprehensive policy of population-control is vigorously followed, every increase in income may be dissipated by an increase in population.

Effective control of population is considered to be an important pre-requisite for economic development.

All advanced countries have passed through three phases of population growth. In the first phase, both birth and death rates are high. During the second phase, birth rate continues high but death rate declines because of better health services, more nutritious food, sanitary living, etc., made possible by an increase in incomes; this results into a rapid increase in population. In the third phase, both birth and death rates become stable at a low level. Birth rate declines in the third phase because of a number of reasons. Urban industrial life removes ignorance and creates an awakening among the masses. Calculation takes the place of tradition. People start calculating the comparative pleasure from an additional child and from a rise in the standard of living. Availability of a large range of goods and means of recreation decreases the importance of sexual pleasure in life. Economic development increases social mobility. A person with a smaller family stands a better chance of not only raising himself but improving the status of his children. With economic advancement, children become less of an asset and more of an expense. The opportunities for child labour decrease and the cost of bringing up children increases because of the availability of greater opportunities for education and training. Advancement in civilisation brought about by economic development and urbanisation tends to replace joint family system by nuclear families consisting of wife and husband and their children. In a joint family, the responsibility for supporting children of a couple is widely diffused; this encourages early marriage and a large number of children. In a nuclear family, the obligations for supporting children are exclusively of the parents. People, therefore, tend to marry only when they can support a family; this tendency raises the normal age of marriage. Rise in the marriage age considerably lowers birth rate because the fertility is far higher in the earlier than in the latter period. Further, when parents alone are responsible for supporting their children, they tend to have a smaller number of children. When the death rate is high, people tend to have larger families to cover the risk of death of some children at one or the other stage. In trying to cover the risk of death they, often, overcompensate themselves. Decline in death rate brings a decline in birth rate by decreasing the need for having children to cover the risk of death.

Most of the advanced countries have passed through the first two phases of population growth and are living in the third phase of low birth and low death rates. Countries in the early stage of development are, generally, in the second phase of population-growth. In the early stages of development, birth rate continues high but death rate declines. Sometimes, birth rate may even rise because with the increase in income, people can afford larger families. Forces which reduce the birth rate have to overcome strong social resistances while the forces reducing death rate do not meet any such resistances. At this stage of development, if the rate of increase in income is not faster than the rate of population-growth there is the risk that the process of development may be frustrated. Rapid increase in population decreases the capacity to save. In some countries, savings are not sufficient to maintain even the per capita income with the population growing at current rates; per capita income in such countries is maintained with the funds borrowed abroad.

It is held by some that no development is possible till population growth has been controlled. Does it mean that we should wait for the development program till the population growth is effectively controlled? Certainly not. Some population growth will occur even if the state does not follow a deliberate development policy. Growth in population through a decline in death rate cannot be checked by refraining from economic development. With the spread of medical knowledge, decline in birth rate is inevitable. No doubt, medical services will be availed of more fully at higher incomes, these won't remain unavailed at unchanged incomes. Medical services are a bare necessity and it is very probable that a part of the expenditure will be diverted to these from other less important items. Even in underdeveloped countries, some classes are well off and will make full use of the medical service with the spread of medical knowledge. Provision of medical services is considered to be one of the important functions of a government and every popular government will make best efforts to provide these even at unchanged incomes by diverting a part of its expenditure from less essential heads. Medical services are also provided by charitable organisations. Thus to a certain extent, spread of medical services is independent of the rate of growth in income; consequently, population will grow through a decline in death rate whether or not economic development takes place. If the efforts are not made to develop these countries, the growth of population will be checked by the Malthusian misery. Malthusian misery and catastrophes do not check the population-growth permanently. Population cut by the misery, epidemics, starvation, etc. retains its potentiality for growth. This may lead to repeated cycles of growth and decline in population.

If the growth of population is met by the same or by a quicker rate of economic development, the growth of population will be permanently checked after some time through the operation of forces which bring a decline in birth rate. If the rate at which income rises is more rapid than the rate of population-growth, standard of living will rise. Rise in the standard of living combined with new ways of life associated with economic development causes a decline in the birth rate. Ultimately, both birth and death rates become stable at a low level and development takes place at an accelerated rate. The second phase is likely to be shorter in presently developing countries than it was in the case of countries which were pioneers in the field of economic development. Evolution of ideas in the pioneering countries was a very slow process and took a long time. Once the ideas are evolved, these spread quickly. Mere spread of education will lower the birth rate irrespective of whether or not economic development is taking place. It is, of course, true that economic development will expedite the decline in birth rate. In spite of the comparatively advantageous position of the presently developing countries, stabilisation of birth and death rates at a low level through natural forces will take a long time. Meanwhile there may occur a large increase in population. Measures to control population, therefore, are very essential if the development is to be achieved at a fairly rapid rate.

Use of contraceptives is an important method of controlling the birth rate. In a primarily rural country, it, however, involves a number of difficulties. Most of the women are uneducated and, therefore, it is difficult for them to learn and practise contraception. People are too poor to afford the high cost of contraceptives. Training of women in the use of contraceptives requires a large number of lady doctors which are not available in most of the underdeveloped countries. Use of contraceptives is, often, bitterly opposed on moral and religious grounds.

There are certain underdeveloped countries which suffer not from overpopulation but from underpopulation. The problem of both underpopulated and overpopulated countries can be simultaneously solved by encouraging migration. International migration was an important factor in the development of newly settled regions. In present days, however, because of certain political and economic factors, it is doubtful, if international migration can be achieved on a sufficiently large scale. Movement and resettlement of labour requires considerable expenditure in the emigrant as well as in the immigrant countries. Any migration on a fairly large scale requires considerable expansion of transportation. Most of the demand in advanced countries is for skilled labour of which there is shortage within the underdeveloped countries themselves. Immigration is not welcome in advanced countries even when faced with a fear of stagnation. Stimulation of consumption, increase in public expenditure and foreign investments are preferred to immigration for dispelling stagnation. The prejudice against the immigration of non-white people is particularly marked. Partly it is because of the fear that low standard of living of the non-white people will lower the wage rates and thereby the standard of living of the local labour. Racial complexes is another factor obstructing labour movements.

Further, if migration is permitted, it is mostly the young, enterprising and adventurous people who will migrate abroad. Local development of the country will suffer if the efficient labour migrates abroad and only the aged, incapable and incompetent labour is left behind.

Sometimes it has been suggested that population-growth be controlled through fiscal devices. It is, however, difficult to devise a system which discourages larger families and is also equitable.

Development will be followed by an increase in the rate of growth of population only if the consumption is permitted to rise along with the increase in incomes. Increase in the rate of growth of population can be checked by diverting the increased incomes towards investment rather than towards consumption. This method of controlling population-growth will have the additional advantage of accelerating the pace of development. Once the development has reached the stage at which the factors which restrict population growth—urbanisation, education, break-up of the joint family system, etc.—have become operative, increase in consumption can be permitted without any risk of explosive growth of population.

Population-growth, however, is not an unmixed evil. In certain respects it helps the development process. Economies with growing population can adjust to changed conditions more easily than the economies with stationary populations; newcomers can adapt to changed conditions more easily than the old ones. High rate of population growth expands markets and thereby offers incentive for investment. Increase in population lowers wage rates and thus raises the share of profits in total output which stimulates investment. Profits constituted an important source of investment during the development phase of the present developed countries. At the same time, we should not neglect the possibility of lower wages encouraging substitution of capital and thus slowing the rates of capital formation.

Most of the advantages of growing population, however, relate to latter stages of growth when the supply of savings tends to exceed investment opportunities. At this stage, the growing population maintains the growth process by expanding markets. Expanding markets are essential for maintaining the marginal efficiency of capital. In the absence of expanding markets, the economy will move towards a state of secular stagnation. Growing population, however, is not the only way of expanding markets. In the absence of a growing population, markets can be expanded through fiscal and monetary measures which stimulate consumption and investment. Gap between savings and investments opportunites can be filled up by government expenditure.

Population policy: In framing a policy for fighting the problem of overpopulation, the South Asian countries are bound by one rigid value premise which has important practical consequences, that is, the efforts to check the rapid rate of growth of population have to be concentrated only on the fertility factor. Complacency about or even tolerance of a high rate of mortality because it keeps down the rate of growth of population is simply not permissible. All that is reasonably possible must be done to check diseases and premature deaths irrespective of its effect on the rate of growth of population. This value premise is accepted throughout the civilised world.

Measures to lower the birth rate have to be based on the principle of voluntary parenthood, which is, in fact, the basis of population policies in almost all countries. People have to be induced through various ways to have a smaller number of children. Knowledge about birth control must be spread widely and the most effective means to carry it out made available to the masses.

For creating a motivation for birth control, some people have suggested economic penalization of the families with a larger number of children or rewarding those having a smaller number of children. But no country has done this in actual practice. The maximum that has been done is to deprive larger families of certain benefits available from the government, e.g., denial of maternity leave after a certain number of births, limiting health facilities to a certain maximum number of children, etc. The reason is obvious. Since having a larger number of children is the major cause of poverty, such measures would penalise the relatively poor and subsidize the relatively well off. Such a result would not only be contrary to principle of equity but would also be detrimental to the health of the poor families and thus to that of the growing generation.[2]

On the other hand, the South Asian countries should avoid, as far as possible, redistributional reforms in favour of families with a large number of children, who will tend to be poorest and most in need of aid, lest they thereby encourage childbearing. The two objectives of checking fertility and improving the living conditions of children therefore appear to conflict with each other. But the conflict arises mostly when redistributional reforms are carried out by means of cash payments to parents. No doubt, there is an element of redistribution in everything that is done for children, from expanding health, educational, and training facilities to providing school meals, the risk of stimulating childbearing is minimized if the benefits are provided to children in kind and not to parents in cash.

Once the fertility rates are brought down, the population policy should be directed towards an improvement in the quality of population and the welfare of families. The policy of bringing down the birth rate would in itself improve the quality of population and the welfare of children. The children will share the increase in per capita income resulting from a decline in the fertility rate. Further, it is natural that the birth control efforts would be concentrated more on parents who are poor and already have a large number of children. If these efforts are successful, living conditions for the children already born will be improved.

In recent years, many South Asian countries have been groping towards a public policy of bringing down fertility through birth control. India and Pakistan have already started a birth control program with great vigour. Sri Lanka and Thailand have permitted or sponsored studies and pilot projects, and Sri Lanka and Malaya have given government support to private organisations for 'family planning'. Some other countries have also shown interest in formulating a policy of population control. But no country in South Asia has yet succeeded in bringing down the fertility rates to any significant extent. Fertility rates have not declined even in India, which has pursued the policy of birth control most vigorously. The meagre gains from birth control policy have been offset by a decline in mortality rates and a relaxation of fertility-depressing customs.

NATURAL AND ACTUAL RATE OF POPULATION GROWTH

Today developing economies are facing faster rate of population growth than the developed economies during their initial phase of development. Also, the acceleration in population growth of developed economies in their early phase was endogenous phenomenon induced by accelerated economic growth, while in developing economies today it is largely exogenous in nature. According to Wrigley and Birdsall, acceleration in the former was based on increased employment and income that were generated by the productivity growth in the newly established industries, whereas acceleration in the latter was due to importation of health and medical technologies from developed economies.[3] When exogenous population growth in developing economies is explosive and not matched by increases in employment and income, they are destined to face the problem of relative resource exhaustion, economic degradation, and destitution.

To explain the difference in population growth rates among different regions we need to consider both the natural as well as the actual rates of population growth. The natural rate of population growth can be defined as

$$p_n = \frac{b_{cr} - d_{cr}}{10} \qquad \text{... (10.1)}$$

where,

p_n = natural rate of population growth;

b_{cr} = crude birth rate (CBR), which is the number of live births per 1,000 population; and

d_{cr} = crude death rate (CDR), which is the number of deaths per 1,000 population.

Equation (10.1) gives the natural rate of population growth in percentage since CBR and CDR are stated per 1,000 population, when we divide equation (10.1) by 10, CBR and CDR are converted to rates per 100 of population.

The actual rate of population growth can be defined as:

$$p_a = p_n + m \qquad \text{... (10.2)}$$

and $m = m_i - m_e$

where,

p_a = actual rate of population growth in percentage;

m = migration;

m_i = immigrants per 100 population; and

m_e = emigrants per 100 population.

Thus, from equation (10.2) we find that the actual rate of population growth is equal to the natural rate of population growth plus or minus net migration. It implies that the actual rate of population growth will be very similar to the natural rate in countries where immigration and emigration are relatively balanced. If $m_e > m_i$, that is, more people leaving the country than entering, the natural rate of population growth, p_n, will overstate the actual rate of population growth, p_a.

Here one point should be noted that the population growth is controlled not only by CBR and CDR but also by the present population. Therefore, rate of population growth can also be written as:

$$\frac{dN}{dt} = p_n N \quad \text{or,} \quad N = N_0 e^{p_n t} \qquad \ldots (10.3)$$

where,

N_0 = starting population,

N = population after,

p_n = natural rate of population growth,

t = time period, and

e = exponential constant (2.71828...).

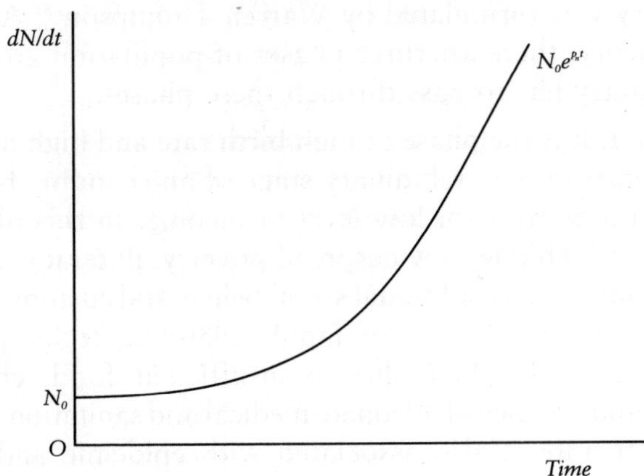

Fig. 10.1

Population grows exponentially if the natural rate of population growth, which is controlled by human behaviour does not change. Figure 10.1 discribes this behaviour of population growth.

ECONOMIC DEVELOPMENT TO POPULATION GROWTH

Economic development requires many human and non-human components, but the human factor is the most important component and is considered to be the basic component that development relies on in any country. In this section we shall analyse how economic development leads to increase in population.

Theory of Demographic Transition

Theory of demographic transition deals with the growth of population due to change in the crude birth rate and crude death rate; and essentially it states that societies experience modernization progress from a pre-modern regime of high fertility and high mortality to a post-modern one in which both are low. F.W. Notestein is regarded as the first proponent of this theory, although Notestein did not refer to his generalisation as 'transition'. The first to use the expression 'demographic transition' was Adolphe Landry in his book entitled *La Révolution Démographique,* published in 1934.[4] The english version of this theory was formulated by Warren Thompson.[5] According to this theory, there are three phases of population growth and every country has to pass through these phases.

Phase I: It is the phase of high birth rate and high death rate which occurs in the preliminary stage of an economy having an agrarian economy with low level of income. In this phase, the birth rate is high due to widespread poverty, illiteracy, universal and early marriage, traditional social beliefs and customs, attitude towards male child, lack of family planning techniques, etc. Death rate is also high due to insufficient food, child care facilities, and absence of adequate medical and sanitation facilities. High death rate is also associated with epidemic and natural calamities. High death rate tends to cancel out relatively high birth rate, so population growth rate is quite low in this phase.

Phase II: It is the phase of high birth rate and low death rate which occurs when economic development starts. In this phase birth rate is high due to the reasons stated in Phase I. Death rate declines due to direct and indirect effect of economic development such as better and adequate food supply, proper housing, pure drinking water, better medical facilities, better sanitation, development of antibiotics, vaccines and introduction of immunization programs, decline in infant mortality rate, etc. This leads to widening the gap between birth and death rates. So, the growth rate of population is very high in this phase.

Phase III: It is the phase of low birth rate and low death rate which occurs when economy becomes developed. In a developed economy birth rate is low because industrialization and urbanization lead to high preference for small families. Death rate is also low because of economic availability of better medical facilities. Low birth rate and low death rate lead to a stable population growth in this phase.

These three phases taken together make up the demographic transition, which can be shown by Fig. 10.2.

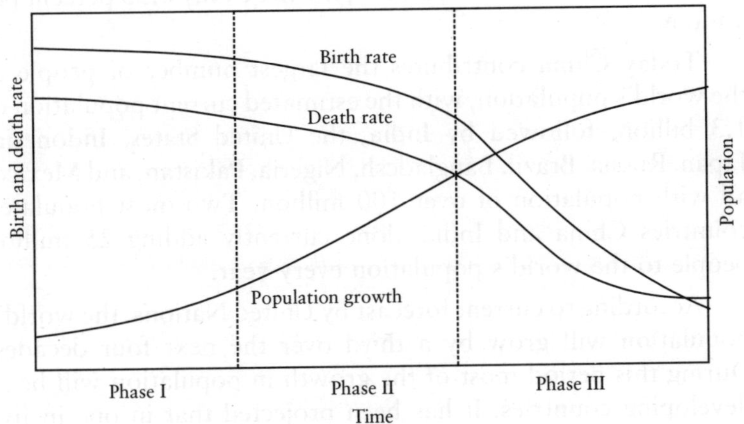

Fig. 10.2

In Fig. 10.2 we see that in phase I both birth and death rates are high leading to low but stable population. In phase II, birth rate is high while death rate is falling. In this phase population grows sharply. In phase III, both birth and death rates begin to fall leading to slow increase in population. In this phase after some time population becomes stable or even declines.

Trends in Population Growth

If we go in the history of world's population we find that at the time of Christ it was approximately 179 million and less than 1000 million till 1800 AD. It has been established that the growth rate of population from AD 1 to 1750 was not more than 0.05 percent per annum and from 1750 to 1850 it was 0.5 percent per annum. From 1900 to 1950, the population of the world grew by 50 percent and then increased by 200 percent over the next 50 years to reach 6.1 billion just before the turn of the twenty-first century.

The world's population is projected to be 8.9 billion in 2050, an increase of 47 percent from the 2000 level. Thus, the average population growth rate over this half-century will be 0.77 percent per annum, substantially lower than the 1.76 percent per annum from 1950 to 2000. If we consider a short span of time, the annual growth rate was 1.22 percent between 2000 to 2005, and between 2045 to 2050, it will be only 0.33 percent per annum.

Today China contributes the largest number of people in the world's population, with the estimated current population of 1.3 billion, followed by India, the United States, Indonesia, Japan, Russia, Brazil, Bangladesh, Nigeria, Pakistan, and Mexico, all with population of over 100 million. Two most populated countries China and India alone currently adding 25 million people to the world's population every year.

According to current forecast by United Nations, the world's population will grow by a third over the next four decades. During this period most of the growth in population will be in developing countries. It has been projected that in one in five developed countries, including Germany, Japan, the Republic of Korea and the Russian Federation, populations are expected to shrink; while in one in six countries, all of them developing countries, population will be more than doubled within the next 40 years. It is assumed that the population of developed countries would peak in 2020 and fall by 7 percent in next three decades. The trend observed over the last half century—the fall in the share of people living in Europe and the increase in Africa—is likely to continue.

It has been estimated that the global working-age population will increase by 1.1 billion by 2050, while the share of developed countries in the total working-age population will decline slightly. Again over the next 15 years, the total number of working-age people currently in developed countries will be less than the new entrants to the labour force in developing countries. This will put an upward pressure on wages leading to an increase in the incentives for movement of labours among potential employees in poor countries and seeking out workers from abroad among employers in rich countries. This will affect the dependency ratio—the ratio of elderly and young to the working-age population. Currently, 49 for every 100 working-age population in developed countries are not working, roughly half of them are children or elderly. While, in developing economies, the ratio is 53 out of which three quarters of the dependents are children. As the economies grow, over the next 40 years, due to lower birth rates the proportion of children falls as they reach working age. The dependency ratio will remain roughly stable in developing countries, just reaching 55 by 2050. On the other hand during this period, the proportion of elderly will rise in developed countries. There will be 71 non-working-age people for every 100 working-age people.

Adjustment of Birth Rates

In the previous section we have seen that the main factor in the growth rate of population is that due to economic development death rate has declined rapidly, while at the same time, birth rate has declined marginally. The decline in death rate can be associated with the increase in the carrying capicity, such as rise in agricultural productivity, of the earth. Improvement in sanitation and health care in developing countries has also contributed to the decline in the death rate.

The high birth rate can be associated with two forms of inertia—(i) macro-inertia, at the level of the overall population, and (ii) micro-inertia, at the level of the family. The high birth and death rates in a developing country make the level of population growth low similar to the developed country, but it has another implication that the population of developing country will be younger than the developed country. This characteristic of developing country tends to keep overall birth rates high even if fertility rates are reduced at different age groups. This is refer to macro-inertia. Micro-inertia which operates at the household level refers to the operation of societal norms regarding children and other socio-economic factors.

In developing countries offsprings are generally considered as substitutes for missing markets, such as institution of social security in old age. People make their fertility choices based on the assumption that some of their children will die, which ultimately leads to a larger number of births.

Suppose that a child will grow up to look after its parents. This probability depends on several factors:

(a) A child may die at the young age.
(b) The diseases of childhood may kill the child up to the age of five or so.
(c) A child may not earn enough to look after its parents.
(d) A child may not look after its parents in their old age.
(e) The parents themselves might not anticipate being around in their old age.

Let p be the probability that a child will grow up to look after its parents and q is the probability that a couple finds acceptable as a threshold probability of receiving support from at least one child. Now our problem is to find out the number of children each having probability p of looking after its parents, so that the overall probability of having at least one child to look after its parents is q.

Suppose one has n children. The probability of none will look after its parents is $(1 - p)^n$. Therefore, one would choose the number of offspring, n, just large enough so that

$$1 - (1 - p)^n > q \quad \text{... (10.4)}$$

If gender bias is considered, i.e., suppose one wishes to get support from a son only, then one would see n as desired number of male offspring only. In that case the value of n derived from equation (10.4) will be doubled.

Parents do not know which child will take care of them. They must make their fertility decisions in advance, i.e., they will have to give birth to n number of children. This is known as *hoarding*, i.e., children have to be stockpiled in advance without knowing which one among them will take care of their parents.

In case of high infant mortality rate, a wait-and-see strategy has high feasibility. A couple can have a child and it takes its next fertility decision on the survival of this child. In this case, the desired number of children can be obtained sequentially. This is known as *targeting*—total number of children need not to be created in advance. A change from hoarding to targeting may lead to a drastic lowering of the fertility rate.

Now, let us consider the cost of child rearing. There are two costs:

(a) Direct costs of children—feeding, clothing, health, schooling, etc.

(b) Indirect or opportunity costs of children—amount of income foregone in the process of bringing up the child. The opportunity cost of child rearing is proportional to the prevailing wage rate multiplied by the number of hours spent in parenting.

In societies having low opportunity costs of child rearing, fertility rates tend to be high. In most societies it is the responsibility of women to look after the upbringing of children. Also in such societies women get low wages compared to their male counterpart. This makes the opportunity cost of having children low leading to a high birth rates. Similarly in the case of high unemployment rate, the opportunity cost of child rearing goes down and this also increases birth rate.

Cost-Benefit Analysis of Having Children

Privately optimal fertility choices may not be the socially optimal. They generally lead to overly large numbers of children.

Government provides a large numbers of social facilities which have an impact on individual's fertility decision. Social infrastructures such as free education, healh facilities, etc. reduce the child rearing cost of an individual leading to high fertility rate. Since the private cost of having children to the family is lower than the social cost, the number of children that people choose to have will exceed the socially optimal.

Using Fig. 10.3 we shall analyse the costs and benefits of having children.

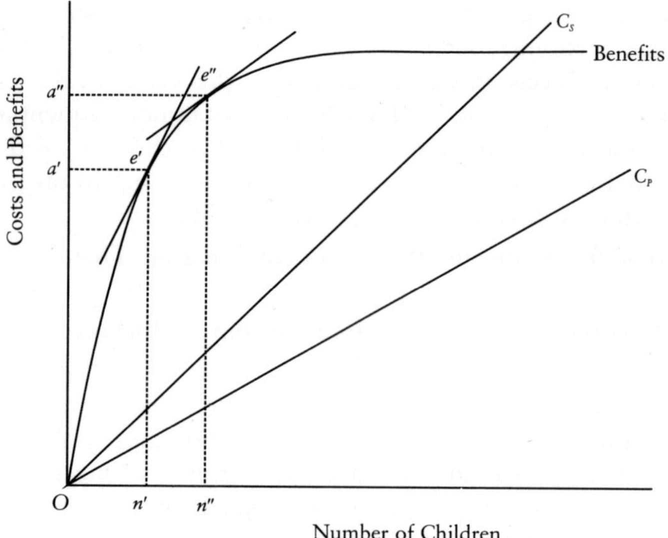

Fig. 10.3

In Fig. 10.3, the line OC_P represents the private costs of an additional child and the line OC_S represents the social costs of an additional child. For simplicity, costs curves have been represented as straight lines, so that each additional child costs the same amount. Since the diminishing returns to having more children operates, the benefit curve has concave shape.

The socially optimal number of children will be obtained at the place where the vertical distance between benefit curve and the social cost line is maximum. The optimum point is obtained by equalising the marginal benefit and marginal social cost, which is point e' in the Fig. 10.3 yielding n' number of children.

On the other hand privately optimal number of children is obtained at the place where the vertical distance between benefit curve and the private cost line is maximum. In Fig. 10.3, this point is represented by e'' yielding n'' number of children. Thus, we see that $n'' > n'$ i.e., privately optimal number of children is more than the socially optimal.

POPULATION GROWTH TO ECONOMIC DEVELOPMENT

High population growth has some positive as well as some negative effects on economic development. It has negative impact on economic development in countries where natural resources are scarce, government policies are ineffective, and property rights are poorly defined. It creates pressures on limited natural resources, reduces private and public capital formation, and diverts additions to capital resources to maintain rather than increase the stock of capital per worker. On the positive sides effects such as economies of scale and specialization, the possible spur to favourable motivation caused by increased dependency, and the more favourable attitudes, capacities, and motivations of younger populations compared with older ones, etc. can be considered. In this section we shall examine how the population growth affects the economic development of a country.

Negative Effects

Let us start with the Malthusian view on the effect of population growth on economic development. According to Malthus, a nation's economic development is determined by the growth in population due to a variety of problems caused by the growth. For example, overpopulation places a pressure on the limited natural resources, more specifically on agriculture, which starts a chain reaction of problems as the nation grows. Since population growth outstrips growth in food supply, the population will be forced to live at the subsistence level of income.

According to Malthus population increases at a faster rate than the food supply. Population grows at a geometric rate, whereas the growth in food production follows arithmetic progression. Therefore, scarce resources will have to be shared among an increasing number of individuals. However, Malthus predicted the existence of some checks that ease the pressure of population explosion. He distinguishes between two categories—(i) the preventive check, and (ii) the positive check.

Preventive check refers to the voluntary limitations of population growth. Individuals make rational decisions about the number of children they want to have, based on their expected income and the quality of life they want to enjoy in future. And the lack of a preventive check leads to the positive check which consists of diseases, famines, wars, and other natural calamities. Malthus pointed out that the positive check acts more intensively in lower classes due to high infant mortality rates and unhealthy conditions of living. Thus, by controlling population growth, both the checks minimise the gap between the level of population and the availability of resources. But, the positive checks create misery and wickedness that cannot be avoided and are beyond the control of human being. In this condition, any increase in the agricultural productivity due to technological improvements will only produce a temporary increase in living standards, but in the long run it will be offset by a correspondent increase in population size.

Malthus believed that monetary transfers from rich to poor will not increase the welfare, eventually it will worsen their living conditions. This is because poor would mistakenly be led to think that they can support a bigger family, which would in turn depress the preventive check and generate higher population growth. Finally same amount of resources has to be distributed among a large population, triggering the work of the positive check to populations. Also, after such transfers, people can afford buying more food, which will bid up the prices of foods leading to a decrease in real wage. This will hurt the poor individuals whose main income comes from their labour. Therefore, Malthus held that it is better for a family to consider its lack of ability to support children before having them, than to deal with subsequent diseases and infant mortality, i.e., it is better to use the preventive check than the positive one.

If the real wage is above the subsistence level, population will begin to grow, resulting a decline in nominal wages due to a large supply of labour to the firms. Also, increase in population would increase the demand for goods leading to an increase in prices and decrease in real wages to their subsistence level. This concept is known as the *Iron Law of Wages*.

Agricultural production and mining activities are characterised by diminishing returns to scale, whereas constant returns to scale operate in the manufacturing sector. Taking this hypothesis with Malthus' population principle will yield a pessimistic scenarios for countries having their productive structure based on manufacturing. In this condition, an increase in population will increase employment in the industrial sector more than the agricultural sector and manufacture supply will be raised more than the agricultural supply. Thus, the population pressure increases both the supply and the demand for goods and induces prices of agriculture products to move up relative to the manufacturing product making the condition of factory workers worse.

Now we will make the use of growth models to analyse the effects of population growth on economic development. People divide their income into consumption and savings. Saved income goes into investment leading to increase in the capital stock of the economy. At the same time population of the economy also grows. All these things can be represented by following Harrod-Domar growth equation.

$$s/\theta=(1+g)(1+n)-(1+\delta) \qquad \text{... (10.5)}$$

where,

s = rate of savings,

θ = capital-output ratio,

g = rate of growth of per capita income,

n = rate of population growth, and

δ = rate of depreciation of the capital stock.

In Eq. 10.5, if all parameters remain constant and the rate of population growth n increases, the rate of growth of per capita income, g, must fall. In this way, population growth has a negative effect on the rate of growth.

In Solow's growth model, with technical change at some constant rate a production function relates capital and labour to the production of output. One remarkable feature of this model is that once the change in the capital-output ratio is taken into account, the steady-state rate of growth is independent of the rate of savings and the rate of population growth. An implicit assumption of this model is that capital and labour can be substituted for each other indefinitely. Due to this assumption, population growth has no ultimate effect on the rate of economic growth. This does not imply that in Solow model population growth has no effect at all. It lowers the steady-state level of the per capita capital stock, expressed in units of capital per effective unit of labour, and in this way affects the level of per capita income, expressed again in units of effective labour. Following equation represents the Solow model with technical progress:

$$(1 + n)(1 + p)\, k(t + 1) = (1 - d)\, k(t) + sy(t) \quad \text{... (10.6)}$$

where,

n = rate of population growth,

π = rate of technical progress,

k = per capita capital stock,

t = time period,

δ = rate of depreciation of the capital stock,

y = per capita income.

From Eq. 10.6, we see that if the rate of population growth, n, goes up, the left-hand side of the equation goes upward and the steady-state level of the capital stock, expressed as a ratio of effective labour, comes down. It implies that in the long-run rate of growth is unaffected by a change in the rate of population growth, but the entire trajectory of growth shifts downward. In this way, the increased population growth has negative level effects on the rate of growth.

There is another negative effect of population growth which has not been considered in the growth models. The aggregate rate of savings decreases due to increase in population because population growth reduces aggregate income and increases aggregate consumption. Due to increase in the young age population dependency ratio in families increases which increases in the consumption because children consume more than they produce leading to decrease in savings rates.

Positive Effects

According to the neo-classical school the population growth is correlated to technological advancement. As population increases, there arises a need for some sort of technological change in order to meet the rising demands for certain goods and services. The effect of population growth on technological progress has two dimension:

(a) High population density creates a pressure for technical progress—a demand-driven view.[6]

(b) A large pool of potential innovators and therefore a larger stock of ideas and innovations are created—a supply-driven view.[7]

Increase in population increases the demands for certain goods and services and to meet this demand some sort of technological change in production is required. On the other hand, increase in population makes available a large and cheap labour force resulting in a huge rise in employment as businesses are more inclined to cheap labour. Low labour cost reduces money wage bill, which can be used in technological advancement resulting in rise in overall outputs by the business and the nation as a whole and making even more population to survive. Thus, increase in population generates demands for goods and results in overall economic growth.

In Julian Simon's view, the long run benefits of population growth in development of developing countries are on the positive balance. He argued that an increase in the numbers of consumers and an increase in income increase the demand for raw materials as well as finished products. This will create a shortage in goods and services, forcing up prices for the natural resources. People will start to search new ways to satisfy the increasing demands leading to finding of new sources and innovative substitutes. These new findings make available cheaper natural resources than existed before. Thus, it will leave the nation better off than before implying that it has gone through a process of economic growth and development.

Everybody in the population has an independent chance of coming up with an idea that can benefit the whole society. No one knows which child will become a great inventor, scientist, or entrepreneur. Stopping the population growth will limit this chance. Newton and Einstein had not been there if population growth had not taken place. We do not have Reliance Industries if parents of Dhirubhai Ambani who had two daughters and three sons, had limited their family to only one son (Dhirubhai was the second one). Thus, the chances of getting genius person are higher if the population is larger.

POPULATION AND ENVIRONMENT

Population and environment are interlinked. Changes in population size, age distribution, fertility, mobility, settlement patterns, and resource availability and consumption patterns put an impact on environment. Population variables interact with consumption patterns, technologies, and political and economic structures to influence environmental change. Due to high increase in population, natural resources are under increasing pressure creating a lot of environmental problems that threaten public health and development. Following are some of the effects of population growth on environment:

(a) Over 12 million people are killed each year, most of them are from developing countries, due to unclean water, along with poor sanitation. Another 3 million are killed due diseases caused by air pollution.

(b) A study of United Nation Food and Agriculture Organisation shows that in 64 out of 105 developing countries the population has been growing faster than food supplies. Due to high population pressure, some 2 billion hectares of arable land have been degraded or converted into concrete areas.

(c) The Earth has limited sources of freshwater, but demand is soaring as population grows and use per capita rises. It has been projected that by 2025, when world's population will be around 8 billion, 48 countries containing 3 billion people will suffer from acute shortages of water.

(d) Due to high population densities and urban development coastal ecosystems has been destroyed. Ocean resources such as fisheries are being overexploited.

(e) The Earth has lost its half of the original forest cover, and each year another 16 million hectares are destroyed. Forests are vital to maintaining healthy ecosystems and they add more than US $400 billion to the world economy annually. Also forests are homes for thousands of species. Nearly 2/3 of the world's species are endangered due to deforestation.

(f) Biological diversity on Earth is crucial for the existence of agriculture and medicinal plants. Increasing population are pushing many thousands of plant and animal species into extinction.

(g) Burning fossil fuels emit greenhouse gases which is the main cause of global warming. Due to rise in global temperature, sea levels would rise, causing widespread flooding.

Due to rapid population growth accompanied with economic development, developing countries are facing urgent need to improve their living standards. As a result they are exploiting natural resources to meet present needs much faster than they can regenerate and are destroying resources needed for the future.

Only from 1960s, awareness regarding global population has increased. A report of the Secretary General of the United Nations entitled "Problems of the human environment" cited the explosive growth of human populations as first among the portents of a crisis of worldwide scope concerning the relation between man and his environment.[8] This report was a crucial step towards making the population problem a worldwide concern. The first world intergovernmental conference on the protection of the environment was called in Stockholm in June 1972.

Today it is a matter of great concern that despite slowing growth, nearly 80 million people are added in world population each year parceling land, freshwater, and other finite resources among more people. It is not possible to find out precisely how an increase in population size affects specific environmental problems. Too many factors interact, and much depends on the time frame under consideration. But the facts such as the loss of half of the planet's forests, depletion of fisheries, and the alteration of atmosphere and climate reveal the truth that the human population which was mere millions in prehistoric times has reached to nearly 6.1 billion today and is creating a huge pressure on natural resources.

The intensity of environmental problem can be better understood from the outcome of the "Declaration of the United Nations Conference on the Human Environment"[9] and the "Action Plan for the Human Environment".[10] The outcome of the conference constituted the basis for activities of the United Nations system on environmental issues during the 1970s and 1980s. The Declaration confirmed that "the natural growth of population continuously presents problems for the preservation of the environment, and adequate policies and measures should be adopted, as appropriate, to face these problems". However, the Declaration also stated that "of all things in the world, people are the most precious", noting that "it is the people that propel social progress, create social wealth, develop science and technology and, through their hard work, continuously transform the human environment". The Declaration also noted that "along with social progress and the advancement of production, science and technology, the capability of man to improve the environment increases with each passing day". The World Population Plan of Action adopted at the United Nations World Population Conference in Bucharest in 1974 took the environmental question in terms of per capita use of world resources.[11] According to the Plan developed countries should adopt appropriate policies in population, consumption and investment, bearing in mind the need for fundamental improvement in international equity.

The second International Conference on Population, held in Mexico City in 1984, framed the environmental issues as a dimension of the population-development relationship on the global scale, directing all countries in which there were imbalances between trends in population growth and resources and environmental requirements to implement policies to redress such imbalances.[12] The Conference also emphasised on the formulation of national population goals and policies in such a way that they must take into account the need for long-term environmentally sustainable economic development. Rio de Janeiro Conference on Economic and Development, held in 1992, was a milestone in the evolution of an international consensus on the relationships among population, development, and environment, based on the concept of sustainable development. Sustainable development is defined as the development that meets the needs of the present without compromising the ability of future generations to meet their own needs.[13] In the Rio Declaration, population policies were considered as an integral element of sustainable development. Principle 8 of the Declaration states that "to achieve sustainable development and a higher quality of life for all people, States should reduce and eliminate unsustainable patterns of production and consumption and promote appropriate demographic policies".

NURKSE'S SURPLUS LABOUR MODEL

According to Nurkse if prevailing unproductive surplus labours in the rural sector are being supported by the productive labours who produce more than they consume, then this difference only represents virtual saving from the point of view of the economy as a whole. This is because the surplus created by the productive labours is fully consumed by the unproductive labours. If the unproductive labours are utilised to produce new capital goods, the virtual savings can be transformed into effective saving creating capital without decreasing in the overall level of consumption of any individual in the economy. In this way supply of finance for the accumulation of capital can be generated internally simply by mobilising the unproductive labours into productive labours. There is no requirement of formal creation of finance or *ex ante* savings other than the reallocation of unproductive labours to capital construction projects. In this case there will be no fall in total agricultural output.

We can show the effect of withdrawal of unproductive labour from agricultural sector on marketed surplus of foodgrains. Let us suppose,

Y_0 = initial total net output,
Y_1 = total net output after development program,
L_0 = total labour available in agriculture sector,
L_1 = productive labour on agriculture,
c = average propensity to consume foodgrains,
d = ratio of gross to net output,
e = income elasticity of demand for foodgrains, and
m = marginal propensity to consume foodgrains.

Then, we have

$$a = \frac{L_1}{L_0} \text{ and } b = \frac{Y_1}{Y_0}$$

where, $0 < a < 1$ and $b > 1$.

Three stages are possible:

(a) Stage I: No increase in output is produced.

(b) Stage II: There is an increase in output as a result of the simultaneous introduction of a development programme.

(c) Stage III: In this stage gross output is also introduced into the picture.

When surplus unproductive labours are withdrawn from the agriculture sector, the increase in market surplus of foodgrains are given by:

In Stage I: $cY_0(1 - a)(1 - e)$, or $Y_0(1 - a)(c - m)$

In Stage II: $Y_0[(b - 1)(1 - ce) + c(1 - a)(1 - e)]$,

or $Y_0[(b - 1)(1 - m) + (1 - a)(c - m)]$

In Stage III: $Y_0[(b - 1)(d - ce) + c(1 - a)(1 - e)]$,

or $Y_0[(b - 1)(d - m) + (1 - a)(c - m)]$

We can also examine the increase in marketed surplus as a proportion of the initial consumption of those withdrawn from the agriculture sector. The following equations represents this proportion.

In Stage I: $(1 - e)$, or $\dfrac{(c - m)}{c}$

In Stage II: $\dfrac{(b-1)(1-ce)+c(1-a)(1-e)}{c(1-a)}$,

or $\dfrac{(b-1)(1-m)+(1-a)(c-m)}{c(1-a)}$

In Stage III: $\dfrac{(b-1)(d-ce)+c(1-a)(1-e)}{c(1-a)}$,

or $\dfrac{(b-1)(d-m)+(1-a)(c-m)}{c(1-a)}$

The gap between the value of total output and net disposable income may become wide automatically as output increases. Nurkse put a question that from where the food will come to feed the labours who will be emloyed to build the capital goods to create an industrial sector. However there are some voluntary savings among the rich urban commercial and landowning classes of poor countries, but they are unlikely to be sufficient to support industrialisation. By reducing conspicuous consumption of higher income classes through formal restrictions or fiscal policy measures savings of the poor countries can be supplemented. But it is difficult to enforce any restrictions on consumption of higher income classes. Due to shortfall of voluntary savings out of existing incomes, poor developing countries will be forced to a vicious cycle of poverty unless alternative sources are not found.

SEN'S SURPLUS LABOUR MODEL

Let us consider a region consisting of identical peasant families. Each family, with a given stock of land and capital, has α members out of which β are working members ($\alpha > \beta$). At a given point of time family output q is the function of labour L is given by

$$q = q(L);\ q''(L) < 0 \qquad \text{... (10.7)}$$

The marginal productivity of labour is assumed either to become zero for a finite value of labour $\left(\bar{L}\right)$, with a maximum output $\left(\bar{q}\right)$ and can be written as:

$$q = Max\, q(L) = q(\bar{L}) \text{ and } q'(\bar{L}) = 0 \qquad \text{... (10.8)}$$

or, to approach zero asymptotically,

$$\lim_{L\to\infty} q'(L) = 0 \qquad \text{... (10.9)}$$

Let u be the personal utility function of every member of the family which is a function of individual income y and v be the personal disutility function related to individual's labour, l. The functions u and v are of the same shape for everyone. The marginal utility from income is positive and non-increasing, and the marginal disutility from labour is non-negative and non-decreasing.

$$u = u(y); \quad u'(y) > 0,\ u''(y) \leq 0 \qquad \text{... (10.10)}$$

$$v = v(l); \quad v'(l) \geq 0,\ v''(l) \geq 0 \qquad \text{... (10.11)}$$

Family welfare, W, is given by

$$W = \sum_{i=1}^{\alpha} u_i - \sum_{i=1}^{\beta} v_i \qquad \text{... (10.12)}$$

Here one point should be noted that the work is equally divided between working members, whereas income is equally divided between all members. When the marginal utility of income is strictly diminishing and the marginal disutility of labour is strictly increasing, egalitarian distribution will be the only one consistent with welfare maximisation. Thus, we have

$$L = \beta \cdot l \qquad \text{... (10.13)}$$

$$q = \alpha \cdot y \qquad \text{... (10.14)}$$

$$W = \alpha \cdot u - \beta \cdot v \qquad \text{... (10.15)}$$

Family welfare is maximised when the following condition is satisfied:

$$q'(L) = \frac{v'(l)}{u'(y)} = \mu \qquad \text{... (10.16)}$$

where, μ is the real cost of labour and is given by the individual rate of indifferent substitution between income and labour. Equation (10.16) shows that labour is applied upto the point where its marginal product equals the real cost of labour.

The amount of the product q can be exchanged for an amount r of some other products. Individual utility can be related to individual share of r and correspondingly we can modify equation (10.10) keeping it of the same analytical type, with positive non-increasing marginal utility.

$$u = u(r_1);\ u'(r_1) > 0,\ u''(r_1) \leq 0 \qquad \text{... (10.17)}$$

where, r_1 is the individual's share in r.

Now suppose that the peasants face a cometitive market for their product, and the price of their product in terms of the product r is taken to be p per unit.

$$r = q \cdot p = \alpha \cdot r_1 \qquad \text{... (10.18)}$$

Maximisation of family welfare is given by

$$q'(L) = \frac{v'(l)}{u'(r_1)} \cdot \frac{1}{p} \qquad \text{... (10.19)}$$

A part of the product q is sold in the market and a part is consumed directly. Suppose q_1 amount of product is marketed and r_1 is the amount of purchased commodity enjoyed by each member of the peasant family. y is the amount of the self-produced output enjoyed by per member of the family. Now we have a more complicated individual utility function involving both r_1 and y. There is non-increasing marginal utility for each good when the amount of it is increased in isolation, or when both goods are raised in the same proportion. Thus, we have

$$u = u(r_1, y) \qquad \text{... (10.20)}$$

such that

$u_y > 0,\ u_{r_1} > 0,\ u_{yy} \leq 0,\ u_{r_1 r_1} \leq 0,\ u_y(r_1, y) \geq u_y(\lambda \cdot r_1, \lambda \cdot y)$, and,

$u_{r_1}(r_1, y) \geq u_{r_1}(\lambda \cdot r_1, \lambda y)$, when $\lambda > 1$.

$$q(1 - q_1) = \alpha \cdot y \qquad \text{... (10.21)}$$

$$r = q \cdot q_1 \cdot p = \alpha \cdot r_1 \qquad \text{... (10.22)}$$

By maximising family welfare, given by equation (10.15), with respect to variations in total family labour (L), and therefore of individual labour (l) and of output (q), and with respect to variations in the share of the product marketed (q_1), we get two allocational rules:

$$u_y = u_{r_1} \cdot p \qquad \text{... (10.23)}$$

$$q'(L) = \frac{v'(l)}{u_y} \qquad \text{... (10.24)}$$

The equation (10.23) states that the product should be divided in such a manner between direct consumption and exchange in the market that the relevant marginal rate of indifferent substitution between the two commodities equals their price ratio. Equation (10.24) equates the marginal product of labour with the real cost of labour at the margin.

Now suppose other than peasants own labour, some other facts are required for production which they have to buy. In this case marginal product of each factor other than labour will equal its price in terms of the product. While in case of labour it is given by the equality of its marginal product with the real labour cost. If p_i be the prices of n other factors f_i in terms of commodity q, then the profit maximising equilibrium conditions are given by

$$\frac{\partial q}{\partial f_i} = p_i; \qquad i=1,2,3,......,n \qquad \text{... (10.25)}$$

and $$\frac{\partial q}{\partial L} = \frac{v'(l)}{u_y} \qquad \text{... (10.26)}$$

A rise in the real labour cost reduces the total output. It can take place because:

(a) an emigration of labour from the family reduces the number of working members (β) in the family reducing the level of total family labour and to maintain the earlier level of labour, each remaining member has to work more raising the marginal disutility of effort.

(b) with less member in the family, there will be a rise in income of the remaining members reducing the marginal utility from income.

These two effects will push up the real labour cost reducing the equilibrium value of family labour and total output. Thus, the existence of surplus labour depends on the marginal utility schedule and the marginal disutility schedule. Only under the condition of flatness of marginal utility schedule and the marginal disutility schedule in the relevent region, a rise in income will leave the marginal utility unchanged and a rise in individual effort will leave the marginal disutility unaffected.

We assume that the marginal utility of income within a certain range is constant implying an insensitivity of the usefulness of income to its quantity within that region. With this assumption and a suitable choice of units, the constant value of marginal utility can be made equal to unity. So, the equation (10.16) becomes

$$q'(L) = v'(l) = \mu \qquad \text{... (10.27)}$$

Suppose the marginal disutility of effort remains constant, say at η, until a certain critical amount of effort l^* is reached, then we have

$$\mu = v'(l) = \eta > 0; \quad l \leq l^*$$
$$v''(l) > 0; \quad l > l^* \qquad \text{... (10.28)}$$

One point should be noted here that the emigration of labour starts in a situation when the amount of labour put in by each working member in a family is l and the total family labour is $\beta \cdot l$. If $l \geq l^*$, there will be no surplus labour. If the withdrawal of labour takes place in divisible units and $l < l^*$ then some labour can be removed without affecting the output. On the other hand, if labour is withdrawn only in units of one person and reorganisation of the land-labour allocation cannot take place after withdrawal of labour from some families, then the necessary and sufficient condition for the existence of surplus labour is given as

$$\frac{\beta}{\beta - 1} \cdot l \leq l^* \qquad \text{... (10.29)}$$

If there are very large number of families and land can be reallocated after the transfer of labour, then the necessary condition for the existence of surplus labour given by equation (10.29) becomes $l < l^*$.

Now we are going to discuss the quantitative response of peasant output to population withdrawal. we shall further assume that:

(a) there are a large number of peasant families in the economy;

(b) constant returns to scale operates in the economy;

(c) non-labour resources are fully divisible; and

(d) non-labour resources can be reallocated after emigration of labour from some families.

With the above four assumptions, the entire peasant economy can be treated as one production unit with a uniform production function given by equation (10.7), considering q as the total output for the economy and L for total labour hours for the economy. Also, there will be a uniform real cost and marginal productivity of labour. The welfare maximisation rule given by equation (10.16) will be uniformly followed and it will be achieved for each peasant family in spite of indivisibility of the number of persons in each family, through redistribution of non-labour resources. We also assume β to be the total number of working members and α to be the total number of all members, i.e., population in the economy. Since, the number of families in the economy is very large, α and β can be treated as continuously divisible. Marginal utility from income and disutility from work both are taken as positive.

Let ϕ be the ratio of the total number of working population to the total population in economy and it is assumed to be constant. This implies when one working member leaves for work elsewhere, he supports his share of the family, which is ϕ members, so that the peasant economy is left with one less working member and ϕ less consuming members, i.e.,

$$\alpha = \phi\beta \quad \text{... (10.30)}$$

From equation (10.16) we have

$$\frac{d\mu}{d\beta}=\frac{\dfrac{dv'(l)}{d\beta}\cdot u'(y)-\dfrac{du'(y)}{d\beta}\cdot v'(l)}{\left[u'(y)\right]^{2}} \qquad \text{... (10.31)}$$

Now, from equations (10.10), (10.11), (10.13), (10.14) and (10.30) we have

$$\frac{dv'(l)}{d\beta}=v''(l)\left[\frac{\dfrac{dL}{d\beta}\cdot\beta-L}{\beta^{2}}\right] \qquad \text{... (10.32)}$$

$$\frac{du'(y)}{d\beta}=u''(y)\cdot\left[\frac{q'(L)\cdot\dfrac{dL}{d\beta}\cdot\alpha-q\cdot\phi}{\alpha^{2}}\right] \qquad \text{... (10.33)}$$

Taking $q''(L)$ as uniformly strictly negative, from equation (10.16), we have

$$\frac{d\mu}{d\beta}=\frac{dL}{d\beta}\cdot q''(L) \qquad \text{... (10.34)}$$

Using equations (10.31), (10.32), (10.33) and (10.34) and solving for $dL/d\beta$, we have

$$\frac{dL}{d\beta}=\frac{\dfrac{v''(l)}{v'(l)}\cdot L\cdot\phi-\dfrac{u''(y)}{u'(y)}\cdot q}{\alpha\cdot\dfrac{v''(l)}{v'(l)}-\beta\cdot\alpha\cdot\dfrac{q''(L)}{q'(L)}-\beta\cdot q'(L)\cdot\dfrac{u''(y)}{u'(q)}} \qquad \text{... (10.35)}$$

For simplification, we have ignored the possibility of $v'(l)=0$. Now we shall define various types of elasticities and the relation between them.

Elasticity of output with respect to the number of working members is given by

$$e=\frac{dq}{d\beta}\cdot\frac{\beta}{q} \qquad \text{... (10.36)}$$

The elasticity of marginal disutility from work with respect to individual hours of work is given by

$$e_1 = \frac{v''(l) \cdot l}{v'(l)} \qquad \text{... (10.37)}$$

The absolute value of elasticity of the marginal utility of income with respect to individual income is given by

$$e_2 = -\frac{u''(y) \cdot y}{u'(y)} \qquad \text{... (10.38)}$$

The elasticity of output with respect to hours of labour is given by

$$e_3 = \frac{q'(L) \cdot L}{q} \qquad \text{... (10.39)}$$

The absolute value of elasticity of the marginal product of labour with respect to hours of labour is given by

$$e_4 = -\frac{q''(L) \cdot L}{q'(L)} \qquad \text{... (10.40)}$$

Solving equations (10.7), (10.30) and (10.35) to (10.40), we get the response equation as

$$e = e_3 \left(\frac{e_1 + e_2}{e_1 + e_2 \cdot e_3 + e_4} \right) \qquad \text{... (10.41)}$$

At extreme case of surplus labour we have $e_1 = e_2 = 0$. This is similar to the case of having flat regions in the marginal utility and the marginal disutility schedules. In equation (10.41), if we put $e_3 = 0$, the same case seems to arise, but this does not strictly follow, because zero value of e_3 requires that the marginal productivity of labour be zero, which requires that the relevant marginal disutility of labour be zero too, which was ruled out in deriving equations (10.35) and (10.41), involving division by $v'(l)$. However, by assuming $q'(L) = v'(l) = 0$ we can get substantially the same result of surplus labour. To assume that it does not only hold trivially for infinitesimally small changes around the point of equilibrium, we need one more assumption that $v'(l)$ stays at zero even when l is increased. Therefore, $v''(l)$ has to be zero over a certain range, which comes to the same thing as e_1 being zero over this range. Having a flat marginal disutility curve in the relevant region, i.e., $e_1 = 0$, we have from equation (10.41)

$$e = \frac{e_2 \cdot e_3}{e_2 \cdot e_3 + e_4} \quad \text{... (10.42)}$$

Thus, the case of surplus labour is that of $e_2 = 0$ which makes $e = 0$.

Since the transfer of peasant labour will be accompanied by a rise in the price of their output, a positive response of output to the price level makes the conditions for the existence of surplus labour less exacting. When a part of the labour force moves out, there is a tendency for the output level to fall. And given the price of the produce, the fall in output may be compensated by a positive response to the price level resulting from the movement of the labour force itself. In the case of agricultural economy that relies exclusively or inclusively on the product market. In this way, the existence of surplus labour depends on the price response.

HUMAN RESOURCE AS HUMAN CAPITAL

Economic activities are carried out by the people and for the people, therefore the importance of human resources in the economic development is self-evident. Since the manpower development is the cornerstone of the development process, the quality of human resources is the most important indicator of the level of development. Since human resource development is a necessary condition for all kinds of growth, it can be considered as a more realistic, reliable, and pervasive indicator of development than any other single factor.

Human capital formation is the process of increasing the knowledge, the skills, and the capabilities of all the people in a society. Human resources are developed in several ways. The most obvious is by formal education, beginning with primary or first level education, continuing with various forms of secondary education, and then higher education including the colleges, universities, and higher technical institutes. Second, human resources are developed "on the job" through systematic or informal training programs in employing institutions; in adult education programs; and through membership in various political, social, religious, and cultural groups. A third process is self-development, as individuals seek to acquire greater knowledge, skills, or capacities through preparation on their own initiative—by taking formal or correspondence courses, by reading, or by learning from others in informal contacts. Two other processes of human capital formation are improvements in the health of the working population through better medical and public health programs, and improvements in nutrition, which increases the working capacity of people, on a man-hour basis as well as over a working life.

Though the concept of human capital formation has gained much importance in recent years, early economists were not unaware of the importance of human resource development. Adam Smith, for instance, emphasized the role of education at various points in the *The Wealth of Nations,* and he specifically included "the acquired and useful abilities of all inhabitants or members of society" in his concept of "fixed capital". "The acquisition of such talents, by the maintenance of the acquirer during his education, study, or apprenticeship, always costs a real expense, which is a capital fixed and realized, as it were in his person. Those talents, as they make a part of his fortune so do they likewise of that of the society to which he belongs."[14] Alfred Marshall emphasized the importance of education "as a national investment" and in his view "the most valuable of all capital is that invested in human beings".[15]

Till recent years, the modern economists did not pay much explicit attention to human resources in economic growth as did some of the great classical economists like Smith and Marshall. Probably because physical capital was measurable, and capital-output relationship was given an apparent quantitative respectability, some modern economists virtually ignored the human resource factor in economic development. But in recent years it has been increasingly recognised that the growth of physical capital depends to a considerable extent on human capital formation. Studies made by Schultz, Harbison, Denison, Kendrich, Moses, Abramovitz, Becker, Mary Bowman,

Kuznets and several other economists show that relatively increasing outlays on education has been an important factor responsible for the rapid growth of the American economy. They show that a dollar invested on education leads to a larger increase in national income than a dollar spent on dams, roads, factories or other tangible capital goods.

While investment in human beings has been a major source of growth in advanced countries, the negligible amount of human investment in underdeveloped countries has done little to expand the capacity of people to meet the challenge of accelerated development. The characteristic of 'economic backwardness' still manifests itself in several particular forms[16]—low labour efficiency, factor immobility, limited specialisation in occupations and in trade, a deficient supply of entrepreneurship, and customary values and traditional social institutions that minimise the incentives for economic change. The slow growth in knowledge is our important restraint on progress. The economic quality of the population remains low where there is little knowledge of what natural resources are available, the alternative production techniques that are possible, the necessary skills, the existing market conditions and opportunities, and the institutions that might be created to favour economising effort and economic rationality. An improvement in the quality of the 'human factor', therefore, is no less important than investment in physical capital. An advance in knowledge and the diffusion of new ideal and objectives are essential to remove economic backwardness and instill the human abilities and motivations which are more favourable to economic achievement.

Recent experience with attempts to accumulate physical capital at a rapid rate in poor countries reveals the need for due attention to human capital. It has been found that effective use of physical capital itself depends upon human capital. If adequate investment is not made in human resources, the rate at which additional physical capital can be productively utilized will be limited since technical, professional, and administrative people are required to effectively use material capital. In many developing countries, it has been found that the absorptive capacity for physical capital is low because the development of human capabilities has failed to keep pace with the accumulation of physical capital. To cite Frederick H. Harbison, "The rate of modernisation of a country is associated with both its stock and rate of accumulation of human capital. High-level manpower is needed to staff new and expanding government services, to introduce new systems of land use and new methods of agriculture, to develop new means of communication, to carry forward industrialisation, and to build the education system. In other words, innovation, or the process of change from a static or traditional society, requires very large 'doses' of strategic human capital. The countries which are making the most rapid and spectacular innovations are invariably those which are under the greatest pressure to accumulate this kind of human capital at a fast rate."[17]

Stressing the importance that should be attached to the growth in the quality of human resources, Professor Schultz illustrates the possible implications of the quality component as follows: "Suppose there were an economy with the land and the physical reproducible capital including the available techniques of production that we now possess in the United States, but which attempted to function under the following restraints: there would be no person available who had any on-the-job experience, none who had any schooling, no one who had any information about the economy except of his locality, each individual would be bound to his locality, and the average life span of people would be only forty years. Surely, production would fall catastrophically. It is certain that there would be both low output and extraordinary rigidity of economic organisation until the capabilities of the people were raised markedly by investing in them. Let me now take a Bunyan-like step and suppose a set of human resources with as many but no more capabilities per man than existed as of 1900 or even as of 1929 in the United States. The adverse effects on production in either case would undoubtedly be large. To continue these speculations, suppose that "lay some miracle India, or some other low-income country like India, were to acquire as it were overnight a set of natural resources, equipment, and structures including techniques of production comparable per person to ours—what could they do with them, given the existing skills and knowledge of the people? Surely the imbalance between the stock of human and non-human capital would be tremendous."[18]

Role of Human Capital in Development

Individuals can save in two distinct forms:

(a) savings as holdings of physical capital or rights to the proceeds from such capital, and

(b) savings by investing in education, which raises the future market value of the labour.

Now we shall introduce these two forms of savings in the Solow model of growth, considering just two inputs of production—physical capital and human capital. Thus, our production function will be like

$$y = k^{\alpha} h^{1-\alpha} \qquad \text{... (10.43)}$$

where,

y = output,
k = physical capital, and
h = human capital.

In equation (10.43), the parameters y, k, and h are in aggregate or per capita magnitudes, considering the overall population as constant. Here, the effects of unskilled labour and the depreciation have not been considered.

Now, suppose a part of the output is consumed and the remaining part of the output can be used in two ways. A fraction, s, of the remaining output is saved leading to the accumulation of the capital as

$$k(t + 1) - k(t) = sy(t) \qquad \text{... (10.44)}$$

and another fraction, q, is used to augment the quality of human capital as

$$h(t + 1) - h(t) = qy(t) \qquad \text{... (10.45)}$$

where, $qy(t)$ can be considered as the quantity of physical resources spent on education and training.

From equations (10.43), (10.44), and (10.45), we have

$$\frac{k(t+1)}{k(t)} = s \cdot \frac{y(t)}{k(t)} + 1 = s \cdot \frac{k(t)^{\alpha} h(t)^{1-\alpha}}{k(t)} + 1$$

$$= s \cdot \frac{h(t)^{1-\alpha}}{k(t)^{1-\alpha}} + 1 = s \cdot r(t)^{1-\alpha} + 1 \qquad \text{... (10.46)}$$

and,
$$\frac{h(t+1)}{h(t)} = q \cdot \frac{y(t)}{h(t)} + 1 = q \cdot \frac{k(t)^{\alpha} h(t)^{1-\alpha}}{h(t)} + 1$$

$$= q \cdot \frac{h(t)^{-\alpha}}{k(t)^{-\alpha}} + 1 = q \cdot r(t)^{-\alpha} + 1 \qquad \text{... (10.47)}$$

where, $r(t) = h(t)/k(t)$ is just the ratio of human to physical capital.

Dividing equation (10.47) by equation (10.46), we get

$$\frac{h(t+1)/h(t)}{k(t+1)/k(t)} = \frac{q \cdot r(t)^{-\alpha} + 1}{s \cdot r(t)^{1-\alpha} + 1}$$

$$\frac{h(t+1)/k(t+1)}{h(t)/k(t)} = \frac{q \cdot r(t)^{-\alpha} + 1}{s \cdot r(t)^{1-\alpha} + 1}$$

$$\frac{r(t+1)}{r(t)} = \frac{q \cdot r(t)^{-\alpha} + 1}{s \cdot r(t)^{1-\alpha} + 1}$$

$$r(t+1) = \frac{r(t) \cdot \left\{q \cdot r(t)^{-\alpha} + 1\right\}}{s \cdot r(t)^{1-\alpha} + 1} = \frac{q \cdot r(t)^{1-\alpha} + r(t)}{s \cdot r(t)^{1-\alpha} + 1}$$

$$= \frac{q + r(t)/r(t)^{1-\alpha}}{s + 1/r(t)^{1-\alpha}} = \frac{q + r(t)^{\alpha}}{s + r(t)^{\alpha-1}}$$

$$= \frac{q}{s} \cdot \frac{\left(1 + r(t)^{\alpha}/q\right)}{\left(1 + r(t)^{\alpha-1}/s\right)} = r(t) \cdot \frac{q/r(t) + r(t)^{\alpha-1}}{s + r(t)^{\alpha-1}} \qquad \text{... (10.48)}$$

From equation (10.48) we find that

(a) if at any period of time t, $r(t) > q/s$, then $r(t) > r(t+1) > q/s$, and

(b) if at any period of time t, $r(t) < q/s$, then $r(t) < r(t+1) < q/s$.

Equation (10.46) gives the growth rate of physical capital as

$$\frac{k(t+1)-k(t)}{k(t)} = sr^{1-\alpha}$$

Equation (6.47) gives the growth rate of human capital as

$$\frac{h(t+1)-h(t)}{h(t)} = qr^{-\alpha}$$

These two growth rates are same in the long run, therefore we have

$$sr^{1-\alpha} = qr^{-\alpha}$$

or,

$$r = \frac{q}{s} \qquad \text{... (10.49)}$$

From equation (10.49) we see that the larger is the ratio of saving as human capital relative to that of physical capital, the larger is the long-run ratio of the former to the latter. Since all the variables grow at the same rate in the long-run, we can use any of the preceding growth-rate equations to calculate the long-run growth rate. Using equation (10.49) and the growth rate of human capital equation, we get

$$\frac{h(t+1)-h(t)}{h(t)} = qr^{-\alpha} = q\cdot\frac{q^{-\alpha}}{s^{-\alpha}} = s^{\alpha}q^{1-\alpha} \qquad \text{... (10.50)}$$

The long-run growth rate of all the variables, including per capita income, can be given by the equation (10.50).

On introducing the human capital, the coefficients of saving rates and population growth rates will be significantly larger in absolute terms than those predicted by Solow model. This is because an increase in savings increases national income leading to a greater accumulation of both physical and human capital.

Productivity of Investment in Human Capital

Estimation of the productivity of investment in human resources is a highly complicated problem. We discuss below some of the approaches to the problem.

Rate of return approach: Several efforts have been made to calculate this for the United States, based on measurement of income flows of individual's earnings assumed to result from education, and then measuring the present value of these by using one or several discount rates. For instance, Gary S. Becker measured income differentials attributable to the cost of acquiring a college education in the United States. The resulting rates of return for urban white males were 12.5 in 1940 and 10 percent in 1950.[19] Another approach, using Schultz's earlier estimates of total earnings foregone and expenditures for high-school, college, and university education in the United States, calculated an average return to education of between 5 and 10 percent over the period 1900 to 1950.[20] A related method, involving the measurement of how much various amounts or levels of education are worth in dollar terms in the United States for different age groups, was used to show that (for example) the capital value at age fourteen of lifetime income (after taxes, discounted at 6 percent) was $25,380 at the completion of eight years of schooling, $33,466 at the completion of high school, and $41,432 after the completion of four or more years of college or university.[21]

Such measures of the return from education, however, involve several difficulties. In the first place, earnings at different educational or age levels are not solely the result of formal education but are also on account of differences in natural ability, on-the-job training, experience, social status, family income, and other such factors. Some of the studies mentioned above have tried to make allowances, for these factors. Secondly, such measures take in account only the direct material benefit and completely ignore the external economies of education—the direct and indirect benefits accruing to the country from improvement in the levels of education of the people. Thirdly, since one level of education leads to another, the comparisons of those with a primary education and those who lack it may underestimate the value of primary education as a stepping stone to further education. A recent study concludes that recognition of the value of the option to obtain additional education may raise the expected 1939 rate of return on primary or elementary education to 54 percent from 35 percent in the United States.[22] This assumes, of course, that further education is available to all who desire to exercise the "option"—an assumption which does not hold true in many developing countries. Fourthly, most of these estimates are measurements of 'private' rates of return to individuals receiving education. They assume that differences in earnings in a market economy reflect differences in productivity. But collective efforts by various groups (such as doctors, or manual workers through trade unions) and other factors may distort relative earnings in the national economy. Fifthly, private rates of return cannot be evaluated where the costs of running the school are negligible as is the case with single teacher schools being run without any fee in many Indian villages. Finally, prices of educated labour used in the estimation of rate of return must reflect the relative scarcities of factors involved. But where the major portion of investment costs on education are borne by the government, prices of educated labour do not reflect scarcities of factor inputs determined in competitive markets.[23]

In spite of the qualifications and limitations of these estimates, the results obtained for the U.S. economy do offer rather consistent (some might say surprisingly consistent) support for the notion that education, on the average, has paid significant financial as well as non-financial rewards. The difficulties involved in identifying earnings differentials with productivity differentials force one to be somewhat more cautious in drawing sweeping conclusions as to the effect of education on national output.

Residual approach in determining contribution of education to GNP: Several economists have tried to measure what portion of the increase in gross national product in the United States over a period of time can be attributed to measurable inputs of capital and labour and then considered the "residual" as a consequence of, among other things, improvements in the quality of labour force resulting from education. One of the first attempts, however, concentrated on determining the increase in GNP due to increased use of capital, with the remainder "attributable to technical change". Under assumptions of a linear homogeneous production function and a "neutral" technical change which does not affect the rate of substitution between capital and labour, Robert M. Solow thus calculated a "residual" equal to 87.5 percent of the increase in output per man/hour in the United States between 1909 and 1949.[24]

Edward F. Denison has attempted to determine in greater detail the sources of growth in the United States. His computed "residual", unaccounted for by increase in labour and capital inputs, is smaller because he has tried to identify and measure a number of factors such as education and the effects of shorter hours on the quality of labour inputs. The resulting residual is also broken down into several components, of which "advance of knowledge" and "economies of scale" are the most significant.[25] To cite Denison's conclusions in his own words, "From 1929 to 1957 the amounts of education the average worker had received was increasing almost 2 percent a year and this was raising the average quality of labour by 0.97 percent a year, and contributing 0.67 percentage points to the growth rate of real national income. Thus, it was the source of 23 percent of the growth of real national income per person employed. Additional education contributed only a little more than half as much to growth between 1909 and 1929 as between 1929 and 1957."

The residual approach has serious limitations, some of which are well recognised by those who used it. The interrelation between capital formation, technology, and the growth of knowledge means that the "residual" attributed to increased knowledge may really include some capital formation in terms of improved quality of capital assets. Further, what is attributed to "education" is not more specific than that; no distinction is made between formal and informal education, or of difference in the quality or content of education.

In spite of these limitations, this approach has had the merit of bringing to attention of economists and policymakers the obvious contribution to national output made by improvements in the quality of human resources through the engineers (themselves the product of education) who improve technology and the quality of capital equipment.

Inter-country correlations of school enrolment ratios and gross national product: The principal work on this has been done by Svennilson, Edding, and Elvin for the Organisation for Economic Cooperation and Development (OECD). They compared enrolment ratios in three age groups (5 to 14, 15 to 19, and 19 to 24) in 1958 (or nearest year) for twenty-two countries with the GNP per capita in the United States dollars at 1959 prices for these same countries. The correlations are most striking at the higher age groups. To cite the conclusions in the words of authors, "...it is obvious that a country with a low GNP per capita cannot afford to have most of its young people between 15 and 19 in full-time education and thus withheld from gainful employment. On the other hand, a highly industrialized country with a high GNP per capita can hardly afford to break off the education of most of its young people at the age of 14. Moreover, in a rich country there is a high demand for education as current consumption and the margin of income available to satisfy this demand is large.... Generally speaking, the income-level as expressed by GNP per capita seems to set the lower limit of educational effort. But above that limit there is a wide margin for choice, whether it be determined by private consumer preferences or by political decision to invest heavily in education in order to accelerate economic development."[26]

Relationship between expenditure on education and income or physical capital formation: Theodore W. Schultz has analyzed this, relationship in the United States for the period 1900 to 1956, measured in constant dollars, and has shown that "the resources allocated to education rose about three and a half times (a) relative to consumer income in dollars, (b) relative to the gross formation of physical capital in dollars...."[27] In other words, the "income elasticity" of demand for education was about 3.5 over the period, and alternatively, education visualised as an "investment" might be considered as 3.5 times more attractive than investment in physical capital. Schultz further states that "the underlying private and public motives may have been cultural in ways that can hardly be thought of as 'consumption' or they may have been policy determined for purposes that seem remote to investment".

Schultz has also attempted to measure the total stock of "educational capital" at different points in time.[28] By adding together the possible earned income foregone by those enrolled in schools, colleges, and universities (i.e., the "opportunity cost" of education) and the expenditures for formal education of all types (with allowance for depreciation), he computed a figure for the total annual investment in education in the United States by decades from 1900 to 1956. For high-school education this "investment" in education increased 135 times from $81 million in 1900 to $10,944 million in 1956; and for college and university education the increase was 110-fold from $90 million in 1900 to $9,903 million in 1956, all expressed in 1956 figures. The total stock of "educational capital" in the labour force of the United States rose from $63 billion in 1900 to $180 billion in 1930 and $535 billion in 1957, in 1956 prices. It is also significant that the ratio of the stock of educational capital to the stock of reproducible non-human wealth (physical capital) rose from 22 percent in 1900 to 42 percent in 1957.

Another attempt to measure the costs of all types of education in the United States included estimates for "education in the home" (earnings foregone by mothers staying at home to educate their preschool children), "training on the job", "education in the Church", "education in the armed services", as well as costs of formal education, special schools, other federal expenditures, and costs of public libraries. The total cost for 1956-57 was calculated at over $60 billion, or 12.9 percent of adjusted gross national product. The comparable figures for 1955-56 were over $51 billion and 11.8 percent of GNP.

Some general observations: In spite of the importance attached to investment in man by several economists and their efforts to bring at within the realm of economic theory, most economic-development planners normally give only peripheral consideration to the analysis of human resources. While they recognise that some investments in education are "economic" because they directly promote economic growth, they argue that other expenditures for education and human resource development are primarily "social investments" and should be determined residually.

In view of the difficulty of ascertaining how much is really consumption and how much represents investment, it is almost impossible to calculate the rate of financial return on an educational project in the same manner as on a dam or factory. While it is misleading to analyse the human resource development solely in economic terms, it is equally fallacious to contend that education and other means of human development should be considered "human rights" irrespective of their contribution towards production of goods and services. Education for citizenship, education for "life adjustment", or education for enhancement of the freedom, dignity, and worth of man are legitimate goals, but they express only in part the aspirations of modern societies. The purely humanistic approach, like the limited economic approach to human resources, does not truly reflect the aspirations of modern man and modern societies.

In fact, there is no conflict between the economists and the humanists. The development of man for himself may still be considered the ultimate end, but economic progress can also be one of the principal means of attaining it. Human resource development systems can be so designed as helps to increase production of essential goods and services and at the same preserves and enhances the freedom, dignity, and worth of the individual.

Problems of Human Capital Formation

Development of human resources gives rise to a number of problems. The first problem is to determine at what phase of development the formation of intangible capital is most significant. It can be argued that a high rate of increase in the demand for improvements in the quality of inputs appears only at a fairly advanced phase of development. The early industrialization in Western Europe, for instance, was attained without requiring as prerequisites marked improvements in skills and knowledge and health of workers. In the American economy, while capital investment was more important in the earlier decades, investment in the development of resources has been most pronounced in the more recent decades. But, unlike the earlier historical situation, it may now be necessary to have a relatively high level of skill and much more knowledge to take benefit of the more complex equipment and techniques which are available from advanced countries.

Another problem concerns what types of education should be emphasized, to what degree, and how soon. Some economists are of the view that the developing countries do not yet have an effective demand for a large number of educated workers; and they cannot afford to pay for as much education as can rich countries. The immediate requirements for accelerating development call for stress on vocational and technical training and adult education rather than on a greatly expanded system of formal education. In view of its high cost and the problems of absorption that it creates, even the case for universal primary education is questionable.

In developing countries, the deficiency in secondary education is more serious than the lack of universal primary education. The most critical manpower requirements tend to be for people with a secondary education who can be managers, administrators, professional technicians (scientists, engineers, agronomists, doctors, economists, accountants, etc.), or sub-professional technical personnel (agricultural assistants, technical supervisors, nurses, engineering assistants, bookkeepers, etc.).

High priority should also be accorded to the infusion of new skills and knowledge into the agricultural sector. In order to attain a system of modern agriculture, the quality of labour in agriculture needs to be improved as an input in its own right and also to make possible the use of better forms of non-human capital (equipment, seeds, insecticides, etc.). In many countries that have experienced substantial increases in productivity, the key factor has been the introduction of new skills and knowledge and not the new land brought under cultivation nor the physical capital.

In their enthusiasm to spread higher education the underdeveloped countries have a tendency to open too many universities without trying to improve the standard of education. No restrictions are placed on higher education with the consequence that the proportion of failures at the higher secondary and university level is very high. Mass failures and the general lowering of academic standards tends to lower efficiency and does not promise well for the formation of a dynamic leadership for economic development. This leads to wastage of human resources. Further, there is little manpower planning and no efforts are made to match the demand and supply of different types of critical skills. This results in graduate unemployment and frustration.

TECHNOLOGICAL PROGRESS

In a wider sense technological progress includes all the ways in which advances of knowledge promote economic growth. It includes all the productivity benefits of increased education, and product innovations attributable to research, of economies of scale, of the introduction of money into agriculture, the predominant sector of the economy which is partly non-monetized, and of import substitution. This list could be continued indefinitely to include anything which would bring an increase in productivity in technological progress. In a narrower sense, technological progress refers to the introduction of new or improved procsses, which required fewer or cheaper inputs per unit of output, and of new or improved products; increased mechanization and automation provide an example of the former while plastics and computers exemplify the latter. In this, sense, there could be either "process" or "product" innovation. J.A. Schumpeter summarises the nature of the technological progress as understood by the English classical economists in the following words: "Technological improvement may impinge upon the productive process from outside, that is to say, through some innovation that revolutionizes the technological horizon of producers (changes their production functions). The "classic" writers thought exclusively or almost exclusively of this case and hardly ever realised—an exception was Barton—that there is another case the effects of which differ substantially from the first; machines may also be introduced that are no novelties to producers and, so far technological knowledge is concerned, could have been introduced but were not introduced before, because it would not have been profitable to do so. Owing to a change in the relative prices of factors (e.g., an increase in wage rates), their introduction may, however, become profitable. Here we have no change of technological horizons but a change in the combination of factors within unchanging production functions. A third case was recognized by Adam Smith, namely, the case where the introduction of a machine that had been known before becomes profitable as soon as output expands beyond a certain figures."[29]

Thus, the classical economists viewed technological progress in a very narrow sense. According to them the main factors responsible for technological progress are invention, changes in relative factor prices, and opportunities for mechanisation arising from an expansion in output. The contribution of better educated labour stock was given a subordinate position and the productivity benefits of increased education and skill attainment, of managerial efficiency, and of increased research and development efforts were not given a significant place among the components of technological progress.

How Societies Progress Technologically

Technological progress results from a combination of research, invention, development and innovation. Research and invention are the activities which "create" knowledge, and development and innovation are the activities which apply new knowledge to the task of production. Though these are all basically economic activities, the study of the way in which societies progress technologically, and the speed of progress, is not the preserve of only the economist. The economist can identify the mainsprings of progress, but their pervasiveness and acceptance in societies is not a purely economic matter. The spread of knowledge, for instance, depends on its rate of adoption and diffusion and this raises questions of individual motivation, the willingness to assimilate new ideas and to break with custom and tradition, which impinge heavily on the field of development sociologists. The relative importance of different factors contributing to progress, and the speed of progress itself, will differ from country to country according to its stage of development and a whole complex of social and economic forces. Analysed below are the three major sources of progress which are of potential significance to any society.

The first important source of improvement in technology and progress is the inventive and innovative activity of the native population. All societies are endowed with some potential supply of inventors, innovators and risk-takers and, in the absence of imported technology and personnel, it is on the emergence of this class that technological progress mainly depends in the early stages of development. Economic backwardness in many countries has been the result of a relative shortage of inventors, innovators and risk-takers. It is fairly well established that some cultures and some environments are more congenial to change than others, and in the past have produced a greater supply of entrepreneurs. It is often maintained that the major source of growth during Britain's industrial revolution was mainly technological progress fostered by an abundant supply of inventors, innovators, entrepreneurs and risk-takers, with the accumulation of capital playing an essentially secondary role.

In a closed economy, invention is a necessary but not a sufficient condition for progress. In an open economy, it is not even a necessary condition because technology embodying new knowledge can be imported from foreign countries which are more technically advanced. Societies' exposure to new goods may be a powerful factor in economic development by acting as an incentive to producers and workers to increase their surplus for exchange. The spread of technology and ideas may also take place through the general process of commercial intercourse, and the exchange of information through trade.

A third way in which societies progress technologically, gradually raising their efficiency and productivity, is the process of 'learning by doing', which refers to the accumulation of experience by workers, managers and owners of capital in the course of production which enables productive efficiency to be improved in the future.

Role of Technological Progress

While the pivotal role of capital formation in economic development is well recognised, there is tendency among several economists to underestimate the role of technical progress in originating and accelerating economic development. In fact, technical change is a principal contributor to economic growth. To cite Schumpeter, "The slow and continuous increase in time of the national supply of productive means and savings is obviously an important factor in explaining the course of economic history through the centuries, but it completely overshadowed by the fact that development consists primarily in employing existing resources in a different way, in doing new things with them, irrespective of whether those resources increase or not."[30]

Technology in Underdeveloped Countries

A low level of technology is an important characteristic of the underdeveloped countries. In these countries the techniques, particularly in the field of agriculture, have stagnated for centuries. In contrast, during the past two centuries, the science and technology have progressed very fast in the advanced countries. Consequently the gap in the technology of the underdeveloped and the advanced countries has widened, particularly during the last century. Two types of forces were responsible for the all-round fast technological progress in the advanced countries, *viz.*, (i) inducements to invention, and (ii) permissive conditions. The first kind included the ambition to avail of the opportunities offered by the expanding markets, the desire to search solutions for many practical production problems, and the desire to economise the consumption of relatively expensive factors of production. The second type of force (i.e., premissive conditions) created environments favourable to inventions. Extension of specialisation broadened the field for inventions. Certain social forces and occupational stimuli engendered the spirit of enquiry and experimentation in the society as a whole. Even now the rate of technological progress is higher in advanced than in the underdeveloped countries and consequently the gap in their technologies is widening still further.

No doubt the new technology developed in the advanced countries has entered the underdeveloped countries but its impact on their economies has been extremely limited in extent and depth. It has affected only certain limited sectors and the major fields of production remain unaffected. The modern technology has entered the underdeveloped countries mostly along with foreign capital and enterprise which are primarily concentrated in the primary industries producing for export or public overheads which reinforce the export sector. In some countries the foreign investments have concentrated in plantations, mining enterprises and foreign trading firms. In Thailand, for instance, large amounts of foreign investments have concentrated in rubber plantations, tin mines, teak export and rice trade; "the rice farmer clings to the methods and techniques handed down from generation to generation. He uses about the same instruments of production, prepares his fields in the same way, and harvests the grain by hand, just as his father did."[31] The sectors on which the new technology has concentrated and the manner in which it is associated with foreign capital and enterprise leaves hardly any hope of the modern technology automatically spreading to the broader fields of the economy. "Unless a special effort is made", a United Nations Study observes, "the process of technological development in the underdeveloped countries will be relatively slow and the gap in technology will continue to grow wider as the cumulative scientific progress of the developed countries accelerates".[32]

A considerable increase in production, particularly in agriculture, can be obtained by introducing simple and inexpensive technological improvements. Use of fertilisers, better seeds, better crop rotation, insecticides, improved implements, etc., for instance, can considerably increase agricultural production. Presently developing countries are in a privileged position as compared with countries who were pioneers in the field of economic development. It took centuries for the pioneer countries to evolve modern technology. Underdeveloped countries are not required to evolve modern technology anew. There exists a vast store of tested technical and scientific knowledge in developed countries. What is required in underdeveloped countries is simply its utilisation.

Problems of Change in Technology

Utilisation of modern technology existing in advanced countries, however, involves a number of difficulties and problems. In developed countries evolution of modern technology was very slow and spread over centuries. Traditions and cultural pattern could keep pace with the progress of technology. In underdeveloped countries, traditions and cultural patterns have remained practically unchanged. Fitting of modern technology into old traditions and cultural pattern involves several difficulties. In traditional agriculture, for instance, there is often a strong resistance to technical education and to change in working processes. Old traditions and cultural patterns will have to be overhauled before modern technology can successfully be transplanted.

Masses are uneducated. It is difficult for them to learn and practice modern techniques. A comprehensive program of education at all levels is required for enabling the producers to grasp the use of modern technology. A large number of experts and technicians are required to train people in the new methods of production. Underdeveloped countries are highly short of technical personnel. A nation-wide education and training program will involve huge expenditure.

Radical changes are required in the economic, social, religious, legal and political institutions of the country before modern technology can successfully be introduced. The entire outlook of the people has got to be changed to make them receptive to new methods of production. The problem, however, is not insuperable. Experience shows that people readily respond to new methods, to the use of machinery, to new products, once it is made clear to them that these bring larger reward.

Use of modern technology requires modern equipment and a number of other facilities. Not to talk of costly machinery, most of the producers in underdeveloped countries are too poor to buy even the most inexpensive modern equipment, *viz.*, better implements, better seed, fertilizers, insecticides, etc. Provision of basic facilities (*viz.*, irrigation, electric power, transportation, etc.) requires huge amounts of investment. Use of modern technology, thus, requires vast amounts of capital. A United Nations study has aptly remarked:

> Capital and technology are joint inputs in one process, the use of either of which involves necessarily the use of the other. Technological progress involves necessarily the investment of capital in human beings and in training and instructing them in the new technology, and administrative processes for its transmission, in capital goods embodying it, and in capital works and facilities supporting and developing the whole process.[33]

According to Ragnar Nurkse, an advance in technical knowledge in the abstract may be of no economic relevance if there is no capital in which to incorporate it and with which to take advantage of it in the process of production.[34]

The rate at which modern technology can be introduced is to a large extent limited by the role of investment. Most of the technology existing in advanced countries has been developed keeping in view the environments and needs of these countries. It has got to be adapted to the resources and needs of the underdeveloped countries which are different from those of the developed countries. A system of crop rotation suited to the land and climatic conditions of developed countries may not be very successful in underdeveloped countries with different climatic conditions. Land in underdeveloped countries may be rich in elements in which the land in developed countries is highly deficient. Land in underdeveloped countries may be deficient in certain other elements. If this is so, land in underdeveloped countries will need different types of manures. A fresh research may be required to find out the best crop rotation system, fertilisers, strains of plants, breeds of cattle, manufacturing process and equipment suited to the environments and climatic conditions of underdeveloped countries. Advanced countries are abundant in capital and scarce in manpower. All their research efforts, therefore, are directed to finding out techniques which economise labour and offer outlets for savings. The needs of underdeveloped countries are quite the reverse. These countries possess vast amounts of unemployed and underemployed labour and are very short of capital. The techniques best suited to these countries, therefore, are those which require more labour and less capital. In this connection, Nurkse's observation is very pertinent:

> In overpopulated agricultural countries, in building a road, for instance, it would be fantastically uneconomic to equip each worker with a bulldozer. Much simpler tools and equipment may be appropriate to the relative factor endowment of countries of this type, in the early stages of development. The same capital intensity as in economically advanced countries should be neither desired nor permitted. We should not expect the new investment worker at once to work on capital-formation at a much higher level of efficiency. But at least they would be working, producing, and contributing to the expansion of their country's production capacity. They would no longer be unemployed in disguise.[35]

Some economists have suggested a more dynamic approach to the problems. They argue that in order to take advantage of the labour-intensive investments, it is essential to undertake capital-intensive investments. When a program of industrialisation is planned in 'complementary interacting fashion, the suitability of a single industry from the angle of capital intensity must be judged in the light of the complementary contribution of that particular industry to the whole economy. This would mean that a country should adopt technology appropriate to its factor endowments after providing for investments in capital-intensive overhead industries. It suggests use of capital intensive modern technology on the "growing points" of the economy so that once the development is initiated, the supply of capital would expand and make application of modern technology possible on a wider scale in other sectors.

As regards the objective to be achieved, there is not substantial difference between the two approaches. The first approach envisages growth through expansion of production and employment. The second aims at achieving growth through heavy investment on the 'growing points' so as to raise the rate of capital formation and then expand production and employment in the economy. The first approach does not appear to give adequate importance to the intermediary link between production and employment, that is, capital formation. The second attaches importance to lump investments in those industries which help other industries to expand at a later stage. It appears to be more balanced because it takes into consideration not only the prevailing factor proportions, but also envisages a change in them and the consequent gradual change-over to modern technology. The difference in the two approaches, in fact, is only of degree. Neither the first excludes modern technology altogether, nor does the second rule out adjustments in accordance with the existing factor endowments.

The problem, thus, is not simply of transplanting technology available in advanced countries. Knowledge available in advanced countries has got to be tested and adapted to the particular environments and needs of the underdeveloped countries. Fresh research is required into fields in which developed countries are not interested but are of vital interest to the underdeveloped countries. This requires vast amounts of money and talent of a high calibre, both of which are lacking in underdeveloped countries. A chain of research institutions has got to be established within the underdeveloped countries. Maximum possible use should be made of research facilities available in advanced countries for studying the problems of underdeveloped countries. Research institutions set up within the underdeveloped countries should hire the services of foreign experts for studying the problems of these countries.

In the initial stages of development, the underdeveloped countries will require the services of a large number of foreign experts. This involves a number of difficulties. The developed countries themselves are short of competent experts and technicians. Competent technicians can easily find well-paid jobs at home. The underdeveloped countries, therefore, find it difficult to procure the services of foreign experts and technicians. The United Nations and its agencies and governments of several advanced countries are making efforts to provide underdeveloped countries with the services of foreign experts. Wage rates are far higher in advanced countries than in underdeveloped countries. Foreign experts cannot agree to serve abroad at salaries lower than those which they are receiving in their home country. Employment of foreign experts at wages they are receiving in their home country leads to a wide disparity between the remuneration of local and foreign experts. This is resented by the local experts and the masses at large. It is dubbed as exploitation of underdeveloped countries by foreign imperialists. To avoid the resentment of local experts and masses, foreign personnel should not be employed for works which can be handled with equal efficiency by the available local experts.

But no country can afford to permanently depend upon foreign experts. Apart from the scarcity and high cost of foreign experts, national experts will be more useful than foreign experts. National experts are better familiar with the environments and needs of the country. They will work with greater zeal out of patriotic sentiments. They hold permanent interest in the country in which they are employed while most of the foreign experts come only for a short period and their permanent interest lies in their mother country. Foreign experts who come for a short period do not feel perfectly at home and consequently their efficiency tends to suffer. Further the development process that is a imported from abroad cannot be self-generating. New techniques will show better results when these are completely assimilated in the social structure of the country and start developing as an integral part of the whole economic and social structure.

There is a lack of competent teachers for imparting training. The scarcity of teachers can be overcome by importing foreign teachers to train local teachers or by sending selected nationals abroad to learn the technique of training teachers. Training of administrators and business executives raises special difficulties. Successful administrators and business executives cannot be trained in training institutions. Techniques of administration can be learnt best at the job. In colonial countries, nationals do not get an opportunity to participate at higher levels in the administration of the country. In underdeveloped countries, a major part of the modern commerce, industry, mining and plantations is in the hands of a limited number of people. People outside this group do not get an opportunity to participate in the activities at higher levels. Where these activities are in the hands of foreigners, local people are often excluded from employment at the executive levels.

One way of acquiring managerial techniques is to send young enterprising persons abroad for working in foreign concerns. This was done on a large scale by Germany and Japan in the initial stages of their development. There are, however, difficulties in the way of young people in finding jobs at the executive level in foreign countries. The difficulties are particularly marked in the case of coloured people against whom there exists a prejudice and hatred in white countries. Governments and private organisations in advanced countries can assist the underdeveloped countries by providing young people of these countries with opportunities to serve at higher levels in their countries.

For rapid economic progress, "mass education" is very important. This requires a vast outpouring of men who have received training for a year or so to work in fields where people with four to six years training usually work in advanced countries.

> It is impossible to reach the masses if only men of the highest qualifications are to be employed as teachers, physicians, dentists, bridge-builders, agricultural extension workers or the like. There is much to be done that can be done after a short training, and much that can be done better after a short training than it is done by persons further removed from the people. Economic development will be held up if underdeveloped countries are compelled to adopt the expensive standards of the more advanced countries.[36]

NOTES

1. Gunnar Myrdal, *Asian Drama,* Vol. II (New York, 1958), pp. 1392-93.
2. Gunnar Myrdal, *Asian Drama,* Vol. II (New York, 1968), pp. 1502-04.

3. Wrigley 1969; Birdsall 1988.
4. A. Landry, *La Révolution Démographique* (Paris, 1934).
5. W.S. Thompson, 'Population', *American Journal of Sociology*, 34 (1929), pp. 959-75.
6. Boserup (1981).
7. Simon (1977) and Kuznets (1960).
8. United Nations, 1969.
9. United Nations, 1973b, chap. I.
10. *Ibid.*, chap. II.
11. United Nations, 1975, chap. I.
12. United Nations, 1984, chap. I, sec. B (III and IV).
13. World Commission on Environment and Development, 1987, overview entitled "From one earth to one world", sec. I, p. 8.
14. Adam Smith, *An Inquiry into the Nature and Causes of the Wealth of Nations,* Cannan ed. (reissued by Modern Library), 1937, pp. 265-66.
15. Alfred Marshall, *Principles of Economics,* 8th ed. (London, 1930), pp. 216, 564.
16. Hla Myint, "An Interpretation of Economic Backwardness", *Oxford Economic Papers,* June, 1954, pp. 132-63.
17. Frederick H. Harbison, "Human Resources Development Planning in Modernising Economies", *International Labour Review,* May, 1962. Reprinted in Gerald Meier, *Leading Issues in Economic Development* (1970), p. 613.
18. T.W. Schultz, "Reflections on Investment in Man", *Journal of Political Economy,* Supplement, October, 1962, pp. 2-3.
19. Gary S. Becker, "Underinvestment in College Education", *American Economic Review* (Papers and Proceedings), May, 1960, p. 347.
20. E.F. Renshaw, "Estimating the Returns to Education", *Review of Economics and Statistics.* August, 1960, pp. 318-24.
21. H.S. Houthakkar, "Education and Income", *Review of Economics and Statistics,* February, 1959, p. 26.
22. A. Weisbrod Burton, "Education and Investment in Human Capital", *Journal of Political Economy* (Supplement), October, 1922, p. 12.
23. Ingvar Svennilson, in association with Friedrich Edding and Lionel Elvin, *Targets for Educaticn in Europe in 1970,* Vol. II, Policy Conference on Economic Growth and Investment in Education (Paris, 1962).

24. Robert M. Solow, "Technical Change and the Aggregate Production Function", *Review of Economics and Statistics,* August, 1957, pp. 312-30.

25. Edward F. Denison, *The Sources of Economic Growth in the United States and the Alternative Before Us,* Supplementary Paper No. 13, Committee for Economic Development (New York, 1962).

26. Ingvar Svennilson, in association with Friedrich Edding and Lionel Elvin, *Targets for Education in Europe in 1970,* Vol. II, Policy Conference on Economic Growth and Investment in Education (Paris, 1962), p. 73.

27. "Education and Economic Growth", in Nelson B. Henry (ed.), the Sixtieth Yearbook of the National Society for the Study of Education, Part 2, *Social Forces Influencing American Education* (Chicago, 1961), p. 60.

28. Schultz, *Ibid.,* pp. 64-73, and "Capital Formation by Education", *Journal of Political Economy* (December, 1960), pp. 571-83.

29. J.A. Schumpeter, *History of Economic Analysis* (1954), p. 679.

30. J.A. Schumpeter, *The Theory of Economic Development* (Cambridge, Mass, 1949), p. 68.

31. James C. Ingram, *Economic Change in Thailand Since 1850,* p. 28.

32. United Nations, *Measures for the Economic Development of Underdeveloped Countries* (New York, 1951), p. 28.

33. United Nations, n. 19, p. 30.

34. Ragnar Nurkse, *Problems of Capital Formation in Underdeveloped Countries* (Oxford, 1955), p. 3.

35. *Ibid.,* p. 45.

36. United Nations. n. 19, pp. 33-34.

11

Planning for Economic Development

After going through this chapter, you will better understand:

- importance of planning
- functional planning vs structural planning
- planning from above vs planning from below
- flexibility in planning
- balances in planning
- physical and financial planning
- execution of the plan
- public ownership
- implementation through direction
- implementation through inducements
- voluntary cooperation

Planning means an extension of the size of the unit of control involving an enlargement of the field to be surveyed while taking economic decisions.[1] In an unplanned economy, decisions regarding prices and output are taken by individual enterprises ignorant of the decisions of other enterprises. Under perfect competition—which is complete negation of a planned economy—each firm controls so small a part of production that it cannot influence the price of its product, prices of the factors of production which it buys and the scale of output of other firms. The unit of control may be extended to an industry, to a number of industries, or to the whole economy. Under the most comprehensive form of planning (known as centralised planning), the unit of control extends to the whole economy. Under centralised planning decisions regarding prices and production in an industry are made keeping in view the whole economy.

Importance of Planning

Because of a number of reasons, economic activities will be better organised in a planned economy than in an unplanned one. In an unplanned economy, each individual enterprise controls a very small part of an industry. While deciding its production, it is unaware of the production plans of other enterprises in the same industry. This often leads to either overproduction or underproduction. Cobweb cycles in agriculture are an interesting example of this phenomenon. Small individual enterprises do not take into consideration the social repercussions of their actions. The social loss may far outweigh the private gain from certain activities of private enterprises, e.g., competitive advertisement with the objective of bluffing and deceiving consumers rather than informing them. In some lines of production, social gain may be far larger than the private profits, e.g., industries which generate considerable external economies. The central planning authority, in contrast, while considering production plans for any industry is fully aware of the production plans of other industries which provide demand for its products and supply the inputs required by it. By maintaining a balance in the rate of growth of different industries, it can avoid overproduction and shortages. Further it can stimulate production in lines in which social gain is larger than private profits and discourage production in those lines in which social costs are higher than the private costs.

The central planning authority in a planned economy can take not only a wider but also a longer view of things. It can foresee the developments sufficiently in advance and make provision for these. It can better safeguard the interests of the posterity.

Unplanned economies are marked by a repeated occurrence of business cycles. Business fluctuations arise, mainly, because of divergences between savings and investment. Divergences between savings and investment arise because of a lack of direct contact between the people who save and those who invest. The central planning authority can avoid the wastes and agonies resulting from business fluctuations by maintaining a proper balance between savings and investment and between production and consumption.

Laissez faire creates extreme inequalities in the distribution of income and wealth. The central planning authority can take measures to reduce economic inequalities. Reduction in inequalities will diminish class struggle and the wastes resulting from it. Cordial relations between labour and capital will increase the efficiency of production. When increased productivity benefits not only capitalists but also labourers, the latter will put heart and soul in their work.

A planned economy can adjust to rapidly changing conditions much more easily than a free enterprise economy. Suppose, for illustration, that a hundred per cent increase is required in the production of shoes in one year and an equivalent decrease in production in the next year. Under the freely working price mechanism, hundred per cent increase in the production of shoes will considerably raise the prices of the factors of production required in the shoe industry during the first year. Required hundred per cent decrease in production will considerably depress the prices of these factors in the next year. In a planned economy, the required increase and decrease in production can be achieved without violent fluctuations in the prices of factors of production.

FUNCTIONAL PLANNING VS STRUCTURAL PLANNING

Functional planning means planning within the existing socio-economic order. It aims only at repairing damaged spots in the economy. The idea is not to change the structure of the society but only to repair and improve it. This type of planning does not create a new social order and only improves the working of the existing order. Structural planning, in contrast, means planning of an entirely new order with radical and far-reaching changes in the structure of the economy.

Planning in the erstwhile U.S.S.R. and in other socialist countries provide examples of the structural type of planning.

The structure of most of these economies has changed very fast. The planning adopted in India is by and large of a functional type.

In the course of time, step by step, even functional planning may change the entire socio-economic order of the economy. Similarly, structural planning may yield place to functional planning after some time. The planning in the erstwhile U.S.S.R., for instance, after a few plans, started working within the given socio-economic structure and thus became functional in nature. Thus there is no permanent demarcation line between the two types of planning.

The advantage of functional planning is that it can be carried out even with meagre resources and scanty technical staff. This type of planning, however, fails to remove all economic ills. The structural planning which overhauls the socio-economic structure, may face strong opposition from the privileged sections of society whose interests are adversely affected thereby.

PLANNING FROM ABOVE VS PLANNING FROM BELOW

The planning can be done at the top or at the bottom or at both the levels. Planning from above implies organising the organised or semi-organised sector in a more precise manner. This type of planning has the merit of being comparatively easy. It is also more coordinated and accurate. The benefits of this type of planning, however may not accrue to those sections who need these most. This approach may, therefore, not be very realistic.

Planning from below is more realistic and more fully takes into consideration the local requirements. But it cannot adequately take into consideration the overall picture of the economy. There is, however no necessary conflict between the two types of planning. The two types can be combined to produce an accurate and realistic plan. In the erstwhile U.S.S.R., the planning is done both from the top downward and from the bottom upwards.

FLEXIBILITY IN PLANNING

Flexibility in planning implies scope for adjustments and readjustments in the plan in regard to targets relating to production, outlay, etc. As the plan progresses, there may occur changes in human wants, techniques of production, availability of productive resources, etc. For successful planning, therefore, it is very essential that the plan is sufficiently flexible so that it can be quickly adjusted to the changed conditions. Flexibility is particularly important when the plan is of a long-term nature and the economy is passing through a transitional stage. To cite Durbin, "Planning does not, and should not imply any dogmatism about future. It is not possible to tell in details what will happen to human tastes, to technical inventions, to general standards of security and well-being. It would, therefore, be foolish in the extreme to attempt to lay down plans which could not be amended quickly in the light of changing social requirements."[2] Speaking in the House of Commons on February 5, 1946, Dalton pointed out that, "These plans must not be mere essays. They must be consistent with practical possibilities. They must not be too rigid or hidebound. They must be capable of continuous adjustment in the light of changing conditions.... Eternal vigilance is the price of successful planning."

Though an adequate amount of flexibility is very essential and highly desirable, it should not go to the extent of changing the very character and structure of the plan. While changes in details may be freely made, the basic structure of the plan should not be tempered with; otherwise planning would become a farce. A certain amount of rigidity, therefore, is necessary in regard to the basic structure of the plan.

BALANCES IN PLANNING

With a view to ensure internal coherence or consistency of the plan as a whole, it is essential to obtain a number of balances. In the absence of this, the plan will lead to 'gluts' or 'shortages' in different sectors of the economy. It is essential to draw up various balances even before the final production targets or schedules in important sectors of the national economy are laid down. There are three main types of balances, *viz.*, (i) Crosswise Balances, (ii) Backward Balances, and (iii) Financial or Monetary Balances. To begin with the first type, the crosswise balance is an attempt to attain equilibrium between the aggregative output targets and the total available resources of the community. Any discrepancy between the two would lead to serious problems for the economy and also for the smooth working of the plan. If the aggregate output targets fall short of the resources available, some of the resources will go unutilised or under-utilised. On the other hand, if the output targets are in excess of the resources available, there would occur shortages and inflation.

In order to ensure that every physical target is itself consistent internally, it is essential to attain what is called "backward balance". The backward balance is an attempt to achieve an equilibrium between the final product and its various inputs. While fixing production target for any industry, the planning authority should ensure that the labour, raw materials, power, etc. required for its production are available. Successful planning also requires that the attainment of production target in one industry should be related to its utilisation in other industries or in consumption. This is necessary because economic activity is closely interdependent and the output in one industry constitutes the input for another.

This highly complicated task has been facilitated by the recently evolved technique of input-output analysis. The input-output analysis enables the planners to lay down final output targets which are internally coherent or consistent. The basic idea involved in this analysis is that the output of one industry constitutes the input for another industry. The analysis implies the various physical units required to obtain specified outputs of various commodities. The basis of this analysis is an elaborate matrix table which enables the planners to study the inter-industry relationships and to establish the necessary inter-industry balances. This type of analysis pre-supposes the availability of detailed statistical data in regard to the technical relationships between the inputs and outputs of every type of industry. Because of the non-availability of adequate and reliable statistical data, this technique can be applied in underdeveloped countries only to a limited extent.

The third type of balance is the monetary balance which aims at maintaining a monetary equilibrium in the economy. For maintaining a monetary equilibrium, it is essential to have a proper relation between aggregate income and the volume of goods available, between savings and investment, between that part of income which is used for investment and the volume of investment goods made available and between foreign payments and receipts.

PHYSICAL AND FINANCIAL PLANNING

Physical planning means planning in terms of real resources like labour, raw materials, equipment, etc. Every plan for development or construction requires real resources. While formulating a plan, the planning authority has got to assure itself of the availability of real resources for the execution of the plan; otherwise there would appear bottlenecks during the execution of the plan. The physical plan should also lay out in advance how the output of each production unit is to be utilised either in consumption or in further production. In contrast, financial planning means planning in terms of money. Since a payment has to be made for obtaining any physical resources, financial planning is also very necessary.

The two types of planning are not rival of each other; in fact, they are complementary to each other. Physical planning is very necessary for giving precision to the efforts. But finance is the mobiliser of physical planning. Neither of the two techniques alone can set the things moving in a smooth manner. Discrepancies between physical and financial plans will lead either to certain resources remaining unutilised or to inflation. The two types of planning, in fact, are two parts of a single indivisible process.

Fixation of targets and allocations in terms of money does not involve much difficulty. But fixation of targets and allocations in terms of men, materials and power is a highly complicated job. In physical planning, it is essential to coordinate different targets in the same segments and the targets of one segment with another. Physical planning involves formidable difficulties in underdeveloped economies. There is lack of statistical data and information in regard to the available physical resources. There is also the problem of balancing different segments of the economy. Because of the inherent structural difficulties, it is not easy to attain internal consistency of a high order. The country may not have reached the stage of technology required for attaining the stipulated targets. There may be unexpected failure of crops resulting in a decline in the supply of agricultural commodities. Lange suggests that to provide for such contingencies the input-output and consumption balances must make provision for certain reserve stocks.

In the erstwhile U.S.S.R., with an elaborate system of statistics, detailed information about various technical co-efficient derived from the norms were collected as a matter of routine by various enterprises and departments. Required correlations were worked out by the methods of balances and during the last so many years they had attained internal consistency of a very high order. The economy of the erstwhile U.S.S.R. was an integrated economic system and the various coefficients and correlations in physical and financial fields were scientifically worked out. They had a system of correct balancing along with internal consistency.

EXECUTION OF THE PLAN

Once the plan has been formulated, there arises the question as to how it should be implemented. Following are the main ways in which it can be implemented:

(a) All productive resources may be nationalised. If the state acquires ownership of all productive resources, it can utilise these in accordance with the national plan without any difficulty.

(b) If the state does not want to acquire the ownership of all productive resources, it can implement the plan through direct controls over the activities of private enterprises and those of the factors of production, *viz.*, rationing, licensing, labour direction, production direction, etc.

(c) Private individuals and enterprises may be induced to work according to the national plan through monetary and fiscal instruments, *viz.*, rate of interest, rate of exchange, taxation, subsidies, loans, etc.

(d) The plan may be implemented through voluntary cooperation of the people. Let us briefly discuss these methods of executing a plan.

Implementation Through Direction

The state lays down targets of production for all industries. Each industry is allocated the amount of raw materials, machinery and labour required for achieving its targets. Labour is directed to plan employments. A detailed scheme is laid down for the utilisation of the production of each industry, i.e., how much is to be consumed, how much is to be exported, how much is to be used for capital formation, so forth and so on. The amount of produce allocated for consumption is distributed among consumers through rationing and licensing. Equity is assured by allocating a fair share of the product to each citizen. Full employment is assured because the plan provides for the utilisation of all productive resources. Replacement of the criterion of private profits by that of social contribution increases the economic welfare of the community. Smooth adjustments can be made to rapidly changing conditions which lead to violent fluctuations in prices under freely operating price mechanism.

A number of objections, however, have been raised against this method of implementing the plan. The most important objection is that it threatens personal freedom. Consumers are not free to spend their purchasing power in any manner they like. The products which they can buy are decided by the planning authority. Similarly, the workers are not free to choose the profession they like. The profession and the place at which they are to work are decided by the planning authority.

Administration through direction may lead to wrong decisions resulting into huge wastes. An economy is too complicated to be comprehended in all its aspects by any central planning authority, however efficient and stable its staff, and however well equipped with statistical and other information. Every economic activity creates so wide repercussions in the whole of the economy as cannot be traced by the planners. The planners can take into consideration only the direct and the main indirect repercussions of any economic activity. Price mechanism, on the other hand, reflects even the minutest and farthest repercussions of an economic activity. No doubt, private entrepreneurs also make mistakes; the consequences of their mistakes are not so disastrous as those of the mistakes of the central planning authority.

Direct controls lead to corruption, favouritism and black-marketing which tend to demoralise the national character. Administration of controls requires a considerable amount of manpower. Price mechanism, on the other hand, works automatically and requires little manpower to administer it. Further, controls are clumsy, inefficient and wasteful as compared with a properly functioning price mechanism. The individuals and enterprises have to move according to the direction of the central planning authority. No scope is left for the enterprise and initiative of individuals which have been the mainsprings of the progress made so far.

Implementation Through Inducements

The shortcomings of the direct controls mentioned above have led the people to think of implementing the plan through monetary and fiscal incentives. Suppose, for illustration, that the planning authority decides to increase the production of cloth. Instead of directing labour and other factors of production into textile industry, it should create conditions in this industry which attract additional factors of production, i.e., it should raise the reward of the factors of production employed in textile industry as compared with the reward of those employed in other industries. Reward of the factors of production employed in textile industry can be increased by the payment of subsidies. Similarly, if the planning authority considers it to be in the national interest to decrease production of opium, it should encourage a transfer of resources from the production of opium to that of other commodities by lowering the reward offered to the factors of production employed in the opium industry. Reward to the factors of production in opium industry can be decreased by the imposition of taxes. Consumption can be regulated in the same way as production. The state should subsidise the goods whose consumption is to be encouraged and tax those whose consumption is to be discouraged. Business cycles can be controlled and full employment maintained through monetary and fiscal measures. Inequalities in the distribution of wealth and income can be reduced by taxing the rich and spending the tax-proceeds on the poor. Thus the national plan can be implemented through the monetary and fiscal measures without infringing upon the personal freedom of people and without involving the evils of direct controls. The funds for the payment of subsidies will be collected from the imposition of taxes.

In underdeveloped countries, the extent to which the economic activities can be manoeuvred through monetary and fiscal instruments is strictly limited. Agriculture which constitutes an overwhelmingly large part of the economy is not very responsive to monetary incentives. Agriculture is more a way of life than a business proposition. Monetary incentives may do the trick where economic activities are guided mainly by commercial considerations. Commercial considerations do not play an important role in underdeveloped countries. Producers retain a large part of the produce for domestic consumption and sell very little in the market. Similarly, they buy very little from the market. People are ignorant and lead a traditional life. They are not very responsive to monetary incentives. Not to talk of underdeveloped countries, even in developed countries the response to monetary incentives is very meagre in agriculture.

Monetary incentives may do the trick in advanced countries where only marginal changes are required. It is doubtful if these can be successful in underdeveloped countries requiring fundamental and structural changes.

Monetary incentives take time to be effective. It takes time for the information about incentives to reach the people concerned. The people concerned take further time in responding to incentives. Directive measures can achieve the same objectives immediately.

Monetary incentives tend to increase inequalities in the distribution of income. Suppose, for illustration, it is considered desirable to shift part of the textile industry from centre *A* to another centre *B*. Encouragement of the movement through incentives may require a considerable increase in the wages of labour employed in centre *B* and a decrease in the wages of the similar labour employed in centre *A*. Private enterprises may require unduly high profits before they agree to increase production. This would accentuate the inequalities in the distribution of income.

Planning through inducements assumes that sufficient funds will be forthcoming from taxes imposed for discouraging production in certain lines to finance the payment of subsidies for stimulating production in other lines. In case the need for stimulation is much more than for discouragement (i.e., funds required for subsidies exceed), which is very likely to be the case in actual practice, there arises the problem of obtaining additional funds. If the additional funds are obtained by levying taxes in addition to those necessary for discouraging production in some lines, adverse effects may by caused on the economy. The adverse effects of taxes when these cross a certain limit are too well-known to be narrated here.

The extent to which inequalities in the distribution of income and wealth can be diminished through taxes and subsidies without causing adverse effects on production is very much limited. Any diminution of inequalities will require taxation on such a large scale as will adversely affect production to a considerable extent.

Monetary and fiscal measures may not succeed in lifting the economy from a grim depression marked by an extreme wave of alround pessimism. Directive measures can immediately lift the economy out of such a depression.

PUBLIC OWNERSHIP

Public ownership of all means of production is the most effective way of implementing a plan. In addition, it is claimed that production will be organised more efficiently under state ownership than under private ownership. State ownership will avoid the wastes of competition. The state can cut out the overlapping services of competing firms. It can spend on research sums far larger than those which the individual enterprises can afford. Labourers will work more sincerely because the additional output resulting from the sincere and hard work will benefit the whole society and not only a few capitalists.

On the other hand, it is contended by some that production will be less efficient under state ownership than under private ownership. State employees, with fixed salaries, and promotion, primarily, by seniority won't have the incentives of efficiency which profits provide for private enterprises. Under the competitive system, inefficient enterprises are eradicated through recurrent losses. Elimination of competition may breed lethargy and inefficiency in state enterprises. Administration in state enterprises is more cumbersome, slow, wasteful and rigid.

On the whole, the case for state ownership is stronger in case of public utilities and other heavy industries which are monopolised even under private ownership than in case of manufacturing and trading requiring flexibility and quick decisions.

VOLUNTARY COOPERATION

It is doubtful if any national plan can be implemented through the voluntary cooperation of people on a national scale. Whenever there is a conflict between the personal interest and the national interest, it is the former which will prevail over the latter. Suppose, for illustration, the national plan requires an increase in the production of cloth and a decrease in that of sugar. If the rate of profit is higher in sugar industry than in textile industry, private enterprises will have a tendency to shift resources from the production of cloth to that of sugar inspite of a reverse shift required by the national plan. Speeches by topmost leaders from high platforms cannot persuade private enterprises to any significant extent to go against their self-interest. In the actual world, self-interest rules above everything else. In such a world it will be living in a fool's paradise to think of implementing the plan through voluntary cooperation alone.

To conclude, a combination of all the methods discussed above will be much more effective and useful than any of these alone for implementing a plan. Wherever and to the extent possible, the plan should be implemented through voluntary co-operation and monetary inducements. This will avoid the evils, generally associated with the directive measures, *viz.*, threat to personal freedom, corruption, inefficiency, etc. Directive measures should be used wherever the monetary inducements fail to get the needful done. Public ownership will be useful in case of public utilities and other heavy industries.

NOTES

1. E.F.M. Durbin, *Problems of Economic Planning* (London, 1955), p. 44.
2. *Ibid.*, p. 43.